Peace as Government

Peace as Government

The Will to Normalize Timor-Leste

Ramon Blanco

LEXINGTON BOOKS
Lanham • Boulder • New York • London

Published by Lexington Books
An imprint of The Rowman & Littlefield Publishing Group, Inc.
4501 Forbes Boulevard, Suite 200, Lanham, Maryland 20706
www.rowman.com

6 Tinworth Street, London SE11 5AL

British Library Cataloguing in Publication Information Available

Library of Congress Cataloging-in-Publication Data

Library of Congress Control Number:2019957132

ISBN 978-1-4985-8177-6 (cloth)
ISBN 978-1-4985-8179-0 (pbk)
ISBN 978-1-4985-8178-3 (electronic)

To Fernanda and Maria Isabel

Contents

Acknowledgments

This book took too long to see the light. Throughout its research, I had the help, support, and encouragement of many individuals and institutions without whom this whole enterprise would not even have begun, much less being published. I would like to dedicate this moment to express my gratitude to them. I am perfectly aware that this is a very difficult task. I will certainly make omissions, forget someone, and be unjust to others. Nevertheless, I would like to acknowledge and thank some individuals and institutions that were pivotal to the publication of this book.

I would like to thank, initially, for the financial support of the Portuguese Foundation for Science and Technology (Fundação para Ciência e Tecnologia—FCT, SFRH/BD/43498/2008) and the European Union (under COST Short-Term Scientific Mission, ECOST-STSM-IS0805-050911-007628). These financial instruments were fundamental for the proper development of the research herein presented. I would like also to thank the Center for Social Studies and the Faculty of Economics of the University of Coimbra for hosting this research and for providing such an enriching and theoretically stimulating environment. At the University of Coimbra, I would like to namely thank Paula Lopes for all the patience, generosity, and guidance, and all the professors for the rich discussions. Still in Coimbra, I must acknowledge some friends who were crucial for the proper development of this research, namely Fernando Ludwig, Gilberto Oliveira, and Fernando Cavalcante.

I would like also to thank the editor of this book, Joseph Parry, and all the people of Lexington Books involved in this book, for all the support through the publication process. Parts of the chapters of this book were published as: Blanco, Ramon. (2017). Normalizando Anormais na Sociedade Internacional: Operações de Paz, Foucault e a Escola Inglesa. *Relações Internacionais*

(Lisboa), p. 83–107; Blanco, Ramon (2015). The UN Peacebuilding Process: An Analysis of Its Shortcomings in Timor-Leste. *Revista Brasileira de Política Internacional*, v. 58, p. 42–62; Blanco, Ramon (2015). A Construção da Paz em Timor-Leste: Uma Visão Crítica. In: Maria Raquel Freire. (Org.) *Consolidação da Paz e a sua Sustentabilidade: As Missões da ONU em Timor-Leste e a Contribuição de Portugal*. 1ed. Coimbra: Imprensa da Universidade de Coimbra, p. 37–67; and Blanco, Ramon (2014). Del Mantenimiento de la Paz al Processo de Formación del Estado: Un Esbozo de los Esforços de la ONU para la Paz Internacional. *Foro Internacional*, v. 216, p. 266–318. I would like to thank the journals for providing the proper permissions.

This whole enterprise would not be possible without my family. Therefore, I would like to thank my father, André, who, by being such an outstanding role model, I owe everything that I am. I would like also to thank Deise, Alice, and Rita for all the support and love, without which this research would not be possible. Finally, to dedicate this book to Fernanda and Maria Isabel is definitely downplaying their role in it. Their mere existence gives me the strength and the love necessary to think, to research, to write, and, most importantly, the very reason to live. Therefore, it is only fair to both of them to say that this book is as much theirs as it is mine.

Introduction

There is little doubt that the overcoming of violent conflicts throughout the globe is one of the most pressing international issues nowadays. Consequently, international peace becomes a fundamental pillar of current international relations.[1] Accordingly, in this setting, peace operations[2] deployed to post-conflict scenarios have become a crucial international policy. In fact, they currently are the very epicenter of a triangular narrative that merges, apparently distant, notions of security, development, and peace.[3] The rationale behind such narrative is quite simple. As this triangular narrative goes, without security there is not the possibility of having any kind of development; development, by its turn, not only reinforces but in fact is an indispensable condition for the increase of security; both, together, are the mandatory pillars for the transformation of violent conflicts throughout the globe and the consolidation of a sustainable peace in post-conflict states. Not by coincidence, peace operations are often portrayed as a mere technical instrument deployed to post-conflict scenarios seeking to overcome violence, both direct and structural,[4] in these places and reconstruct war-torn countries. Hence, under this narrative, peace operations are a technical international tool designed to restructure the political, economic and social spheres of these countries in order to build peace.

Nevertheless, reflecting about current efforts of building peace in post-conflict scenarios, this book proposes a problematization that is developed through the operationalization of two theoretical approaches that are often placed in diametrical opposite epistemic poles—the analytical tools developed by Michel Foucault and the English School. Under this proposed theoretical framework, the book argues that peace operations have a very precise function in current international scenario—the maintenance of international order. More precisely, the book argues that peace operations should be understood as a pivotal international *dispositif*—for now, an heterogeneous assemblage of actors, concepts, institutions, and practices—that is essential to both the fostering and the maintenance of order within a particular international society—a (neo)liberal-democratic one.[5]

Consequently, under this rationale, the construction of peace in our time is understood as an attempt of international normalization of post-conflict states and their populations. International dynamics include mechanisms, tools and rhetoric portrayed as being directed toward the prevention, management, and even the transformation of violent conflicts throughout the globe, contributing to building peace. In this book, the construction of peace is herein understood as the pursuit of shaping and conducting post-conflict states' behaviors so they start behaving less as abnormal states and more as normal states in the international scenario. Examining current international reality, abnormal states are considered as those states labeled as failed ones, or the ones that might become failed, and normal states as the liberal democratic states. Hence, in short, to normalize post-conflict states and their populations means to shape, conduct, and structure their behaviors in order to make them resemble more like liberal-democratic entities.

As the argument goes, such function is rendered operational through the attempt of normalizing post-conflict states and its populations. The pursuit of this normalization is operated through the government, the conduct of conducts in a Foucauldian sense, of post-conflict states and their populations' lives at the international society. Hence, as the argument goes, this normalization attempt occurs in two levels. At the international level, this government operates through discipline, rewarding and punishing post-conflict states seeking to shape their behaviors as individuals in the international society. At the national level, government operates through biopolitics, which functions through the administration and control of life-supporting processes of mass population in these post-conflict states. Hence, bringing Foucault and English School's analytical tools a bit closer, one can clearly perceive that peace operations are in fact a normalizing *dispositif* that seeks the maintenance of a liberal order in the international society.

When mentioning the word *government*, perhaps one of the very first things that come to one's mind is the state and the wide range of institutions it involves. With this kind of understanding in mind, studying government would imply addressing certain questions such as who holds the power? How is this power legitimized? Is it representative? What is the source of this power? (Dean, 2010: 16; Rose, 1999: 1). The understanding of government advanced by Foucault seeks exactly to develop an analytical framework that enables the reflection about the political power exercised precisely outside, above, permeating, across, and beyond the state (Larner and Walters, 2004: 2; Rose and Miller, 1992). Briefly defining government as the conduct of conduct (Foucault, [1982] 2000: 341), Foucault enlarges its meaning to cover the scope adopted in this book, which encompasses processes and mechanisms that are designed to conduct, drive, or shape the conduct and behaviors of individuals or group of individuals ([1980] 2009: 18).

It is precisely due to this Foucauldian enlargement of the meaning of the word that one can analyze government, the conduct of conducts, being rendered operational both on individuals, through the exercise of discipline, and on mass populations, through biopolitics. In regard to the construction of peace, this is an effort that happens in two dimensions. At the international level, this government is rendered operational through the attempt of disciplining the post-conflict state. Discipline seeks to *correct* the individual post-conflict state behaviors in the international sphere. This works through instruments of knowing, assessing, monitoring, individualizing, and ranking and seeks to reward and punish individual post-conflict states for having, or not having, a determinate set of behaviors. These instruments include, for instance, standardized data collection, periodic reports, performance benchmarking, auditing techniques, access to credit lines, funding of projects, conditionalities, and even sanctions. At the national level, government operates through biopolitics. Biopolitics functions through the exercise of a great amount of influence, supervision, and control over life-supporting processes of post-conflict populations, such as health, education, employment, food, fertility, or housing. It works through the transformation of the post-conflict state into a governance state (Duffield, 2007: 82), which is a state that has a form of contingent sovereignty in the sense that its fundamental spheres—the disciplinary, political, and economic governance, and the socio- and biopolitical ones—are under a great amount of international supervision, influence and control (Duffield, 2007: 82).

In order to render its argument operational, the book focuses on the United Nations' (UN) engagement with Timor-Leste, which was, in essence, a deep state-building effort. State-building is herein understood to embrace not only the construction and strengthening of state institutions but also the practices that seek to shape, direct, and conduct the relations between post-conflict states and their population. Therefore, in current post-conflict reconstruction processes, state-building is, not rarely, the most fundamental element of peace operations. Timor-Leste was subject of five UN peace operations: UNAMET (1999), UNTAET (1999–2002), UNMISET (2002–2005), UNOTIL (2005–2006), and UNMIT (2006–2012). Furthermore, Timor-Leste was also subject to two multilateral international interventions— INTERFET (1999–2000) and ISF (2006–2013). Therefore, the country clearly stands out for having in its territory five consecutive UN peace operations and two interventions. Observing the UN engagement with post-conflict scenarios, it is clear that there is no other case with this number of operations, with the range of levels of engagement and the depth of involvement as the UN engagement with Timor-Leste. Moreover, now that the UN presence in

Timor-Leste, in the form of a peace operation, have finished for more than a couple of years, one is in a privileged position to have a more comprehensive understanding about the UN peacebuilding efforts in Timor-Leste, especially its shortcomings. Consequently, Timor-Leste presents itself as the most suitable case to have a refined and, most importantly, comprehensive analysis of UN post-conflict state-building efforts.

The book, while analyzing the UN state-building process in Timor-Leste, delineates the process in which Timor-Leste emerges as an urgent need in the international scenario which should be unequivocally handled. It is precisely this perception of Timor-Leste as an international urgent need—which happens after a very long and bloody path of foreign colonization, occupation, and annexation—that triggers the formation of an international state-building *dispositif* in order to deal with it and, consequently, its deployment to the country. It is this state-building *dispositif* that will seek to normalize Timor-Leste, seeking to prevent it from turning into an abnormal state, a failed one. The overall goal is to make Timor-Leste resemble a normal state, namely a liberal-democratic one.

Throughout the analysis, the book delineates some fundamental limitations of the overall UN state-building process in Timor-Leste. Furthermore, and most importantly, it evinces the UN attempt to conduct and shape not only the Timorese state per se and its very functioning, but also several of its pivotal spheres in a clear attempt to normalize Timor-Leste seeking to making it a liberal democratic state. In this regard, the book analyses the pivotal spheres of a state—namely the disciplinary, political and economic governance, and the socio- and biopolitical spheres—and sheds light on the process in which these spheres, in the case of Timor-Leste, are highly influenced, structured, shaped and supervised by internationals. The book elucidates how several institutions, processes and practices within each of these fundamental spheres are severely supervised by internationals, who constantly seek to shape them toward a determinate end, toward a liberal-democratic functioning. Remarkably, this process does not end, and in fact becomes denser, after Timor-Leste restores its legal independence. In addition, the book delineates the very instruments which, although having a power-denying technical and bureaucratic tones, are fundamental to rendering this normalizing *dispositif* operational in Timor-Leste.

The main point here is not of condemning/praising the efforts done by the UN so far in the country. Approaching the UN intervention in Timor-Leste as a manner of good or bad is certainly not the best way to problematize UN state-building strategies. The path pursued here is essentially to unnaturalize the natural. This means that the path taken seeks to expose a wide range of actions and relationships that might pass as unproblematic and which are the very ones that are pivotal instruments that the UN used in its attempt to normalize Timor-Leste. The critical problematization of the state-building process is of utmost relevance in our present time. After all, as already mentioned, state-building has become a pivotal practice of the contemporary international scene. This importance lays essentially on the fact that state-building has become a key instrument employed by both states and international/regional organizations, as a manner of addressing, at once, three main international discourses of current international relations—international security, poverty reduction, and the construction of peace. Indeed, state-building is often understood, by those who have a more orthodox understanding of the international reality, as the most appropriate tool to merge these discourses and deal with the issues of security, development and peace simultaneously. What agglutinates these issues, within a mainstream rationale, is the notion of state fragility, understood as the weak institutions and governance systems with a limited capacity to deliver key public goods. This fragility is perceived, simultaneously, as the main source of global insecurities, a fundamental barrier to the overall development of the whole globe, and as a source to violent conflicts since, under this line of reasoning, underdevelopment might lead to poverty which could easily lead to violence.

In order for state-building processes to operate smoothly in the international scenario, this notion of state fragility which is rendered operational by the idea of failed states must be coupled with a reinterpretation of the idea of state sovereignty. The idea of sovereignty has always been the very bedrock of international relations. Nevertheless, this was a concept that suffered a distinct reproblematization after the Cold War when the state (in)capacity emerged as a fundamental element of analysis of the international scenario. This process could hardly be developed without a differentiation and (re)categorization of the concept of sovereignty, without the development of the notion of *gradations* of sovereignty (Keohane, 2003). Robert Jackson, for example, makes his distinction in terms of *positive* and *negative* sovereignty (1990). Whereas the positive sovereignty is the possession of state characteristics *de facto* and *de jure*, the negative one is the absence of the *de facto* characteristics, even though possessing the *de jure* ones (Hill, 2005: 146). For the orthodox thinking, it is precisely this space between both kinds of sovereignty, de jure on the one hand and de facto on the other hand, that constitutes the main obstacle to global peace, security, and prosperity (Ghani, Lockhart, and Carnahan, 2005: 4). For Stephen Krasner, sovereignty is analyzed in terms of three *attributes*: (1) domestic sovereignty, being the capacity of internal governance; (2) Westphalian/Vattelian sovereignty, being the self-government and political autonomy; and (3) international legal sovereignty, being the formal juridical independence (2004: 87–88). It is precisely this differentiation that enables state-building processes, while being portrayed as merely seeking to strength weak state institutions and reduce their fragility, to be easily described as a beneficial enterprise that actually *en-*

hances a post-conflict state's sovereignty and autonomy instead of a practice that in fact limits their range of possible actions.

Therefore, not by coincidence, in a state-centric rationale such as the one which clearly permeates and underpins current international relations, state-building is understood as a crucial element for both the pursuit of international security and for the very preservation of world order (Rotberg, 2003: 1). Moreover, it is understood that state-building, through the enhancement of the state's capacities, is an essential element in overcoming underdevelopment and therefore increasing the standard of living across the globe. These two elements—security and development—are considered to be essential pillars of peace. Hence, it easily follows that state-building is fundamental to the construction of international peace in today's world (Brahimi, 2007). In fact, closely observing the main efforts of building peace in several post-conflict scenarios, this is exactly what is taking place (Richmond and Franks, 2009). This is how state-building emerges in the international scenario as the fundamental node of a triangular narrative of peace, security, and development.

Surprisingly, notwithstanding such centrality in the current international scenario, very frequently, the discussions about state-building deal with its technical aspects or instrumental improvements and the ways in which it can be rendered operational (Chandler, 2006: 5–6). Such studies are obviously relevant and important. Nevertheless, they tend to be limited in their analysis. Merely analyzing state-building processes by themselves, neglecting the entrenched and deep power relations underlying them, is missing most of the picture. Evincing these power relations, which constitute the fundamental element of these processes, can only emerge with a critical reading of the state-building process. Hence, critically analyzing such crucial processes renders these relations more visible and offers a better understanding of the functioning of their devices, opening up new areas for discussion, rethinking, and change which is of high importance. It is fundamental, while doing such analysis, not merely to see the state-building processes but especially to observe them. It is their close observation that brings the deep power relations entrenched in the process to light. For this enterprise, especially in terms of evincing entrenched power relations, the theoretical and analytical tools developed by Michel Foucault are of great help.

They enable an analyst to rethink how she perceives and makes sense of the construction of peace. In addition, it also allows not only the exposition of the shortcomings of the state-building process carried out by the UN in Timor-Leste but also offers a distinct understanding of it. Moreover, it makes possible the evincing of deep and hierarchal power relations entrenched in the very process of building peace. It allows for a more comprehensive understanding of the state-building practice performed in Timor-Leste, and certainly other post-conflict scenarios, by rendering visible power relations, which shape the attempt to normalize it. This kind of theoretical tools offers the possibility of shedding light on the fact that the very construction of peace, rather than a technical or apolitical enterprise toward reconstruction, is in fact a mechanism of putting in place a surveillance framework, composed by several instruments, that is pivotal to the normalizing assemblage operating in any post-conflict state, especially in Timor-Leste. It facilitates precisely a sophisticated analysis by making it possible to observe that this surveillance framework is what enables the conduction of one's conducts to be rendered operational *through* the very construction of the other's freedom. Therefore, it enables reflecting on government being rendered operational through the very construction of freedom and independence, as it is exemplary in post-conflict scenarios, especially in Timor-Leste. Most importantly, it enables the observation of the fact that this surveillance framework is pivotal to placing Timor-Leste under a constant and frequent international scrutiny and observation, which aims to closely monitor whether Timor-Leste, as a country, and its population are being conducted toward what is understood by the state-builders as the right direction—making Timor-Leste a liberal democratic country.

Furthermore, this kind of analysis enables the observation that the construction of peace, in Timor-Leste, was in fact a process that ended up transforming the country into a governance state. Consequently, what is observed is a top-down approach toward peace that is poorly embedded within Timorese social, political, and economic structures. This, in turn, in addition to structure Timorese conducts, lays a fragile basis for the future development of Timor-Leste. It makes the constant international monitoring and supervision a permanent need, so the overall thin stabilization of the country achieved so far can be sustainable.

Moreover, the kind of analysis herein advanced enables the delineation of deep power relations entrenched in the UN engagement with Timor-Leste being rendered operational precisely through power-denying notions. Among the buzzwords of post-conflict (re)construction efforts, one can find, for instance, good governance, capacity-building, empowerment, mentoring, advising, and even local ownership. Approaching state-building using Foucauldian theoretical and analytical tools makes possible to evince the attempt of government being operated precisely *through* good governance, capacity-building, empowerment, mentoring, and ownership. Remarkably, closely observing post-conflict reconstruction efforts, rather than being a camouflage or a rhetorical mask for real and deep power relations, they are actually some of the very tools *through* which government and the normalization effort pursued are exercised. The framework herein used enables the observation that exactly because of that, they are clearly power-denying. They are power-denying in the very sense that they enable a great amount of power to be exercised precisely through the negation of its exercise. This certainly resembles what David Chandler (2006) conceptualizes as an empire in denial. With this concept Chandler (2006: 10) seeks to capture how non-western states and populations are internationally intervened, while at the same time such intervention is constantly evading from any kind of responsibility or account-ability. To Chandler (2006: 11), the denial is not due to the fact that there is less regulation of the non-Western states and societies. On the contrary, for him there is much more regulation attached to aid and assistance than before. The denial comes with the fact that this regulation is precisely clothed in technical, bureaucratic, and non-political tones. In order to clearly perceive this process, it is of great help to bring a bit closer the problematizations, on the one hand, in regard to the international society developed by the English School and, on the other hand, the technologies of power theorized by Mich-el Foucault. It is toward this delineation that the book now turns.

INTERNATIONAL SOCIETY AND
TECHNOLOGIES OF POWER

Arguing that peace operations have a precise function in current international scenario, serving as a pivotal *dispositif* that is essential to both the fostering and maintenance of order within a particular international society—a liberal-democratic one—seeks to bring a bit closer two problematizations that are not often operationalized together—the theoretical and conceptual tools de-veloped by the English School and by Michel Foucault.[6] This certainly might appear as, to say the least, an eccentric move. After all, both problematiza-tions definitely have a lot of differences. The major of them is epistemic, and some of these differences are perhaps even irreconcilable. Not by coinci-dence, both problematizations are often placed, quite correctly, in different poles of the so-called great debates[7] within the discipline of international relations.

Nevertheless, seeking to observe beyond their distance, which is some-thing real, it is certainly possible to seek bringing them a bit closer and peace operations is perhaps the most appropriate international practice that an en-able such movement. Both problematizations are herein understood as hav-ing the capacity of illuminating different aspects of peace operations as an international practice and the process of building peace around the globe. It is only by bringing the conceptual and theoretical tools developed by the Eng-lish School and Michel Foucault that one can properly apprehend, for in-stance, the reasoning, even though unconsciously, underneath such process. The assumption, even though not spoken, is that international relations are constituted by an international society, where its members, in this case states, share certain values and behaviors, (neo)liberal ones, and that individuals of this society who does not have this kind of behavior should be intervened so they have their conducts shaped in this direction. In this sense the English School analytical tools provide the understanding about the scenario and the environment where the peace operations operate, whereas the conceptual tools advanced by Foucault enable the perception of the function and the role that they have in this environment. It is to the elucidation of these elements that this book now turns.

International System and International Society

Perhaps the first delineation that is important to make while bringing the English School's analytical tools is the distinction that the school makes between international system and international society. Both terms are part of the basic triad of concepts, which also includes the notion of world society, from where the English School's thought is developed (Buzan, 2014: 12). Whereas the latter plays a more marginal role in the English School's problematizations, the distinction between the other two, on the contrary, has a fundamental place within it (Buzan, 2014: 15). Each one of the three notions represent a particular understanding about the international environment and the kind of relationship among the actors within it will predominate. These concepts derive from three distinct traditions of thought,[8] respectively: (1) the Hobbesian or realist tradition; (2) the Grotian or internationalist tradition; and (3) the Kantian or universalist tradition (Bull, 1977: 23). To Hedley Bull (1977), these traditions reflects both an understanding about international politics and a set of conducts that are expected, and also prescribed, in the international sphere (Bull, 1977: 23).

Consequently, the distinction between international system and international society[9] rests on essentially different world conceptions and on different degrees of relationship among its members. On the one hand, in the view of Hedley Bull (1977), the international system, or a system of states, departs from a Hobbesian tradition and emerges not with the mere existence of two or more states. The main issue regarding the notion has to do more with the contact among the units, states, than with the mere existence of them. For Hedley Bull (1977), the international system emerges when the states have not only enough contact among them but also a degree of relationship that makes them part of a whole (Bull, 1977: 9). Consequently, the emergence of an international system occurs when, in addition to this relationship among states, such relationship is sufficiently relevant to make them take it into account when problematizing their own behaviors (Bull, 1977: 10).[10] These regular contacts among states may vary and also take place in different spheres. They can range from conflict to cooperation, or neutrality/indifference and take place in difference spheres, such as the political, economic social and so on (Bull, 1977: 10).

International society, on the other hand, departs from a Grotian tradition and presupposes a much denser degree of relationship between the actors of the international scene, which continue to be essentially states. In fact, the existence of an international society presupposes the existence of an international system. However, the opposite is not true. An international system can certainly exist without emerging an international society (Bull, 1977: 13). The notion of international society is at the very core of the English School's understanding about international relations. An international society, in the view of Hedley Bull (1977), is about the perception and understanding, among states, that they share some common norms and kinds of behaviors internationally. Moreover, in this rationale, the states conceive themselves as not only bound by this set of norms, but also part in the efforts in the very maintenance of these norms and conducts through different set of international institutions (Bull, 1977: 13).

A common parallel made for understanding the notion of international society, a society of states in Bull's words (1977: 13), is observing what takes place within the states. Barry Buzan (2014), for instance, makes this connection when he says that just as individuals influence and are influenced by the society in which they live, states also influence and are influenced by the international society (Buzan, 2014: 13). However, while making this kind of association, one should be very careful about not falling on what Bull named as the domestic analogy (Bull, 1977: 44), which could very much be named as the domestic fallacy. Hedley Bull understood this rationale that he named as domestic analogy as the core of the counter-argument against the notion of international society. According to this notion, which the English School certainly disagrees, [11] since the international relations are anarchical, in the sense of the absence of a political entity above states, the states do not form together a society. As this argument goes, states would only form a society if they abdicate their sovereignties and subordinate themselves to a common political authority (Bull, 1977: 44). On the contrary, for the English School, states can form a society, even though an anarchic society, even not submitting themselves to higher form of political power (Linklater, 2005: 84). For the English School, there is a high level of order, a certain disposition of the international practices that organize the international reality (Bull, 1977: 16), despite the fact that the international condition is one of anarchy (Bull, 1977: 16). That is why Bull argues about an anarchical society in the international sphere (Bull, 1977).

It is precisely the parallel with the domestic society, without falling of course on what Bull named as the domestic analogy, that allows the approximation with the problematizations advanced by the French philosopher Michel Foucault. The analytical tools developed by Foucault are powerful instruments that enable the reflection about some mechanisms present in the international scenario that are fundamental for the maintenance of order in the international society. As aforementioned, it is herein argued that peace operations are one of these instruments. In order to perceive this, the paper now turns to the delineation of some analytical tools developed by Michel Foucault.

Opening Foucault's Toolbox

The French philosopher Michel Foucault is a decisive thinker of the twentieth century. Due to his mastery in analyzing and uncovering hidden power relations, a key asset of Foucault's thought is the strength that his research has in providing analytical and theoretical tools which are very useful in investigating and scrutinizing a wide variety of issues and subjects of very distinct fields. In fact, the use of Foucauldian analytical tools has a strong impact and it is ubiquitous in a wide range of disciplines in social sciences in general. In a sense, this is might be understood as a consequence of Foucault's perception about his own work as a provider of analytical tools. This is straightforwardly clear in the way Foucault himself understands his own work—as a sort of a toolbox from where other researchers can find a tool to use in other areas ([1974] 1994: 523–524).

Inside Foucault's toolbox, *dispositif* and normalization are certainly among these useful tools. *Dispositif*[12] is a decisive term in Foucault's thought. Nevertheless, interestingly enough, Foucault never devoted a major work to it or gave a concrete definition of the term (Agamben, 2009: 2). It was other scholars, like Gilles Deleuze (2007), for instance, who tried to delineate a clearer understanding of the term. Although not offering a complete definition, Foucault comes close to it when he delineated what a *dispositif* was during an interview (Agamben, 2009: 2) when he points to the understanding of a *dispositif* as an heterogeneous assemblage composed by different kinds of elements, such as discourses, institutions, procedures, laws, architectural elements, moral statements, administrative measures, and so on, that form a system of relations. The *dispositif*, in Foucault's understanding, has, in a given moment in history, the purpose of responding and answering to a certain urgent need (Foucault, 1980: 194–196).

Stretching even further the already loose Foucauldian understanding of *dispositif*, Giorgio Agamben understands the *dispositif* as anything that can, in any way, shape or conduct the ways in which someone behave, think, or express one's thinking (2009: 14). Therefore, the *dispositif* is essentially a heterogeneous assemblage composed by different, and quite often competing and conflicting practices, institutions, administrative measures, legislations, actors, concepts, theories, kinds of knowledge, and so on, that emerges in order to deal with a certain issue. To be more precise, the *dispositif* emerges in a determinate moment in order to address something that, at that particular moment, starts to be perceived as an urgent need, seeking to shape, conduct and orient it in a specific manner.

Whereas, on the one hand, the *dispositif* can be understood as the analytical grip that binds a wide range of elements that, although disparate, conflicting, and quite often not related, are part of a comprehensive whole that emerges in order to address an urgent need; normalization, on the other hand, can be understood as a process of handling this urgent need. It can be rationalized as the approach in which this urgent need is shaped and conducted in a specific manner. In this regard, one must notice that, from the start, this notion of normalization is entrenched by an underpinning, though very often silenced, distinction between normal and abnormal conditions.

In the normalization process, the normal condition is the primary element and the norm is deduced from it. It is clear though that there are normalities that are more acceptable than others; there are ones that are more normal than others, and therefore the latter become the abnormal ones, while the former the normal ones. Hence, those abnormal ones must be intervened to become more like the normal ones (Foucault, [1978] 2007: 63). The normalization process seeks thus to bring the abnormal elements to resemble more as the normal ones. Therefore, the abnormal ones are intervened, through a variety of institutions, techniques, and practices, in order to make them behave more like the normal ones. In Foucault's studies, the abnormal ones were the sick, the pervert, the delinquent, the mad, and so on. In a variety of manners, such as through hospitalization, psychoanalysis, schooling, incarceration, beating, among others, the ones understood to be the abnormal ones within a specific society have their behaviors and actions intervened in such a way so their behaviors look more like to what was perceived as a normal behavior within that society.

This normalization process is rendered operational by a range of technologies of power.[13] Technologies of power, for Foucault, relate to the conduct of individuals and their submission to certain ends (Kelly, 2009: 44). They are technologies that have the objective of shaping one's conduct with a dual purpose: on the one hand, directing it to a desired effect and, on the other hand, deterring undesired outcomes (Rose, 1999: 52). When Foucault talks about power, this is merely an abbreviation for what he really advances as the object of his analyses—the relationships of power (1994: 11). These, understood by Foucault as the ways in which one seeks to conduct and shape the conducts and behaviors of the other, are present in any society (Foucault, 1994: 18). Hence, Foucault problematizes power as a relationship where one attempts to produce, direct and determinate the behaviors of others (Foucault, 1994: 11). He sees that, throughout time, although the nature and essence of power did not change, its technological functioning did (Kelly, 2009: 42). Therefore, Foucault perceives that what really changes throughout time in regard to the exercise of power is its functioning, the manner in which and through what instruments it is exercised (its technological devices), and not its very essence—the attempt of shaping behaviors. This is where Foucault differentiates the technologies of power such as government, discipline, and biopower.[14]

Placing the notion of government as a guideline (Foucault, [1978] 2007: 363) to his investigations, Foucault introduced a new dimension for investigating power relations which can now be problematized from a different angle, from the conduct of conducts standpoint (Bröckling, Krasmann, and Lemke, 2011: 2). Briefly defining government as the conduct of conduct, Foucault notoriously plays with the double meaning of the word *conduct* and consciously sees it as a proper analogy to understand power relations ([1982] 2000: 341). Whereas as a verb, to conduct, means to lead, to guide, or to direct, as a noun, conduct refers to the human actions and behaviors (Dean, 2010: 17). Linking these two meanings, government as conduct of conduct seeks to capture the attempts to shape and outline the behaviors of oneself or the others, in light of a specific set norms or rules (even though they are not written at all), toward a particular objective (Dean, 2010: 18).

Understanding government as the conduct of conduct frees the reflection about the exercise of power from the common sense. Government in the Foucauldian sense is much more than the bureaucratic image that might emerge once reading the word. For Foucault, government is dispositional. Government is about the disposition of a variety of elements, arranging them in a convenient way, in order to achieve a particular end (Foucault, [1978] 2007: 99). Consequently, to govern becomes more than the mere management of state structures and legal apparatus. In fact, to govern, within this framework, means essentially to structure the area in which the possible actions and behaviors of the other can be performed (Foucault, [1982] 2000: 341). Therefore, government does not simply refer state structures. It refers to the way in which one can direct and shape the behaviors and conducts of individuals or groups toward a specific kind of behavior and conduct. It is in this sense that one can speak about the government of the sick, the families, the soul, the communities, the workers, and so on (Foucault, [1982] 2000: 341). Hence, government becomes an activity that does not operate solely at the state level and institutions but indeed turns out to be apparent in the everyday aspects and places of an ordinary life such as at schools, factories, hospitals, business enterprises, religious sites, families, and so on.

The normalization process is rendered operational through government, the conduct of conduct. This can be developed in two dimensions—either focusing on individuals or on populations. This is where the notions of discipline and biopower are helpful. In regard to discipline and biopower, Foucault observed these two technologies of power emerged during the modern period and are, respectively, micro- and macro-political. Although these technologies have the general features of all technologies of power, they allowed a more productive and a closer direction of behaviors and conducts, in regard to both individuals and populations, than was possible with other kinds of technologies of power (Kelly, 2009: 43). In addition to the magnitude of the possibilities of their actions, these technologies of power were also different in regard to the manner in which they were exercised. Discipline and biopower are exercised through *correcting* individuals and *enhancing life*, respectively. A key element of these technologies of power visualized by Foucault is that they operate in different levels and scales and operate through different instruments. This fact is what allows one technology to exist without the extinction of the other. Indeed, this allows these technologies function simultaneously and complementarily.

In essence, discipline seeks to correct the individual behaviors that are considered inappropriate. Due to its essence of *correcting*, and therefore changing behaviors, discipline is a type of power that is very much connected to the notion, previously presented, of normalization. Indeed, the ultimate aim of discipline is to normalize, which makes the detailed dissociation of normalizing and disciplining processes impossible. Indeed, for Foucault a disciplining mechanism is in essence a normalization mechanism. ([1978] 2007: 56). This is a result of the fact that discipline is at the same time an individualizing and a relational process. This might sound paradoxical at first but, in fact, these characteristics are very much complementary. Being the essence of discipline the correction of the behaviors of deviant individuals, the operative word here is certainly the adjective *deviant*. In this sense, the disciplinary mechanism visualizes what should be the *correct* behavior and mold the incorrect and *deviant* ones toward this *correct* model of behavior. Consequently, discipline is a technology of power that seeks to shape the individual behavior both rewarding what understands as a correct behavior and punishing what perceives as a deviant one. This is nothing but a normalization process. Therefore, discipline can perfectly be understood as one of the mechanisms in which a normalization process can be rendered operational, in the individual level. It is through punishing and rewarding techniques that abnormal behaviors are molded and corrected, and the normal ones invested and stimulated.

From the second half of the eighteenth century onward, Foucault visualizes the appearance of a new technology of power that operates on the opposite pole of discipline—biopower.[15] Biopower in essence is a macropolitical power. Whereas discipline is exercised on the individual, biopower is exercised on the collectivity having the population as its target (Kelly, 2009: 43). Consequently, this is a technology of power that is not concerned with the individual wo/man, but with wo/men as living beings (Foucault, [1976] 2003: 242). In contrast to discipline, biopower is applied to the individual as a living being (Foucault, [1976] 2003: 242). As a result, whereas discipline is applied to a multiplicity of people because this whole can be divided into individuals who can be put under surveillance, series, hierarchies, and, if necessary, be punished, biopower acts exactly in the opposite way. It is addressed to a multiplicity of people in the sense that these individuals, collective, are affected by overall and agglutinating processes like death, health, jobs, birth, incarceration, housing, and many others (Foucault, [1976] 2003: 242–243). Therefore, biopower is a technology that is exercised not over the individual body, as in discipline, but is fundamentally exercised over the populations' life. Consequently, rather what is perceived is the emergence of a biopolitics (Foucault, [1976] 2003: 243).

Consequently, biopolitics is the management of overall processes that affect the groups of people as living beings (Rabinow and Rose, 2003: 6). Hence, it is a kind of politics that entails the supervision and the management of the processes that affect the lives of a population as a whole (Duffield, 2007: 5). Hence, biopolitics starts to problematize a whole set of phenomena that bind population together, that makes it a coherent whole. It problematizes all the biological processes concerning a population (Foucault, [1976] 1978: 139) and, consequently, its demographic characteristics (Smart, 2002: 99). Consequently, this new regulatory power is concerned essentially with the government of groups of human living beings, in the form of populations (Duffield, 2007: 6). As a result of that, biopolitics problematizes and rationalizes the whole set of processes surrounding the populations' life intervening in phenomena such as birth, death, production, working conditions, nutrition, illness, fertility, health, employment, life expectancy, housing, education, standards of living, and so on, and with all the conditions that surround and might have an influence on them (Duffield, 2007: 6; Foucault, [1976] 1978: 139).

One should remember that these technologies of power do not operate solely. In fact, they operate simultaneously and complementarily to each other. For Foucault, what links all these different domains is that they shared a common focus—the government, at once, of each and all (Gordon, 1991: 3). The common element that is pervasive throughout these disparate domains is the concern of how to govern individuals and collectivities. They form a structure of power that seeks to conduct the conducts of the other, individually or *en masse*, assuring the correction and the optimization of each and all (Rose, 1999: 23). They form a structure of power that seeks the government, the conduct of conducts, being operated both on individuals, through the exercise of discipline, and on mass populations, through biopolitics. At the core of this structure of power, there is the norm. The norms plays a key role, since it circulates between both discipline and biopolitics (Rose, 1999: 253). It is in light of the norm that the normalization, rendered operational through the conduct of conduct, working through discipline and biopolitics, depending of the level, functions. As Foucault properly remembers, the norm is what one applies toward an individual who one wants to be disciplined and toward a population that one wants to be regularized (Rose, 1999: 253).

PEACE OPERATIONS AS A NORMALIZING *DISPOSITIF*

The construction of international peace went through a lot of modifications throughout time. They modified in regards to the extent, depth, and range of the activities performed on the ground.[16] During the Cold War, peace operations were a light-armed force that was understood as an instrument deployed to the ground in order to act as a buffer between two belligerent states (Newman, Paris and Richmond, 2009: 5; Paris and Sisk, 2009b: 4). From the end of the Cold War onward, peace operations started enlarging the activities performed on the ground. In addition to incorporating civilians in its activities, they started to perform practices such as the supervision of elections, constitution drafting, reconstructing security sectors, mainstreaming gender, fostering human rights, and acting on the social, political and economic sectors of post-conflict societies, to name a few. Most importantly, peace operations became very much connected with state-building. In fact, state-building—the process of not only constructing and strengthening of state institutions but also the practices that seek to shape, direct and conduct the relations between post-conflict states and their population—became the very core of peace operations.

With that in mind, the analytical tools aforementioned are very useful in the (re)problematization of the construction of peace in the international relations. The analytical tools enable the problematization of the role that peace operations have in international politics, operating in the international society as normalizing *dispositif* directed to post-conflict states and populations. In this sense, peace operations are understood as a *dispositif* that emerges as a response to what is perceived as an urgent need in the international society. Therefore, peace operations can be understood as a normalizing technology that seeks to govern post-conflict states and populations, to conduct their conducts, both through the attempt of disciplining the post-conflict state as an individual entity in the international society and through the constant exercise of a biopolitical power over life-supporting processes of its population. Consequently, peace operations are a normalizing *dispositif* designed to act on both societies—of the first and second order.

The elements of this normalizing *dispositif* are the actors, theories, discourses, concepts, practices, instruments, institutions, and so on, which are comprised by a peace operation and deployed to the ground seeking to shape and conduct the behaviors of post-conflict states and their populations. The notion of *dispositif* applied to the comprehension of peace operations deployed to post-conflict scenarios facilitates the understanding of the wide and distinct series of actions, experts, practices, procedures, and concepts that are part of the reconstruction process. These elements, in fact, may not be inter-related at all and quite often can be very conflicting. Nevertheless, they can be understood as part of one comprehensive and coherent whole. It is precisely this sense that this notion of *dispositif* seeks to capture.

As mentioned before, a *dispositif* emerges in order to respond to an urgent need. Nevertheless, although a certain situation might be characterized as an urgent need by those who live under this condition, this does not mean that this situation is understood as an urgent need within the international society. The emergence of an urgent need in the international society, and the legitimation of the operationalization of the normalizing *dispositif* that peace operations materializes, are usually underpinned by two operating notions—state fragility and the transformation of the understanding of sovereignty into state capacity. These notions are closely linked, by the mainstream thinking, to violence, insecurity, and poverty. Under this rationale, it is the uneasiness of a place becoming a fragile state or a state with limited capacity—and potentially being harbor for violence, insecurity, and poverty—and, in turn, becoming a threat to the stability[17] of the international society that sparks the emergence of the *dispositif* that peace operations materialize. Connecting both notions, on the one hand, the *dispositif*, while designed to address state fragility, is construed as a fundamental instrument designed to deal with what is perceived as an urgent need in order to enhance the security and well-being in the international society. On the other hand, since it is portrayed as closing the post-conflict states' sovereignty gap,[18] peace operations are not viewed as a problematic external intervention, since they are portrayed as working on the domestic, or *de facto*, sovereignty of post-conflict states while maintaining intact their international legal, or *de jure*, sovereignty. In fact, through both notions, peace operations are portrayed as *enhancing* post-conflict states capacity. Indeed, the processes rendered operational by peace operations on the ground are often represented as a beneficial relationship between the external actors and the post-conflict states being intervened, in the sense that the former are portrayed as reinforcing the sovereignty and independence of the latter.

In addition, perceiving that peace operations function as a normalizing *dispositif* within the international society, one is able to clearly observe that underpinning the functioning of this technology, there is an inherent understanding of what constitutes the normal and the abnormal behaviors of this international society. In Foucault's reflections, those that should be normal-ized—the abnormal ones—were the sick, the pervert, the delinquent, the mad, and so on. These were the ones that needed to be intervened in order to be normalized and to become more normal elements within the society in general. In the international society, it is clear which are constructed as the normal and abnormal elements. The normal elements are the Western-liberal-democratic states while the abnormal ones are the ones that do not have this kind of behavior in the international society. It is from this understanding of the international society that is deduced the norm that is rendered operational through the discipline of post-conflict states as individuals of the international society and the biopolitical exercise of power over post-conflict populations. The norm is that the states should resemble liberal democracies. This is the norm against which the abnormal states are intervened in order to make them resemble more like the normal ones.

However, one should not forget that the normal and abnormal are not inherent and natural conditions of the international society. The normal and abnormal conditions need to be constructed as such, so they become crystallized and constituted as facts. These conditions are fundamental for determining which values and behaviors are construed as shared and, most importantly acceptable, and which ones are not acceptable within the international society. Although both conditions are constructed, those working on peace operations move on the ground having both conditions assumed, even though most of the time unconsciously, as true facts and therefore they are the background that shapes the practices on the field. It is the Mozambican novelist Mia Couto who perhaps best captured the essence of this construction when he writes in one of his novels that "the facts are only true after being invented" (Couto, 2002: 111). Regarding the normal behavior within the international society, the construction of this condition is underpinned by a dual narrative and understanding: (1) that the state formation in Western Europe as *the* path of organizing a political entity and becoming states, and (2) the equaling of liberal values with peace and prosperity. This is what is construed as the fundamental shared, and most importantly acceptable, values and behaviors that the whole international society must abide. In this framework, those who do not share, or are perceived as not sharing, these values and behaviors are intervened in order to have what is understood as an appropriated behavior within the international society. This dual narrative materialized and merged in the notion of good governance. In the case of the abnormal condition, this abnormality is constructed through the idea of state fragility and the failed state notion.

Considering the former, instead of understanding the process of state formation in Western Europe as a process that is located both in time and space, and not at all replicable, this process is understood, even though sometimes unconsciously, as the normal historical path of creating and forming states. Therefore, the normalization process of post-conflict states seeks to place these states in this normal historical path. Francis Fukuyama, in his *The Origins of Political Order* (2011), perhaps best sums up this understanding of what is this normal path for the creation of a state, which is highly shared by the peacebuilders. For him, a successful state would combine a stable balance of three important political institutions—the state itself, the rule of law, and an accountable government—and the result of a twofold interaction—among the states themselves and among the social groups within the state's society. Therefore, in Fukuyama's eyes, a successful state formation process produces a state that on the one hand, concentrated the power, made the citizens compliant with the laws, and defended itself and its population from outside threats; and, on the other hand, had a rule of law and an accountable government limiting state's power, making it operate within certain rules, and ensuring that the state would be subordinated to the will of the population (Fukuyama, 2011: 15–16).

Interestingly, observing the practices developed on the ground in a post-conflict state, it stands quite clear that the normalization process is much more than the attempt of *correcting* these states' institutions, behaviors and practices; it is as if peacebuilders seek to *correct* these states' history. Even though current post-conflict peacebuilders rhetorically argue that each place has its own specificity and characteristics, and as a consequence has its own developing path, this could not be farther from the reality on the ground. In fact, the attempt of implementing in post-conflict states the resulting elements of a very-long-time process that took place in Western Europe—the state itself, the rule of law, and an accountable government—has a silenced element. Indeed, through the pursuit of inserting these elements in post-conflict states, peacebuilders demonstrate an understanding that the process that took place in Western Europe is the normal and correct historical path of the formation of states. Therefore, even though this might not consciously be perceived by peacebuilders, what is pursued is more than the mere institution-building. It is the very *correction* of post-conflict states' history itself that is pursued. In this sense, peace operations become an instrument through which peacebuilders can seek to place post-conflict states within *the* normal and correct historical path, speeding up their passage through this path.

In regard to the second narrative that underpins what is construed as being the normal condition in the international society, it has to do with an understanding that equates the liberal values with peace and prosperity. Hence, the consequential norm taken from this understanding, rests fundamentally in the notions advanced by thinkers such as Immanuel Kant (1905 [1795]), Joseph Schumpeter (1966 [1919]), Montesquieu (2002 [1748]) and others that liberalism—in political, economic, and social terms—has a pacifying effect on states, both internally and externally (Richmond, 2008: 89–90). Consequently, according to this argument, those states that have liberal institutions would be more peaceful and prosperous than non-liberal ones (Newman, Paris and Richmond, 2009: 11). Therefore, the adherence to liberalism is equated with the way toward peace and prosperity. This narrative is materialized in the international society through the liberal peace[19] argument, which construes liberalism as a fundamental shared value, and consequently adequate behavior, within the liberal international society in regard to which its members should comply.

The dual narrative underpinning the construction of the normal behavior in the international society is materialized and epitomized by the notion of good governance. Since the 1990s, several international organizations, especially those working on development assistance and the provision of finance support, started to embrace a new motto—good governance (Wouters and Ryngaert, 2005: 69). Indeed, it was the World Bank who played a key role in disseminating the good governance notion among the international organizations (Zanotti, 2005: 468). Actually, the idea of governance is important since it frames the area of intervention. For the World Bank, governance means "the manner in which power is exercised in the management of a country's economic and social resources for development" (1992: 92). Despite the importance of the term *governance*, what is the key operative word of the notion is the adjective *good*. At this point, it is perceptible that whereas the financial institutions emphasized the macro-economic reforms as a borrowing requirement, the political ones placed more attention to democratic principles, human rights and rule of law (Wouters and Ryngaert, 2005: 69–77).[20] Hence, the function of the notion good governance is twofold. Firstly, through the idea of governance, it structures the very area that should be intervened, and therefore it delineates *where*—namely the state structures, its *modus operandi*, and its relationships with its own population—the internationals should focus their actions and influences. Secondly, through the idea of good, it delineates *how* those areas intervened should in fact behave. It frames the kind of outcomes expected from the intervention performed. Regarding the construction of peace in post-conflict scenarios, this notion of good directly refers to a neoliberal-democratic polity with respect for human rights and underpinned by rule of law.

Furthermore, the implicit and unsaid idea of the good governance notion is that there is a *bad* governance. While there is a good and correct governance, which should be stimulated and fostered in the international society, the other side of the coin is the bad and inappropriate governance which must be intervened and corrected. This correction of the bad governance toward a good one would come through economic, political, and social reforms like the reduction of trading barriers and tariffs, privatization of state-owned properties, deregulation and liberalization of the economy, marketization of public services, budgetary discipline, respect for human rights, NGO engagement, rule of law, and so on (Wouters and Ryngaert, 2005: 73; Zanotti, 2005: 468). More profoundly, this correction can come through the very delineating and shaping of the *modus operandi* of the institutions built in post-conflict institutions. It is Zanotti, for instance, who elucidates that good governance "became the organizing concept for UN interventions in diverse fields, the key for achieving not only democracy but also development and peace"

(2005: 469). This is an important element of the normalization process under which post-conflict states and populations suffer by the normalizing *dispositif* that peace operations materialize.

In addition, one should not forget that the abnormal condition also needs to be construed as such. It is in this construction of abnormality and at the normalization process that the failed state notion works perfectly. This is a *contrario* concept. It incorporates a subliminal dichotomy, unspoken, of what it is a successful/normal state (Pureza et al., 2007a: 3), which, as already mentioned, is the (neo)liberal-democratic one. This concept is at the heart of the very existence and need of the normalizing *dispositif*. The notion is a fundamental operating concept of the process. As already discussed, peace operations emerge in the international society in order to address the question of fragility, and this question is rendered operational through the notion of failed states. This concept emerges when the orthodox rationale observing the international society problematizes the fragility and the lack of capacity of some state structures, or their bad governance (Doornbos, 2006: 2). Under this line of thought, the failed states are those states that failed to behave as normal states. In addition, those states are constructed as pathologies of the international society that need to be cured. They are portrayed as abnormal states in the international society through analogies such as: "degenerative disease" (Zartman, 1995: 8), "serious mental or physical illness" (Helman and Rather, 1992: 12), or even "dead leaves that accumulate in a forest" (Krasner and Pascual, 2005: 155), to name a few. Therefore, the failed state notion has a fourfold function, even though they are not, most of the time, clearly visible. They are: (1) relational, in the sense that it construes the problematization of these states in relation to other states; (2) constructive, in the sense that constructs these states as abnormals; (3) hierarchical, in the sense that, while problematizing these states in relation to other states and constructing them as abnormals, clearly hierarchizes the states in the international scenario; and (4) prescriptive, in the sense that while delineation the reality that interests to describe, it also inherently frame what should be enhanced and where the interventions should focus (Pureza et al., 2006: 2–5).

Therefore, the notion of failed states not only works making the normalizing *dispositif* emerge as a proper instrument of the international society but also as a sort of negative parameter, essential in the ranking processes of the states and indispensable for any normalization process. It is precisely while characterizing certain states as failed or fragile that one is, subliminally and essentially, ranking these states in comparison with other states—the normal ones. More than that, this ranking process is done while intimately connecting the failure or fragility of these states with the international insecurities and underdevelopment. It is such mechanism that creates the *urgent need* of reforming these states and correcting their behaviors so they stop being failed. Otherwise, the international society, under the orthodox line of thinking, becomes highly insecure and its overall development is impaired. Moreover, these corrections and interventions are portrayed as a beneficial relationship due to the possibilities open by the reinterpretations of sovereignty as *capacities* and *gradations*. It is this twist that enables such deep social structural reengineering process to be performed through power-denying notions of capacity-building, advising, or mentoring, and be portrayed as in fact enhancing post-conflict states range of actions, rather than limiting them.

Consequently, peace operations advance numerous economic, political, and social reforms that are carried out, in light of the notion of good governance and underpinned by the liberal peace argument, aiming precisely at making these states stop being, even though potentially, a threat to the international society and stop having a deviant behavior in the international society. It is under this framework that, for instance, all the institutions that are built in post-conflict environments should be perceived. Therefore, rather than a mere exercise of institution-building, these several (re)structuring enterprises are the very operation of the exercise of the dispositional power over post-conflict states and their populations in the sense of correcting their *modus operandi*; correcting how each one of these spheres should properly behave. These practices, as might be quite clear at this point, are essential to the normalization process that states and their populations are subject. It is through their internal normalization, the normalization of first-order societies of post-conflict states, that their international normalization, the second-order society, is achieved. It is under this framework that, for instance, structural adjustments imposed by the International Monetary Fund, stimulating certain kinds of economic conducts and blocking others, by the post-conflict states through, for example, the concession (or denial) of funding and credits to these post-conflict states, should be understood. In essence, it is aimed so that the economy in general behaves in a specific way. One might also think about the vast and profound reforms in the political sphere such as, for instance, the creation of whole juridical, legislative, and executive systems (or in fact exercising these powers),[21] constitution writing, definition of electoral systems, or the writing of laws. On the social sphere, it is clear, for instance, the management of a variety of key areas of the lives of the populations in question, including movement in the territory, education, health, food programs, demographics, housing, or jobs, to name a few. Under this framework, all these actions are essentially conductions of conducts which have the objective of stimulating, or discouraging, certain kinds of behaviors, so the state and the population in general behave accordingly. Intervening on the levels of the state and of the population, the normalizing *dispositif* that peace operations materialize places both levels in a complex power network whose the objective is to conduct their conducts so they can become more similar to a liberal-democratic state and population.

Therefore, to normalize these abnormal and failed states in the international society means finding instruments to render operational a good kind of governance, which is underpinned by the liberal peace normative framework and argument, which in essence means to implement normality in these countries. In fact, this can be pursued through several instruments ranging from sanctions to war. However, in post-conflict contexts and within the narrative of building peace, it is the *dispositif* materialized by peace operations that emerges as the fittest instrument to intervene in post-conflict states in order to correct their behaviors, to make them resemble more like liberal democracies and, in essence, to normalize them and their populations. Hence, in a normalization process happening in the international society through peace operations, not only post-conflict states are intervened aiming at their normalization, to make them behave in accordance to an established international norm, but also their relationship with their own populations and how the populations themselves should behave are sought to be normalized. Indeed, the peace operations function as a *dispositif* that seeks to normalize the post-conflict state's conducts so they start to behave accordingly international norms; accordingly what was constructed was a normal behavior expected from the states within the current international society—being a liberal-democratic-market-oriented state.

METHODOLOGICAL REMARKS AND
STRUCTURE OF THE BOOK

This book departs from the understanding of peace operations as a *dispositif*—an assemblage of actors, concepts, narratives, theoretical notions, institutions, and practices. In order to grasp, in Foucault's own words, such heterogeneous ensemble of disparate elements, this book is, as it could not be otherwise, methodologically anchored essentially on a qualitative approach. This is the kind of approach that not only allows the observation of the power relations entrenched on the whole state-building process but also enables the refined understanding of the relationship between these elements that composes it and their role in the very functioning of the state-building process. In order to render its theoretical argument operational, this book makes use of the empirical illustration of the UN state-building process in Timor-Leste.

In this sense, this endeavor started initially by critically reviewing the secondary sources of the UN peacebuilding efforts and state-building processes in general and then complemented this literature with the ones dealing with the UN engagement with Timor-Leste. Supported by this analysis of secondary sources, this book lays extensively on primary sources in regard to the UN engagement with Timor-Leste. In order to collect the relevant information about this process, and to render its argument operational, the book laid essentially on the combination of two methodological instruments: archival research and fieldwork (direct observation and interviews). In regard to the first instrument, relevant documents include mainly UN documentation—resolutions, reports, and evaluations from the UN system—but also documents from other international organizations, non-governmental institutions, research centers, and think-tanks, as well as national reports and legislation. During this process, this book benefited a lot from the fact that nearly all UN documentation, and most of the documentation of the aforementioned actors, at least in regard to its engagement with Timor-Leste, is available online. The UN online and open-source archival proved to be an essential and invaluable resource, since it allowed most of the archival documents to be collected mainly electronically.

In addition to the archival analysis, this book complemented the collection of primary sources with fieldwork, which enabled the invaluable opportunity of firsthand observation of how the state-building process has been consolidated and, simultaneously, provided access to key actors in the process. The fieldwork consisted mainly of qualitative semi-structured interviews and direct observation. In addition to a first-hand observation of the process, the fieldwork also enabled supplementing of the documentation already collected. The fieldwork was pivotal mainly to the conduction of interviews with key actors of the process.[22] In regard to the actors interviewed, the research reached high-level officials from international organizations, international agencies, state cooperation agencies, embassies, and international financial institutions. In addition, the research also included interviews with high- and mid-level officials, both in office and former ones, of the Timorese state, members of local NGOs, along with Timorese academics. In regards to the spheres, the interviews covered a wide range of the fields that characterize the UN intervention in Timor-Leste. Notwithstanding the fact that these spheres are hardly differentiated on the ground, they can be characterized as: (1) the disciplinary sphere, which namely covers the police, the army, and the justice system; (2) the political and economic governance sphere; and (3) the socio- and biopolitical sphere, which essentially covers the area of the life-supporting processes of the Timorese population and its surrounding conditions. In regard to the first sphere, the interviewees were actors such as, for instance: high- and mid-level officials and advisors of the UN and Timorese Police, a former Timorese Minister of Defense, leaders of NGOs active in the security sector, and high-level officials of the Timorese justice system. In regards to the second sphere, the actors interviewed can be characterized, for instance, as: high-level advisors of the Timorese president, a former Timorese president and prime minister, high- and mid-level officials and representatives of the Timorese government, of the UN, of other international organizations such as the Asian Development Bank (ADB) and the WB, of foreign governments and development agencies, as well as leaders and activists of Timorese NGOs. In regard to the last sphere, the actors interviewed can be characterized as high- and mid-level officials and policy advisors of the UN and its agencies, as well as of the Timorese government, leaders of Timorese NGOs, and also Timorese academics.

The fieldwork was also instrumental in allowing direct observation. While in Timor-Leste, the research profited very much from the fact that it was the parliamentary election period. This allowed a close observation of the campaigning period and the electoral process. Furthermore, the research was certainly enriched by the fact that the author was able to be an international accredited electoral observer in the 2012 parliamentary elections. This is a relevant point because an election process' importance, in a post-conflict context, is mainly twofold: (1) on the one hand, an election process is a fundamental element of the UN state-building process in any post-conflict scenario; indeed, in a not very distant past, this even functioned as an key milestone to spark UN exit plans; (2) on the other hand, an election process is a crucial element of the normalization process carried out by the UN in a post-conflict state, due to the fact that the occurrence of elections is perceived as a pivotal element of a democratic process, which, in turn, is understood as crucial to a normal behavior of the political sphere of a normal state. This electoral observation proved to be very much informative and insightful in the sense that provided the opportunity to observe part of the normalization process that Timor-Leste is subject from within.

As already mentioned, this book renders its argument operational through the empirical illustration of the UN state-building process in Timor-Leste. Timor-Leste emerges as the most suitable choice due to the unique position and relevance that the case has within the conflict-resolution and peacebuilding rationale of the UN. On the one hand, the country is very often presented as a success case in regard to UN engagement in post-conflict scenarios. On the other hand, the UN engagement with the country is noticeably characterized by: the distinct kinds and large variety of UN peace instruments deployed to the country; the depth of its engagement; and the wide range and the kinds of activities carried out in Timor-Leste. Therefore, one can perfectly argue that Timor-Leste is a paradigmatic case within the UN rationale in regard to the consolidation of peace. Indeed, very few places, if any at all, had an UN engagement for so long as Timor-Leste had and as many peace instruments deployed, which in Timor-Leste were nearly all at UN's hand. This makes Timor-Leste not only a very appropriate case, but also, and most importantly, it makes the critical analysis of the state-building process there something of the utmost importance.

Many aspects regarding the Timorese case have already been studied. One could mention, for instance, the detailed historical analysis of its annexations during World War II and the mid-1970s, and its independence quest, (Dunn, 2003; Kingsbury, 2009; Magalhães, 2007), along with the Portuguese and Indonesian diplomatic negotiation process regarding its independence (Teles, 1999b), or even the multidimensionality of the process of the construction of the Timorese identity (Mendes, 2005). Indeed, the case of Timor-Leste has already been used for larger critiques within the IR discipline when, for instance, José Pureza, departing from the case, poses a critical questioning of the dominant reading of international relations (2001). In regard to UN involvement with Timor-Leste,[23] it ranges from mere balloting monitoring, during the referendum carried out in the country, to profound state-building missions, as profound as not only (re)creating governmental institutions but in fact exercising the executive, the legislative and judicial powers (S/RES/1272: 2). In fact, several dimensions of the state-building process there were already evinced (Mendes and Saramago, 2012). Regarding this unprecedented involvement (Goldstone, 2004: 84) were already uncovered several elements, for instance: the evolution of Timor-Leste's juridical system (Santos, 2002), the ill-configuration of the missions (Suhrke, 2001: 2), and the reluctance to include Timorese participation in decision-making processes (Chopra, 2000: 31). Even the contradiction of the UN, through the voice of Jean-Christian Cady, Deputy Special Representative of the Secretary-General of UNTAET, declaring Timor as an "undeniable success" (Goldstone, 2004: 83) while a rigorous analysis shows the neglect of the everyday needs of the Timorese population (Richmond and Franks, 2009: 86), and their inheritance of a "failed state" (Goldstone, 2004: 95) was delineated.

The path herein proposed adds further clarifications and elucidations to those already made in the literature. The first one is refining the problematization of the UN state-building process in Timor-Leste. Consequently, different set of practices and relations that are entrenched to the process that are often silenced can be observed. In addition, and most importantly, it enables the reproblematization of highly visible practices that are carried out during the UN state-building process in Timor-Leste and quite often perceived as a normal kind of engagement. The path of examination herein proposed allows the observation that these practices, rather than unproblematic engagements, are very much arbitrary. Furthermore, it helps the observation that those actors, practices, and procedures carried out on the ground, even though conflicting and contrasting with one another, are part of a comprehensive whole that seeks to direct Timor-Leste toward a determinate direction.

Indeed, observing the case of the UN engagement with Timor-Leste, it is enabled the visualization of deep power relations and social reengineering process being operated *through* power-denying notions such as capacity-building, advising, or mentoring. Most importantly, it renders visible the attempt of normalization and government of Timor-Leste and its population being operated *through* the very narrative of constructing Timorese autonomy, fostering the country's independence, and enhancing the sovereignty of a post-conflict state. Moreover, the *terra nullis* mentality and the sense that Timor-Leste was being built from scratch (Goldstone, 2004: 85; Richmond and Franks, 2009: 111, note 86; Suhrke, 2001: 13), which was (and still is) pervasive throughout the UN engagement with the country provide a rare opportunity to investigate and evince the arrangement of things, the disposition/functioning of the technologies of power and conceptual tools delineated by Michel Foucault. In fact, even though Foucault did not have in mind, when problematizing his theoretical and analytical tools, neither the construction of peace nor Timor-Leste, the country provides a solid case for the observation of the formation, and operation, of a surveillance framework, characteristic of any normalization process, operating both internally and externally in Timor-Leste. It elucidates how the UN closely monitors and seeks to conduct each movement of the country in several spheres—the disciplinary; the political and economic governance; and the socio- and bio-political one—and seeks to shape the Timorese behavior, and attempts to ensure the proper behavior of each one of these spheres and, as a consequence, of Timor-Leste as a country. Most importantly, it allows the clarification of toward what end this process heads to and through what procedures and techniques this process is operated.

Consequently, such enterprise allows the observation of different processes and elements present throughout the construction of peace in Timor-Leste. It is precisely this kind of effort that not only gives visibility for many concerning aspects of the whole process, which frequently pass as natural and unproblematic, but also, and most importantly, opens the space for questioning the processes carried out throughout the construction of peace in our current international scenario, which certainly gives room for the very transformation of them.

In order to develop its argument, the book is structured in five chapters followed by some concluding remarks. The first chapter presents the object of analysis of this book, the construction of peace in the international scenario, and how it was transformed throughout time. The chapter is dedicated to the discussion of pivotal practices in regard to international peace namely peacekeeping, peacebuilding, and state-building efforts led by the UN. It delineates how UN peace instruments in regard to addressing violent conflicts and peace were transformed from the Cold War period to the characteristics of the current endeavors. Therefore, chapter 1 outlines the main elements of, and activities performed by, each of these efforts, and how they changed over time, and also discusses the normative framework that underpins these processes. Chapter 2 takes a step back and provides a contextualization and exposition of the process that led Timor-Leste to emerge in the international scenario as an urgent need. It is precisely this recognition of Timor-Leste as an international urgent need that triggered the deployment of a state-building *dispositif* to the country. Chapter 3 focuses the analysis of the

UN engagement with Timor-Leste and the discussion of its major shortcomings. Initially, the chapter analyses the UN peace operations deployed to Timorese soil—namely UNAMET (1999), UNTAET (1999–2002), UNMIS-ET (2002–2005), UNOTIL (2005–2006) and UNMIT (2006–2012). In addition to bringing attention to the main aspects of each one of them, the chapter evinces the linear mindset entrenched in the UN engagement with the country and its reactive character. Furthermore, it also delineates some of the pivotal shortcomings of the UN state-building process in Timor-Leste as well as some fundamental strands of the Timorese reality that were evidently neglected by the UN while carrying out its state-building process in the country. Chapter 4 delineates the surveillance framework which Timor-Leste is subject and that is fundamental to the functioning of the normalization process pursued in the country. The normalization *dispositif* under which Timor-Leste is subject and its transformation into a governance state, to be merely operational, must be accompanied by the setting up of a series of steering, monitoring, and structuring instruments which are dispersed throughout and over Timor-Leste. It is precisely the elucidation of these surveillance instruments that is the core of this chapter. These instruments, although neither centralized nor unified and quite often unrelated, form a surveillance framework that is fundamental to the normalizing assemblage operating in Timor-Leste. After all, this framework is what enables the close monitoring of the Timorese conducts since it places Timor-Leste and its several spheres, along with its population, under a constant and frequent international scrutiny and observation. Finally, chapter 5 problematizes the transformation of Timor-Leste into a governance state and sheds light on the width of the normalizing state-building *dispositif* deployed by evincing several spheres and levels in which the UN attempts to conduct the Timorese state's and population's conducts. This conduction is attempted essentially through the pursuit of structuring the field of possible actions of the Timorese state and its populations and also through seeking to influence and control pivotal spheres of the country.

NOTES

1. Following a non-written convention of the literature, the capital letters will be employed herein in reference to the academic discipline (international relations, IR). Although the author acknowledges the erosion of the division inside/outside (Walker, 1993) when talking about IR nowadays, the lowercase is used in reference to the dynamics that take place majorly in the international scenario and that involve majorly actors that are external to a determinate state.

2. Following the UN terminology, this thesis uses the term *peace operations* to mean operations deployed to conflict scenarios seeking to prevent/manage/overcome violent conflict, or even reduce the chances of their reemergence (UN, 2008: 98). Hence, the term encompasses, in line with the UN understanding of the term, the key instruments used by the UN to address violent conflicts throughout the globe, ranging from peace prevention to peacebuilding and state-building efforts.

3. This distance was shortened by the elucidations, for instance, of Mark Duffield (2007, 2010).

4. For more about direct and structural violence, see (Galtung, 1969).

5. A short and modified version of this argument was developed at (Blanco, 2017).

6. The delineation of the whole range of both problematizations is far beyond the scope of this book. For this, see for instance, for the English School (Bull, 1977; Burchill et al., 2005: Chapter 4; Buzan, 2014; Dunne, 1998; Linklater and Suganami, 2006; Watson, 1992) and for Foucault (Bröckling, Krasmann and Lemke, 2011; Burchell, Gordon and Miller, 1991; Kelly, 2009; Rabinow, 1984; Rabinow and Rose, 2003; Smart, 2002).

7. For more about the great debates of the discipline, see for instance (Fernandes, 2011). For some critiques of this manner of organizing the discipline, see for instance (Ashworth, 2002; Wilson, 1998).

8. This triad of traditions is derived from the work of Martin Wight. For more about it, and the characteristics of each tradition, see for instance (Bull, 1977: 23–26; 1992; Wight and Porter, 1992; Wight, 1987).

9. For the purpose of the argument herein presented, the book focuses on these two notions. For the notion of World Society, see for instance (Bull, 1977: 269–282; Buzan, 2014: 13).

10. For a delineation of different types of international systems, see for instance (Watson, 1990; Wight, 1977).

11. For the critic about it advanced by Hedley Bull, see (Bull, 1977: 44–49).

12. Usually the word *dispositif* used by Foucault is translated as apparatus to English. Nevertheless, in order to avoid unproductive translation discussions or misperceptions about the term (Kelly, 2009: 174, footnote 12), the book uses the original word *dispositif.*

13. For a detailed account of the Foucauldian account of the term technology, see (Kelly, 2009; Rose, 1999).

14. A denser delineation of these conceptual tools is beyond the scope of this paper. For a comprehensive account of them, see for instance Foucault lectures *Society Must Be Defended* ([1976] 2003), where he gives a clear explanation about his thinking on those technologies of power, delineating the framework that will be returned to and developed further later in his lectures *Security, Territory, Population* ([1978] 2007) and *The Birth of Biopolitics* ([1979] 2008).

15. This concept has been developed differently by contemporary philosophers such as Giorgio Agamben (1998), Antonio Negri and Michael Hardt (2000). For a contrast of theirs and Foucault's use, see (Rabinow and Rose, 2006).

16. A wide and extensive delineation of these transformations is beyond the scope of this paper. For more about it, see for instance (Blanco, 2014; Guerra and Blanco, 2018; Kemer, Pereira and Blanco, 2016; Kenkel, 2013; Newman, Paris and Richmond, 2009; Paris and Sisk, 2009b).

17. For a comprehensive account of this rationale, see for instance (Brainard, Chollet and LaFleur, 2007; Ghani and Lockhart, 2008; Ghani, Lockhart and Carnahan, 2005; Ingram, 2010; Rice, 2003, 2007; Rotberg, 2003, 2004).

18. This would be the distance between the sovereignty *de jure* and the sovereignty *de facto.* For more about this notion, see (Ghani, Lockhart and Carnahan, 2005).

19. For decisive works in this regard, see for instance (Duffield, 2001; Fischer, 2000; Heathershaw, 2008; Paris, 2004; Richmond, 2006, 2007b; 2008: 89–95). For a detailed discussion of the different nuances, gradations and discourses of the liberal peace see for instance (Heathershaw, 2008; Richmond, 2006, 2007b).

20. For more in regard to this relationship, especially between democracy and good governance, see for instance (Knight, 2007).

21. Timor-Leste was one of these cases where the United Nations exercised the legislative, executive and judicial power in the country. For a shorter critical account of the UN peacebuilding effort there, see (Blanco, 2015).

22. The instrument of the interview was used to have a more comprehensive context and a deeper sense of the post-conflict reconstruction process as a whole, rather than an instrument for looking forward to quote any interviewee directly. On the contrary, in order to have the

interviewees speaking freely and frankly, it was agreed with them that the future publications of the research would not quote them directly. Most importantly, since most, if not all, of interviewees are still active in the field (in Timorese politics, the UN or at a NGO), this was agreed also in order to preserve their identities and, therefore, not taking the risk of jeopardizing, in any way, either their careers or the author's future research in the field.

23. UNAMET (1999), UNTAET (1999–2002), UNMISET (2002–2005), UNOTIL (2005–2006), UNMIT (2006–2012).

Chapter One

A Genealogy of the UN Approaches toward International Peace

Peacekeeping, peacebuilding, and state-building efforts carried out by several international actors, and in especial those led by the United Nations (UN), have become pivotal elements of the current international scenario. Indeed, they constitute the very core of international policies in regard to peace, development, and security in our time. Nevertheless, this was not always the case. Indeed, this was possible only with the end of the Cold War. This is a direct consequence of the transformation of the shared international rationale in regard to peace, which went from the maintenance of a negative peace to the attempt of building a positive peace in the international scenario.[1]

Moreover, it is also very much clearer that the actors and institutions involved in this process of seeking to build a positive peace share, even though sometimes loosely, the same understanding of what peace means and how it should be achieved. This is what Oliver Richmond (2004b: 91–92) calls the peacebuilding consensus. It is precisely the discussion of this consensus and the delineation of the main elements of these operations throughout time, along with their transformations, from the end of World War II until nowadays, that is the core of this chapter. Following the approaches to the reflection about peace delineated by Richmond (2008: chapter 5), this chapter is divided in five sections. Firstly, it delineates the attributes of peace operations that were characteristic of the Cold War period focusing on both the main configuration of such operations and the main elements that influenced their transformation after the end of the Cold War. Secondly, while dealing with the normative framework that underpins current peace operations, the liberal peace, evincing its main rationale and elements, it discusses the reconfigurations that peace operations had after the Cold War. Thirdly, it deals with the transformation that peace operations had during the post Cold

War period discussing the peacebuilding consensus that shapes these operations. Fourthly, this chapter discusses a pivotal element of current post-conflict reconstruction efforts, the state-building process, and evinces its relation to state-fragility. Finally, on the fifth section, the chapter not only differentiates it from other processes, namely nation-building and peacebuilding, but also further delineates what is a post-conflict state-building process.

THE UN PEACE DURING THE COLD WAR

During the period of the Cold War, the main UN type of intervention regarding international peace was traditional peacekeeping (Bellamy, William and Griffin, 2010: 173–174). This kind of approach to peace falls on what Oliver Richmond (2008: 99) calls the first generation of theory regarding peace and conflict studies. This first generation, in Richmond's view, derived from conflict management reflections toward ending conflicts. Due to its realist posture regarding peace, it was very state-centric.[2] Therefore, this was an understanding that focused essentially on state-related matters and that excluded non-state actors and non-state-centric issues. Furthermore, this was a type of peace that problematized very little, if at all, the internal sources of the conflicts. Indeed, this was a rationale regarding peace that was directed toward a negative peace; it was an approach that its ultimate concern was the attempt to produce order, both internal and international, without the presence of open violence between states (Richmond, 2008: 99).

At that time, peacekeeping usually meant the deployment of a small military force aiming just to monitor a cease-fire or patrol a neutral territory between former combatants (Paris and Sisk, 2009b: 4). Peacekeeping was usually a military force that acted as a sort of buffer between two states (Newman, Paris and Richmond, 2009: 5). Therefore, peacekeeping was reflected as a mere instrument of managing or containing a conflict. The objective was the overcoming of the symptoms and not the transformation of the violent conflicts. (Ramsbotham and Woodhouse, 2000: 5). In fact, quite often, this instrument directed to peace would find itself framed by the bipolar rivalry of the Cold War and used to maintain the international order. Indeed, peacekeeping often functioned as an instrument, operationalized by the great powers of the time, for preventing a violent conflict from escalating. Consequently, the objective was the preservation of a certain stability so a political agreement between the belligerent states could be achieved (Newman, Paris and Richmond, 2009: 6). Since the international order and stability, on the one hand, and violent conflict between states, on the other hand, were perceived as the main objective and challenge, respectively, in regards to the international scenario, peacekeeping missions were usually deployed by states to peacefully overcome their violent disputes (Newman, Paris, and

Richmond, 2009: 6). Not surprisingly, the vast majority of peace operations during the Cold War was directed to deal with classic inter-state conflicts and very few had a civil war in its horizon (Newman, Paris, and Richmond, 2009: 6).

These operations are the best example of what Alex Bellamy, Paul Williams, and Stuart Griffin call traditional peacekeeping (2010: 173–174). These operations were underpinned by what they call the holy trinity of consent, impartiality, and minimum use of force (Bellamy and Williams, 2010: 173–774). There were essentially six reasons for this kind of configuration of the operations: (1) the lack of a very specific reference of this kind of activity in the UN Charter; (2) the limitation, present in the UN Charter, of intervening on domestic affairs of states; (3) the belligerent parts were usually unwilling to accept a third-party involvement greater than the monitoring/patrolling; (4) the international scenario was embedded in a bipolar logic; (5) the manner in which pivotal concepts, such as sovereignty and security were understood; and (6) the approach in which international violent conflicts were problematized (Paris and Sisk, 2009b: 4; Santoro and Blanco, 2012). Reflecting about UN practices toward international peace during the Cold War, Edward Newman, Roland Paris, and Oliver Richmond highlight some peace operations that are emblematic of this period. They mention, for instance, the UN Emergency Force deployed to Egypt after the Suez War (1956–1967), the UN Military Observer Group deployed to supervise a cease-fire between India and Pakistan (1949), and the UN Peacekeeping Force in Cyprus (1964), among others.[3]

The scholarly literature of that time regarding peace operations tended to be very light on theoretical reflections and sought to provide heavily detailed descriptions of particular missions (Paris, 2009). They focused very much on defining and itemizing the characteristics of such operations, while offering little systematic cross-case analysis.[4] In the view of Cindy Collins and Thomas Weiss, this literature was not concerned, for instance, in developing new theories and problematizations. The discussion was focused on merely describing the processes and events, evaluating the mechanisms deployed and prescribing policies to future peace operations. (1997: 1). An important element of the discussion of that literature had to do with the effectiveness of peace operations and the delineation of the elements influencing their success or failure (Denis, 1999; Diehl, 1994; Diehl, 1993; Durch, 1993; James, 1995). For Paris and Sisk (2009b: 6), the two major volumes edited by William Durch (1993, 1996) are the most iconic example of the literature at that time which, although path-breaking and important, shed little light on the underlying assumptions of such missions and had a very atrophied theoretical stance. It is quite fair to say that the vast majority of the literature of that time fell into what Robert Cox labeled as a problem-solving approach (1981).

Notwithstanding the fact that there is indication that these operations significantly decrease the chances of the recurrence of war (Fortna, 2004), some fundamental problems were identified: (1) their difficulty in preventing the belligerent parties from breaking the cease-fire agreements or enforcing the resolutions agreed (Bellamy, William, and Griffin, 2010: 183); (2) their blindness regarding a wide variety of issues, such as identity, institutional fragility, and economic underdevelopment (Bercovitch and Dean, 2012: 7); and (3) their focus on short-term solutions and lack of concern for addressing the deep root causes of violent conflicts (Bercovitch and Dean, 2012: 7), to name a few. This kind of operation proved to be very poor at achieving the resolution of violent conflicts (Bellamy, William, and Griffin, 2010: 190).[5]

It was only with the end of the Cold War that the nature of peace operations changed. It is true that some analysts caution, somewhat rightly, that there is not a clear-cut division between peace operations deployed during the Cold War and afterward (Bellamy, William, and Griffin, 2010: 7), or that the end of the Cold War does not provide the entire explanation for this change (Jakobsen, 2002). Notwithstanding these cautions, it is hardly disputable that the end of the Cold War, and its consequences, are pivotal elements in this transformation of peace operations. Indeed, the end of the Cold War played a crucial role in making the resolution and transformation of the intra-state violent conflicts, rather than their mere management, the main concern in regard to violent conflicts throughout the globe (Bures, 2007: 9–10).

In addition to the failures of the conflict management approach, there were four main reasons underpinning this change. Firstly, with the end of the Cold War several issues gained more relevance in the international agenda (Alves, 2001), and many of them were rationalized differently. This was the case of intra-state violent conflicts. Contrary to common sense, intra-state violent conflicts constitute the vast majority of the conflicts since the end of World War II (Themnér and Wallensteen, 2011: 526). Nevertheless, these conflicts were, during the Cold War, problematized within the bipolar mentality and framework, which was shaped by the ideological rivalry between the super powers. Consequently, the internal matters of these conflicts were most of the times invisibilized in the analyses. As a result of the different rationalization of intra-state violent conflicts, their internal sources started to be problematized. Therefore, the internal dimension of these conflicts became relevant and the main concern of the analysts dealing with these conflicts was redirected to the resolution of the root causes of these violent conflicts. This meant that the previous configuration of peacekeeping interventions had to be rethought in order to address a different set of elements.

Secondly, with the end of East-West tensions, both countries—the United States of America (USA) and the Union of Soviet Socialist Republics (USSR) and later Russia—were not willing to maintain high levels of military expenditure, or of economic assistance, to allies perceived as non-strategic in this new international scenario. This retraction of the major powers had, at least, two important consequences. First, it made latent discontentment within several countries, often suppressed by the super powers, visible and quite often violently. As a result, not only new violent conflicts emerged throughout several countries but also an issue that was usually handled by the superpowers started to fall on the hands of the international community at large. Second, this retraction of the superpowers allowed other international actors, such as the UN and its agencies, to become much more active in the processes of ending/transforming violent conflicts throughout the globe. Consequently, new situations where conflict transformation, especially headed by the UN, was needed emerged. These consequences led to a high demand of peace operations at the international scene: the number of peace operations deployed in the decade ranging from 1989 to 1999 was more than the double of the number of operations deployed in the previous four decades (Paris, 2004: 16–17).

A third reason pivotal to the transformation of the characteristics of UN peace operations after the Cold War is the reconceptualization of crucial concepts of the international narrative. This was the case of concepts such as sovereignty, security, and development. Whereas the idea of sovereignty, during the Cold War, was a notion that was strongly unitary and indivisible, after the Cold War, sovereignty became a notion that could be divisible (Jackson, 1990), much more flexible, and started to have different gradations (Keohane, 2003) and be divided into several attributes[6] (Krasner, 2004: 87–88). It is precisely this shift that allows the profound restructuring of post-conflict states and societies, which are the essence of current peace operations, to be portrayed as a beneficial practice that actually *enhances* the post-conflict state's sovereignty, rather than a deep intervention that limits their capacities of action. Similarly, the notion of security, during the Cold War, was an idea problematized from a realist, militarist and strategic approach (Buzan and Hansen, 2009: 13). However, a process of enlarging/deepening of the concept initiated during the 1980s led to the argument that security should be engaged with life in general, be aware of sources of *in*securities, have the individual as the referent of its concerns, and pursue the overcoming of physical and human constraints as its ultimate objective (Peoples and Vaughan-Williams, 2010: 17). For Ken Booth, such constraints would be war, poverty, political oppression, and poor education, among others (1991: 319). Regarding development, during the Cold War, the notion was monopolized by a narrow state-centric economic understanding (Ruttan, 2003: 103). After the end of the Cold War, development began to incorporate other elements into its rationale, becoming closely associated with overcoming several constraints that affected human lives, such as tyranny; social, economic, and political deprivations; intolerance; poverty; hunger; illiteracy; repression; and diseases. As a result, the enhancement of the individual's lives became the main objective (UNDP, 1990: 10). These reconceptualization processes are central to the characteristics of peace operations after the Cold War.

The fourth reason which underpinned the change of the nature of UN peace operations after the Cold War is the international *zeitgeist* that emerged with the end of the ideological dispute between the superpowers. Without the Cold War ideological tension and the triumphant spirit of the West—perhaps most iconic in Francis Fukuyama's *End of History* (1992)—there was little debate about how the internal domestic design of the states should look like. Indeed, as a US State Department's Deputy Director, Fukuyama even proclaimed the "end point in mankind's ideological evolution and the universalization of Western liberal democracy as the final form of human governance" (1989: 4). The end of the ideological debacle brought an international *zeitgeist* where liberal democracy was understood by several international actors as "the only model of government with any broad legitimacy and ideological appeal in the world"[7] (Diamond, Linz, and Lipset, 1990: x). This was clearly evinced, for instance, by Paris (2004: 20) when he remembers that, in the period of 1990–1996, more than three dozens of countries started to adopt liberal democratic constitutions for the first time. This fact raised the number of liberal democracies in the world from 76 to 118.

The Liberal Peace Argument

After the Cold War, there was little doubt that the states should all resemble liberal democracies and peace operations were transformed accordingly. The modifications of the characteristics of peace operations deployed between early and late 1990s make the kind of peace pursued during this period falls on what Richmond (2008: 101) calls the second generation of approach to theorization regarding peace and conflict studies. This generation rests on conflict-resolution approaches, and, therefore, has a more ambitious stance regarding peace. This framework perceives the deprivation and the repression of basic human needs as the foundation of protracted violent conflicts. Consequently, it is an approach concerned with overcoming direct and structural violence and is directed toward individuals (Richmond, 2008: 102; 99). Even though the materialization of such approach was still limited and Eurocentric, it not only pushed the discussions about peace beyond state security and concerns, including other issues, such as political participation and development, but also included other actors in this debate, such as civil society and NGOs, in particular, though the state remains the prominent actor (Richmond, 2008: 102–103). Most importantly, this approach to peace, with all its limitations and shortcomings, represents a movement from the attempt of merely maintaining a negative peace in the international scenario, toward the pursuit of building a positive peace in post-conflict countries.

This rationale reached the international policies directed to peace, especially the UN's. At the early 1990s, the UN released an important document dealing with international peace—*An Agenda for Peace* (A/47/277). This document rapidly became a pivotal text regarding international peace in the post-Cold-War world precisely because it is there where the UN delineates its instruments directed to the construction of international peace, and because it is a document that clarifies the UN's own understating about what peace is. These instruments directed to the achievement of peace at the international level became denser and deeper from this document onward, and permeate UN publications regarding international peace since then.

The instruments established by the UN are namely five: conflict prevention, peacemaking, peace enforcement, peacekeeping, and peacebuilding[8] (UN, 2008: 17–18). Conflict prevention is an instrument that deals essentially with the implementation of a series of instruments, either structural or diplomatic, that seeks to prevent a certain tension and disputes, either intra- or inter-state, to escalate to violence. These instruments vary from the Secretary-General's good offices to the implementation of measures seeking building confidence among the parties (UN, 2008: 17). Peacemaking, by its turn, is usually directed toward a violent conflict already in progress and involves diplomatic measures seeking to bring the parties to a negotiated peace agreement. It may include, for instance, the use of envoys from different kinds of organizations (governments, group of states, regional or global organizations, and so on) (UN, 2008: 17–18). The instrument designed as peace enforcement deals with the use, with the due authorization from the Security Council, of a series of coercive measures (including the military one) to restore peace and security (UN, 2008: 18).

Peacekeeping[9] is understood as an instrument designed to preserve peace, even tough a very limited one, in order to assist peacemakers implementing the measures agreed in peace agreements (UN, 2008: 18). Lastly, peacebuilding[10] involves a set of measures seeking to reduce the chances of a violent conflict (re)emerge. It aims to deal with the deep-root causes of a conflict, usually concentrating on the state and its apparatus (UN, 2008: 18). These instruments are designed to deal with violent conflicts in their different phases of escalation. Notwithstanding, the clear-cut distinction between each of these instruments is not an easy enterprise and to precisely say where one instrument begins and the other ends on the ground is very subjective. In fact, these instruments quite often overlap.

Whereas a traditional peacekeeping mission is easily identifiable on the ground, one would clearly have difficulties finding a peacebuilding mission. In fact, the Security Council (SC) does not authorize *peacebuilding* missions, per se. In fact, most of the missions authorized by the SC can be understood as the merging between both peacekeeping and peacebuilding instruments (Olsson, 2010: 395). This is what the UN calls multi-dimensional peacekeeping operations (UN, 2008: 22). These are missions that, while still having traditional peacekeeping elements, perform also peacebuilding activities such as: disarmament, demobilization and reintegration (DDR) of combatants; demining activities; security sector reform (SSR) and other rule-of-law-related activities; protection and promotion of human rights; electoral assistance; and support to the restoration and extension of state authority (UN, 2008: 26). Therefore, rather than understanding peacebuilding as a kind of a mission that can be clearly identifiable on the ground, it makes more sense to understand it as a sort of a strategy to be pursued, which can be developed through several elements such as electoral assistance, (re)construction of state institutions, humanitarian assistance, DDR, policing, and so on.

Since internal sources of intra-state violent conflicts and overcoming their deep root causes became a main concern after the Cold War, the developments advanced by peace studies pioneers (Ramsbotham, Woodhouse, and Miall, 2005: Chapter 2), such as John Burton (1990), Edward Azar (1990) and Johan Galtung (1969), started to make more sense to the UN. Building on the failures and limitations of the conflict management approach to peace operations deployed during the Cold War, the UN understood that in order to transform intra-state violent conflicts it had to pay attention to human needs and overcoming structural sources of violence (Bercovitch and Dean, 2012: 10). The UN answer to that was very clear, as early as 1992, in the UN *An Agenda for Peace* when the organization perceived that it should focuses at the causes of violent conflict, which for the UN were: economic despair, social injustice, and political oppression (A/47/277). UN peace operations started to change and to include more peacebuilding activities.

Indeed, Roland Paris makes a clear characterization of what would be the typical peace operation during the 1990s. For him, it included: (1) in the political sphere, the promotion of civil and political rights, the organization of elections, the writing of constitutions, and the (re)structuring the state infrastructure, to name a few; (2) in the social sphere, it includes, for instance, promotion of a civil society and the transformation of belligerent groups into political parties; and (3) in the economic sphere, the measures would include, for instance, the promotion of a free market, the reduction of the state participation in the economy, the elimination of barriers of capital and goods, and a series of marketization programs, to name just a few (Paris, 2004: 19). Roland Paris and Timothy Sisk (2009b: 6), in addition, rightly remember that, at that period, the missions' mandates, typically, tended to be limited in time. Furthermore, to them (2009b), at this time, little attention was directed to the construction, or strengthening, of institutional structures inside those states. In very few words, one can argue that the major focus of these missions was the rapid democratization and marketization of post-conflict states (Paris, 2004: 19).

These characteristics are consequences of the fact that the transformation of peace operations did not occur in an ideological vacuum. An international environment embedded in a liberal triumphant spirit had an unquestionable influence in the kind of activities performed by peace operations and the outcomes expected from these activities. In such international scenario, it was highly shared that political and economic liberalism was *the* route to deal with several international issues, ranging from poverty and underdevelopment to violent conflicts. This understanding rests on a liberal peace[11] argument. According to Oliver Richmond and Jason Franks, the liberal peace is, at the same time, a narrative, a framework, and a structure that have a very specific ontology and methodology underling its functioning (2009: 4). This is an understanding of peace that rests essentially in some very specific pillars, such as: democratization, rule of law, human rights, and neoliberalism (Richmond and Frank, 2009: 4). Therefore, notwithstanding the fact it does not have a completely unitary understanding,[12] it is very clear that underpinning such approach to peace is an understanding that peace in post-conflict states must be achieved through fostering and implementing some specific elements and norms, such as the democratization of the government, a neo-liberal market economy, the establishment of the rule of law and the dissemination of human rights (Richmond and Frank, 2009: 4).

Mark Fischer (2000), for instance, delineates the understanding that is often assumed as the two pillars in which this notion is sustained: democracy and liberalism. Both terms are, per se, essentially a conceptual quicksand. Nevertheless, Fischer seeks to characterize how both pillars are understood under the notion of liberal peace. On the one hand, he argues that democracy, succinctly put, means that each member of a collective should have the same weight in the decisions on how this collective should be governed (2000: 2). Conversely, liberalism, under this rationale means that the individual has a range of rights that must be respected, especially from the rulers, in order to assure the freedom of the individual (Fischer, 2000: 2). These are essentially negative and positive rights. Liberal institutions, as the argument goes, seek to guarantee and foster these rights through the establishment of a constitution which enumerates the rights and limits of each individual, and at the same time limiting the power of the rules over the latter (Fischer, 2000: 2). Additionally, these institutions seek also to guarantee, in the view of Fischer, the private property, the freedom of goods and services, and the limitation of regulations and taxations (Fischer, 2000: 2). The combination of both understandings, according to Fischer, is what is understood by liberal democracies (Fischer, 2000: 3).

This rationale, when transposed to the area of peace, leads to the argument for the transformation of post-conflict states into liberal democracies, which is underpinned by the understanding that liberal democracies are more prone to peace. This rationale has its main roots at the theoretical formulations, for instance, of Immanuel Kant, Joseph Schumpeter, and Montesquieu who have argued that liberalism has a pacifying effect in political institutions (Richmond, 2008: 89–90). This is underpinned by an assumption, and very often construction, that directly relates the possession of liberal values with peace and prosperity.[13] Under this line of reasoning, liberal states are more developed, peaceful, and, most important, stable both domesticly and internationally. This argument, in the international narrative, is clearly epitomized on the formulations of the democratic peace theories[14] (Newman, Paris, and Richmond, 2009: 11). This understanding is sustained by the proposition that established democracies do not engage in wars with each other. This argument rests on two interrelated pillars: (1) democracies are less prone to war and (2) economic interrelationships are a solid basis for peace.

The first pillar is underpinned by the First Definitive Article of Perpetual Peace of Immanuel Kant (1905 [1795]). For Kant, due to its constitutionalism and popular representation, this political organization would bring various institutional restraints in regard to the directions of foreign policy (Doyle and Recchia, 2011: 1435). Therefore, in this rationale, due to internal institutional constraints, leaders in democratic countries find it more difficult in initiating, and engaging in, a violent conflict (Newman, Paris, and Richmond, 2009: 11). Additionally, under this argument, democracies perceive other democracies in the international scenario much more favorably than they perceive non-democratic countries, which also constitute a restraint of war. The second pillar rests on the understanding that a war between trading countries would disrupt trade and economic relations, which would be a great discouragement for engaging in a violent conflict. This pillar rests essentially on the ideas of the Baron de Montesquieu (2002 [1748]) and of Joseph Schumpeter (1966 [1919]). For Montesquieu, peace was a pivotal part of the very spirit of the commerce (2002 [1748]: 338). His point is developed in the very first pages of the book XX of his *The Spirit of the Laws* when he argues that peace is the natural effect of commerce, since two trading nations would became dependent from each other (Montesquieu, 2002 [1748]: 338) . Therefore, it will be of no interest engaging in a war with each other because no nation would profit from it. In this regard, Schumpeter adds another point when he associates the monarchies with imperialism and, as a consequence, with war (1966 [1919]: 54–64). He perceived monarchies as a war machine (1966 [1919]: 24). Furthermore, Schumpeter perceived democracy and capitalism as forces for peace (Doyle, 1986: 1153). He argued that capitalism is fundamentally in opposition to war (Schumpeter, 1966 [1919]: 70), since the majority of people would never engage in something that only a small minority would profit, since only aristocrats and war profiteers would benefit from wars (Doyle, 1986: 1153).

Consequently, under the liberal peace argument, peace must come through the liberalization of states in several domains: political, economic, and societal. This argument reached the international policies that are directed to peace and became the normative framework (Richmond and Franks, 2007: 27) which shapes the configuration of the current UN peace operations. Under this rationale, to transform violent conflicts throughout the globe, to achieve peace, and to develop post-conflict states means to render operational in those territories the liberal peace argument. [15]

Hence, as the argument goes, peace meant that the political and economic spheres of post-conflict states should be intervened in order to liberalize them and transform these states into liberal democracies. Therefore, on the political realm, it was pursued the implantation of democratic regimes in these countries. This process, nevertheless, was underpinned by a very strict, and procedural, understanding of democracy. In this context, the democratization of post-conflict states simply meant holding elections periodically, being the first one usually within the first years of formal peace. On the economic side, this meant the construction of an open-free-market-oriented economy. This was pursued through several instruments ranging from the reduction of the state's role within the economy to the stimulation of the free flow of capital and through conditional loans. In the 1990s, the liberalization of the social sphere was still limited. This scenario would change profoundly from the 2000s onward.

Notwithstanding the fact that this approach to peace represented an attempt to pursue a positive peace, it had several flaws. The very first one was the assumption that the normative framework of liberal peace, with its one-size-fits-all approach, could be unproblematically exported throughout the globe, irrespective of the singularity of each post-conflict scenario. Moreover, this kind of approach to peace, quite often, did not avoid the relapsing of violence in these conflicts (Paris, 2004). Finally, rather than creating an encouraging environment for the development of a lasting peace, this rationale produced, in Paris's and Sisk's view (2009b: 2), several destabilizing effects in different countries, such as: the elections serving as a catalyst element for the renewal of the conflict in Angola in 1992; the resurgent of not only war, but the occurrence of a genocide in Ruanda in 1994; the reversion of the democracy to a despotic form of rule by the elected officials in Cambodia in the 1990s, with Hun Sen, and Liberia after 1997, with Charles Taylor; the reinforcement of the power of the nationalist elements and the increasing of power of those operating in the black markets after the Dayton Accords; and the reproduction of the sources of the conflict in Nicaragua, El Salvador and Guatemala (Paris and Sisk, 2009b: 2); to name a few.

The Peacebuilding Consensus

All those elements indicated that peace operations had to be rethought. Strangely, rather than motivating a pulling back from the enterprise or the

rethinking of its underpinning normative framework, the failures and limitations of the early 1990s brought the conclusion that more needed to be done
in terms of time frame, range, scope, and depth of the activities performed. In
fact, it emerged a situation which can be characterized as a peacebuilding
consensus (Richmond, 2004a, b).

The peacebuilding consensus certainly does not mean that all the actors of
the international scenario completely agree in regard to every kind of issue
when the subject debated is international peace. This could not be further
from reality. However, it is clearly perceptible that despite the differences
and variety of actors within the international scenario involved in peacebuilding efforts—international non-governmental organizations, states, international organizations, and so on—especially those working under the UN
system, it is shared, to a wide degree, an understanding of the overall strategy
to be pursued, in order to achieve a stable and lasting peace and a prosperous
world. This understanding rests on a much denser version of the liberal peace
argument. In this version, more than the ending of the direct and violent
conflict, it is pursued the (re)construction, toward a profound liberalization,
of the whole post-conflict state and society (Newman, Paris, and Richmond,
2009: 10–11). Therefore, peace became the mere institutionalization of *one*
kind of governance, namely the liberal-democratic one, and this became even
more solidified as the cornerstone which sustains current peace operations.

Following Richmond's (2008) understanding regarding the approaches to
peace, this characterizes a third generation. This approach mobilizes large-
scale and multidimensional processes in order to achieve peace (Richmond,
2008: 99). This is a kind of peace that intervenes in post-conflict states
aiming to make them meet international standards in disparate areas such as:
security sector, border control, human rights, corruption, development, rule
of law, and many others. Richmond rightly remembers that this approach in
fact pursues peace through the reform of governance. This is a consequence
of the fact that peace operations rapidly incorporated into its multidimensionality the major focus on state-building (Richmond, 2008: 107; 105)—herein
understood as a practice that embraces both the construction and strengthening of the state and its governance institutions, and also the practices that
seek to shape, mold and direct the state-society relations between post-conflict states and their populations. At this point, state-building became a pivotal activity within peace operations.

Notwithstanding the fact that the liberal peace argument is quite disputable in several fronts, this argument has a strong and widespread support
internationally (Newman, Paris, and Richmond, 2009: 11), particularly in
terms of conflict transformation in post-conflict countries. This is clearly the
cornerstone which underpins external interventions, especially those regarding peace and development, particularly those led by the UN. A direct consequence of this line of thinking is the crystallization, and quite often the

legitimization, of the understanding that fostering liberal democratic values globally directly means the propagation of prosperity and peace throughout the world; even when this is pursued at gunpoint, as it was argued in the case of the US invasion of Iraq or Afghanistan.

Nevertheless, contrary to what those working under this understanding try to portray, this approach to the transformation of violent conflicts and peace is far from unproblematic and universal. It essentially fosters, and therefore sustains, one particular understanding of the world, namely a (neo)liberal-democratic-northern-Atlantic one (Bellamy and Williams, 2004b). Nevertheless, what is silenced, and even bluntly denied, is that in order to such understanding of peace to find a nurturing environment to develop, a specific kind of post-conflict state, society, and relationship between both is needed. The perverse side of this is that, in the absence of such environment, those working under this rationale seek precisely the profound and structural transformation of the post-conflict state and its population.

Indeed, for Roland Paris (1997), this kind of approach to peace is in effect a social engineering experiment, which involves the transplantation of the Western modes of organizing the political, the economic, and the social spheres to post-conflict scenarios (Paris, 1997: 56). Having in mind that state-building, throughout time, became a pivotal activity in regard to peace-building, there is little room for doubt in terms of what kind of state is being sought to be built and what kind of state-society relationship is being pursued by this approach to peace. In fact, in the current international scenario, being a liberal-democratic state became a non-written norm, and it is through state-building that this norm is sought to be implemented in post-conflict states.

By the end of the 1990s, and the beginning of the 2000s, peace operations were transformed in order to incorporate this rationale. They became longer in time and a major focus was directed toward the construction of governmental institutions in the intervened states (Paris and Sisk, 2009b: 2). From late 1990s onward, operations started to incorporate such concern and even those already on the ground were reconfigured. Indeed, following security and development conceptual trends, the missions became deeper and wider; not only their mandates were much more expansive, but also the institutional structures of the states became a fundamental part of the interventions (Paris and Sisk, 2009b: 7). Newman, Paris, and Richmond (2009: 8–9) delineate the wide scope of the goals and the activities performed by these operations.[16] They, for instance, encompass areas such as: (1) security, which includes the support of the cease-fire, the demobilization and disarmament of former combatants, and their reintegration into society, security sector reform, the police enforcement capacity-building and strengthening the rule of law, to name a few; (2) economic, which might include the stabilization of the economy, employment creation, basic welfare provision, the delineation of the currency and its stability, and so on; and (3) political, which leads to activities like establishing a democratic system (including the organization of elections and the regulation of parties, strengthening public service delivery, strengthening governance institutions and the drafting of constitutions, to delineate just a few examples). For Newman, Paris, and Richmond, some emblematic cases of this kind of intervention were, for instance, Timor-Leste, Haiti, Kosovo, or Bosnia[17] (Newman, Paris, and Richmond: 7), among others.

This manner of pursuing peace certainly has a lot of flaws. Roland Paris (2010), for instance, points out several shortcomings, such as: (1) the little consideration regarding the tensions and contradictions inherent to the whole process; (2) the democratization and marketization efforts without considering local institutional conditions; (3) the limited knowledge about the local environment; (4) the posture of not taking enough consideration about the variations among post-conflict societies; (5) the little ownership by the locals over the strategic and daily decision-making within the missions; (6) the often insufficiency of resources directed to the missions; (7) the lack of continuity of the tasks undertook within peacebuilding efforts; (8) the lack of coordination among the innumerous actors engaged in such operations; or even (9) the lack of definition of what success means in such efforts (2010: 347).

Just as peace operations on the ground suffered modifications from late 1990s onward, within the academia new kinds of literature about them were also burgeoning. Not only more cross-case comparisons started to appear, but also studies became much more refined theoretically (Paris and Sisk, 2009b: 7). Paris and Sisk (Paris and Sisk, 2009b: 7) identify several burgeoning branches, such as: (1) the comparison of different types of interventions in order to better understand the durability of peace after civil wars; (2) the research of the role of natural resources and conflict economies, seeking to understand the "greed and grievance" argument[18] in violent conflicts; (3) the examination of these practices through neo-Marxist, cosmopolitanism and post-strutcturalist approaches; (4) the problematization of spoilers of peace processes; and (5) the observation of elements such as regional dimensions, transitional justice, and gender issues of peace operations (Paris and Sisk, 2009b: 7).

In addition, three main lines of argumentation within the literature can be identified (Chandler, 2008: 2–3; Paris, 2010; Paris and Sisk, 2009b: 12–13). In essence, they argue that: (1) too much is being done, that the whole activity is too interventionist and ambitious (Englebert and Tull, 2008; Grindle, 2004; Walton, 2009), and that the intervention should not happen in the first place (Herbst, 2003; Luttwak, 1999; Weinstein, 2005); (2) the whole enterprise lacks commitment and resources (Chesterman, 2005), which is a point acknowledged by the UN (A/55/305: 10–11), and the international community needs to do more (Fearon and Laitin, 2004; Ignatieff, 2003;

Mallaby, 2002); and (3) focus should be placed on the coordination problem among the different actors and wide range of resources deployed (Jones, 2001; Paris, 2009; Rubin, 2006), which is a point that the UN concedes (A/ 50/60: Paragraph 81) and the very creation of the Peacebuilding Commission aims exactly to address this issue.

Many other arguments were made and aspects elucidated by those studying peace operations. This was the case, for instance, of issues like: the elements of success/failure of such activity (Gürkaynak, Dayton, and Paffenholz, 2009; Lijn, 2009); their mixed records (Berdal, 2009; Doyle and Sambanis, 2006; Fortna, 2008; Howard, 2008); the interrogation whether such operations in fact have a positive effect in avoiding the recurrence of violent conflicts (Gilligan and Sergenti, 2008; Quinn, Mason, and Gurses, 2007); their unintended consequences (Aoi, Coning, and Thakur, 2007); their political economy (Pugh, 2005); and the underlying paradoxes and contradictions of this enterprise (Baranyi, 2008; Jarstad and Sisk, 2008; Paris and Sisk, 2009a). Furthermore, there is also, for example, the effort of studying statebuilding processes not just as a current practice but putting it into a more historical perspective. In this sense, there are authors who problematize current state-building processes in relation to the practices that were performed, for instance, by the United States in Japan and Germany, or by the League of the Nations in its administration of the Saar Basin (Chesterman, 2004; Dobbins et al., 2005; Wilde, 2007). Indeed, for those who have a more critical reading[19] regarding the reconstruction efforts, it is quite clear the attachment of the state-building efforts in Afghanistan, Bosnia, and Kosovo, for instance, to a clear picture of imperial practices (Bendaña, 2005; Encarnación, 2005; Ignatieff, 2003). Not by coincidence, there are those who also draw parallels between current state-building practices and the *mission civilizatrice* of the past (Paris, 2002).[20]

Another element that is not left out of the discussion is the underlying ideological assumptions of the processes. It is Roland Paris (2004) and Oliver Richmond (2007b), for instance, who clearly delineate the origins, conceptual antecedents, and theoretical cornerstones of current peace efforts, evincing their distinct liberal tone. Following this path, Beate Jahn (2007a, b) also exposes the long-term history of these policies and their firm roots in the liberal ideology. To Kirsti Samuels and Sebastian Einsiedel (2003), though rarely explicitly stated, "[t]here are strong implicit assumptions underlying the state-building agenda, particularly the notion that a Western-style liberal democracy is the outcome sought" (2003: 3). Therefore, this is pursued through a one-size-fits-all model regarding the construction of peace that is indiscriminately applied throughout every post-conflict scenario. Oliver Ramsbotham, for example, calls it a "standard operating procedure" (2000: 170). For Marina Ottaway, this model is underpinned by a series of prescriptions that "in essence list the institutions and processes that need to be in place in a modern, Weberian, democratic state" (2002: 1009). Furthermore, Mark Duffield (2001) elucidates how this process becomes an instrument of containing conflict-affected people in their own countries.

In addition, it was already exposed not only that the process represents in fact a specific social engineering, but also its destabilizing effects and its possibilities of reproducing the very sources of violent conflicts (Paris, 2004). Observing some consequential effects of the operations, some authors focus, for example, in the correlation between post-war elections and the occurrence of violence.[21] Jack Snyder (2000) explored this hypothesis when evinced that democracy promotion, in early stages of the democratization process, might enhance, rather than reduce, the probability of violent conflicts. For Paris (2004) the rapid move to elections, before having proper institutions in place, is what leads to violence. Edward Mansfield and Jack Snyder (2005) add that the postwar electoral process introduces new kinds of uncertainties and that might leave the recovering society vulnerable to violence. This line of thought is supported by Paul Collier (2009), who also brings empirical support regarding the dangerous of premature election's promotion.

Other analysts focus more on the local context. Beatrice Pouligny (2006), for instance, seeks to understand how local individuals and groups perceive their relationship with UN missions. Furthermore, Roger Mac Ginty (2008) also problematizes the local context when focusing on local peacemaking practices. He observes indigenous peacemaking efforts and interrogates how those can relate to Western forms of peacemaking. Other observers evince, for instance, the failure of such missions to engage with the local people. Richmond and Franks, for example, expose lack of engagement of UN missions with local cultures, identities and everyday life (Richmond, 2009; Richmond and Franks, 2009). More recently, other analysts problematize the question of political hybridity. They illustrate the combination of elements of both the Western and local modes of governance (Boege et al., 2008: iii; 2009, 2010) and, consequently, illuminating the hybrid political orders that emerge from such interaction between internationals and locals.

Many of these critiques clearly fit in what Oliver Richmond (2008: 97–117), labeled as the fourth generation regarding the reflections about peace—the critique of peace-as-governance. This generation is composed by a wide range of scholars, usually departing mainly from critical approaches to IR, who has pointed out several flaws on the reflections of the third generation. For instance, they have evinced not only the limitations of the previous generation in terms of its emancipatory potential, but also its fixed focus on the state sovereignty and limitations in regard to elements such as identity or culture. Most importantly, they have also brought light not only to the underling cultural assumptions of such project, but also its neo-colonial posture (Richmond, 2008: 97–117).

Therefore, observing the debates aforementioned, it is clear that the series of challenges, shortcomings, and failures of peace operations can be divided into conceptual/theoretical, normative, political, and practical challenges (Bercovitch and Dean, 2012: 179–182). Nevertheless, interestingly enough, the efforts of (re)transforming UN peace operations address only a narrow part of the challenges. Even when they are rethought and reprogrammed, this effort is still embedded by the same normative framework of the liberal peace. To be fair, even those who criticize the enterprise do it, quite often, departing from this same normative framework. As a result, although peace operations were reprogrammed to tackle previous perceptions of failures, they were restructured within the same framing. Hence, even performing different and deeper activities, they still operate within their original Euro-centric ontology and near-imperialist attitude. This makes the reframing of such operations, which is the essence of this book, even more important. This is what makes the path of challenging the very manner in which the post-conflict state-building is framed and problematized much more relevant and urgent. Nevertheless, before advancing any further, it is essential to have a closer observation of what state-building means.

STATE-BUILDING AND STATE FRAGILITY

In an international environment, such as the current one, where state fragility is increasingly a significant concern, it is not a coincidence that state-building has emerged as a fundamental process within peacebuilding efforts. Indeed, state-building became a pivotal tool to deal with international security concerns, development advancement aspirations, and transforming violent conflicts, globally. Consequently, state-building became a crucial instrument regarding peace and a pressing topic in the contemporary international agenda. Additionally, nowadays, state-building is not anymore something that takes place only after a humanitarian/military intervention, as in the cases of Kosovo, Afghanistan, or Iraq; a peacebuilding effort, as in Bosnia or Timor-Leste (Chandler, 2010: 1); or after a natural catastrophe as in Haiti. Indeed, state-building is no longer an activity that happens solely in post-conflict settings. Even though not being labeled as such, the EU's relationship with Southeastern Europe (Chandler, 2006: chapter 5–6; 2010: chapter 5), the International Monetary Fund's (IMF) relations with South America during the 1980s and 1990s, or even the current *troika*—IMF, European Central Bank, and European Commission—practices performed in the European context during the current crisis are clear examples of this.

Nevertheless, state-building is a practice that is more clearly perceptible in post-conflict scenarios. Despite several attempts to clarify the process, contemporary international state-building remains to some extent a blurry term (Goetze and Guzina, 2010). For Catherine Goetze and Dejan Guzina (2010), this happens due to three difficulties: (1) its close relation to an even more debated concept—state; (2) the concept is already somewhat loosely, and incorrectly, employed by some historical sociological literature to study the *longue durée* processes of state formation in modern Western Europe; and (3) the very often confusion, sometimes intentionally, with nation-building processes.

In order to deal with these difficulties and to analyze state-building processes in the international scenario, one could start by further delineating the words *state* and *building*. Regarding the state side of the term, there is no doubt that the concept state is central to most political analysis. Consequently, it is a concept widely employed, very difficult to define, and heavily contested (Hay and Lister, 2006: 1). Herein, state[22] is understood as a political entity which has the monopoly of both the legitimate law-making and the use of the force (Weber, [1922] 1978: 54). In addition to these Weberian aspects, which are commonly understood as the main elements of statehood; this political entity must also possess other pivotal attributes, which were formulated and agreed in the Montevideo Convention on Rights and Duties of States (1933), and remains the most accepted criteria for statehood (Caplan, 2005a: 52). They are: a permanent population; a defined territory; a government; and the capacity to enter into relations with the other states (League of Nations, 1936: article 1/page 25). Regarding the building part of the term, a brief semantic note is sufficient. A clear semantic distinction should be made between state *formation* and state-*building*. This should be done due to the fact that this best represents the very manner in which each process is performed. Departing from the Cambridge Dictionary (2008), formation brings a sense of a process that is naturally developed and mainly internally made, which can somewhat represent better the processes that took place in Western Europe.[23] In opposition, the word *building* brings a sense of a process that is externally incited and performed by the disposition of components in a determinate manner, which gives a clearer picture of current post-conflict state-building processes.

State-building emerged as a central instrument to deal with post-conflict states and populations. This is a result of a process that ended up transforming state-building into the epicenter of a triangular narrative that merges, apparently distant, notions of security, development, and peace.[24] As this narrative goes, without security there is no possibility of development; development, by its turn, reinforces and is a pivotal condition for the increase of security; both, together, are the indispensible pillars for the transformation of violent conflicts throughout the globe and the consolidation of a sustainable peace in post-conflict states. Despite the apparent distance between these discourses, currently, they are very interrelated. It is the centrality of the question of fragility underpinning mainstream rationales regarding these narratives that bind them together. These discourses, in an orthodox understanding, have as a pivotal concern overcoming the fragility of states. Fragility, within this perspective, is grounded in three pillars: (1) weak, or nearly nonexistent, institutions and governance apparatus; (2) deficiency in delivering fundamental public goods to its population; and (3) the insufficient capacity of protecting its own population (Ingram, 2010: 4). Under this line of reasoning, fragility is perceived as a barrier to the increase of development and security of a country and, as a result, as an obstruction to the consolidation of peace in post-conflict states. Consequently, and mostly importantly, fragility becomes understood as a barrier to the increase of development and security, and the consolidation of peace, of the whole world. Hence, as it would be expected with this line of thinking, state fragility lays at the very heart of the state-building debate. It is precisely this understanding of the world that makes the reverse of this same coin—state-building being a pivotal instrument in order to address international security and development issues—also true. The rationale behind it is that, while tackling state fragility, state-building is handling post-conflict internal disturbances and, in fact, avoiding their spill over to the international system and, consequently, enabling the enhancement of international stability.

This international concern with state fragility is rendered operational through the conceptualization of failed states. This is a concept that the orthodox thinking regarding international relations developed to conceptualize states in the periphery of the international system in a very hierarchal and even prejudicial manner. In this reasoning, failed states are failed because they do not perform, perform badly, or unwilling (Gros, 1996), or even unable to perform (Jackson, 2000), functions that are perceived as core functions of states, such as the provision of basic services, security, the monopoly of the legitimate use of violence, controlling the borders, and rule-of-law enforcement (Doornbos, 2006: 2; Zartman, 1995: 5). The bad performance is understood as a direct consequence of the weakness of the institutions and governance systems. As a result, these states are perceived as a potential source and harbor of poverty, diseases, terrorists, fluxes of drugs, illegal migration, and so on. Connecting both discourses of security and development, Fukuyama (2004) understands failed states as the most privilege locus to be the source of the world's insecurities, ranging from poverty to terrorism (2004: ix). Indeed, this is a concept that is an important element not only in approximating both discourses, but also highly relevant regarding each of the discourses separately.

On the one hand, in the international security discourse, the mainstream narrative goes on the direction of directly connecting failed states with international (in)security. This linkage is perhaps most emblematic on the first National Security Strategy (NSS) of US President George W. Bush's Administration, where it is stated that failing states are the biggest threat to America

(NSS, 2002: 1). Although the attention regarding failed states, as a source of threat to US *interests*, can be traced back to President Bill Clinton's last NSS, President Bush goes even further connecting these states to the threats of US *national security* (Rice, 2003: 2). This document, due both to its relevance inside the security environment and the relevance on the international scenario of the state that advances it, is central to this shift inside the international (in)security rationale. Although arguing that the document does not a proper course of action for dealing with the issue, Susan Rice (2003) clearly welcomes the document's focus on this kind of threat (2003: 1). In addition to the understanding that these states are a likely environment to the emergence or settlement of terrorist organizations, this linkage between failed states and international (in)security is made through other associations. One can mention, for instance, the fact that these states are also perceived as places where insurgents are more likely to exist, which could threat regional and international stability, or even the fact that these states are understood as sites for entry, transfer or transit of chemical, biological or nuclear weapons materials (Newman, Paris, and Richmond, 2009: 10).

On the other hand, within the international development discourse, the fragility of states is also seen with a great amount of concern. Fragility is understood as an obstacle to the overall development of the globe. According to a UNDP/World Bank's policy paper, developed by Sue Ingram (2010), delineating the role of state-building in the world, it is state's fragility that, on the one hand, threatens the world's security and, on the other hand, prevents the enhancement of global development (Ingram, 2010: 4). Hence, under this rationale, an international scenario with more fragile states is an international scenario farther away from a more developed world. This link between fragility and underdevelopment is done through the argument that these states, due to their fragility, cannot deliver public goods to their own population. This, per se, is something of great concern; however, these countries are also perceived as an important element in the development and dissemination of, for instance, contagious diseases around the globe. Therefore, for those working under this line of thinking, these states constitute a regional and international threat (Newman, Paris, and Richmond, 2009: 10).

Furthermore, another side of this line of thought is that this severe limitation of public services is also a condition that might lead to poverty. However, the most worrisome issue emerges with the easy and direct connection that this kind of thought makes between poverty and violent conflicts.[25] In this view of things, fragility is very often associated with violent conflicts, being both their cause and consequence (Ingram, 2010: 5). In a clear highjack of the development discourse by the security rationale, the argument is underpinned by the assumption that poor states are more prone to experience instability and violence. This would pose a threat not only for its populations, but to its regional neighbors and the world (Brainard, Chollet, and LaFleur,

2007: 1). Susan Rice, former US Ambassador to the UN, best summarizes this connection when she says that poor states, in a globalized world, might be, even though indirectly, a threat to other states that are faraway from them (2007: 33). For her, poverty produces insecurity (Rice, 2007: 31).

Because state fragility is a central matter in the international scenario, it is not a surprise to see that the whole state-building agenda emerges as policy thought to deal with, and overcame, it (Ingram, 2010: 5). Another point to take in consideration is that according to mainstream thinking, both within international security and development discourses, states are understood to be the very bedrock of the international scenario. Therefore, according to this rationale, state fragility threatens the very foundation of this system (Rotberg, 2003: 1). Not by coincidence, state-building, under this line of thinking, becomes "one of the most important issues for the world community" (Fukuyama, 2004: ix) and it is one of the critical moral and strategic imperatives of our time (Rotberg, 2004: 42). According to Ashraf Ghani and Clare Lockhart, state-building is solution for issues like global insecurity, poverty, and underdevelopment (2008: 4). Therefore, state-building becomes not only crucial to the security, well-being, and peace of the state and population subject to a state-building enterprise; it is a crucial instrument also to the security, well-being, and peace of the whole globe. Unsurprisingly, state-building, especially in post-conflict scenarios, is perceived as a fundamental practice that, while (re)shaping these states internally, is consequently enhancing the very maintenance of the international system.

THE POST-CONFLICT STATE-BUILDING

Herein, the post-conflict state-building is understood to embrace not only the construction, strengthening, and enhancement of post-conflict state institutions, but also the practices that seek to shape, mold, and direct the relations between post-conflict states and their populations. Therefore, since there is a frequent misunderstanding between terms like state-building, peacebuilding, and nation-building, before advancing any further, it is important to clarify the distinctions between them.

Due to the fact that many, if not most, of contemporary peacebuilding activities in post-conflict scenarios are centrally concerned with state-building efforts (Brahimi, 2007), both terms are quite often used synonymously. Indeed, for some, peacebuilding *is* state-building (Barnett and Zürcher, 2009: 25). Although they share some fundamental attributes, perform complementary and quite often overlapping activities, and are hardly differentiated on the ground, they are still distinct processes. In fact, sometimes they might even be contradictory (Call, 2008; Chopra, 2009; Rocha Menocal, 2009: 14–17). Peacebuilding, as the UN definition points out, refers to a wide range of measures addressing root causes of violent conflicts aiming at the creation of conditions to reduce the risk of relapsing into violence. State-building, by its turn, while focusing on the (re)construction and strengthening of post-conflict state institutions and on post-conflict state relations with its own population, is usually a crucial part of the current peacebuilding activities performed by the UN (Paris and Sisk, 2009b: 14).

Although a precise demarcation from each other is hardly an easy task, it is perceptible that although both processes have several overlapping activities—such as political settlements, security sector reform, constitution-making, elections, strengthening of core governance institutions, and delivery of basic social services, among others—they also have their own particular ones. Whereas peacebuilding addresses, for instance, issues such as critical infrastructures, employment, refugees and internally displaced people, transitional justice and disarmament, and demobilization and reintegration of former combatants, state-building comprehends activities like the restoration of administrative and civil service capacity, strengthening of the financial management, decentralization, supporting the governance capacity in the executive, legislative and judiciary, supporting also the civil society, and the development of governance capacity. Obviously, this differentiation is very disputable. However, the most important point, rather than making an exact catalogue of which activity lies under what process, is to evince that although closely related, state-building is not peacebuilding. Hence, in post-conflict scenarios, although complementary and sometimes overlapping, state-building is better understood as a pivotal part of a more comprehensive activity of building the peace.

Another very frequent confusion of terms happens between state-building and nation-building, which are often used interchangeably. This happens particularly outside the academic circles, in spheres such as the media, among donors, and within think-tanks and NGOs (Scott, 2007: 3). This might be explained by the well-known change of mind of George W. Bush regarding the term *nation-building*. While a campaigner in 2000, Bush was very much worried about using the term nation-building in regard to US military interventions. By the time of the US intervention in Afghanistan, as president, he viewed this intervention as an ultimate nation-building mission (Miller, 2010). Therefore, from that time onward, much of the narrative in regard to post-conflict scenarios was permeated by a nation-building discourse.[26] This is something perceived mainly in the US discussions about the theme, but due to the relevance of the country this narrative also influenced the overall debate about the matter.

Nevertheless, although both processes might be sometimes related, state-building and nation-building are very distinct phenomena. Sometimes, they can even be very conflicting processes (Ottaway, 1999). On the one hand, as already observed, state-building deals with the (re)construction/strengthening of post-conflict state institutions and with shaping post-conflict state relations with its population. Nation-building, on the other hand, refers to processes dealing with the (re)creation or (re)construction of a cultural or political identity.[27] In fact, these identities can be correlated, or not, with the territorial limits of a state. Moreover, the formation of the state, and the state power, can definitely be a defining force in this process. Indeed, this process might even be the result of the process of both the formation and the (re)construction of the state. However, they are hardly the same process. Paris and Sisk (2009b), for instance, argue that nation-building has to do with the strengthening, on the one hand, of the collective identity of a population and, on the other hand, with its sense of uniqueness and unity (2009b: 15). Therefore, nation-building, in contrast with state-building, has to do with the activities in the sphere of language, values, memory, culture, myths, signs, religion, and several other spheres that would comprehend the formation of a common identity of the population in question. Hence, although sometimes the processes of the creation of state institutions and the management of state-society relations, and the formation of cultural, political, and collective identities can be related, and even be operated simultaneously, state-building and nation-building should not be understood as synonymous processes.

As a practice performed at the international scene in post-conflict scenarios, state-building[28] can have more than one understanding. Under a very broad view, state-building might be understood as a process under which a state improve its capacity to perform its tasks (Whaites, 2008: 4). However, other understandings are much more specific. In a narrower perspective about the process, state-building is merely institutional. It is a process that focuses on the (re)construction of states through the strengthening and/or the (re)creation of its institutional apparatuses. Under this rationale, state-building simply means institution-building. In this understanding, post-conflict state-building is a part of the reconstruction efforts which the primary objective is the (re)construction of political institutions (Bickerton, 2007: 96). Under this understanding, this process is a part of peacebuilding activities and seeks to create effective and legitimate governmental institutions (Paris and Sisk, 2007: 1), that are to be endowed with governance instruments and that are to be capable of providing physical and economic security to its population (Chesterman, 2004: 5). In this sense, under this line of thinking, state-building is intimately connected with state capacity (Fukuyama, 2004) and its internal governance (Rotberg, 2004). In this view, state-building refers to the process of (re)constructing the governance structures of a state, or even building it from the scratch (Caplan, 2005b: 3). Paris and Sisk's definition of post-conflict state-building as the processes of strengthening or building legitimate state institutions in post-conflict countries (2009a: 14) best sums up this understanding about the process.

This understanding is certainly not held without criticism. The first criticism is the notorious attempt to depoliticize the whole state-building process. Notwithstanding the deeply entrenched ideological dimension of the process, state-building is presented as a merely administrative, purely bureaucratic, response to violent conflicts throughout the world (Bendaña, 2005). Presented in a bureaucratic/administrative manner, state-building is portrayed as something that can be operated, without problems, bypassing popular support and agreement (Chandler, 2005). As a result, an issue that is essentially political is transformed into a merely technical topic and, consequently, into something requiring purely technical solutions and approaches (Bickerton, 2007).

This leads to a second criticism which argues that by bypassing the public dimension and by being represented in such technical and bureaucratic terms, state-building ends up creating institutions with little, if any, legitimacy/representation because they are not endowed with the will of the population. Consequently, the resulting institutions have a very weak political and social support (Bickerton, 2007). This kind of state created in post-conflict scenarios is what David Chandler calls phantom states. For him, phantom states are states that exist on paper, in juridical terms, but are not independent political entities and possessors of self-government (Chandler, 2006: 43–44). Notwithstanding having institutions in place and some degree of governance, these states are not perceived as the embodiment of the political will of their societies. Therefore, in addition to lacking popular support and legitimacy, these states end up having their political realm atrophied. Hence, through the construction of institutions that have little legitimacy and by downplaying the political connotation of the whole process, state-building builds not only very weak foundations but also creates entities that, in order to merely survive, are highly dependent on external assistance. Consequently, state-building processes very often become state-failure ones (Bickerton, 2007: 100).

On the other hand, state-building processes might also be problematized through a wider understanding of the process. In a much wider sense, state-building is analyzed beyond that primary institutional approach to the process. In this sense, state-building is analyzed as an international engagement with domestic governing mechanisms of other states and their respective societies. Therefore, this understanding seeks to analyze practices beyond the scope of the (re)construction and strengthening of state institutions. It also reflects upon the whole set of practices in which internationals seek to manage and regulate state-society relations of a particular country, such as international assistance, strengthening the regulatory capacity of the state, conditionalities, debt relief, international loans, poverty reduction strategies, and many others (Chandler, 2006). This is a more comprehensive understanding of state-building practices and allows the problematization of its practices not only during reconstruction periods, but also in different sets of relationships between states. In a post-conflict peacebuilding setting, for instance, this requires the analyst to observe not only the post-conflict state institutions that are being (re)constructed/strengthened but also the whole set of practices that seek to shape and direct the relations between these post-conflict states and their own populations.

This understanding regarding state-building, once confined to those who have a more critical stance about the subject, seems to be precisely the understanding policy-oriented reflections are heading to nowadays. Observing some key policy papers, for instance, of the Organisation for Economic Co-operation and Development (OECD) (2008, 2010), the Department for International Development of the United Kingdom (DFID) (2009, 2010) and UNDP/WB (Ingram, 2010), it is clear that they are seeking to respond to the aforementioned criticisms of depolitization, technicality and lack of legitimacy. Observing the approaches directed to state-building practices, it is clearly perceived that the understanding of what state-building means has evolved considerably from the mere institution-building and capacity enhancement framework to a focus on state-society relations (Rocha Menocal, 2009: 6). Among policy-oriented reflections, the key state-building definition that sets the discussion for all other policy papers is given by the OECD. The organization defines state-building as a endogenous process, driven by state-society relations, seeking to enhance the capacity, the institutions and ultimately the legitimacy of a certain state. (2008: 1). The DFID, by its turn, also adds to the discussion that state-building is majorly focused on strengthening the state-society relationship and building ways to enhance such relation (2009: 4). Unpacking the elements of these definitions, Sue Ingram (2010: 6) visualizes four topics where the discourse in regard to the understanding about state-building shifted: (1) state-society relations are at the centre stage; (2) while dealing with state-society relations, state-building becomes characteristically political; (3) state-building is not a technical process; and (4) state-building is principally an endogenous process. Hence, nowadays, in post-conflict scenarios, the relations between post-conflict states and their populations are at the heart of state-building concerns and efforts.

This certainly does not mean that in the past state-society relations were not targeted during state-building processes. However, they were a consequence of the institutional building/enhancement attempts. In contrast, current state-building processes are essentially concerned with this relationship. Nowadays, state-building is concerned about how a state interact with its society. Consequently, state-builders became more concerned with not only how the state perform its functions but also how it interacts with its own population (Ingram, 2010: 7). Hence, whereas in the past the major focus of state-builders were the (re)construction of the state institutions, nowadays the greater amount of attention is directed, without dismissing the institution building efforts, to the relationship between the intervened state and its own population; to the design of how this relationship should perform itself.

Nevertheless, three elements remain silenced and often denied. First, state-building practices have become even more invasive and profound. Whereas in the past state-building efforts were basically about institutions, nowadays these processes are much more capillary in their reach. Second, the aforementioned *how* the state should perform and *how* it should interact and engage with its own society is internationally pre-given, rather than open for discussion. Finally, it is also brought to light that certainly there is action and agency inside post-conflict countries; however, those actions are conducted by international state-builders toward a pre-given *how*. In fact, whole populations are conducted toward this pre-determined *how*, toward not only *how* states should relate to society but also *how* society should act and also relate to the state. These are some of key aspects to take in consideration while analyzing state-building processes in the current international scenario that this book elucidates.

CONCLUSION

This chapter discusses how the practices toward peace in the international scenario were transformed throughout time, namely from the end of the World War II onward. Focusing on the period of the Cold War and afterward, it delineates the configuration and the main elements of peace operations during both periods, how this configuration was modified from one period to the other, and the identification of elements that allowed such transformations. Furthermore, this chapter evinces that peace operations were transformed into operations where a major focus is directed to state-building. Therefore, (re)creation of institutions and public administration systems, the establishment of judicial institutions, the creation of political parties, the strengthening of the state's capacity to provide services to its populations, and the relationship between the post-conflict state and its own population became a major part, if not the very essence, of the UN approach to building and consolidating peace in such post-conflict contexts. Most importantly, this chapter indicates that even though the UN sought to overcome, in a variety of manners, the challenges, shortcomings, and failures of its peace operations, these actions still depart from the same normative framework of the liberal peace. Therefore, they remain far from being a driving force for building peace. This indication makes the reproblematization of the very reflections about these operations and the reframing of state-building practice crucial. This effort allows the perception of different kinds of interactions, engagements, and possibilities which can, in turn, bring new ways of seeing and understanding such practices that, in the end, allows for their very transformation.

NOTES

1. For more on positive and negative peace, see (Galtung, 1969).
2. For a better delineation of the realist posture toward peace and also of other different approaches within the IR theories, see (Richmond, 2008).
3. For further missions of this kind, see (Newman, Paris and Richmond, 2009: 6–7).
4. Representative studies of this period are, for instance, (Diehl, 1994; Durch, 1993, 1996; Heininger, 1994; Mayall, 1996; Ratner, 1995).
5. For a more extensive delineation of the challenges and weakness of this kind of peace operations, see for instance (Bellamy, William and Griffin, 2010: 190–192; Bercovitch and Dean, 2012: 82–83).
6. For more in this regard, see for instance (Jackson, 1990; Keohane, 2003; Krasner, 1999, 2004).
7. To be fair, Paris (2004: 21) remembers that this view of the world was not universally shared.
8. It is worth to mention that the very name of some of these instruments is already present in publications of Johan Galtung (1976). Indeed, the UN itself acknowledges Galtung's and Peace Studies' influences in the formulation of its peace instruments (UN, 2010b: 1; 45).
9. Peacekeeping is a very disputed concept. For other definitions of the term, see for instance (Bellamy, William and Griffin, 2010; Butler, 2009: Chapter 4; Diehl, 2008: Chapter 1; Diehl et al., 2010; Durch and Berkman, 2006). For an overview of how this concept evolved throughout time and how it was rendered operational by different international organizations, such as UE, NATO, or OSCE, see for instance (Pinto, 2007).
10. For other definitions of the term and the different understandings of peacebuilding among different international actors, including within the UN, see for instance (Barnett et al., 2007; Chetail, 2009; Gourlay, 2009: 3–48). For an evolution of the concept within the UN, see for instance (UN, 2010b: 45–49).
11. For decisive works in this regard, see for instance (Duffield, 2001; Fischer, 2000; Heathershaw, 2008; Paris, 2004; Richmond, 2006, 2007b; 2008: 89–95).
12. For a detailed discussion of the different nuances, gradations and discourses of the liberal peace see for instance (Heathershaw, 2008; Richmond, 2006, 2007b).
13. For a deeper understanding of these relationships, see for instance (Oneal and Russett, 1999). For a critique of this pacifying effect of liberalism see for instance (Doyle, 2004).
14. For a deeper understanding about these formulations, see for instance (Doyle, 1983a, b; Elman, 1997; Oneal and Russett, 1999; Owen, 1994; Russett, 1993). For a critique of the democratic peace book, see for instance (Gates, Knutsen and Moses, 1996; Rosato, 2003).
15. To be fair, it should be noted that David Chandler, to a some degree, disputes that the current peace operations are informed by the liberal canon when he argues that, in fact, the underpinning paradigm of the whole practice is what he calls "post-liberal governance." For more in this regard, see (Chandler, 2010: Chapter 4).
16. This delineation is merely illustrative and by no means exhaustive. For other delineations of this kind, in order to complement this one, see, for instance (David, 1999; Ramsbotham, 2000: 182).
17. For more examples, see for instance (Newman, Paris, and Richmond, 2009: 7).
18. This "greed and grievance" argument is developed by Paul Collier and Anke Hoeffler (2001).
19. For a deeper discussion in regard to the importance of having a critical reading about these processes, see for instance (Bellamy and Williams, 2004a, b; Paris, 2000; Richmond, 2007a).
20. For a similar argument in regard to the UN engagement with Haiti, see for instance (Guerra and Blanco, 2017).

21. For a broader discussion about this theme, see for instance (Sisk, 2009).

22. For a deeper discussion regarding the concept, see for instance (Hay, Lister, and Marsh, 2006; Vincent, 1992).

23. For more regarding this process, see for instance (Blanco, 2013; Ertman, 2005; Poggi, 2004; Tilly, 1975a, b).

24. Distance very much shortened by the elucidations, for instance, of (Duffield, 2001, 2007).

25. For more regarding the direct link between poverty and violence, see for instance (Brainard, Chollet and LaFleur, 2007; Miguel, 2007; Rice, 2007). For an oppositional view, see for instance (Sen, 2008).

26. It is important to notice that in the United States, the term *nation-building* is frequently used to soften the interventions and invasions done abroad. This is clear in the cases of Afghanistan and Iraq. This effort is obviously underpinned by some US think-tanks. The most iconic example is perhaps the RAND which defines nation-building, in 2003, as "the use of armed force in the aftermath of a conflict to underpin an enduring transition to democracy" (Dobbins, 2003: 17), and in 2007 "as the use of armed force as part of a broader effort to promote political and economic reforms with the objective of transforming a society emerging from conflict into one at peace with itself and its neighbors" (Dobbins et al., 2007: xvii).

27. For more regarding the concept of nation, see for instance (Anderson, 1983; Gellner, 1983; Hobsbawm, 1992; Smith, 1998; Smith and John, 1994).

28. For other contexts where state-building might take place, see for example (Fritz and Menocal, 2007: 17).

Chapter Two

The Emergence of Timor-Leste as an International Urgent Need

At the beginning of the year 2002, the eastern half of the small island of Timor, in Southeast Asia, entered in the realm of the international system as a newly independent state. Timor-Leste became an independent democratic republic on May 20th 2002, under the auspices and conduction of the UN. To be more precise, on May 2002, Timor-Leste restored its legal independence. This process was neither short nor smooth. On the contrary, Timor-Leste had a very long, tortuous, and violent road toward regaining its legal independence. In fact, the UN state-building process in Timor-Leste was the instrument used by the international community to deal with the international urgent need that Timor-Leste had become over the years. After all, the process of seeking to build a liberal peace and to construct a liberal democratic state in Timor-Leste is a process that sought to put an end to a long and violent period of occupations, violence and killings in that part of the island (Richmond and Franks, 2009: 83). In addition, due to the extreme conditions in which the country found itself after long years of Portuguese colonization, Japanese occupation during the Second World War, and, from 1975 onward, bloody violent Indonesian occupation, it is also clear that UN state-building was also a process of seeking to address issues of development, security, and state fragility in Timor-Leste. Simultaneously, due to the range, scope, depth, and novelty of activities performed on the ground, employing nearly all the instruments at its disposal, the UN engagement with Timor-Leste, according to Oliver Richmond and Jason Franks, is an important symbol of the liberal state-building process internationally (2009: 83). Indeed, Timor-Leste, due to the unprecedented scope of UN engagement, is considered as a test case regarding state-building processes (Suhrke, 2001).

In this sense, this chapter process traces the long road that Timor-Leste travelled until the UN state-building enterprise and clarifies the process through which Timor-Leste emerged in the international scenario as an urgent need. Throughout this whole process, Timor-Leste and its independence not only became part of the international agenda but also, and most importantly, progressively relevant in the international scenario to the point of unavoidability. The elements herein analyzed, combined, are fundamental parts of the process in which Timor-Leste became an urgent need within the international scene and the intervention in the country highly necessary, which led to the formation of the state-building *dispositif* that was directed and deployed to Timor-Leste. The chapter is organized around three sections. The first one presents the trajectory of Timor-Leste until the Timorese struggle and despair started to become less invisible internationally. It addresses the Timorese path until the Indonesian invasion, annexation, and occupation of Timor-Leste. The second section discusses pivotal episodes in the process of Timor-Leste becoming an urgent need within the international scenario during the Indonesian occupation. Furthermore, it addresses the tripartite negotiations of the Timorese Referendum of 1999 and the massive violence which occurred before it. The third section delineates Timor-Leste as an international urgent need. It discusses the bloody violence occurred during and after the results of the referendum process which led, firstly, to the deployment of a military international force to Timor-Leste in order to restore security, and, secondly, to a massive state-building *dispositif* in order to deal with the country.

TIMOR-LESTE AS AN INVISIBLE URGENT NEED

Timor-Leste was a Portuguese colony from the eighteenth century[1] until mid-1970s, but the Portuguese presence in Timor dates back to the sixteenth century (Cristalis, 2009: xiii; Kingsbury, 2009: 28–30). The Portuguese, however, firmly established themselves in their part of the island of Timor only during the latter part of the nineteenth century. Initially, the ruling method of the Portuguese colonial process was essentially based on the ruling via local chiefs and the exploitation of local alliances/rivalries. This kind of arrangement was modified over time. By the beginning of the twentieth century, an administrative structure was imposed, which was formed by councils (*conselhos*), divided into posts (*postos*), formed by villages (*sucos*) encompassing small groups of houses (Kingsbury, 2009: 35–36).

In nearly every colonial domination relationships, any political and economic change in the metropolis certainly has its effects in the colony, and this was not different in the relationship of Portugal and Timor-Leste. In the first three decades of the twentieth century, Portugal went through a series of economic and political turbulences, ranging from a revolution that deposed the monarchy, the implementation of a short-lived republic, and the beginning of an authoritarian government under the leadership of António de Oliveira Salazar (Kingsbury, 2009: 37). Under Salazar's *Estado Novo*, the notion of civilizing mission in the colonies strengthened and the control of the colonies became tighter (Kingsbury, 2009: 38).

During the Second World War, Timor-Leste, due to its strategic position, had foreign troops on its soil, such as the Dutch and the Australian who, respectively, sought to protect its Dutch East Indies and use Timor as a buffer zone against the Japanese expansion. The attack on Pearl Harbor by the Japanese led the Dutch and Australian to send four hundred troops, on December 17th 1941, to the island aiming to pre-empt a possible Japanese takeover (Kingsbury, 2009: 38; Taylor, 1999: 13). This was understood by the Japanese as a clear indication that Timor-Leste was not neutral anymore and that the Allies sought to use it as a military base in the Pacific War. Consequently, the Japanese sent two thousand troops and invaded the island (Kingsbury, 2009: 38; Taylor, 1999: 13).

The war led to massive devastation. James Dunn (2003) says that official estimates suggest that 40,000 Timorese died as a result of the war (22). Nevertheless, applying the typical population growth rate of Timor-Leste, he argues that the figure can easily reach 60,000 (Dunn, 2003: 22). For António Magalhães (2007), this might represent from 11.4 percent to 15 percent of the Timorese population; a figure just comparable, for him, with the ones of the Soviet Union and Poland (2007: 9). Moreover, in addition to the impressive figure of dead people, main cities and villages were completely destroyed, and the population was starving (Taylor, 1999: 14). Dunn (2003) gives a graphic picture of the aftermath situation when he states that Timor-Leste seemed to have returned to the Stone Age (2003: 23). After the war, Timor-Leste returned to Portuguese authority (Cristalis, 2009; Kingsbury, 2009: 39) and the reconstruction efforts were tremendous for Portugal.

Only on December 15th 1960, Timor-Leste entered the UN agenda when it was placed into UN's list of non-self-governing territories (A/RES/1542). In theory, according to chapter XI of the UN Charter, Portugal was required to promote, among other things, "the well-being of the inhabitants" of the territory (UN, 1945: article 73 paragraph B) and also "to develop self-government and take due account of the political aspirations" of its people (UN, 1945: article 73 paragraph B). Furthermore, the UN General Assembly, on December 1960, passed Resolution 1514 on "the granting of independence to colonial countries and peoples" stating that colonialism was very much contrary to the UN Charter (A/RES/1514). All this put Portugal in an uncomfortable and isolated position internationally (Kingsbury, 2009: 40). Nevertheless, in practice, Portugal maintained that the territories listed by the General Assembly, Timor-Leste included, were overseas provinces of Portugal. Consequently, Portugal had no obligations under chapter XI (UN, 1999b) and continued to administer Timor-Leste until the mid-1970s.

During the mid-1970s, Portugal experienced a revolution that ended its authoritarian regime. In a revolution that became known as the *Revolução dos Cravos* (Carnation Revolution), the *Movimento das Forças Armadas* (Armed Forces Movement—MFA) deposed Marcelo Caetano, who replaced Salazar in 1968, on April 25th 1974. One of the pillars of this movement was the general dissatisfaction with the costly and failing colonial wars. Therefore, following the revolution, the independence process of the Portuguese colonies became possible (Kingsbury, 2009: 43). The revolutionary process at the metropolis certainly opened a window of opportunity for Timorese to think politically about its future and this undoubtedly meant to think in terms of its own independence. Facing this clear chance of political independence, local Timorese political activists formed three major political parties, which supported three different paths for Timor: (1) the *Associação Popular Democrática Timorense* (Timorese Popular Democratic Association—Apodeti), which pursed the integration with Indonesia; (2) the *União Democrática Timorense* (Timorese Democratic Union—UDT), which sought the continuation of the relationship with Portugal; and (3) the *Associação Social-Democrata Timorense* (Timorese Social Democratic Association—ASDT), which was later renamed as *Frente Revolucionária de Timor-Leste Independente* (Revolutionary Front for an Independent East Timor—Fretilin) and sought the complete independence of Timor-Leste (Kingsbury, 2009: 43–44).

The Indonesian Invasion and Annexation

By mid-January 1975, UDT and Fretilin agreed on a coalition. Two months later, the coalition agreed with Portugal to have a three-year transitional government that would end with the Timorese full independence (Taylor, 1999: 39). Nevertheless, as it is already known, this window of opportunity for the Timorese legal independence rapidly closed. By this time Indonesia had already decided to annex Timor-Leste. This Indonesian decision had the concurrence of major regional and global powers such as Australia, New Zealand, the United Kingdom, and the United States of America (Kingsbury, 2009: 48). There were essentially two factors underpinning this decision. The first one had to do with the Cold War rationale of that time, which led to the perception that Indonesia had a crucial role in the region in regard to the containment and avoidance of communist revolutions to spread. After all, one should not forget the impact that the communist revolutions in Vietnam, Laos, and Cambodia had among the north-American policy makers both in regard to the revolutions themselves and in regard to Indonesia as a key regional player (Kingsbury, 2009: 48). Magalhães (2007: 174–176) evinces precisely that this fear of domino effect that was present in the North American society at that time, in regard to those revolutionary processes, is best captured by a whole series of articles published, for instance, in *Times*, *Newsweek*, and other well-known North American magazines. In this context, Indonesia was perceived by policy makers as the major, if not the unique, barrier capable of holding the advance of this communist wave at that part of the world.

The second factor has to do with the notion, that was publically sustained by Australia's prime minister, that small states were not viable (Kingsbury, 2009: 48). Having in mind, just as most of the western political leaders of that time, the events in Southeast Asia, Gough Whitlam declared to the President of Indonesia, General Hadji Suharto, that the annexation would be the best solution for the Timorese and for the region (Magalhães, 2007: 179). Additionally, one should not forget that, as Magalhães (2007: 197–204) argued, the Australian interest in appropriating the gas and oil of Timor's Sea also played a key role in the Australian position in regard to the Indonesian invasion and then annexation of Timor-Leste.

Under what became known as *Operasi Komodo* (Operation Komodo),[2] Indonesian agents started to disseminate a wide range of false information throughout Timor-Leste as part of a clear misinformation strategy (Dunn, 2003: 73; Kingsbury, 2009: 48). They disseminated, for instance, hostile information regarding Fretilin through UDT supporters, which consequently strengthened the argument against, and the group opposing, the coalition between the UDT and the Fretilin. Consequently, the coalition ended later on May 27th 1975 (Kingsbury, 2009: 48). Due to this misinformation strategy, the UDT was led to believe that Fretilin would perform a coup on August 10. Aiming to anticipate this movement, the UDT performed its own coup, supported by the police, in order to demonstrate its own strength. With the support of junior army officers and by the majority of local troops, Fretilin responded to that coup. As a consequence, a very bloody, although brief, civil war[3] took place in Timor-Leste (Kingsbury, 2009: 49). It was by the end of August that the Fretilin's military support, reorganized as *Forças Armadas de Libertação e Independência de Timor-Leste* (National Armed Forces for the Liberation of East Timor—Falintil), could re-establish the order throughout Timor-Leste (Kingsbury, 2009: 49).

In this rough context, the UDT and Apodeti members reached to Indonesia and sought its support. They presented this support plea as if it was something grounded on the wishes of the Timorese population (Taylor, 1999: 51). This plea led to the invasion of Timor-Leste by Indonesian troops, firstly under the overall perception of being members of UDT troops, on October 8th and 16th. As Indonesia continued to send more troops, its presence on the territory could not be disguised anymore. On November 24th Fretilin appealed to the Security Council (SC) asking for the withdrawal of the Indonesian troops from Timor-Leste (Taylor, 1999: 63). Observing that an Indonesian invasion seemed close, Fretilin thought that a declaration of independence would help weighting in their favor. They sensed that an independent state would increase the chances of success in two spheres—on the external and on the internal fronts. On the one hand, in regards to the external sphere, it was thought that the UN would help an independent state. It was sensed that the UN would be inclined to deliberate favorably if Timor did not have to rely on Portugal. On the other hand, on the internal sphere, based on the feelings coming from the military front, it was sensed that the independence declaration could motivate the soldiers. It was thought that if they were going to die, they would prefer to die for their own country. Hence, on November 28th 1975, the Fretilin declared the independence of the territory. The new born country was the *República Democrática de Timor-Leste* (Democratic Republic of East Timor)[4] (Taylor, 1999: 63).

Although Timor-Leste was recognized as an independent state by twelve countries, these states did not have enough influence in the international scenario. Those states had neither international nor regional weight. The independence was not recognized, for instance, by the states that supported Indonesia's annexation—such as the United States, Australia, or the UK—by its former colonial power Portugal, and also by the UN (Kingsbury, 2009: 49). In the next day, members of UDT and Apodeti, having the Indonesian authorities behind, along with two other minor political parties signed in Bali, Indonesia (and not in Balibo Timor-Leste) the Balibo Declaration, which was drafted by Indonesian intelligence. This document argued that the Timorese population was claiming for the integration with Indonesia (Magalhães, 2007: 213). In fact, the document was signed by UDT and Apodeti members, without any consultation with the population, and the document was in reality an Indonesian pretext to invade Timor-Leste. This set the scenario for Indonesia to call for a full-scale military invasion, by sea and air on December 7th in what became known as the *Operasi Seroja* (Operation Lotus). This movement was welcome by international and regional powers, such as the United States of America and Australia. In fact, the US President Gerald Ford and his secretary of state Henry Kissinger were in Jakarta and met with President Suharto the day before the invasion (Dunn, 2003: 243; Magalhães, 2007: 186–187). This is a clear indication in regard to their concurrence and approval of the whole operation and also the role that the Indonesian invasion had within the international chess game of that time, which was also shared by Australia and the UK.

In the very day of the invasion, Portugal cut diplomatic relations with Indonesia and later presented a plea at the UN Security Council. The plea was accepted and the Council condemned the Indonesian military invasion and called upon Indonesia to withdraw all its forces from Timor-Leste (S/RES/384). Nevertheless, no concrete action was pursued (Magalhães, 2007:

285–286). In few days, Indonesia had seventy thousand troops on the ground (Kingsbury, 2009: 50). By mid-December, a provisional government which was formed by UDT and Apodeti leaders was installed. Furthermore, a few months after the beginning of the invasion, at the end of May 1976, the Indonesian government chose thirty-seven Timorese that were forced to sign a plea in which a People's Assembly (*Assembleia do Povo*) asked that Timor-Leste would become part of Indonesia. After obtaining the approval of the Congress, President Suharto accepted this plea on July 16th 1976 and Timor-Leste became Indonesia's twenty-seventh province with the official name of Timor Timur (Magalhães, 2007: 211). In spite of all this, the UN, the SC, and the General Assembly continued to consider Timor-Leste an autonomous territory under the administration of Portugal (Magalhães, 2007: 211). By that time, both Falintil and Fretilin members retreated into the hills and began what would be a twenty-four-year war of attrition, survival, and resistance[5] (Kingsbury, 2009: 50).

The Indonesian invasion was extremely brutal (Kingsbury, 2009: 50), precipitating massive killings throughout the country. Magalhães (2007) states that the precise statistics are difficult to obtain; especially in a territory that was almost totally closed to the world for a long period of time. Nevertheless, he advances the figure of dead people ranging from 180,000 to 308,000 (around 30 to 45 percent of the Timorese population) and above 80 percent destruction of people's livelihoods, mainly agriculture and cattle. In addition to the many thousands of people that died, many more were tortured, including children and elders, and many women were raped (2007: 215). James Dunn (2003) argues that after the four years of the invasion, Timor-Leste was only comparable to the worst conflicts, like Bosnia (2003: 292). For Magalhães (2007), the invasion of Timor was, without a doubt, one of the worst humanitarian tragedies of the twentieth century (2007: 215). Indeed, the Indonesian actions in Timor-Leste can be described as a bloody genocide that had the acquiescence of major international and regional powers.

But the Indonesian brutality certainly did not stop there. Dunn (2003) points out several other bloody examples throughout Indonesian occupation, such as: (1) 2000 people killed in the area of Dili in the fisrt week of the invasion; (2) the massive killings in 1976 that took place at Suai and Aileu; (3) in 1977 in the area of Bobonaro and Quelicai; (4) in 1978, when thousands were killed in the area of Matabian; and (5) in June of 1908, with the executions after the attack by Fretilin (2003: 292). Furthermore, two other massacres should be mentioned—the Lacluta massacre of September 1981 and the Creras massacre of August 1983. Regarding the former, apparently part of the Fretilin guerrilla was captured with their women and children. Part of the women was taken away by the Indonesian military, while the rest, along with the men and children were killed. In addition, their bodies were covered with dry grass and leaves and set on fire (Dunn, 2003: 292). Even pregnant women were not spared. Their stomachs were open and had shapen instruments inserted into their vaginas (Gama, 1995: 102). Four hundred people are said to be killed in this tragedy (Dunn, 2003: 292). In regard to the latter, the Creras massacre was one of the worst (Dunn, 2003: 292). The massacre was a reprisal for the killing of fifteen or seventeen Indonesian military men by Fretilin. This massacre, which took place allegedly on August 1983 21st and 22nd, was carried out after the raping and killing of some Timorese girls, including a wife of a Timorese official (Dunn, 2003: 292). According to Dunn (2003), around 200 Timorese were burnt alive at their own houses and 500 were killed at the Be Tuku River (Dunn, 2003: 292). Moreover, he evinces that there were solid evidences that more than 1000 Timorese, of all ages, were killed in this particular massacre (Dunn, 2003: 292). Indeed, this systematic killing and massacres evinces, most importantly, that the extermination directed toward the Timorese was genocidal (Dunn, 2003: 293).

In spite of all this, the Indonesian government was very much successful in obtaining the silence of the western media through several actions such as the murder of journalists; the total blockage of the access to the territory; attending the interests of the powerful states involved; and through a large misinformation strategy. Without all this, the enormous silence, and invisibility, that surrounded the Timorese case would be simply impossible (Magalhães, 2007: 217). Magalhães (2007: 219–228) argues that for thirteen years Timor-Leste was almost absolutely closed to the outside world. The Indonesian government, greatly limiting its presence, carefully selected the journalists and the humanitarian agencies that had access to Timor-Leste. This lack of, or poor, information in regards to the Timorese reality was certainly in the interest of Indonesia. Without information in the media regarding Timor-Leste, the Indonesian government could frame the reality in favor of its own position. Most of the people did not even know where Timor-Leste was located. This informative shield led to a complete invisibility and silence regarding the critical situation in Timor-Leste and the series of killings that was taking place in the country. Due to this informative blockade, the situation in Timor-Leste did not appear on the news; and not being on the news, it was practically as if Timor-Leste was virtually nonexistent.

Therefore, as grave as the situation in Timor-Leste was, it did not, at that time, result in an international *dispositif* to address the situation. The situation in Timor-Leste was certainly brutal and definitely there was *need*; in fact, an *urgent* one. Nevertheless, the situation in Timor-Leste was not perceived as an *international* urgent need. In reality, at that time, due to the fact that the Indonesian government was very effective in shielding the country in regard to information, the situation in Timor-Leste was barely visible at all.

Hence, it is not that the elements of a *dispositif* do not exist. Certainly, some of these elements are created and designed in the very moment when an urgent need emerges. However, most of the time, the narratives, concepts, institutions, actors, and other elements of a *dispositif* already exist. But they need to be construed as a coherent whole so they form a consistent assemblage. In the case of the state-building *dispositif*, in general, the urgent need that this *dispositif* must address lays very much on the notion of failed states, or the mere possibility of their emergence, and on the idea of these states becoming a threat to the international security. In other words, the mere possibility of the emergence of a failed state somewhere can spark the necessity of the deployment of a state-building *dispositif*. However, in order to this possibility to be sensed, the situation in question needs to be, firstly, at least visible and this was what started to happen in regard to Timor-Leste.

THE CONSTRUCTION OF TIMOR-LESTE AS AN INTERNATIONAL URGENT NEED

The invisibility of Timor-Leste within the international scenario only started to change almost two decades after the Indonesia invasion. A series of events made the Timorese situation *visible* in the international scene and built up the need for addressing it internationally. Some of these events include the Santa Cruz Massacre (1991), the Nobel Peace Prize awarded to José Ramos-Horta and Bishop D. Carlos Filipe Ximenes Belo (1996), the dinner of Nelson Mandela and Xanana Gusmão at the Presidential Palace in Jakarta (Indonesia), as well as the pre- and post-referendum violence. Each of these events is highly relevant per se. However, perceived collectively, they were certainly decisive to the construction of Timor-Leste as an *international* urgent need. With this new visibility of the Timorese situation, not only the intervention was perceived as inevitable but also the state-building *dispositif* was considered the fittest instrument to be deployed. This state-building *dispositif* would have to address, simultaneously, the triangular and self-reinforcing narrative of security, development, and peacemaking in the case of Timor-Leste.

The Santa Cruz Massacre

The Indonesian informative shield was to some extent cracked after the Pope's visit of Dili on October 12th 1989. It can be said that John Paul II somewhat put Timor-Leste on the international press map with his visit. The Timorese youth and the resistance sought to benefit from the fact that, for the first time, there were numerous international journalists in the country due to the coverage of the Pope's visit. They could organize their first public manifestation and the whole world would see it (Magalhães, 2007: 390). If this information shield was somewhat cracked with the Pope's visit, it was completely shattered after the Santa Cruz Massacre on November of 1991.

The Santa Cruz Massacre, where around 270 people died (Kingsbury, 2009: 62), was certainly not the worst and the bloodiest massacre conducted by the Indonesian military in Timor-Leste. Nevertheless, despite all brutal massacres carried out by the Indonesian military, only after November 1991 that the world had a small vision of the massacre of the Timorese (Dunn, 2003: 292). The Santa Cruz Massacre opened the eyes of the world to the situation in Timor-Leste. In October 1991, a Portuguese delegation, in concurrence with the Timorese resistance, was scheduled to visit Dili. This visit was cancelled by the Indonesian government which led to a protest on October 28th (Kingsbury, 2009: 61). One of the organizers of the protest, Sebastião Gomes Rangel (eighteen years old), was identified by the Indonesian government and killed at the Motael's Church. Several other protesters were detained and one more killed. In the following days, there were several incursions made by the Indonesian military in numerous houses in different parts of the country often beating the families (Magalhães, 2007: 401).

On November 12th, many people headed to the Santa Cruz cemetery in a procession honoring Sebastião Gomes. Two thousand people were gathered in the cemetery seeking to benefit from the presence of journalists to peacefully demonstrate against the Indonesian occupation and expose the Timorese desire for self-government (Magalhães, 2007: 401). Moreover, they thought that the presence of the UN Special Rapporteur on Torture in Dili would prevent the Indonesian government from employing the usual violence against them. Still, the military surrounded the cemetery, blocked the entrance and shot 2,000 unarmed and pacific protesters at the Santa Cruz cemetery. During the following days, those that were wounded and were in the hospital were murdered, and about eighty more protesters were also killed on November 15th and the following days (Kingsbury, 2009: 61; Magalhães, 2007: 401).

This massive killing was not left unheard, and the journalists played a key role in its dissemination. Many reports were certainly crucial to the wide diffusion of the tragedy; nevertheless, it were the images of the British journalist Max Stahl that woke the world up and gave a graphic picture of the cruel situation in Timor-Leste (Magalhães, 2007: 402–403). This film was sent out of Timor-Leste and hit the television broadcasts and "it leapt to prominence around the world, replayed over and over. This footage of the carnage at Santa Cruz became the signature image of East Timor for world's television audiences" (Kingsbury, 2009: 61). This was in sharp contradiction with the Indonesian discourse that Timor-Indonesia's relationship was smooth, everything was settled in the territory and that the Indonesian rule was welcome by the Timorese (Kingsbury, 2009: 61; Magalhães, 2007: 402–403).

The Santa Cruz Massacre definitely gave a new momentum for the global solidarity campaign for Timor-Leste. There were many protests all over the world, including Portugal and Australia (Kingsbury, 2009: 63; Magalhães, 2007: 403). Some states started to change their relationship with Indonesia. Damien Kingsbury (2009), for example, argues that Lisbon started to defend the Timorese cause in several international for a, including the UN (2009: 63). The situation was also discussed at the European Parliament since Portugal was a member of the European Economic Community (Magalhães, 2007: 405).

The Timorese issue also penetrated through the US Congress. José Ramos-Horta, for instance, was very active in galvanizing US members of Congress support for the Timorese cause. Nevertheless, the Congressional voice was not heard in the executive branch. The US executive, since President Jimmy Carter, and throughout the administrations of Presidents Ronald Reagan and George H. W. Bush, supplied the Indonesian government not only with diplomatic support but also with money and arms (Dunn, 2003: 314; Taylor, 1999: 214). Days after the Santa Cruz massacre, the situation changed following a Congressional declaration on Timor-Leste calling for the suspension of the US military training funds for the Indonesian government (Dunn, 2003: 314; Taylor, 1999: 214). However, the manifest change in the US policy toward Indonesia only occurred when President Bill Clinton took office. This was a clear influence of his vice-president Al Gore, who was active regarding this matter in the Senate (Dunn, 2003: 314; Taylor, 1999: 214). Australia was also timid about revising its relations with Indonesia. The farthest that Australia went was to pressure Indonesia to produce a credible investigation report. This report, despite its contradictions, was sufficient to maintain the United States, the Australian, and the Japanese support and their continuing cooperation with Indonesia (Magalhães, 2007: 404). However, other countries, such as the Netherlands, Canada, and Denmark, decided otherwise, suspending their support and assistance to Indonesia (Magalhães, 2007: 404).

Nevertheless, the most important fact was that, from November 1991 onward, Timor-Leste and the atrocities carried out there were not restricted to a few people anymore. The misery and the poverty, in which the Timorese population lived, along with the bloody brutality of the Indonesian, were not invisible anymore to the eyes of the rest of the world. Due to both the dissemination work done by the journalists through the printed media and the striking video that circulated over and over throughout international televisions, the closed argument and constructed discourse of the necessity of the Indonesian annexation became, to say the least, very much questionable. The massacre of Santa Cruz put firmly Timor-Leste and, most importantly, the Timorese despair on the international agenda. This undoubtedly represented a turning point in regard to Indonesia's occupation of Timor-Leste. It was a moment in which Timor-Leste and the situation of the Timorese population started to become not only as an international concern but also to emerge as an international urgent need that had to be addressed.

The Nobel Prize Award and the Dinner at the Presidential Palace

José Ramos-Horta, along with Xanana Gusmão, is one of the most well-known leaders of the Timorese resistance. Despite the fact that Timor-Leste would only become a UN member in 2002, its people and the resistance were already represented at the organization, mainly through the work of Ramos-Horta who often integrated Mozambique's or Vanuatu's missions. This work was pivotal to aggregate friends and allies sympathetic to the Timorese cause (Magalhães, 2007: 437). He also developed a campaign to have Timorese Bishop Ximenes Belo awarded with the Nobel Peace Prize in 1995, which was not successful. However, the following year, the Nobel Peace Prize was awarded to both Bishop Ximenes Belo and Ramos-Horta (Nobel Foundation, 1996).

The Nobel Peace Prize placed the Timorese struggle into a higher level in the international agenda. To some extent, the prize represented the international community's recognition of the importance of the Timorese struggle. Furthermore, the prize not only *recognized* the struggle but also, and most importantly, associated it with a notion that has, consciously or unconsciously, a heavy positive weight worldwide—peace. This symbolic sign brought consequences that went farther than the symbolism of the gesture, which was already very important in itself. It brought also very practical consequences. The Nobel Peace Prize was a ceremony that was broadcasted by the vast majority of the televisions of the world (although not in Indonesia). Therefore, the prize gave the Timorese cause a high and broad attention worldwide, which not only gave more visibility for the cause but also associated it, due to the very characteristic of the prize, with peace and the pursuit of it (Magalhães, 2007: 438–439).

The prize set the stage for the Timorese voice to be heard worldwide. In the prestigious and internationally visible stage which is the Nobel lecture, Ramos-Horta (1996) remembers that the violence of the Indonesian government is not restricted to the Timorese and was also directed also to the Indonesian people. Moreover, in his lecture, Ramos-Horta, side the Timorese with the oppressed people of the world (Horta, 1996). Most importantly, Ramos-Horta argues for the Timorese right of self-determination (Horta, 1996) and delineate his vision of a peace plan. As a result of the prize, many diplomatic doors, political and religious leaders, and personalities in general, which were once closed to the leadership of the Timorese resistance, were now wide open. Consequently, the prize not only brought more international attention to the Timorese cause, but also opened new perspectives in terms of struggle and new diplomatic paths (Magalhães, 2007: 438–439).

In addition to the Nobel Peace Prize awarded to Ramos-Horta and Ximenes Belo, it is necessary to mention another event that was also crucial to raise the Timorese cause globally and construe it as an international urgent need—the dinner of Nelson Mandela and Xanana Gusmão at the Indonesian Presidential Palace in Jakarta (Indonesia). In a state visit to Indonesia, the South-African President Nelson Mandela expressed his wish of meeting Xanana Gusmão, the leader of the Timorese resistance, who was in jail since November 20th 1992 (Kingsbury, 2009: 63). Unable to refuse a desire from President Mandela, one of the most prestigious political leaders of the world, President Suharto conceded Mandela's request. On July 15th 1997, Suharto gave permission to Xanana Gusmão to leave the Cipinang prison and visit Mandela at the guest house of the Presidential Palace in Jakarta (Magalhães, 2007: 441).

This dinner had both practical and symbolical consequences. After the dinner, Mandela expressed publicly that he was greatly impressed with Xanana Gusmão. He expressed his impression regarding the exceptional political and humane feature of the former, and that he would ask Suharto to release not only Xanana Gusmão but also other Timorese political prisoners (Magalhães, 2007: 442). In practical terms, the gesture of the dinner completely changed the status of Xanana Gusmão in Indonesia. Until then, he was treated by Indonesian authorities and the press as a common prisoner. Dining at the Presidential Palace left this attitude simply unsustainable from that moment onward. On the symbolical side, but not having any less practical consequences, through the simple act of dining with Xanana Gusmão, Mandela was giving him an enormous international prestige. More than that, being himself in a similar position—of a prisoner leading a resistance struggle—in the recent past, before becoming the president of South Africa, Mandela was clearly indicating not only the prominence of Xanana Gusmão, but also the he could in fact become the president of an independent Timor-Leste. Indeed, symbolically, the dinner with Mandela framed Xanana Gusmão as the Timorese Mandela (Magalhães, 2007: 440–441).

The Road to the Timorese Referendum

Around the year 1996, the situation in regard to Indonesia started to change. The financial community, who had, to some extent, supported President's Suharto economic miracle during almost thirty years, stopped supporting the Indonesian military government (Magalhães, 2007: 445–450). By the year 1997, a serious economic and financial crisis affected Southeast Asia in general, but this crisis was much more severe in Indonesia in particular (Magalhães, 2007: 450). From August 1997 onward, the Indonesian economy was beginning to collapse, with the rupiah, the Indonesian currency, going through a fast devaluation process. By the beginning of 1998 the rupiah had experienced a free fall, which led to some important events, such as: (1) the disappearance of Indonesian middle class savings, (2) the inflation of prices of basic food products, and (3) the vanishing, in a few months, of the economic gains seen under the Suharto's period (Kingsbury, 2009: 65). The economic performance was the major pillar of support of the Indonesian military regime. Therefore, when this pillar disintegrated, significant parts of Indonesian society started withdrawing their support to the military regime— students, business leaders, and also part of the military itself (Kingsbury, 2009: 66). The economic-financial crisis was so severe that President Suharto resigned on May 21st 1998. This paved a solid path not only to Indonesia's democratization, but also opened a large window of opportunity to a serious reconsideration of the Timorese issue (Magalhães, 2007: 451; Martin and Mayer-Rieckh, 2005: 126).

Bacharuddin Jusuf Habibie, Indonesia's vice president, succeeded Suharto. He started to consider the fact of Timor-Leste having a special autonomous status within Indonesia. Therefore, he started the discussions on the issue with Portugal, who was still the legal and recognized authority of Timor-Leste, with the mediation of the UN.[6] At the end of January 1999, on the eve of a high-level negotiation round between the Portuguese and Indonesian officials at the UN, Junus Yosfiah, the Indonesian minister of information, announced President Habibie's decision to start a consultation process asking the Timorese people whether they preferred a large and special autonomy within Indonesia or its independence (Magalhães, 2007: 462).

In practical terms, a Timorese referendum on its political future was clearly on the table. This meant that what was decided, in fact, was that if the Timorese population, after a process of popular consultation, rejected the autonomy proposal, Indonesia would grant Timor-Leste its independence. This consultation process should be a direct and universal vote, under the auspices of the UN, and without the presence of a peacekeeping mission (Teles, 1999a: 389). Indonesia, Portugal, and the UN agreed, on March 11th 1999 that the organization would be responsible for organizing and supervising the referendum, which should take place that year, probably July or August,[7] and it would include the Timorese population within the territory as well as the diasporas (Teles, 1999a: 390). Obviously, this decision was received with deep reluctance by the Indonesian Army (TNI), especially its commander-in-chief, General Wiranto (Kingsbury, 2009: 68) and also by most of the Timorese leaders, including Xanana Gusmão (Kingsbury, 2009: 68).

According to Patrícia Teles (1999a: 390), this window of opportunity led to different actions from the different actors involved. Envisioning the prospect of an independent Timor-Leste, a possible transition period was beginning to be planned by Portugal and the UN. On the one hand, the Portuguese created a workgroup constituted by different ministries to elaborate a transition plan for both scenarios—autonomy and independence. The UN, on the other hand, created a contact group formed by the United States, Japan, Australia, New Zealand, the United Kingdom, and Canada to supervise the mediation role performed by the organization. The European Union and Portugal offered to be responsible for the financing of the organization of the popular consultation and even for a possible transition period to independence (Teles, 1999a: 390).

On May 5th 1999, Portugal and Indonesia, under the auspices of the UN, signed in New York three agreements on the issue of Timor-Leste. In the first agreement, it was established that the UN would be responsible for the organization of a mission to carry out and supervise the popular consultation—which would be based on a direct, secret, and universal ballot—on the Indonesian autonomy proposal. The second agreement dealt with the modality of the consultation. It covered aspects such as: (1) the date of the consultation, (2) the questions to be put to the Timorese, (3) the entitlement to vote, (4) the schedule of the consultation process, and (5) the funding, security[8] and operational phases of the consultation (Portugal and Indonesia, 1999b). The third agreement was centered on the issue of security and stated that Indonesia was the main responsible for this matter. Moreover, Indonesia would be responsible for the general maintenance of law and order, as well as for the security of UN personnel (Portugal and Indonesia, 1999c).

Most importantly, the agreements were underpinned by an understanding, which was shared by the parts involved, the UN Secretary-General (S/1999/ 862) and the Security Council (S/RES/1262), that the whole referendum process was composed essentially by three phases (Teles, 1999a: 417). After phase I, which was the consultation process itself, there would be an interim phase (phase II) which comprised the period after the popular consultation and the implementation of the results (S/1999/862). Later, phase III would be the actual implementation of the results of the referendum. In case of acceptance, by the Timorese, of the autonomy proposal, on the one hand, Indonesia had to start the constitutional arrangement in order to accommodate this new legal framework; on the other hand, Portugal had to initiate the process of properly removing Timor-Leste from the UN list of non-self-governing territories and the removal of the issue of Timor-Leste from both General Assembly and SC agendas (Portugal and Indonesia, 1999a; Article 5). However, if, on the contrary, the Timorese people rejected the autonomy proposal, Indonesia had to initiate the proper legal measures in order to restore the status that Timor-Leste had under the Indonesian law prior to July 17th 1976, and both Indonesia and Portugal would transfer the authority in Timor-Leste to the UN. The UN, by its turn, would have to initiate the process of enabling

Timor-Leste to begin the process of independence (Portugal and Indonesia, 1999a; Article 6).

From the UN side, on May 7th under resolution 1236 (S/RES/1236), the Security Council welcomed the May 5th Agreements, and on June 11th 1999, under resolution 1246 (S/RES/1246), the SC established, until August 31st 1999,[9] the United Nations Mission in East Timor (UNAMET). The main objective of UNAMET was to organize and conduct the Timorese consultation in regard to the constitutional framework proposed by Indonesia (S/RES/1246) advanced by Indonesia.

The Pre-Balloting Violence

The decision of letting the Indonesian responsible for the security of all the territory was seen as something risky and extremely dangerous, since the very beginning of the negotiation process (Magalhães, 2007: 466). This was a concern shared by both the Timorese leadership and the UN. Nevertheless, at that time, it was understood also that this narrow window of opportunity of having a referendum should be seized; even if this meant leaving the Indonesians in charge of the security of the balloting process (Magalhães, 2007: 466). However, the option of having Indonesia responsible for the provision of a secure environment was negligent, to say the least, for anyone with an attentive perception of the developments on the ground even before the May 5th agreements. Indeed, this decision would in fact prove to be catastrophic.

Since a massacre that took place on November 16th 1998 in Alas, where nearly fifty Timorese were killed, it was clear that the Indonesian army were creating and sponsoring, once more, militias in order to maintain the control and terrorize the Timorese population without clear military involvement (Magalhães, 2007: 468). In January 1999, President Habibie's decision of letting the Timorese be independent in case of rejection of the autonomy proposal, which collided with General Wiranto's view of Indonesia's future, set the stage for a looser establishment, and use, of the TNI-associated militias in Timor-Leste (Kingsbury, 2009: 68). The militias would do the repressive and violent work that the military did not want to do directly (Magalhães, 2007: 468). The militias were constituted mainly by elements from the police, the military, pro-integration people and also by pro-independence people that, through death threats, were forced to integrate the armed groups (Magalhães, 2007: 474).

The violence led by the TNI-associated militias was gaining momentum. From January to April, many pro-independence activists and supporters were killed, tortured and had their homes ransacked and destroyed (Martin, 2001: 25). In late-January 1999, another massacre, this time led by the Mahidi militia, in Ainaro, resulted in around thirty dead people (Magalhães, 2007: 468). Nevertheless, the Liquiçá massacre would become the most emblematic example of the militia's violence and the Indonesian military acquiescence. On April 6th 1999, militia BMP, supported by the TNI and assisted by the police, surrounded a church in the city of Liquiçá where pro-independence activists were sheltered following the burning of their houses in the previous days (Kingsbury, 2009: 69). Around noon, the police launched tear gas inside the church forcing those in the interior to come out (Kingsbury, 2009: 69). When the people were coming outside, the militiamen, supported by the TNI, entered the church and its surroundings, shooting people and attacking them with machetes (Kingsbury, 2009: 69). Although the official number of casualties was sixty-one, it is widely believed that around two hundred were killed in this massacre (Kingsbury, 2009: 69). This was in fact the worst massacre since Santa Cruz in 1991 (Martin, 2001: 25). In the next day, sixteen more people were killed in Ermera and fifteen others in Maliana on April 14th (Magalhães, 2007: 470). On April 17th at a large gathering of pro-integration militia and supporters, Eurico Guterres, who was the commander of the militia Aitarak, in Dili, spoke along with João Tavares, head of the militia Halilintar, in Bobonaro, Guterres literally urging "all pro-integration militias to conduct a cleansing of all those who betrayed integration (…) [c]apture and kill if you need" (Quoted in Martin, 2001: 25). After this, the BMP and Aitarak militias attacked several pro-independence homes (Martin, 2001: 25). The situation in Timor-Leste was bloodily violent.

TIMOR-LESTE AS AN INTERNATIONAL URGENT NEED

Oddly enough, it was within this environment that the security dimension was accorded to lay under Indonesia's responsibility on May 5th. The violent events continued even after the signing of the agreement. Nevertheless, despite all the obvious concerns regarding security, the main Timorese leadership, along with the Portuguese, thought that they had to explore the opportunity of independence. It was perceived by them that they might not have a second opportunity. In addition, it was also understood that the occupation had been bloody brutal for more than twenty-three years and this would certainly not change at that moment. Since there was no safe environment to perform the pro-independence campaign, the UN Secretary General sent its Director for Asia, to consult Xanana Gusmão on whether canceling or not the consultation. Xanana Gusmão demonstrated no big concerns since he was confident that the Timorese would choose for independence. For him, as long as the registration proceeded,[10] the pro-independence supporters would win[11] (Magalhães, 2007: 470–473). Despite all the intimidation, threats and violence perpetrated by the Indonesian militias, the registration encompassed 98 percent of the possible voters (Magalhães, 2007: 473). This represented just over 450 thousand Timorese inside and outside the territory[12] (Kingsbury, 2009: 70).

As already mentioned, the organization of the vote by UNAMET proceeded within an environment of embedded violence, destruction and intimidation. This, along with some operational problems, delayed the actual vote to August 30th (Kingsbury, 2009: 72). The wave of terror and threats was clearly increasing with the proximity of the referendum (Kingsbury, 2009: 72). On August 26th many militiamen gathered in Dili organizing widespread violence, killing at least eight people (Magalhães, 2007: 477). In addition, there was also the real threat of a civil war in case the pro-autonomy proposal failed (Magalhães, 2007: 477). This threat was somewhat worldwide known, since Timor-Leste and the atrocities carried out there were not invisible anymore and this concern of a civil war was circulating even on the pages of important international newspapers such as the *Washington Post* and the *International Herald Tribune* (Magalhães, 2007: 477). In addition, there were also warnings coming from high-level officials on the ground. The Military Commander of Timor-Leste, Coronel Noer Muis, for instance, warned even about a bloodbath in the case of victory of the pro-independence movement (Magalhães, 2007: 477).

In fact, clear signs of open violence were coming from militias' head. Eurico Guterres, head of Aitarak, for instance, was quite clear about transforming Timor-Leste in a sea of fire in the case of pro-independence victory and whether the independence actually came to reality (Kingsbury, 2009: 72; Magalhães, 2007: 477). By that time, it was already known the actions of the militias few days prior to the ballot. The militia was consistently rioting, destroying, killing, torturing, and burning houses in order to intimidate the Timorese, which also represented a clear escalation of the violence (Magalhães, 2007: 478). The issue was even a matter of discussion in the Security Council days before the ballot (S/PV.4038). This led to nearly sixty thousand Timorese to abandon their houses and take refuge in the mountains just a couple of days before the ballot in order to avoid such wave of violence (Magalhães, 2007: 478).

Considering the amount of violence perpetrated throughout all the years of occupation and the crescent spiral manifested in the prior days to the voting, the actual day of the vote was relatively calm (Kingsbury, 2009: 72; Magalhães, 2007: 478). There were some cases of outbreaks of violence, but since early in the morning there were long lines at the ballot stations of Timorese waiting to vote for their destinies (Kingsbury, 2009: 72; Magalhães, 2007: 478). Many of them had walked long distances through the night to have their voices heard and many others were wearing their best clothes in a clear sign of the importance of the occasion (Kingsbury, 2009:72–73; Magalhães, 2007: 478–479). Around nine o'clock in the morning, almost 50 percent of the registered voters had already voted (Teles,

1999a: 406). Despite all the intimidation and violence campaign perpetrated by the pro-autonomy militias, with a tacit consent of the TNI, the consultation process had an outstanding voter turnout of 98.6 percent (Martin, 2001: 160). The result was crystal-clear. In an unquestionable indication of the Timorese desire for independence from Indonesia, 78.5 percent rejected the autonomy proposal while 21.5 percent supported it (S/1999/944).

Following the day of the vote, the security situation deteriorated once more and after the announcement of the results the situation became extremely violent. The pro-autonomy militias and the Indonesian military, supported by the non-action of the police, started a large-scale destruction campaign. Indeed, it was a scorched earth campaign with the clear consent of the TNI. Despite all denials of supporting the militias, General Wiranto said that the military would not stop the militias (Kingsbury, 2009: 73). They wanted to spoil the bases of any possibility of a viable independent Timorese state. According to Teles (1999a: 411), the first half of September was stage of a systematic policy of disappearances, rapes, murders, looting, forced dislocations, deportations, and all sorts of destruction of infrastructures and houses. In a short period of time, an estimate of two thousand Timorese were killed, around 230,000 were forced to flee to West Timor, and other several hundred thousand were internally displaced (Beauvais, 2001: 1103). Moreover, more than 70 percent of the territory's infrastructure was completely destroyed (Kingsbury, 2009: 73). Even the UN staff was evacuated by the Australian Defense Force to Darwin under what became known as the Operation Spitfire (White, 2008: 82).

Certainly, this widespread violence was not a result of random events. They were coherently targeting specific places and people. This understanding of a systematic and deliberated planning of the killings was also substantiated by a report developed by the UN High Commissioner for Human Rights Mary Robinson, where she informed that what took place in Timor-Leste was a series of systematic killings and destruction of property. This was carried out by the militia groups and also by the security forces (E/CN.4/S-4/CRP.1: paragraph 50). Moreover, she stated that there were indications that the forcible displacements were previously planned (E/CN.4/S-4/CRP.1: paragraph 29). Robinson ends the report concluding that there was an unequivocal evidence that the what happened in Timor-Leste was a serious and systematic violation of human rights (E/CN.4/S-4/CRP.1: paragraph 47).

Pairing these allegations, Patrícia Teles (1999a: 412) also argues that this post-referendum violence was carefully orchestrated by the Indonesian authorities. This understanding was also shared by the Security Council. In fact, on the ground, a mission of the Security Council deployed to Jakarta and Dili to investigate the tragedy, concluded that there was a strong evidence of violations of the international humanitarian law (S/1999/976: paragraph 21). Moreover, it evinced the impunity within which all the violence was carried out by the pro-autonomy militias (S/1999/976: paragraph 14). For the mission, all this violence simply could not have occurred without the involvement of high-level officials of both Indonesian military and police (S/1999/976: paragraph 19). Indeed, for the SC mission it was clear that a large part of the Indonesian military and police was involved, either organizing (S/1999/976: paragraph 19). In regard to the degree of destruction of Timor-Leste, a UNAMET report is bluntly clear when states that there were plenty of evidence of a scorched earth policy directed by the Indonesian military (S/1999/976: paragraph 1 and annex).

Timor-Leste as a Threat to Peace and Security

This massive violence led to a huge international outrage. Consequently, this led to a series of protests and a wide solidarity campaign worldwide. It should be noticed, for instance, the protests vocalized by the Australian and Portuguese governments and population (Kingsbury, 2009: 74). It was clear by that time that the most effective means of a rapid response would be a UN-sanctioned multilateral intervention (Martin and Mayer-Rieckh, 2005: 131). Nevertheless, no country was willing to intervene without Indonesia's authorization or Security Council's approval. The latter would depend on the consent of both China and Russia, who would only approve such kind of intervention after Indonesia's consent. Therefore, gaining Indonesia's consent was a key element in this intervention process. Indeed, Indonesia was subject to a crescendo amount of diplomatic pressures from different sides, which was led mainly by UN Secretary-General Kofi Annan and Australia's Prime Minister John Howard (Martin and Mayer-Rieckh, 2005: 131).

The bloody wave of violence perturbed also the United States of America who joined the diplomatic pressure on Indonesia to accept an international peacekeeping force on Timor-Leste. The pressure came through several channels, essentially: (1) military pressure by the commander-in-chief of the US forces in the Pacific, Admiral Dennis Blair, who said to General Wiranto, on September 8th in Jakarta, that the military ties between both countries could be suspended; (2) private pressure inside the IMF with US officials saying that the Fund could deny financial assistance to the country, which at that time was critical for Indonesia's recovery from the financial crisis; and (3) through US officials (Kingsbury, 2009: 74). Chief among them was President Bill Clinton who publicly said that Indonesia should accept the international community assisting the restoring of the security in Timor-Leste. (Quoted in Kingsbury, 2009: 74). The pressure came also from regional actors. On a meeting of the Asia-Pacific Economic Cooperation (APEC), scheduled to take place in New Zealand on September 9th, Canada pressured successfully the organization to hold a Special Ministerial Meeting with Timor-Leste on the agenda. Usually, the organization kept its meetings strictly attached to economic matters. Therefore, Indonesia expected that its regional allies would be absent of this meeting. However, nearly all participants attended the meeting showing a great regional concern over the Timorese situation (Martin and Mayer-Rieckh, 2005: 131–132).

With this amount of pressure, Indonesia ended up accepting an international peacekeeping intervention on September 12th 1999. On September 15th, in the SC, the situation of Timor-Leste was acknowledged as a threat to international peace and security, and it was decided that a course of action should follow this conclusion. Under resolution 1264 (S/RES/1264), affirming that the Timorese situation constituted a threat to peace and security (S/RES/1264), the SC authorized the creation of a multinational force to intervene in Timor-Leste—the International Force in East Timor[13] (INTERFET). Acting under chapter VII of the UN Charter, the force was created to restore peace and security in Timor-Leste. The INTERFET, which was led by the Australian Major General Peter Cosgrove, was authorized to use all the means necessary to carry out its duties, which is the diplomatic language for permission for the use of force.

In regard to the deployment of INTERFET, an important point should be mentioned before advancing any further. The deployment of INTEFET represents a turning point in regard to the status of Timor-Leste within the international agenda; not so much because of the operation per se, but due to what it represented. It is true that Timor-Leste is somewhat part of the UN agenda since December 1960 when the territory entered the UN list of non-self-governing territories (A/RES/1542). Furthermore, it is also true that the situation in Timor-Leste was highly grave, to say the least. Nevertheless, it is also true that Timor-Leste was not understood, for a long time, as an *international* emergency, as painful as it is for the Timorese living under an unspeakable situation. As a consequence of the visibility that Timor-Leste already had and the long history of bloody violence, at that moment, an armed intervention in Timor-Leste could not be avoided anymore. At that point, Timor-Leste *had* to be intervened.

Nevertheless, the intervention could be done without changing the status that Timor-Leste had in the international scene. This was certainly not the case of Timor-Leste. The framework under which Timor-Leste was intervened at that point is that what is instructive here. The very fact that the UN, through the good offices of its SG, was overseeing the negotiations between Indonesia and Portugal and the fact that the UN deployed, passing inevitably by the SC, a mission to organize and oversee the referendum indicates that Timor-Leste was already in a way part of the international concern. However, one should not forget that INTERFET was deployed under chapter VII of UN Charter. The chapter is undoubtedly clear regarding its function within the international scenario; it addresses any threat to *international* peace and security. Indeed, its first paragraph is crystal-clear in this regard when says that this is the chapter that guides the actions directed "to maintain or restore international peace and security" (UN, 1945: chapter VII, paragraph 39). Evoking chapter VII while deploying INTERFET, the UN is not only symbolically, but in fact legally, framing the situation in Timor-Leste as a threat to international peace and security. Therefore, the deployment of INTERFET under chapter VII of the UN Charter represents precisely the peak of the process of the emergence of Timor-Leste as an international urgent need. Indeed, this is the point where Timor-Leste became more than just an international concern but in fact became crystallized as an urgent need in the international scene.

On the ground, despite several occasions when a large-scale conflict between INTERFET and TNI could erupt (Kingsbury, 2009: 74), the Australian-led multinational force efficiently controlled the violence in a matter of weeks. Due to this fact, the mission was often praised as a successful peace enforcement operation (Beauvais, 2001: 1103, footnote 10). On the INTERFET's arrival, the situation in Timor-Leste was of vast destruction. There were not only hundreds of thousands of people displaced, either in the mountains or across borders but also most of the buildings and houses were burned by the TNI and the militias (Kingsbury, 2009: 75). In the first periodic report of the INTERFET, of September 29th (S/1999/1025), it was reported that the security situation improved in Dili, although it remained critical in Timor-Leste in general, and there was no effective civil administration in place (S/1999/1025: paragraphs 11 and 22). Lastly, the report stressed the importance of the agreement on the transition to the phase III of the May 5th Agreements, and its implementation.

According to Teles (1999a: 419), in the field, it was sensed a vacuum of both power and authority. Therefore, the UN had to strength phase II and to expedite phase III of the May 5th Agreement. According to phase II, in case of rejection of the proposal, Indonesia would still be responsible, during an interim period, for the maintenance of peace and security in Timor-Leste. However, it was clear that this was not the case anymore. Therefore, bearing in mind that the situation in Timor was critical, the Secretary-General, on a report to the SC (S/1999/1024), proposed a series of measures, such as the redeployment of UNAMET; the deployment of 460 civilian police officers; the dispatch of legal experts to provide legal advices and evaluate the legal and judicial systems; and the deployment of civil affairs officers and experts in local administration to make the preparations for setting up an administration in Timorese territory.

In order to address phase III of the agreement, the UN addressed the process of enabling Timor-Leste in the pursuit of its independence. This was sought in a context where Timor-Leste was already framed as an international urgent need and the harsh reality on the ground, which was palpable not only in regard to the widespread destruction of Timorese infrastructure but especially in regard to lives of the Timorese, was highly visible. In addition, one should not forget that this whole process developed within an international scenario where the notion of failed state, or the threat of it, has a considerable weight. An international scenario where the issues are extensively framed departing from the notion of failed state, the Timorese situation of vast destruction, misery, lack of institutional support to deal with the crisis, along with the vacuum of power and authority that was visualized by the UN, becomes an international urgent need, under mainstream rationale, not only in humanitarian terms, but also in security terms.

Therefore, the crystallization of Timor-Leste as an international urgent need was followed by the emergence of a correspondent *dispositif*. This *dispositif* should address the situation, which means to shape this urgent need properly. This *dispositif* should put an end to a long and brutal history of invasions, dominations, and violence in Timor-Leste. Consequently, and most importantly, to shape the urgent need properly, this *dispositif* would have to address, simultaneously, the triangular narrative of: (1) security; by seeking to overcome Timorese fragility by pursuing the institutional strengthening and (re)construction of its state and therefore attempting to avoid the transformation of Timor-Leste into a failed state within the international scenario; (2) development; by seeking to exercise a profound influence and supervision over several life-supporting processes of the Timorese population; and (3) peace, by pursuing a negative and positive peace and by underpinning the whole activity carried out by this *dispositif* with the normative framework shaped by the liberal peace argument. It is against this background that state-building emerges as the fittest instrument to address the situation in Timor-Leste.

Therefore, in this context, still considering the situation in Timor-Leste a threat to peace and security, the UN created on October 25th 1999, under resolution 1272 (S/RES/1272), the United Nations Transitional Administration in East Timor (UNTAET). The mission would have something unprecedented—it would be empowered with the executive, legislative and judicial powers over Timor-Leste (S/RES/1272). The mission would be responsible for several activities such as: (1) to provide security and maintain the law; (2) to establish an effective administration; (3) to assist in the development of civil and social services; (4) to ensure the coordination and delivery of humanitarian assistance, rehabilitation and development assistance; (5) to support capacity-building for self-government; and (6) to assist in the establishment of conditions for sustainable development (S/RES/1272).

Therefore, all the power was with the UN and they would act to transform almost every part of Timor-Leste and Timorese life. Indeed, the general feeling was that not only it was urgent to act on Timor-Leste, but also, under the shared understanding that Timor-Leste represented a "true meaning of emptiness," it was understood that the UN had to literally "invent" Timor-

Leste (Traub, 2000: 74). Indeed, according to Richmond (2011), the situation provided the environment for a standard liberal state-building process (2011: 84). This state-building process, as many others in different parts of the globe, was directed toward the implementation of a neoliberal state in a remote and one of the poorest countries of the globe (Richmond, 2011: 84). After all, at that time, Timor-Leste was already crystallized as an international urgent need, and nothing more rational and natural, to the mainstream understanding, than the emergence of the state-building *dispositif* and its deployment to Timor-Leste. Most importantly, nothing more natural than, through this state-building *dispositif*, transforming the overall disorderly situation of the country and normalize it by seeking to make Timor-Leste behave more like a normal state of the international scenario, to make it resemble more like liberal democracies. After all, under the rationale of those working within the state-building *dispositif*, this is *the* path to form a state and to achieve peace and prosperity.

CONCLUSION

This chapter process traces the path in which Timor-Leste became an urgent need within the international scenario. This is an essential element to the emergence of a *dispositif*. In the case of Timor-Leste, the country experienced a long history of violence and despair. This was a consequence of the fact of being a former colony of Portugal, invaded by Japan during the Word War II, and invaded and annexed by Indonesia on December 1975. Nevertheless, this whole process was simply invisible to the rest of the world. This situation began to change and Timor-Leste started to emerge as an international urgent need due to series of events, such as the highly broadcasted Santa Cruz massacre, the Nobel Prize awarded to José Ramos-Horta and the Bishop D. Carlos Filipe Ximenes Belo, the dinner of Nelson Mandela and Xanana Gusmão at the Presidential Palace in Jakarta, and the pre- and post-referendum violence. These events not only put Timor-Leste on the map of the international media but were also part of the process of construing the country as an international urgent need. This process reached its peak with the referendum of 1999 and deployment of INTERFET, after the Liquiçá Massacre, under chapter VII of the UN Charter. The deployment of INTERFET both symbolically and legally crystallized the situation in Timor-Leste as a threat to international peace and security, as an international urgent need that should be addressed. As a result, a *dispositif* emerged in order to address this urgent need properly. Addressing the urgent need that Timor-Leste became meant that the *dispositif* should address essentially three aspects simultaneously—security, development, and peace. It is at this point where the state-building *dispositif*, underpinned by the liberal peace normative framework, emerges as the fittest instrument to the task of addressing the situation in Timor-Leste properly and normalizing the country.

NOTES

1. For a comprehensive approach of Timor-Leste's history see for instance (Carey and Bentley, 1995; Dunn, 2003; Kingsbury, 2009: Chapter 2; Magalhães, 2007; Molnar, 2010; Taylor, 1999). For an account of Timor-Leste in the history of Portugal see, for instance (Oliveira, 2004).

2. This is a plan that was designed by an Indonesian think-tank named Center for Strategic and International Studies based in Jakarta aiming at the annexation of Timor-Leste largely through subversive actions (Dunn, 2003: 73; Kingsbury, 2009: 48).

3. From 1,500 to 2,000 lives were lost in this civil war (Dunn, 2003: 278). For more see, for instance (Dunn, 2003: chapter 8).

4. Francisco Xavier do Amaral was sworn in as the country's first President; Nicolo Lobato was appointed Prime Minister; Mari Alkatiri as Minister of State for Political Affairs; and José Ramos-Horta the Minister for Foreign Affairs and External Information (Kingsbury, 2009: 49).

5. For a comprehensive and deep account of this period, see for instance (Dunn, 2003: chapter 11; Gama, 1995; Kingsbury, 2009: chapter 3; Magalhães, 2007: volume 2). For an account from one of the resistance movement leader's perspective see for instance (Niner, 2000).

6. For a deeper insight of the tripartite negotiation period see, for instance, (Teles, 1999b). For a personal account of one of the main negotiators, former Secretary-General Personal Representative Ambassador Jamsheed Marker, see (Marker, 2003).

7. The referendum was initially agreed to be held on August 8, but actually took place on August 30.

8. Although Indonesia would be responsible for the whole security dimension of the consultation process, a number of UN security personnel along with a number of international civilian police would be deployed to Timor-Leste.

9. The mission would be later extended firstly, under resolution 1257 (S/RES/1257) until September 30, 1999, and then, under resolution 1262 (S/RES/1262), until November 30, 1999. For more on the financing of the mission see, for instance (A/54/380).

10. The registration, which was supposed to begin on June 22, in fact began on July 16 despite the serious security situation. The registration process should last until August 4 but it was extended until August 6 (Teles, 1999a: 401).

11. One the one hand, the pro-autonomy side was namely composed by the *Front Bersama Pro-Otonomi Timor Timur* (United Front for East Timor Autonomy—UNIF), which was constituted by the pro-autonomy parties—the *Barisan Rakyat Timor Timur* (Forces of the East Timorese People—BRTT) and the *Front Persatuan Demokrasi dan Keadilan* (Forum for Unity, Democracy and Justice—FPDK)—and the militia umbrella organization PPI. On the other hand, all the pro-independence supporters were under the *Conselho Nacional da Resistência Timorense* (National Council of Timorese Resistance—CNRT) (Teles, 1999a: 404–405). For a deeper account of both pro-autonomy and pro-independence sides and their evolution, see for instance (CTF, 2008: 48–53).

12. This number is the sum of the 437,200 Timorese in Timor-Leste and the 13,090 abroad (Teles, 1999a: 403).

13. For a more comprehensive account on the INTERFET, see for instance (Breen, 2001; White, 2008).

Chapter Three

The UN Engagement with Timor-Leste and Its Shortcomings

Although in a very limited manner, Timor-Leste was somehow under the United Nation's (UN) radar for quite some time. One should remember, for instance, that: in late 1960s the General Assembly (GA) positioned Timor-Leste in its non-self-governing territories list; in mid-1970s the UN immediately repudiated the Indonesian invasion of the territory and never recognized the Indonesian claim over the country; and since early 1980's, at the request of the General Assembly (GA), successive Secretaries-Generals (SG) resorted to their good offices with Portugal and Indonesia holding regular talks with them and Timorese representatives, aiming at resolving the status of Timor-Leste. Nevertheless, the UN never had an actual presence in Timorese territory. The UN started to have a deeper relationship with Timor-Leste in 1999 when the Timorese tragedy became internationally visible and, most importantly, Timor-Leste emerged as an urgent need in the international scenario. This fact triggered the deployment of a vast state-building *dispositif* toward the country. Since 1999, the United Nations deployed five different peace operations to Timor-Leste: UNAMET (1999), UNTAET (1999–2002), UNMISET (2002–2005), UNOTIL (2005–2006) and UNMIT (2006–2012). Timor-Leste stands out for having in its territory five consecutive UN peace operations. There is no other case in the UN with so many missions with different levels of engagement and depth of involvement. Collectively, the manner in which the UN sought to deal with Timor-Leste as an international urgent need constitute in an overall project aimed at overcoming years of civil war and foreign oppression through the implementation of a liberal democratic state in Timor-Leste (Richmond and Franks, 2009: 83).

This chapter discusses the UN engagement with Timor-Leste and its shortcomings. This, of course, does not intend to be an exhaustive account of each one of the missions deployed to the country. On the contrary, the intention is to present them so they can be understood not individually but collectively, which is more instructive to understand the UN engagement with Timor-Leste. This chapter is structured around five sections. The first section deals with the delineation of UN peace operations deployed to Timor-Leste bringing attention to the main elements and characteristics of each one of them. The second section evinces the linearity of the mindset underpinning the UN conflict-transformation rationale which was behind the overall UN engagement with Timor-Leste, while the third one focuses on the reactive, rather than preventive, nature of this engagement. The fourth section sheds light on some structural shortcomings of the whole UN state-building process directed at Timor-Leste. Finally, the fifth section discusses the 2006 crisis and also evinces several pivotal strands which were fundamental regarding the Timorese reality but were clearly neglected by the UN state-building effort in the country and which are underneath the 2006 crisis.

THE UN'S PEACE OPERATIONS IN
TIMOR-LESTE: AN OVERVIEW

The relationship between the UN and Timor-Leste only become denser when the country emerged as an international urgent need. The UN, after a tripartite negotiation with Portugal and Indonesia, was entrusted to organize and conduct a referendum in Timor-Leste regarding their political future. On June 11th 1999, under the Security Council (SC) resolution 1246 (S/RES/1246) the SC established the United Nations Mission in East Timor (UNAMET). The mission was initially mandated to be on the field until August 31st 1999. However, due to an environment of widespread violence and intimidation on the ground and to technical issues acknowledged by the SG himself (S/1999/830), the mission's end date was extended twice: firstly, under resolution 1257 (S/RES/1257), extending the end date to September 30th, 1999; and secondly, under resolution 1262 (S/RES/1262), until November 30th 1999.

The mission's mandate was "to organize and conduct a popular consultation" (S/RES/1246: 2), which was initially scheduled to happen on August 8th, 1999, regarding the Indonesian autonomy proposal, which should be based on secret and universal ballot (S/RES/1246: 2). In order to fulfill this mandate the mission had essentially three components: (1) a political one, which would be responsible for overseeing the political environment of the balloting process, in regard to fairness and the freedom of all the parties involved on the process to carry out their activities; (2) an electoral one, which would be responsible for everything related to the balloting process, namely the registration and the actual voting; and (3) an informational one, which would be responsible for explaining on the ground the terms of the Indonesian proposal, and the consequences of each choice, and for providing information regarding the procedures of the voting (S/RES/1246).

On August 30th, 1999, the voting day, around 98 percent of the registered voters casted their vote and the vast majority of the Timorese (78.5 percent) voted against the autonomy proposal (S/1999/944; Martin, 2001: 160). This was a clear indication of the Timorese will for independence. Following the clear rejection of the autonomy proposal, the security situation deteriorated drastically and a massive violence, perpetrated by the TNI-sponsored militia, was experienced throughout the country (Teles, 1999a: 411). Due to the widespread violence, the Indonesian government suffered a huge international pressure and agreed with an international intervention force to deal with the situation. Hence, on September 15, the SC, under resolution 1264 (S/RES/1264), authorized the deployment of an Australian-led multinational force—International Force in East Timor (INTERFET)—to Timor-Leste in order to handle the security situation. Notwithstanding the vast destruction found when arriving in Timor-Leste, not only in terms of infrastructures, but also in terms of people displaced, the actual direct violence in the country was successfully contained and controlled in a short period of time (Beauvais, 2001: 1103, footnote 10).

It was only on October 19th 1999 that the Indonesian government formally recognized the Timorese rejection of its autonomy proposal. Only after this formal recognition of the referendum, the UN could begin the procedures to assist the Timorese on their road toward independence. Therefore, on the October 25th 1999, the SC, under resolution 1272 (S/RES/1272) chapter VII of the UN Charter, established the United Nations Transitional Administration in East Timor (UNTAET) initially until January 31st 2001. Later on, the mission would also be responsible for assisting the Timorese on two major elections: (1) on August 30th 2001, for the Constituent Assembly, which would be responsible for writing the Timorese Constitution and saw Fretilin (*Frente Revolucionária de Timor-Leste Independente*) winning 57.4 percent of the votes (UN, 2001); and (2) on April 14th 2002, the presidential election (which was won by Xanana Gusmão[1]) (UN, 2002b). Due to delays in the timetable of the elections, the mission was extended twice: (1) on January 31st 2001, under resolution 1338 (S/RES/1338), until January 31st 2002; and (2), January 31st 2002 under resolution 1392 (S/RES/1392), until May 20th 2002.

The mission was essentially responsible for paving the Timorese road to independence, and it was endowed with all the legislative, executive, and judicial authority on the country (S/RES/1272). Therefore, the UN, in a unprecedented manner,[2] actually assumed the sovereignty of the territory (Richmond and Franks, 2009: 87; Suhrke, 2001: 1). Furthermore, the UN mission sought to act upon and shape nearly all aspects of not only the future

Timorese state and but also of population's lives. Notwithstanding all this power and the vast scope of the mission, it is important to notice that INTER-FET still remained in command of the military operations in Timor-Leste. Only on February 2000 the command was transferred from INTERFET to UNTAET (UN, 2006).

In addition to the provision of security and the maintenance of the law and order throughout the territory, the mission was also responsible for several activities, such as: the development of civil and social services; the coordination and delivery of humanitarian assistance; and the assistance to the development of the country. Nevertheless, the pivotal objective of UN-TAET was to establish a state administration; to literally create a Timorese state and support the Timorese on their path to legal independence. Essentially, UNTAET was responsible for both creating the fundamental political bases of the future Timorese state and to form its police and defense forces. This would be pursued essentially through something that literally became a permanent mantra throughout all the engagements between the UN and Timor-Leste—capacity-building (S/RES/1272).

In order to fulfill its mandate, the mission was structured around three main components: (1) a governance and public administration one, which, through good governance, would oversee the development of governance, administrative and rule of law activities, and would head, in addition to the work of the district administrators, five divisions—(a) judicial affairs, (b) civilian police, (c) economic, financial, and development affairs, (d) public services, and (e) electoral operations; (2) humanitarian assistance and emergency rehabilitation, which would be responsible for ensuring a comprehensive delivery of humanitarian assistance, facilitate the reintegration of the displaced persons and refugees, and to undertake emergency rehabilitation of the critical infrastructures and services, to promote social well-being and the restoration of the civil society; and (3) a military one, which, with the approved strength of up to 8,950 troops and up to 200 military observers, would be responsible for maintaining a secure environment throughout the Timorese territory (S/RES/1272).

Before the restoration of the Timorese independence, which would happen on May 20th 2002, the UN established, under resolution 1410 (S/RES/1410) and still under chapter VII, the United Nations Mission of Support in East Timor (UNMISET), which would be mandated, initially, until May 20th 2003. The mission was responsible chiefly for assisting the development of the newly independent Timorese state. As already indented in the mandate, and also due to the very unstable security environment, UNMISET was extended three times: (1), on May 19th 2003, under resolution 1480 (S/RES/1480) until May 20th 2004; (2), on May 14th 2004, under resolution 1543 (S/RES/1543) until November 20th 2004; and, (3), on November 16th 2004, under resolution 1573 (S/RES/1573) until May 20th 2005.

In order to assist Timor-Leste to attain self-sufficiency, the mission's mandate had essentially three aims: (1) to assist to the administrative structures vital to the viability and stability of Timor-Leste, (2) to provide the public security and develop a law enforcement structure, and (3) to assist in the external and internal security (S/RES/1410). The manner in which these objectives would be pursued was, once again, through technical assistance and capacity-building. In order to achieve these aims, the mission was structured around three components: (1) a military one, which would be composed by an initial strength of up to 5000 troops, including 120 military observers; (2) a civilian police one, which would be initially composed by 1250 officers; and (3) a civilian one, composed by three units: (a) a civilian support group, (b) a serious crimes unit, and (c) a human rights unit (S/RES/1410).

In spite of a violent environment on the ground and the persistence of some alarming challenges, which will be later delineated in this chapter, the UN presence in Timor-Leste, in the form of a heavy peace operation, was scaled down in 2005, and UNMISET ended on May 20th 2005. However, the UN presence continued to be felt in Timor-Leste. It was felt not only through its agencies but also in terms of a mission, though lighter than the previous ones. On April 28th 2005, the SC, under resolution 1599 (S/RES/1599), established the United Nations Office in Timor-Leste (UNOTIL). The mission, which was mandated initially until May 20th 2006, was thought to be an UN political mission in Timor-Leste whose main objective would be to consolidate the activities carried out by UNMISET.

According to the mandate (S/RES/1599), the mission had three objectives, namely: (1) to support the development of critical state institutions, (2) to support further development of the police and of the Border Patrol Unit, (3) to provide training regarding democratic governance and human rights, and (4) to monitor and review progress of all the previous objectives. Once again, the manner in which these objectives would be pursued would be, similarly to all the engagements of the UN with Timor-Leste, capacity-building through the mentoring and advising of the experts. Therefore, to fulfill these objectives, the UN dispatched several advisers, which would be totaling forty-five directed to objective one, seventy-five to objective two, and ten to objective three. They would focus on transferring skills and knowledge in order to build capacity of the Timorese public institutions (S/RES/1599). Notwithstanding the fact that UNOTIL was a narrower mission in terms of scope, the mission was still very much focused on capacity-building the state structures and the structuring of the Timorese governance.

This was a mission that represented the process of scaling down, and phasing out, of the UN in Timor-Leste. Nevertheless, nearly a year after the beginning of this process, on April–May 2006, Timor-Leste and particularly the capital Dili experienced a bloody wave of violence. Oliver Richmond and

Jason Franks (2009), for instance, go as far as saying that Dili experienced a
widespread gang violence. This was a kind of violence not seen since the
Indonesian withdraw in 1999 (2009: 84). Responding to a request of the
Timorese government to the UN (S/2006/319), an international force, the
Australian-led Joint Task Force 631[3]—the International Stabilization Force
(ISF)—was deployed on May 27–30th 2006 to deal with the situation (CIGI,
2009: 3). These events had a big impact within the UN and lead the Security
Council to extend UNOTIL's mandate three times.[4] In fact, the UN was
trying to buy some time before figuring out how to deal with a devastating
process that became known as the 2006 crisis, which will be delineated later
on this chapter, and the kind of engagement it would have with Timor-Leste
from that time onward. A crisis that began with discrimination complains
within the Timorese army, escalated so seriously that had grave consequences in several different dimensions: humanitarian, economic, political,
security, social, to name just a few.

In order to respond to this severe and multi-dimensioned situation, on
August 25th 2006, under resolution 1704 (S/RES/1704), the Security Council
decided for the establishment of a fifth peace operation. It established a
multidimensional integrated mission—the United Nations Integrated Mission
in Timor-Leste (UNMIT)—which was mandated until February 25th 2007,
but there was already the intention to renew it for further periods until its end
on December 31st 2012. The mission's mandate was extremely vast and
dealt with several dimensions. This is demonstrated by the fact that UNMIT
had nothing less than fourteen objectives. Apart from protecting UN personnel and property, and monitoring and reviewing the progress of its activities,
the mission should (S/RES/1704): (1) support the government and its institutions enhancing their democratic-governance culture, as well as facilitate the
national reconciliation process; (2) support all aspects of the presidential and
parliamentary elections scheduled for 2007, which included technical support, policy advice, verification, as well as all the security arrangements; (3)
restore and maintain public security, including law enforcement, in the country until the reconstitution of the national police (*Polícia Nacional de Timor-
Leste* (PNTL) in Portuguese), and support the national police through training and institutional strengthening; (4) support the state in the maintenance
of a continuous presence in three border districts; (5) assist the government
in reviewing its security sector, which meant reforming the whole security
framework, including the armed forces, the ministry of defense, the police
and the ministry of interior, through advising and capacity-building; (6) build
capacity of governmental institutions in areas where specialized expertise
was required, such as the justice sector; (7) further strength the national
institutional and societal capacity, as well as instruments for monitoring and
reporting the human rights situation, and promote justice, including for wom-
en and children; (8) facilitate relief and recovery assistance; (9) assist in the

implementation of relevant recommendations in the Secretary-General's report on Justice and Reconciliation, including the assistance of the Office of the Prosecutor-General and the provision of personnel to resume the activities of the former Serious Crime Unit; (10) cooperate with other UN agencies and support Government and relevant institutions, in designing poverty reduction and economic growth policies and strategies to achieve the development plan of Timor-Leste; (11) mainstream gender, children, and youth perspectives through policies, programs, and activities; and (12) provide information to the population regarding the 2007 election, disseminate the work of UNMIT, and build local media capacity.

In order to achieve these objectives, the SG recommended the mission to be structured along three components: (1) a police one, which would comprise of up to 1608 police personnel and should be responsible for maintaining law and order, advising and assisting the rebuilding of PNTL and help the police in providing a secure environment during the pre-election and post-election phases (S/2006/628: 34); (2) a military one, which would be composed essentially by thirty-four military liaison and staff officers, and in addition to providing the security for the mission's headquarters, would be responsible for assisting the UN police when necessary in terms of public security, to provide liaison with the international security force, and also to provide advice to the Timorese security forces (S/2006/628: 34); and (3) a civilian component, which should engage with a wide range of dimensions, such as political affairs, planning and best practices, elections, legal affairs, human rights and transitional justice, administration of justice, democratic governance, economic development, humanitarian affairs, gender, HIV/ AIDS, public information and outreach, joint operations and joint mission analysis centers, and some administrative tasks (S/2006/628: 36–40). All these areas would be pursued through the same UN *modus operandi* so far in its engagement with Timor-Leste—capacity-building through experts. Unsurprisingly, UNMIT's mandate was extended six times.[5] The mission's mandate was extended several times due to an unsecure and violent environment in Timor-Leste (including gang violence and an attack, on February 2008, against the president and the prime minister) and because of two major election seasons, for both the parliament and the presidency, scheduled to take place in the country.

The first election season, from April to June 2007,[6] saw José Ramos-Horta being elected President, in a second round, with nearly 70 percent of the votes.[7] On the parliamentary elections, Fretilin, led by Mari Alkatiri, had around 29 percent of the votes.[8] On the second election season, during the first semester of 2012,[9] it was Taur Matan Ruak, the last commander of Falintil (*Forças Armadas de Libertação e Independência de Timor-Leste*), who was sworn in as president of Timor-Leste with nearly 60 percent of the votes.[10] A few months later, during the parliamentary elections, the party led by Xanana Gusmão, *Congresso Nacional de Reconstrução de Timor-Leste* (National Congress for the Reconstruction of Timor-Leste[11] [CNRT] in Portuguese), was the first-most voted with nearly 36 percent of the votes. It was only after Xanana Gusmão was sworn in as the country's President, that the UNMIT, on December 31st 2012, ended its mandate.

THE LINEAR MINDSET IN THE
UN ENGAGEMENT WITH TIMOR-LESTE

Observing the UN engagement with Timor-Leste, the first thing that strikes the analyst is the width and depth of the scope the missions. After all, it is more than clearly observable that UN activities included, for instance: the actual sovereignty over the territory; the creation of state institutions and the structuring of their *modus operandi*; actions taken in the realm of population's health, education, and others; and even the fostering, through the power-denying notion of good governance and capacity-building, of certain values—liberal democratic ones. Secondly, another thing that stands out, while analyzing the UN peace operations deployed to Timor-Leste, is their number and their duration. Timor-Leste was subject of five UN peace operations and they were on Timorese soil for more than a decade. As already indicated, no other case in the UN was subject to this kind of engagement. Nevertheless, in addition to all this, there is another element of the whole UN interaction with Timor-Leste that does not stand out so clearly while analyzing it and that even pass unnoticed by an inattentive analyst—its underpinning linear mindset. It is only by taking a step back and seeking to understand the UN peace operations deployed to Timor-Leste collectively that it is possible to perceive the linearity of the conflict-transformation approach, underpinning the UN peace rationale, behind the whole UN engagement with Timor-Leste.[12]

    This, obviously, does not mean that one can find a carbon copy of the UN peace rationale on the ground. Furthermore, it is certainly very difficult to clearly delineate each distinct conflict-resolution instrument adopted by the UN when analyzing post-conflict environments. Indeed, it is even harder to look at the reality on the ground, on any post-conflict scenario, where there are more gray zones than clear-cut phases and conflict-resolutions instruments overlap, and seek to precisely outline which phase of the conflict is developing or even to match it with a conflict-resolution instrument. Notwithstanding the fact that it is impossible to find a perfect match between conflict phases and peace instruments, this step back makes it clearer that it was precisely that what was sought by the UN in Timor-Leste—to match different phases of the conflict with an analogous conflict-resolution instrument. Taking this step back and understanding the UN peace operations as a whole also clarifies not only the fact that the UN deployed to Timor-Leste most of its peace instruments, but also, and most importantly, their linear progression, which went from peacemaking to peacebuilding. Indeed, it is perceptible that, collectively, each phase of the conflict was correspondent to an UN conflict-resolution instrument. Michael Smith and Moreen Dee (2006: 454–455), for instance, also point to this matter. Hence, the delineation developed below builds upon their work and goes further. In fact, a more comprehensive understanding of this picture is achieved by bringing to the scene periods of UN engagement with Timor-Leste that the authors overlook, namely the UN Secretary-General's good offices and negotiations that reached the May 5th 1999 agreements, UNOTIL and UNMIT.

The first peace instrument used in the UN engagement with Timor-Leste might be characterized as peacemaking. The peacemaking, as a conflict-resolution instrument, for the UN "normally includes measures to address conflicts in progress and usually involves diplomatic action to bring hostile parties to a negotiated agreement" (2008: 17). In Timor-Leste, therefore, the peacemaking phase might be argued to involve all the SG's good office efforts and all the negotiations, developed under the UN auspices, which led to the agreement signed in New York on May 5th 1999. As already mentioned, this agreement would determine the establishment of a mission designed to carry out and supervise a Timorese referendum on the Indonesian autonomy proposal. Indeed, the process of ballot conduction, and therefore the UNAMET, should also be understood as part of this peacemaking phase since it was not only a direct consequence of the negotiations, but also because this process was as a pivotal element of bringing all the key parties of the conflict—Timorese, Indonesians, and Portuguese—together.

In addition to the peacemaking, Timor-Leste was also subject to the deployment of the instrument of peace enforcement. As aforementioned, the peace enforcement instrument is understood by the UN (2008: 18) as the employment, under the authorization of the SC, of coercive actions, which certainly include the use of the military force, in order to deal with a situation which the SC understands to be a threat to international peace and security. In the case of Timor-Leste, this instrument might perfectly be understood to be deployed twice. The first occurrence was with the deployment of the INTERFET mission, which was a military mission that sought to restore order in Timor-Leste right after the announcement of the rejection by the Timorese of the autonomy proposal offered by the Indonesian government. This peace instrument was also deployed, for a second time, to Timor-Leste with the deployment of the International Stabilization Force (ISF) in order to respond to the April–May 2006 crisis.

The third peace instrument deployed to Timor-Leste was peacekeeping. As already aforementioned, peacekeeping, as a conflict-resolution instrument, for the UN (2008) is understood as "a technique designed to preserve the peace, however fragile, where fighting has been halted, and to assist in implementing agreements achieved by the peacemakers" (2008: 18). In the case of Timor-Leste, one might understand that this instrument was more present, although in different degrees, during the period of the missions of UNTAET, UMISET, and UNMIT. In these periods, not only there was, in the UN's eyes, a peace to be kept, but also the UN was a fundamental element in the very maintenance of the security of the country. In fact, for some periods, and not short ones, the UN was *de facto* responsible for this realm. Indeed, this responsibility, in different periods, was materialized in the form of the actual policing of the country and the responsibility of even the security of the borders.

Lastly, the other peace instrument that Timor-Leste was subjected to was the peacebuilding. This instrument is understood by the UN (2008) as already mentioned, as a conflict-resolution instrument that involves a set of measures aiming at the prevention of the (re)lapsing of a violent conflict, through the strengthening of the national capacities for managing conflicts (2008: 18). Aiming to address the deep-rooted, structural causes of violent conflicts, it concentrates its activities on both the functioning of the state apparatus and its relationship with the population (UN, 2008: 18). Hence, the main objective of this instrument is to create the conditions for a sustainable and long-lasting peace. Observing the UN engagement with Timor-Leste, this instrument might be understood as being present, in different degrees, during the missions of UNTAET and UNMIT. This instrument, due to the scaling down of the UN presence on the field, became reduced at the UNOTIL. Nevertheless, as a response to the 2006 crisis, this peace instrument became deeper and wider with UNMIT.

Observing the UN engagement with Timor-Leste as a whole, it is clear that the conflict-resolution instruments deployed to the country were seeking not only to deal with the amount of violence that was perceived on the ground but also to match a phased and linear understanding of the conflict and its transformation. This linear and phased understanding of the conflict cycle[13] means less a clear-cut delimited phase sequence of each instrument than the progression from peacemaking toward peacebuilding, with several overlapping and grey zones among the peace instruments. In fact, this is precisely the kind of understanding that underpins the UN rationale regarding its approach to peace, which is delineated in the Capstone Doctrine (UN, 2008: 19).

From the period of the UN Secretary-General's good offices to the period of the UNMIT, the UN engagement with Timor-Leste might be characterized as passing through nearly all conflict-resolution instruments; going from peacemaking to peacebuilding. The point here is certainly not to distinctly and decisively divide the Timorese situation into clear-cut periods. Instead, the point is precisely to evince that this kind of a linear rationale, although hardly feasible in reality, was behind the UN engagement with Timor-Leste.

In fact, until the April–May 2006 crisis, it could even be argued that Timor-Leste passed through the whole conflict-cycle. Therefore, being subject to nearly all conflict resolution instruments designed to the whole conflict cycle, Timor-Leste, under this rationale, should be characterized at that time as a country experiencing a strong path of development. However, this could not be further from the reality on the ground. Indeed, the 2006 crisis came to prove precisely the opposite. The crisis evinced the fragile basis of the linear and phase mindset underpinning the UN conflict-resolution rationale, and consequently, of the whole engagement with Timor-Leste.

This linear and phased conflict-resolution approach, if successful, could make a positive and strong argument for this kind of understanding in regard to the transformation of violent conflicts throughout the globe with Timor-Leste as its best-case example. Nevertheless, the mere occurrence of the 2006 and 2008 crises, along with the very slow development of the country, shows precisely the opposite. It makes the case, at least, for the severe questioning, if not the entire rethinking, of this linear rationale, which underpins the UN rationale in general and its engagement with Timor-Leste, in particular. Instead, precisely the opposite occurred. Due to the depth of the UN intervention, the number of missions, the range of the instruments deployed and of the activities performed, Timor-Leste *has*, more than any other post-conflict country, to be a successful case. Since so much is at stake for the UN in the case Timor-Leste, namely the whole conflict-resolution rationale and peace-building approach of the organization, rather than rethinking its approach, Timor-Leste is increasingly presented as a success. Otherwise, the very credibility of this kind of rationale and of the UN as a conflict-transformation actor would be imperiled. This, more than any achievement on the ground or the kind of peace created, is a pivotal reason of the effort of portraying of Timor-Leste as a successful case of conflict transformation.

THE REACTIVE NATURE OF THE
UN ENGAGEMENT WITH TIMOR-LESTE

In addition to its linearity, the UN engagement with Timor-Leste has another distinct characteristic—its reactive, rather than preventive, character. The persistent reactive nature of the UN approach toward Timor-Leste is perceived since the very beginning of the engagement. One might think, for instance, notwithstanding the good offices exercised by successive SGs since early 1980s, the UN hardly sought to prevent the successive violence in Timor-Leste. In fact, the UN engagement with Timor-Leste only became denser, on late 1990s, as a reaction to the fact that the harsh and violent condition under which the Timorese lived became internationally visible and Timor-Leste emerged as an urgent need in the international scenario. Indeed, this reactive nature is perceived persistently throughout the whole UN engagement with the country, when the mission's mandates were certainly modified, adapted and extended, but constantly in a reactive manner, rather than in a preventive one.

On June 11th 1999, taking into account the SG's report to the Security Council[14] (S/1999/595), UNAMET was established to conduct the Timorese referendum, which was initially scheduled for August 8th 1999. Nevertheless, the environment in Timor-Leste was already tense before the signing of the tripartite agreements. The bloody violence perpetrated by the militias, with the consent of the Indonesian military, made UNAMET organize the referendum within a very unstable environment. The cases of destruction, violence, and intimidation were recurrent. Reacting to such unsecure scenario and to some technical issues regarding the organization of the referendum (S/1999/830), the actual voting date had to be postponed to August 30th (Kingsbury, 2009: 72). Consequently, the UN had to extend the end date of UNAMET until September 30th.

In order to prepare the UN role in Timor-Leste after the referendum results the SG (S/1999/862) recommended the restructuration of the mission, which was accepted by the SC. Therefore, on August 27th, under resolution 1262 (S/RES/1262), UNAMET's mandate was again extended, until November 30th, and incorporated the following components: (1) an electoral unit, which would, depending of the results, either work on the elections of a Regional Council if autonomy is accepted or the coming elections if the proposal gets rejected; (2) a civilian police one, which would be composed by up to 460 personnel and would both advise the Indonesian police and prepare the formation of a Timorese police; (3) a military one, which, while being increased to 300 officers and deployed to the thirteen districts, it would, in addition to inform the UN Special Representative (UNSR) in regard to security matter, make a liaison work with the Indonesian military, the pro-integration militias and the Falintil; (4) a civil affairs one, which would also be deployed to the thirteen districts and be responsible for advising the UNSR regarding the political environment on the ground and impacts on the political stability of Timor-Leste. In addition, this component would be responsible for maintaining a liaison with the Indonesian authorities and other actors on the ground, promoting the respect for the rule of law and human rights, and providing humanitarian assistance as well ensuring timely contingency planning for potential humanitarian problems after the elections; and (5) the continuation of the informational one.

Nevertheless, the mission neither sought nor was equipped to prevent a fairly possible consequence of the referendum results in case of a clear choice for independence—the extreme violence of the militias. The country experienced a wave of disappearances, rapes, murders, looting, forced dislocations of the population, deportations, and all sorts of destruction of the infrastructures and houses (Teles, 1999a: 411). Kingsbury (2009: 75), for instance, remembers that a vast majority of the Timorese buildings were burned by the TNI and the militias. In fact, the destruction was not limited to the infrastructure (which more than 70 percent was destructed); it also reached people's lives. Indeed, nearly 2,000 people was killed, around 230,000 forced to go to West Timor, and other several hundred thousand were internally displaced (Beauvais, 2001: 1103). As a reaction to the large-scale violence experience in Timor-Leste, the UN sanctioned the deployment of INTERFET to the country in order to cope with the situation.

As a consequence of the referendum results, the UN would assist the Timorese on its road toward independence and, taking into account the SGRSC (SG, 1999), UNTAET was established. Regarding the path to independence, the National Council of Timorese Resistance (CNRT in Portuguese)—which was the umbrella organization for all the pro-independence supporters during the referendum and which continued to be a pivotal actor afterward—understood, in SG's (S/2001/42) perception of the Timorese political reality, that it should be a two-phased process: (1) the composition of a Constituent Assembly; and, (2) the Constitution drafting. On that same report, the SG admits that the timetable for the first elections, which were planned for the end of 2001, might be postponed due to several reasons, including security. Therefore, merely reacting in regards to the situation, the SC, welcoming the SG's (S/2001/42) recommendations extended the UNTAET's mandate for one year.

During this time, it was still on debate whether the Constituent Assembly would be later sworn in as the country's first legislature or another round of elections would be necessary. This debate divided major Timorese political actors. On the one hand, the former argument was supported mainly by Fretilin's Mari Alkatiri and Francisco "Lu-Olo" Guterres. Fretilin was expected to have a big victory on the elections for the Constituent Assembly and, consequently, having the majority of a future parliament. On the other hand, the latter argument was advanced majorly by Xanana Gusmão and his supporters. They had very little to lose and certainly a lot to gain with another election taking place (Kingsbury, 2009: 100).

On August 30th 2001, the Timorese voted for the Constituent Assembly. In that election, which had a turnout of over 90 percent, the Timorese elected eighty-eight members. As anticipated, the Fretilin won fifty-five seats, which represented a convincing majority of the seats available[15] (Kingsbury, 2009: 100–101; UN, 2001). After this election, a new Council of Ministers, all Timorese, sworn into office and this council along with the Constituent Assembly, was responsible for leading Timor-Leste during the period before its independence (UN, 2002a). Reacting to the coming presidential elections (which were won by Xanana Gusmão) and to the prospect of the declaration of the Timorese restoration of the independence to be postponed to May 20th

2002, the SC, welcoming the SG's (S/2002/80) recommendation, extended the mission's mandate until this date. In fact, May 20th 2002 represented three main events in Timorese political scene, namely: (1) the Constituent Assembly was transformed into the first Timorese Parliament,[16] elevating Mari Alkatiri, Fretilin's Secretary-General, to prime minister (PM) and retaining the political power on Fretilin's side; (2) Xanana Gusmão was sworn in; and (3) Timor-Leste formally entered into the international scenario as an independent state. During an event in Dili, where Xanaxa Gusmão and Mari Alkatiri were sworn in, the UN formally handed over the authority of the territory back to the Timorese, and President Xanana Gusmão formally presented the UN SG Kofi Annan the Timorese request to join the UN (UN, 2006).

Adapting to the new reality, a legally independent Timor-Leste, the UN, very much in line with the SG's recommendations (S/2002/432), established UNMISET in order to assist the Timorese state. Reacting to the inexistence of local expertise to fulfill posts on the Timorese state, the SG recommended a key element to the mission: the Civilian Support Group, which was a group composed by 100 personnel dispatched to fill core functions within the newly independent state (S/RES/1410). They were a small group of experts whose task was to assist the emergent Timorese government (S/2002/432: 10). According to a previous SG's assessment, the UN identified around one hundred positions—which in the UN's view were fundamental for the stability and functioning of the government—that did not have a local expertise, in the eyes of the UN (S/2001/983: 10).

Their distribution rationale would be the following: (1) two-thirds were direct to mentoring (advisory and training) functions; and (2) one-third was directed to direct functions (S/2001/983). The areas covered would be public finance, banking, justice, infrastructure, and other positions necessary for maintaining government functioning (S/2001/983). The SG recommended their distribution to be: (1) forty-two positions directed to financial and central services; (2) twenty-seven positions to internal systems in the Council of Ministers, the Chief Minister's office and various ministers; (3) the legal/justice systems would receive fourteen positions; and (4) essential services, such as water and sanitation, power, roads, housing, ports, and health would receive seventeen positions (S/2002/432: 11). They would provide expertise as well as to capacity-build the Timorese government. Therefore, they were the ones who actually run critical positions in the Timorese state. Those were the few people who would assist in the UN's objective of achieving Timor's self-sufficiency and also those who would constantly monitor, assess and conduct behaviors on a micro-level. Through advising, they would be the ones ensuring that Timor-Leste behave accordingly—as a liberal state.

Regarding UNMISET per se, the SG, due to his perception of a still unsecure environment (S/2003/243), recommended (S/2003/449) the extension of UNMISET's mandate for another year, until May 20th 2004. The security environment in Timor-Leste, in the SG's opinion, had a "sharp increase in the frequency and the magnitude of security-related incidents" (S/ 2003/243: 2). He (S/2003/243: 2) mentions, for instance: (1) disturbances in Baucau from November 18 to 26, 2002; (2) a protest in Dili, on December 4th 2002, which evolved from a protest in front of the parliament building to a riot where several buildings were put on fire, including houses owned by the PM's and his family, and the mosque of Dili was damaged (including the houses of its compound which were burned). In these riots, seventeen Timorese were injured by the gunshots and two of them died; (3) a event, on January 3rd 2003, that a group of nearly thirty armed men, with automatic weapons, attacked villages near Atsabe, in the district of Ermera. In these attacks, five people were killed; (4) another event, on February 24th 2003, where a small group of armed men, with semi-automatic weapons, attacked a bus that was going from Maliana, in Bobonaro, to Dili. In this attack, two people were killed and five injured; and (5) the credible evidence suggesting the return of the militias and armed groups in the country. These incidents, in the SG's understanding, exposed both the scope of the issues that might emerge in the future and the inadequacy of the means available to address these issues (S/2003/243). Therefore, he concluded that the downsizing and phasing out phases had to be rescheduled (S/2003/243).

The security environment, once more, led the UN to revise both military and policing strategies (S/2003/243) and also exposed the shortage of preventive measures. Furthermore, it was clear that the challenges that Timor-Leste would face after May 20th 2004, the forecasted date for UNMISET's end, would be great. It was patent that the previous understanding that Timor-Leste would be self-sufficient in two years was unrealistic. In fact, the SG acknowledges that the plan was prepared "at a time of optimism" (S/2003/ 243: 1). Even Mari Alkatiri, Timor-Leste's PM, asked UNMISET to remain for a period beyond May 2004 (PRTL, 2004). Hence, before the expiration of the mission's mandate, on February 13th 2004 (S/2004/117) and on April 29th (S/2004/333), the SG recommended some structural changes.

Therefore, accepting SG's recommendations (S/2004/117; S/2004/333), UNMISET's mandate was extended twice and structurally redesigned, firstly, to contemplate three objectives: (1) to support Timorese public administration, justice system and the field of serious crimes; (2) to support the development of the law enforcement, which would be responsible for a combination of operational and training tasks; and (3) to be a support for the security and stability of the country, which would be carried out by the military side of the mission. The manner in which these elements would be pursued did not change; it remained the actual performance of tasks and the mentoring and capacity-building through the deployment of advisers and experts; which would be composed by: fifty-eight civilian advisers,[17] 157 civilian police advisers,[18] forty-two military liaison officers, 310 formed troops and an International Response Unit composed by 125 individuals.

Secondly, acknowledging SG's (S/2004/888) further recommendations, UNMISET's mandate was again extended and structurally modified. The SG perceived that several structural issues still remained unanswered. They were, for instance: (1) the fact that Timor-Leste had not yet reached the critical threshold of self-sufficiency; (2) the weakness and fragility of Timorese public administration, especially the finance, banking, and justice sectors (some of the mentors were still performing critical tasks); and (3) the challenges that PNTL still faced, including, in the SG's view the lack of administrative skills, experience in policing, and the adequate infrastructure (S/2004/888: 14). Notwithstanding the fact that none of these issues can be properly solved in six months, the end date of UNMISET remained May 20th of 2005.

It was in such unstable environment that UNOTIL was established. Once more, the UN did not have a preventive approach. In fact, as it will be further discussed later on this chapter, the organization clearly neglected several fundamental strands of the Timorese reality. This neglect culminated on the 2006 crisis, which took place during the process of UN scaling down and almost a month from the end of UNOTIL. As a result of the bloody events of April–May 2006, the state institutions, including the police and the armed forces, simply melted, thirty-eight people were dead, more than 1,650 houses in Dili were damaged or destroyed, and nearly 150,000 people were internally displaced (ICG, 2008: 3). It was literally a humanitarian catastrophe. Reacting to the situation, the UN sanctioned the deployment of the international force—ISF.

However, the violence and the crisis continued. In fact, more people died between August 2006 and February 2007 than during the crisis itself (ICG, 2008: 3). Moreover, in June 2006, there were several resignations: the Prime Minister, the Minister of Defence, the Minister of the Interior, and the Minister of Foreign Affairs, José Ramos Horta. Later, Ramos-Horta was sworn in as an interim Prime Minister (IFP, 2009: 9). The crisis led the UN, once more reactively, to successively extend UNOTIL's mandate. These were serious developments and, on a report on August 8th 2006 (S/2006/628), the SG acknowledges that two-thirds of the Dili population was displaced. Furthermore, for him, these violent events were merely the beginning of a major crisis with political, economic, security and humanitarian repercussions, with deep and long-term issues to be addressed (S/2006/628: 1; 8). In reaction to the grave situation, the SG (S/2006/628) recommended the establishment of a multidimensional integrated mission.

Therefore, the SC decided, in line with SG's recommendation (S/2006/628), for the establishment of UNMIT. UNMIT's mandate, once again reactively, was successively extended. The first extension was on late February

2007. The SG recommend the mandates' extension because there were some serious challenges in the judicial sector, as well as within the PNTL and the military, since the security and political situation remained tense (S/2007/50: 18). Another element that was causing instability in Timor-Leste was the gang groups' violence, which were usually formed by martial art groups.[19] From June 2006 to December 2007, more than a hundred people died and properties were destroyed due to constant political, communal, and gang violence (CIGI, 2009: 4).

In addition, UNMIT's extension was intended also to cover the period of both the presidential and parliamentary elections, which were scheduled to take place in mid-2007. They could potentially trigger instability or even violence. The period of the elections, from April to June 2007, proceeded without major incidents, with only few incidents of violence related to the campaigns (ICG, 2008: 3). The political problems and also violent events would come later with the formation of the government. After the parliamentary elections, Fretilin, led by Mari Alkatiri, had most of the votes but the party did not have an absolute majority or the ability to form a majority government in coalition with other parties. The second-most voted party, Xanana Gusmão's, had nearly 24 percent of the votes. However, bypassing Alkatiri and Fretilin, Xanana could forge an alliance with the third and fourth-most voted parties and formed a majority government named Alliance for a Parliamentary Majority (AMP). The announcement, on August 2007, by the President Ramos-Horta, that Xanana Gusmão and AMP would form the government led to some rioting, with many people with the Fretilin's flag, and throwing of stones and burning down of buildings in Dili, Baucau, and other places (ICG, 2008: 3).

Near UNMIT's end, another incident broke out on Dili's streets. It was an attack against both the president and the prime minister. On February 11th 2008, an armed group led by Alfredo Reinado, a former commander of F-FDTL (*Falintil-Forças de Defesa de Timor-Leste*—Falintil Defense Forces of Timor-Leste), attacked the president, José Ramos-Horta, and the prime minister, Xanana Gusmão. The attack resulted in a nearly fatal injury of the President and the killing of Reinado.[20] Reacting to the attacks, strongly condemning them, and welcoming the SG's (S/2007/711; S/2008/26) recommendations, the SC decided to extend UNMIT's mandate once more.

The mission's mandate would be extended again four times. Firstly, until February 26th 2010, to support the local (*suco*) elections which were scheduled to take place on 2009 and due to the persistent fragile situation (S/RES/1867). Therefore, UNMIT was called, on the one hand to address the critical political and security situation, and, on the other hand, to enhance the democratic governance of Timor-Leste (S/RES/1867), and regarding the justice sector, and the security sectors reforms. Secondly, until February 26th 2011, due to the fact that some of the previous concerns continued, such as the rule of law, development, security, security sector reforms in regard to delineating roles and responsibilities of F-FDTL and PNTL, justice in regards to strengthening legal frameworks, and the enhancement of a culture of democratic governance (S/RES/1912). Thirdly, in reaction to the fact that parliamentary and presidential elections were scheduled for 2012, UNMIT's mandate was once more extended. The mission should pay more attention to the police and armed forces, and focus on the security sector and justice reforms, through training, advising, and capacity-building and strengthening of institutions (S/RES/1969). Finally, UNMIT's mandate was extended, until December 31st 2012 and accepting the SG's (S/2012/43) recommendations, the process of scaling down was started. During the first semester of 2012, Timor-Leste held both the presidential and the parliamentary elections.[21] This, in the eyes of the UN, was a major challenge not only for the Timorese political institutions, but also for the security forces. On May 20th 2012, Taur Matan Ruak was sworn in as president and a few months later, during after parliamentary elections, Xanana Gusmão's party (CNRT) was the winner. The period of both campaigns were relatively calm and with no widespread violence.[22] Despite violent incidents which occurred when Xanana Gusmão announced that he would not form government with Fretilin, and after Xanana was sworn in, the UN thought that UNMIT's job in the country was done and finished the mission.

SOME STRUCTURAL SHORTCOMINGS OF THE
UN ENGAGEMENT WITH TIMOR-LESTE

Although the engagement with Timor-Leste is presented as a success case by the UN (Goldstone, 2004: 83), it had several serious shortcomings from its very beginning. One could begin, for instance, with the very structure of UNTAET. From its start, the mission had key internal structural contradictions. Firstly, one can definitely point toward the very tools assembled. UNTAET was essentially a state-building mission but it was equipped with peacekeeping tools (Suhrke, 2001). Consequently, UNTAET was a mission which was directed toward long-term objectives but was endowed with short-term instruments. One could also bring attention, for instance, to the lack of collaboration, or even competition, between the Department of Political Affairs (DPA) and the Department of Peacekeeping Operations (DPKO), which certainly affected the structuring of the mission.

Secondly, the mission had no structure to accommodate the Timorese participation in the decision-making processes, neither within the administration of the mission itself nor through political consultation (Suhrke, 2001). One should remember that the UN was not mandated to create a Timorese state, organize the country as it wants, and later hand it over the Timorese;

instead, it was mandated to assist the Timorese in this process. Therefore, the lack of a structure to incorporate the Timorese voice was a fundamental shortcoming, creating an uncomfortable situation between UNTAET and the population (Suhrke, 2001: 2). The subsequent missions, as it was already mentioned, had the intention of supporting the development of a post-independence state, namely through institution-building in, and strengthening, the governance, security, and judicial dimensions. Nevertheless, the blocking of Timorese population remained constant. Indeed, according to Richmond (2011: 84–85), the UN focus was directed essentially toward the establishment of liberal state, sidelining the population, notwithstanding the fact that the Timorese were very politicized and active. Indeed, due to the great, and myopic, focus on institution and capacity building a whole set of political experience, history, culture, and needs of the Timorese ended up being marginalized (Richmond, 2011: 87).

Paradoxically, an engagement that would aim to support the Timorese to build their state prevented, sometimes methodologically, the Timorese participation (Chopra, 2002: 981). According to Chopra (2000: 32), this was even rooted in the planning phase of the UNTAET mission which did not include any real contact or participation of the representatives of Timor-Leste. Notwithstanding the effort made by Xanana Gusmão of outlining the Timorese role as a form of Transitional Council, this idea was rapidly rejected (Chopra, 2000: 32). The prevention of the Timorese participation, or information about the whole intervention, might also be observed in the very language on which the laws were written by UNTAET. Despite the fact that Timor-Leste has eighteen languages, the Tetum, despite differences of it between different regions of the country, worked from a long time as a sort of a *lingua franca* (Carvalho, 2001: 65). Nevertheless, very few of the legislative instruments were written in Tetum; only nine to be more precise. The whole set of regulations, directives, executive orders, and notifications promulgated by the UNTAET were available in English and Portuguese, some in Indonesian, and very few in Tetum. Although the Portuguese language played a key role in the genesis of the Timorese cultural and national identity and also on the resistance movement (Carvalho, 2001: 70), the use of the Tetum was more widespread among the population. However, this fact was neglected by the UN. Notwithstanding the fact that the writing of the laws in Portuguese is a good sign, the indication that in any case of a divergence among translations of UNTAET legislation the English text is the one that prevails leaves little space for not interpreting the very language of the laws that the Timorese should comply as a barrier and an obstruction of the full participation of them on the whole process of rebuilding their own country.

On the field, the Special Representative of the Secretary General and the Transitional Administrator, Sérgio Vieira de Mello,[23] had all the powers in his hands since the UN Security Council convened all executive, legislative, and judiciary powers to the UNTAET. Vieira de Mello sought immediately to open a channel of communication with Xanana Gusmão, but this was not adequate to the huge task he had, since this approach was based on a very personal relationship rather than a more institutional and permanent one (Chopra, 2000). This was attempted when, on December 2nd 1999, a National Consultative Council was established to advise the Transitional Administrator in his legislative and executive duties (UNTAET/REG/1999/2). However, they would not have any governing role, or greater say, whatsoever. The views and opinions of the Council were accepted only after the approval of Vieira de Mello (Chopra, 2000: 32). This widened even more the already existent gap between the UN's *de jure* authority on the paper, and the CNRT's *de facto* legitimacy on the field.

This kind of engagement of the UN rested majorly on a sense that Timor-Leste was a sort of *terra nullius* which lacked the proper skills to develop, or to participate in the construction of, a state. Jarat Chopra (2002: 981), former Head of the Office of District Administration of UNTAET, was crystal-clear: the whole project was assumed as an enterprise of institutional invention. Therefore, local political and social structures, which had a broad reach and legitimacy throughout the population, and also cultural considerations, were ignored by the internationals. Those were less important in comparison with quick results regarding the liberal peace implementation in areas such as: politics, security, economy, and state institutions (Richmond, 2011: 86). In parallel with this, capacity building, something that rapidly became a mantra among internationals in Timor-Leste (Richmond and Franks, 2009:100), was thought to be developed through the tutoring of the Timorese state institutions by internationals. Indeed, the Timorese state ended up being created, and key state functions were carried out, by international experts who were deployed along the successive missions. However, this was only possible due to another mantra, the lack of local capacity one, which functioned also as an instrument to legitimate their own control of the Timorese governance (Richmond, 2011: 86). In addition, this lack of capacity mantra also underpinned and to some extent legitimized the recruitment of an international staff, even though most of them had no knowledge regarding the country or the Timorese language and culture (Suhrke, 2001: 11).

While analyzing the UN intervention in Timor-Leste, José Manuel Pureza and other researchers (Pureza et al., 2007b) rightly point out some shortcomings and shortcomings on different dimensions of the process. On the military/security dimension, they evince the expeditious matter of incorporating former rival combatants on the police and the army generated a tension between the two (Pureza et al., 2007b: 23). In fact, uncertainty regarding the status of Falintil delayed the security sector reform. Later, it was decided for the establishment of the FDTL with Falitin as its nucleus (Martin and Mayer-Rieckh, 2005: 134). Those who were not recruited would be assisted and demobilized though the Falitin Reintegration Assistance Programme (FRAP). Nevertheless, resentments with the selection process on both generated a number of security incidents among former Falintil members (Martin and Mayer-Rieckh, 2005: 134). Regarding the formation of the police, this was a slow process since no UNTAET member was initially assigned to carry out this. Hence, the institutional development of the police was initially neglected. Indeed, by the independence day, neither the police nor the army could fully perform the public security and the defense of the country (Martin and Mayer-Rieckh, 2005: 135).

On the political-constitutional dimension, Pureza (Pureza et al., 2007b: 20) sheds light on the case of official language and judicial system as sources of contradictions. They point out, for instance, the arguments advanced by both internationals and locals in regard to the two subjects. Whereas the former advocated for the use of the Indonesian language, or even English, and the use of the common law, the latter advocated for the use of Portuguese and a civil model. Moreover, they point also to contradictions regarding the training of police and judicial authorities. The former were trained in Australia with the UNTAET's regulations as its base, while the latter were trained majorly in Portugal having as its base the legislative projects at the time, which would be adopted later though with modifications (Pureza et al., 2007b: 23). Indeed, Ian Martin and Alexander Mayer-Rieckh (2005: 137) argue that the judicial area had no coordination or an strategy toward the implementation of the rule of law. Moreover, the area lacked constant and appropriate funding.

In regard to the socio-economic dimension, according to Pureza (Pureza et al., 2007b: 23–24), there were little progress in terms of the development on these areas for the Timorese population. Despite several years of intervention, the daily life of the Timorese was barely improved. This is perhaps best epitomized by the disturbing fact that after more than a decade on the ground and millions of dollars spent, not even Timor-Leste's capital Dili does have as basic as sanitation.[24] Richmond (2011: 85), for instance, correctly remembers that the Human Development Index (HDI) of Timor-Leste only marginally improved since 1999.[25] In fact, since 2002, there was a 10 percent increase in the number of those living under the poverty line (Richmond, 2011: 160). Indeed, in 2007, nearly half of the population (49.9 percent) was living in poverty (UNDP, 2011d: vii). Despite more than a decade-long intervention and the great potential to generate revenue from gas and oil,[26] poverty is the still persistent in the country (Richmond, 2011: 160). According to Richmond and Franks (2009: 90–91), the Timorese social-economic situation barely improved since the independence. In fact, they bring a disturbing picture: (1) the economy was quite weak the unemployment was considered to be reaching 20 percent in urban areas such as Dili, and around 44 percent regarding the for urban youth. Consequently, due to its high level of poverty, the Human Development Index (HDI) of Timor-Leste was very low; (2) the infant mortality is 90 per thousand births; (3) the Timorese life expectancy was 55.5 years; (4) 50 percent of the population was illiterate; (5) around 70 percent does not have their own drinking water facilities; and (6) more than 70 percent had no access to electricity.[27] On the psycho-social side, similarly to other peace missions, this was the dimension least focused according to Pureza (Pureza et al., 2007b: 24). The dimension was somewhat touched with the creation of the Commission for Reception, Truth and Reconciliation (*Comissão de Acolhimento, Verdade e Reconciliação*—CAVR) which was a step forward but the short resources directed toward the Commission limited a lot its contribution (Pureza et al., 2007b: 24).

Notwithstanding all this, the whole construction of the Timorese state was portrayed as a success by the UN (Goldstone, 2004: 83). However, according to Richmond and Franks (2009), what was celebrated on May 2002 was in fact a state that existed one in the paper (2009: 93). This interpretation of the Timorese reality is very much connected with the idea of a phantom state developed by David Chandler (2006). For him, this kind of situation occurs when it is perceived that a state may have some governance and administrative structures but it is not endowed with the political will of a society. They might have international legal sovereignty, but their policy-making are extensively controlled and supervised by international institutions (Chandler, 2006: 43–44). Additionally, this links to the Christopher Bickerton's notion of the state-building process as a state-failure process. For him, state-building, while neglecting fundamental strands of the local environment and relegating the local population to a passive role of merely receiving institutions built, is indeed removing the popular will from the political process of their creation. Consequently, the institutions created are not deep-rooted in their societies. As a result, state-building, while building institutions with few social or political foundations, in fact creates institutions with very weak basis and that constantly need the international support to endure (Bickerton, 2007: 93; 100).

STATE-BUILDING AS STATE FAILURE?: THE 2006 CRISIS AND ITS NEGLECTED STRANDS

In fact, the 2006 crisis, and also the 2008 violent events, corroborates this line of thought. All these elements aforementioned led Chopra (2002: 996) to argue about a round of state-failure in Timor-Leste and Richmond (2011: 2), for instance, to refer to an "ever-fragile state" when talking about Timor-Leste. Indeed, Pureza and other researchers (Pureza et al., 2007b: 17) expose that, paradoxically, the processes of state-building and state failure, in Timor-Leste, are not oppositional or dissociated processes. On the contrary, for them, Timor-Leste is the best example to illustrate an apparent contradiction of the state-building being a state-failure process. In fact, the 2006 crisis, with its strands neglected by the UN, is perhaps most instructive of this process. Obviously, this book does not intend to exhaustively deal with, or explain, neither the events nor their deep root-causes.[28] They are discussed herein due to the fact that they are the most iconic illustration of both the fragility of the peace built by the UN and of its state-building enterprise in Timor-Leste, due to UN's neglect of fundamental strands of Timorese reality.

The 2006 Crisis

The open, violent conflicts, which became known as the 2006 crisis, and especially their consequences are something greatly significant due to the fact that they are highly symptomatic in regard to exposing the fragile basis of the state-building process carried by the UN in Timor-Leste. In less than four years after Timor-Leste gained independence, and nearly one year after the scaling down of UNOTIL, Timorese police and army were fighting each other in the streets of the capital. Indeed, these events were the iconic example of the collapse of the security sector in Timor-Leste and a potentially damage to what was built so far in the country. The April–May events, per se, actually had their beginning when, in January 2006, 159 soldiers of the F-FDTL signed a petition, to President Xanana Gusmão (who as President was also the supreme army commander), complaining about discrimination—particularly in regard to salaries, promotions, and accommodation—against the westerners (*Loromonu* in Tetum) and favoring the easterners (*Lorosae* in Tetum)[29] (ICG, 2008: 2). This group became known as the *peticionários* (petitioners in Portuguese).

As a consequence of the fact that the government gave a minimal response to their claim, nearly a month later, on February 17th, nearly 600 soldiers left their barracks on protest and organized a strike (Kingsbury, 2009: 142). The negotiations only served to increase the number of soldiers joining the protests and the ones leaving their barracks (ICG, 2008: 2). After consultation and meetings between the prime minister, the defense minister and the commander of Faltintil-FDTL, they were ordered to return to their barracks; something that was not followed (Kingsbury, 2009: 142). Alleging insubordination, on March 16th, the army's leader, Brigadier-General Taur Matan Ruak[30] decided for the dismissal of 594 soldiers, which was nearly 40 percent of the entire armed forces (CIGI, 2009: 3).

The dismissal led, beginning on April 28th, to a four-day demonstration held by the petitioners, but that also included unemployed youths and members of the organization Colimau 2000, at the government palace (Kingsbury, 2009: 142). At that time, the Police Commander Paulo Martins thought that had the situation under control. However, the situation quickly turned into a riot, and a violent one, with two deaths on the April 28th and three on the 29th. The violence, which was mainly led by the youths who joined the protests, rapidly spread out throughout the streets of Dili and the police was unable to control it. This situation led the prime minister, Mari Alkatiri, to send the armed forces[31] to control the situation and restore the order, which resulted in three deaths (ICG, 2008: 2).

The situation, which already had the potential to be problematic, became even more inflamed. On May 3rd, Major Alfredo Alves Reinado,[32] Chief of the military police, entered on the scene, and, along with his group, became an important player in the violent incidents. He, along with seventeen of his men, breaking their ranks, leaving the chain of command, and taking their weapons with them, deserted to protest on what they understood as a deliberate attack on civilians on the part of the army (CIGI, 2009: 3; ICG, 2008: 2). Although they were not formally part of the petitioners, their claims were similar (CIGI, 2009: 3). However, the next month was stage of a series of violent events between the police and the army, and among the protesters themselves. The International Crisis Group (ICG) (ICG, 2008: 2), a Brussels-based think-tank dedicated to the analysis of violent conflicts throughout the globe, lists, for instance: (1) the murder of a policeman in Gleno; (2) a fight between some army officers and men of the Reinado's group in Fatuahi, near Dili; and (3) an attack carried out by petitioners, armed civilians and police towards the army headquarters in Tacitolu. The attack left five people dead. The escalating violence between the police and the army culminated, on May 25, 2006, in a battle between F-FDTL and PNTL forces, in central Dili, very near the PNTL Headquarters (CIGI, 2009: 3).

The Neglected Strands of the Crisis

As already discussed, the crisis not only shattered the Timorese state apparatus, including the military and the police, but also left the country in a drastic situation with humanitarian, political, institutional, historical, social, and economic outstanding proportions. It is true that, perhaps, the 2006 crisis could not be completely avoided. Nevertheless, it is also true that if the UN sought to have a preventive stance, rather than a successive reactive one, toward its engagement with Timor-Leste and pursued a rigorous understanding of the Timorese reality, the crisis could conceivably have a different proportion. The events of April-May 2006 are better understood as the culmination of a series of events and processes, also violent, which were taking place in Timor-Leste that surfaced. Most importantly, it is essential to have in mind that these events were merely the surface of several other deeper intricate multi-level strands that were apparently neglected or underestimated by the

UN throughout its state-building process in Timor-Leste, which renders visible the fragility of the whole process.

Remarkably, these strands are intrinsically related to fundamental dimensions of the overall post-conflict reconstruction processes—Disarmament, Demobilization and Reintegration (DDR); Security Sector Reform (SSR); the political environment; and the socio-economic dimension. The strands are, for instance: (1) the poor reintegration process that the fighters of the former guerrilla who did not enter in the army; (2) the structural dissatisfactions and divisions present within the armed forces; (3) the poor and tense relationship between the police and the army; (4) the grievances and differences among the Timorese political elite; and (5) the socio-economic condition in which the Timorese lived (and still live), which was desperate, to say the least; to mention a few.

The first strand of the 2006 crisis that immediately emerges is related to the process of DDR, which is a key part of UN post-conflict reconstruction efforts. In Timor-Leste, the program was directed to Falintil during UN-TAET. It was already mentioned that the FDTL has its origins in the transformation of Falintil into a regular armed force. Nevertheless, not all the Falintil fighters were incorporated by the armed forces. The FDTL absorbed some of the veterans but others were left unemployed (ICG, 2006). Those that were left out of the force received a small financial assistance[33] in order to reinitiate their lives within civil society. It is needless to say that this reinsertion was more than difficult and that the money was rapidly spent. Furthermore, these men were twenty-five years in the jungle, with no family, fighting a resistance war, and certainly had difficulties in becoming fisherman or owning a small business. When that money was over, many of them started to regroup,[34] obviously, outside the security framework of the Timorese state. In addition, a deep resentment emerged when these former fighters, which were not incorporated in the military, saw that many of the police officers that were being recruited, vetted and retrained, worked for the Indonesian force during the occupation, being former members of either the Indonesian army or police, while they, who fought for the Timorese independence, were unemployed (ICG, 2006).

A second strand has to do with another fundamental part of UN post-conflict reconstruction efforts—the Security Sector Reform (SSR). It results of tensions that were increasing within the army for some time. Kingsbury (2009: 142), for instance, remembers a long-standing disquiet within the F-FDTL in regard to several issues, such as (1) their status vis-à-vis the PNTL; (2) the general pay and conditions of the organization; (3) the lack of a clear purpose; and (4) a disappointment with the civilian politics. In addition, there were also tensions and divisions within the F-FDTL that date back to the guerrilla time.[35] It has to do, for instance, with the perceived role that each person had during the struggle for independence. The division had to do with the perceived degree of resistance to or connivance with the Indonesian occupation based on geographic distinctions, which divided the people between *Lorosae* (easterners in Tetum) and *Loromonu* (westerners in Tetum).

This division, which in fact did not have much of an echo within the Timorese society, was based on the assumption within the army that those of the resistance who were on the western side of the country, and therefore nearer of Indonesia, had a less prominent participation within the resistance movement or that their participation was less confrontational than those who were on the eastern side of the country who had a more confrontational approach toward the Indonesian occupation, a more prominent participation in the resistance movement, and therefore suffered more during the Indonesian rule (Kingsbury, 2009: 145–146). This was somewhat a false dichotomy, in the sense that easterners and westerners both resisted and were co-opted. Yet, this was something that was claimed by the soldiers; especially by the western soldiers (the majority of those recruited) in regard to the eastern F-FDTL leadership (Kingsbury, 2009: 145–146). Considering that the Timorese military force was in fact the conversion, on February 2001, of the former independence guerrilla force (Falintil) into an army force, this assumption was something that could easily lead to, or be the trigger of, deep tensions. Indeed, this was exactly what occurred. It was precisely this assumption that led to concrete dissatisfactions which had been externalized for a while in Timor-Leste and was downplayed and mismanaged. They include, for instance: (1) on December 2003, forty-two soldiers were discharged after complaining about unfair dismissals, travel distances and poor communications. There was a presidential commission, on August 2004, that suggested some improvements on these matters but they were not implemented; and (2) on February 26, 2005, there was a group of soldiers which started to raise some issues regarding discrimination and mismanagement directly with the President. Indeed, their complains were similar to the ones made, on January 2006, by the petitioners, which was the trigger of the 2006 crisis (ICG, 2008: 2).

The third strand also has to do with SSR; it is the strained relationship between the armed forces and the national police. Firstly, one should not forget the backbone of each organization. Whereas the police had several former Indonesian police officers, and even military, in its organization; the army had as its very core the former Timorese guerrilla men.[36] Therefore, there were in the country two organizations, that due to their ontology are armed, in which it is not hard to imagine that there were people who fought on different sides during the Indonesian invasion and occupation, and the Timorese resistance. In addition, the ICG (2008: 2) also draws attention to the fact that there were no concrete actions to approximate both institutions. As anecdotal as it may be, the ICG remembers that, in the eyes of the US State Department, the only actions that aimed at improving the relationship between the police and the army were a series of high-profile goodwill meetings and a football match that the president was the referee. Therefore, it is hardly not observable that having two, potentially rival, armed divisions of the state, in addition to limited efforts of narrowing the distance between the two and making them collaborate with each other, is the very recipe for a severe instability, to say the least.

In fact, this led to a deep-rooted tension between the two organizations that was externalized through many violent situations, which, in turn, feedback the tension. Indeed, although this tension exploded in the form of the violent events of the 2006 crisis, the crisis was in fact the culmination of a series of incidents that exposed this deep tension between the Timorese army and the national police (ICG, 2008). This tension had grown over the previous years with some incidents, such as the ones mentioned by the ICG: (1) on September 2003, the alleged assault on soldiers by a group of police officers which led to a confrontation at the police station in Dili; (2) on January 2004, clashes during a game of volleyball led to the detention of some police officers by soldiers in Los Palos; (3) on December 2004, soldiers looted the police station in Becora, where one of their officers was detained and allegedly mistreated (ICG, 2008: 2).

The forth strand has to do with a fundamental part of state-building efforts—the political environment. The UN simply neglected the political history of Timor-Leste. The events of 2006 might be also understood as grievances and differences, between Falintil and Fretilin, which dates back to the times of the resistance,[37] being brought into the government politics. During the crisis, it was more than clear that part of the political and the security elite saw it as a political opportunity (ICG, 2006: i). They understood it as an opportunity to, on the one hand, increase their own power, and, on the other hand, liberate their frustrations (Richmond and Franks, 2009: 97). At the surface, the beginning of the events, the dismissal of the soldiers in March 2006, might be understood as part of a power struggle between the PM, Mari Alkatiri, and the president, Xanana Gusmão[38] (ICG, 2006: i). Therefore, it could be seen as an attempt to both destabilize the Fretilin's government, which was led by Alkatiri, and the Xanana's ascendance over the military, since most of the army was personally loyal to him (he was the commander of the Falintil during the guerrilla time). The PM and the president certainly had their differences but they were part of a larger split between Falintil's commander, Xanan Gusmão, and the Fretilin's central committee. This difference is rooted in both political and ideological disputes within the resistance movement.

The origin of these disputes may be found in the early 1980s. Until that time, the politics was the major pillar of the resistance, which made Fretilin's central committee the resistance's most important body. From 1981 onward, the fighting increased in importance and actually superseded the politics.

Therefore, Xanana Gusmão took a larger role in the decision-making (ICG, 2006: 3). Xanana Gusmão, and other leaders, took some decisions that were far from popular among the hardliners of Fretilin, for instance: (1) to initiate negotiations with the Indonesians; (2) to reach out to the Catholic Church and to other parties; and (3) to abandon Marxism in order to increase the united front (ICG, 2006: 3). In 1984, a split took place; some senior members of Falintil, that were also members of the Fretilin's central committee, tried a failed a coup attempt against Xanana Gusmão. Still in 1984, Xanana Gusmão, made another decision that was badly received by the Fretilin's central committee, and lead to another split—he proposed the dissociation of the Falintil from the Fretilin, which was only accepted on December 7th, 1987 (ICG, 2006: 3–4). This dissociation in practice meant that the political side of the resistance was concentrated in the diaspora, with pivotal members of the central committee based in Angola and Mozambique, and the armed side remained in the country and became undoubtedly loyal to Xanana Gusmão. This might be seen as a built-in divide between Fretilin and the military, and consequently Xanana Gusmão[39] (ICG, 2006: 4). In fact, this division had profound implications for the Timorese politics after its independence and still has repercussions nowadays.[40]

Lastly, but certainly not less important, another significant strand has to do with another pivotal element of UN state-building process in Timor-Leste—its socio-economic dimension. The fifth strand is the very environment in which all these events took place. As it was already portrayed, the Timorese socio-economic reality was, and certainly still is, in a desperate condition. Just to give an idea, the 2006 crisis found solid ground to be initiated and to develop in a country where the Human Development Index (HDI) was very low (UNDP, 2006a: 286). Furthermore, the level of poverty was, and still is, very high. Timor-Leste was the poorest country in the region with a *per capita* income of only $370 a year (UNDP, 2006c: 1). In fact, few years earlier in 2001, around 40 percent of the population lived below the poverty line of $0.55 *per capita* per day (percentage higher in rural areas), and the situation barely changed (UNDP, 2006c: 2). More strikingly, 64 percent of the population suffered from food insecurity (UNDP, 2006c: 1).

In an environment such as this, life expectancy can hardly be high. In Timor-Leste, it was estimated at only 55.5 years (54.0 years for men and 56.6 years for women) (UNDP, 2006c: 1). The population was still vulnerable to respiratory, diarrheal diseases, malaria, dengue fever, TB, and leprosy (UNDP, 2006c: 1). In regard to education, the situation was also very difficult. The adult literacy rate was only 50.1 percent (56.3 percent for men and 43.9 percent for women) (UNDP, 2006c: 1). The unemployment rate was around 9 percent, but in urban areas, such as Dili, it could reach around 30 percent (UNDP, 2006c: ii; 8). This figure was much worse among the youth; where it reached 23 percent (UNDP, 2006c: 8) and could be more than 43 percent among urban youth (WB, 2005: 19). This figure was especially disturbing because in such environment with no opportunities and as severe as this one, the martial gangs became much more attractive to the youth, which could be very destabilizing. Therefore, it was not hard to imagine that, in such socio-economic picture, a very small sparkle could literally light Timor-Leste on fire.

Notwithstanding all the concerns that the SG had, one should not forget that by this time Timor-Leste was presented to the whole world as a case of success. Therefore, this was a crisis perceived to be more than a threat to the stability of the newly independent state. Most importantly to the organization's image, the violent events were deemed to be a threat to the credibility of various UN officials pointing Timor-Leste as a success story (Richmond and Franks, 2009: 84). Indeed, what was at stake here, and therefore threatened, was the organization's credibility as an effective conflict-transformation actor and the very rationale which underpins its actions. Nevertheless, the very fact that these strands were neglected, the crisis happened, and that the Timorese institutions simply disintegrated during the events supports the understanding of state-building processes being in fact state-failure ones.

CONCLUSION

This chapter discusses the UN engagement with Timor-Leste through the analysis of the main elements and characteristics of UN peace operations deployed to the country. This elucidation is important to give a panoramic view of the whole UN reconstruction effort in Timor-Leste, which was an effort of creating a liberal peace in Timor-Leste through the instrument of state-building. In addition, the chapter evinces two fundamental characteristics of the UN engagement with Timor-Leste. The first characteristic is the linear mindset underpinning the UN conflict-resolution rationale that characterizes the whole engagement with the country, which made use of nearly all peace instruments at its repertoire—from peacemaking to peacebuilding. The second pivotal characteristic evinced is the reactive nature of the UN engagement. Rather than pursuing a preventive approach, the structural changes, modifications and extensions of the missions throughout the UN engagement with Timor-Leste are mere reactions to what was happening on the ground. The chapter also sheds light on the some structural shortcomings of the whole UN state-building process in Timor-Leste. Most importantly, the chapter evinces, after delineating the 2006 crisis, the several strands of Timorese reality that were neglected by the UN during its state-building process in Timor-Leste and culminated in the crisis. Hence, through the delineation of them, the chapter exposes not only that the UN overlooked fundamental dimensions of the Timorese reality, but also the apparent contradiction that, in Timor-Leste, its state-building process ended up being in fact a state failure one. Paradoxically, the appearance of Timor-Leste as a successful case is fundamental to the UN. Due to the depth of the UN engagement with the country—the number of missions (and their several extensions), their duration and depth and the range of peace instruments deployed—Timor-Leste *has* to be understood internationally as a successful case. Otherwise the whole conflict-resolution rationale and peacebuilding approach of the UN, and the very reputation of the UN as a conflict transformation actor, would be in check.

NOTES

1. Xanana Gusmão won with 82.69 percent of the votes and run against Francisco Xavier do Amaral, who was the first president of Timor-Leste and had 17.31 percent of the votes on that election (UN, 2002b).

2. The UN already had similar missions, such as UNTAC (United Nations Transitional Authority in Cambodia) in Cambodia and UNMIK (United Nations Interim Administration Mission in Kosovo) in Kosovo. Nevertheless, UNTAET was much deeper than them (Richmond and Franks, 2009: 87).

3. The Force was consisted of a 2500-man-strong force composed by Australian, New Zealander and Malaysian troops, in addition to a large contingent of Australian Federal Police (AFP) officers (CIGI, 2009: 3; Richmond and Franks, 2009: 84). Portugal also sent a bilateral force composed by members of its National Guard (GNR—*Guarda Nacional Republicana* in Portuguese).

4. The extensions were all on 2006 (S/RES/1677; S/RES/1690; S/RES/1703).

5. The extensions were: (1) on 2007 (S/RES/1745), (2) on 2008 (S/RES/1802), (3) on 2009 (S/RES/1867), (4) on 2010 (S/RES/1912), (5) on 2011 (S/RES/1969), and finally (6) on 2012 (S/RES/2037).

6. The presidential elections had two rounds: the first one happening on April 9th and the second one on May 9th 2007. The parliamentary elections happened on June 30th 2007.

7. For the detailed results of each candidate of the presidential elections of 2007, see (STAE, 2007b).

8. For the detailed results of the parliamentary elections of 2007, see (STAE, 2007a).

9. The Presidential elections took place on March–April 2012; the first round on March 17th and the second round on April 16th 2012. The Parliament elections took place on July 7th 2012.

10. For the detailed results of each candidate of the presidential elections of 2012, see (STAE, 2012).

11. At that time, CNRT had Xanana Gusmão as President and José Ramos-Horta and Mario Carrascalão as Vice-Presidents.

12. Part of the research of this section was developed under the European-Union-funded COST Short Term Scientific Mission at the Brussels-based think-tank GRIP (*Groupe de Recherche et d'Information sur la Paix et la Sécurité*) under the reference ECOST-STSM-IS0805-050911-007628.

13. For more in regard to the phases of a conflict, see for instance (Ramsbotham, Woodhouse and Miall, 2005: 11–12).

14. As it will be further explored later on the book, the Secretary-General's reports to the Security Council (SGRSC) constitute a valuable instrument of making the situation in Timor-Leste visible, and a valuable instrument to asses, monitor and correct the conducts performed on the ground. The missions, and consequently the actions on the field, were constantly monitored by these recurrent reports and properly adjusted based on them.

15. In order to see the numbers of the seats won by each of the parties on the election race, see for instance (UN, 2001).

16. This movement, lead by Fretilin, still has important repercussions on current Timorese political scene. Two examples of it, to name a few, are for instance: (1) Xanana Gusmão forming majority government with other minority parties, and bypassing Fretilin on the 2007 legislative elections, notwithstanding the fact that Fretilin actually won the elections; and (2) Xanana Gusmão forming a government coalition with other parties and possibly leaving Fretilin out of its next government, notwithstanding the fact that Fretilin was second-voted party on the last 2012 legislative elections.

17. These advisers would be divided in: "19 advisers in the area of finance, 16 in other key ministries, including those related to security, and 8 within other organs of government. It would also include 15 advisers in justice-related areas, including 7 acting judges and judge mentors" (S/2004/333: 6).

18. The advisers would essentially mentor and train the Timorese police, in light of the understanding that this process was based, in line with international standards of policing, on the reinforcement of human rights and rule of law (S/2004/333: 9).

19. It should be noted that these martial arts groups is something that have its origins in the late 1980s during the Indonesian occupation. Therefore, they are neither new nor completely outside the political framework. Some of these martial arts groups, in 2006, were even linked to established political parties—such as the Fretilin, the PD (*Partido Democrático*; Democratic Party in Portuguese), or the PSD (*Partido Social Democrata*; Social Democratic Party in Portuguese), to name a few—the security forces, pro-Indonesia militia, or were led by forms resistance fighters, such as the Colimau 2000, CPD-RDTL, Orsnaco, and the Sagrada Famiglia (Kingsbury, 2009: 153; Scambary, 2006: 4). The discussion of these groups is something that is outside the scope of this book. For more in regard to this subject, see for instance (Kingsbury, 2009: 144–145; 152–153; Scambary, 2006).

20. For more on the 2008 attack, see for instance (Tanter, 2008).

21. The first round of presidential elections took place on March 17th and the second round on April 16th, 2012. The parliament elections took place on July 7th, 2012.

22. The author was an international electoral observer during the parliamentary elections.

23. For a decisive biographical account of Sérgio Vieira de Mello, see for instance (Power, 2008).

24. This is perhaps another result of the disturbing fact that just nearly 10 percent of the assistance allocated to Timor-Leste, July 1999–June 2009 actually reached Timorese economy. For the detailed numbers, see for instance (La'o Hamutuk, 2009).

25. For the numeric of the index see (Richmond, 2011: 218–219).

26. During the first quarter of 2012, the fund was estimated to have nearly US$ 10 billion. For a detailed account of the Timor-Leste Petroleum Fund, see for instance (La'o Hamutuk, 2012).

27. For deeper and concise view of the Timorese statistical profile in regard to the Socio-Economic Development, see for instance (UN, 2011c).

28. For a deeper understanding of the events, see, for instance (Curtain, 2006; ICG, 2006, 2008; Kingsbury, 2009: 138–153; Richmond and Franks, 2009: 89–93).

29. This division will be further explained later in this chapter.

30. He is the current president of Timor-Leste.

31. The organization had no experience in crowd control.

32. For more in regard to his participation in the crisis, se for instance (ICG, 2006: 9–11). It should be noted also that this man also took part on another violent event that happened in Timor-Leste—the murder attempt of the president, José Ramos-Horta, and the prime minister, Xanana Gusmão, in 2008.

33. The amount of this financial assistance was US$ 550 and was part of the FRAP program.

34. Personal Interview, Luís Bernardino, Major of the Portuguese Army (Coimbra, May 16th, 2012).

35. Personal Interview. Nelson Belo, Director of the Timorese NGO *Fundasaun Mahein* (Mahein Foundation in Tetum) (Dili, July 3rd, 2012).

36. The very name of the Timorese armed force, Falintil- Forças de Defesa de Timor-Leste (F-FDTL), is preceded by the name of the armed arm of the Timorese resistance—Falintil.

37. Personal Interview. Nelson Belo, Director of the Timorese NGO *Fundasaun Mahein* (Mahein Foundation in Tetum) (Dili, July 3rd 2012). For a more detailed account of these splits, see for instance (ICG, 2006: 2–5).

38. Indeed, the whole situation became quite worse after an incendiary speech gave by Xanana Gusmão on March 23rd 2006, which clearly collided with the government's decision of dismissing the soldiers (ICG, 2006: 7–8).

39. Another example, still in this strand and related to the splits between Fretilin's central committee and Xanana Gusmão that might be pointed is the case of Rogério Lobato. He was a member of the committee, lived in Angola and Mozambique during the Indonesian occupation, and, as interior minister, he controlled the police. He use to encourage rivalry with the defence force, who were loyal to Xanana Gusmão, and also used the events of the crisis to continue it and also try to increase his power (ICG, 2006: i).

40. Indeed, it is not hard to hear in Timor-Leste that the country is only calm and stable when there is understanding between its three big figures: Xanana Gusmão, Mari Alkatiri, and José Ramos-Horta; otherwise, there is the potential for instability.

Chapter Four

The UN Surveillance Framework

Steering, Monitoring, and Structuring Timor-Leste

This chapter delineates the surveillance framework which is fundamental to rendering operational the normalization process pursued in the country. The normalization *dispositif* under which Timor-Leste is subject to be merely operational and to in fact function must be accompanied by the setting up of a series of steering, monitoring, and structuring instruments which are dispersed throughout and over Timor-Leste. These enable not only the monitoring of the conducts of the Timorese state and its population, but especially their shaping and, most importantly, the proper correction of these behaviors whenever necessary. Nevertheless, notwithstanding its importance to the functioning of the normalization *dispositif*, these instruments are by no means unified or centralized. On the contrary, they are highly decentralized, present in multiple sites, and quite often they have no direct relation at all with each other. Nonetheless, when understood collectively and within the theoretical framework advanced by Michel Foucault, these instruments form a surveillance framework that is pivotal to the normalizing assemblage operating in Timor-Leste.

This surveillance framework is a crucial element to the close monitoring of the Timorese conducts since it places Timor-Leste under constant and frequent scrutiny and observation. This framework enables those intervening to assess whether Timor-Leste, as a country, and its population, are being conducted toward a certain direction, and whether they are conducting themselves accordingly. It further enables state-builders to ensure that Timor-Leste conducts are heading toward a convenient end. A pivotal point in regard to these surveillance instruments is that they might appear at first as merely technical, institutional, and bureaucratic instruments, as normal and

117

natural ones. However, these instruments place Timor-Leste inside a disciplinary mechanism, which is formed by several individual instruments that are
interrelated and that collectively underpins a power framework that seeks to
normalize Timor-Leste. These instruments work in two dimensions—from
outside and from within the country. Although it is difficult to clearly dissociate the two dimensions, since most of the instruments perform on both of
them, it is possible to observe that some instruments were designed to work
more on the steering, monitoring and structuring of the conducts of Timor-
Leste as a state, while others were better designed to work on the surveillance
and structuring of the conducts within the fundamental spheres within the
Timorese state, such as the disciplinary, political, and economic governance,
and the socio- and biopolitical spheres. Furthermore, it can be also observed
that whereas some instruments were designed to work on several spheres at
once, others were designed to deal more with a specific sphere. Nevertheless,
rather than seeking to understand each surveillance instrument individually,
it is more instructive to understand them collectively working in an interrelated manner to form a surveillance framework supervising Timor-Leste.

The presence of such instruments is widespread within the UN relationship with Timor-Leste. Nevertheless, not all of them are essential to the
functioning of the normalization *dispositif* deployed to Timor-Leste. There
are certainly surveillance instruments that are clearly more important than
others. Indeed, some of them are pivotal and essential to the very functioning, and are the very structure, of the normalizing *dispositif* under which
Timor-Leste is subject. This chapter delineates the functioning and the role
of these ones. In order to explore such surveillance instruments, the chapter
is structured in six sections, each one dealing with the functioning of one of
these instruments; respectively: (1) the Secretary-General's Report to the
Security Council; (2) the National Priorities Program; (3) the UNDP Assistance Framework; (4) the Police Arrangement; the Monthly and Local
Governance Reports; and, finally, (5) the Index of Laws of Timor-Leste and
the Accountability Mechanism of Key Institutions.

THE SECRETARY-GENERAL'S
REPORTS TO THE SECURITY COUNCIL

The Secretary-General Reports to the Security Council (SGRsSC) is a key
surveillance instrument which used by the UN to monitor and steer its engagement with Timor-Leste. These reports might be loosely described as a
sort of UN communication channel between the Secretary General and the
Security Council. This is one of the channels, perhaps the most relevant one,
in which the Secretary General, on a regular basis, keeps in touch with the
SC and exposes to the members his/her approach on peace and security

issues. These reports are usually submitted pursuant to statements of the president of the SC, resolutions of the council, or due to the direct request of the body. They can go from elaborating on issues such as the rule of law and transitional justice in conflict and post-conflict societies, to civilian capacity in the aftermath of a conflict, passing through the role of women on peace and security. However, the most frequent, and possibly the most pressing, topic addressed is related to UN peace operations on the field. These reports are a pivotal instrument to the SC in New York so its members can have a clearer picture of how things designed on the mandates are progressing on the field. This is a crucial way for the SC to observe the impacts on the field of its decisions and of the mandates and how to correct them whenever deemed necessary. Therefore, the SG's reports dealing with UN peace operation in the field are important in several aspects. They are fundamental to the disciplinary process carried out by the UN while seeking to normalize the conflict or post-conflict state.

In regard to Timor-Leste, the SG report is an instrument which was operational throughout the whole UN engagement with the country—from its very beginning while monitoring the May 5th Agreements (and their implementation) to the assessments of later UN peace operations.[1] This report operates as a sophisticated instrument of not only periodically making sure that the Timorese state is actually behaving as it is expected and designed, by the UN, but also of signaling where and when corrections on its conducts might be exercised. Hence, as it was aforementioned, the SG report is a pivotal instrument in the normalization process sought by the UN in Timor-Leste. Its importance in Timor-Leste, as in other post-conflict states, is fivefold, all interrelated.

First, the SG's reports are important as an individualizing mechanism. Usually, the SG's reports deal with only *one* post-conflict country and assess it in depth. The report observes the several spheres that are being addressed by the peace operation deployed and assesses each one in depth. This allows each post-conflict country to be observed individually. It is through this instrument that from a mass of several post-conflict states one state can be singled out as an individual post-conflict state to be assessed individually and consequently normalized. Therefore, it is the SG reports that enables the UN to individualize Timor-Leste;[2] to treat Timor-Leste as an individual entity within the international system. It is only by this process that the country can be turned into an individual case to be dealt with. This individualization mechanism is crucial to the normalization process, since what is sought in a normalization process is to shape and alter the behaviors of an individual. This might appear somewhat paradoxical since in a normalization process the individual is shaped in relation to others, to the normal ones. Nevertheless, notwithstanding the fact that this individual is sought to be conducted in relation to others, in the end, it is a set of behaviors of an individual that is sought to be corrected, to be normalized. Indeed, all the SGRsSC in regard to Timor-Leste dealt solely with Timor-Leste and with the UN peace operations established on Timorese soil. Hence, although the actions toward Timor-Leste were always related to other states (how normal states should behave in the international system), it is the Timorese situation that is observed in depth and individually. This is what enables the Timorese condition, and its respective missions, to be dealt with individually by the Security Council. It is due to this individuality that the Timorese behavior can be observed and properly corrected.

Second, the SG reports are important regarding the construction of a field of visibility. It is through the SG reports that the SC and its members actually see what peacebuilders understand as the reality on the ground of a determinate peace operation. It is through these reports that the SC members get familiarized with what is happening in the countries where UN peace operations are deployed during the period covered by the report. This is one of the pivotal instruments that enable the reality in the field to be periodically rendered visible to the SC. In fact, it is only after seeing this reality that the Security Council can act accordingly. In Timor-Leste, this is what enables the reality in the country to become visible to the SC members, therefore constructing a field of visibility to the SC members, so they can shape and correct properly several spheres of Timor-Leste. Along the several SG reports that dealt with Timor-Leste, it is observable that the reports dealt, in a great amount of detail, with a very wide set of spheres of action of the Timorese state and its population. These areas are distinct as governance and public administration, political developments, humanitarian assistance, capacity-building efforts, social processes, administration of justice, security reforms, infrastructure, biopolitical processes such as health and education, jobs, and gender, among other. Usually, the reports are divided by big staring clusters, such as structuring a functioning public administration, political and security developments, economy and infrastructure, promotion of human rights and justice, socio-economic development, or culture of democratic governance and dialogue, followed by a respective disaggregation of key subjects inside these clusters. This division has a very close relation with the SC mandate and with the Council's own requests regarding the areas that it wants to be assessed. In this way the UN is able to provide an analysis both wide and deep regarding Timor-Leste and its reality. Indeed, this is a way of the SC not only keep a close attention whether, and how, its mandate is being implemented, but above all, exam whether the Timorese state is actually making the proper changes that the UN is seeking. This can go from, and be as diverse as, the kind of legislation that is passing in the parliament to the criminal rates of the country or the gender quota within the Timorese police force (among innumerous examples, see for instance S/2011/641). Hence, what happens is that several actions of the Timorese state within a wide range of spheres turn out to be not only visible but in fact under UN surveillance. Since the UN, through these reports, see whether the Timorese state is in fact conducting itself accordingly and can scrutinize several spheres, in the end, it is the whole country that is put under UN surveillance.

Third, the SG reports are also pivotal due to its monitoring character. The reports' monitoring mechanism is clearly not dissociable from the former mechanisms, since they are the ones that enable the proper monitoring of the developments on the ground. Since the SG reports elaborate, and render visible, the several areas which are under UN intervention, it is possible to measure performances, to measure how good or bad the implementation of the mandate, and the whole peace operation, is progressing. This is fundamental as an examination and progress assessment instrument, which is fundamental for future corrections that might take place within the peace operation. In Timor-Leste, this monitoring aspect is clear observable since several aspects of the conducts of the Timorese on several spheres were under UN close observation. In addition, an essential element of this monitoring aspect is not only the range of the spheres under close watch, although this is certainly pivotal, but also the frequency and the regularity of the monitoring. In order to a normalization process to be effective, those under this kind of practice should be, and also *know* that they are, frequently and regularly monitored. Indeed, the SC, on its mandates regarding Timor-Leste, expressly requests the SG to regularly inform of developments on the ground and in regard to the implementation of its mandates. Furthermore, even the timeframe in which the SG should monitor the Timorese situation is expressly requested. During the period of over a decade of UN intervention in the country, there were almost forty SG reports focusing on Timor-Leste. Taking the whole period into account, a simple average indicates that the SG presented a report every four months. However, in the case of Timor-Leste, there are periods where the reporting was much more intense, whereas during other periods the reporting was less regular. In the very beginning of the UN engagement with Timor-Leste, for instance, the SG issued a report almost on a monthly basis. On the opposite pole, there were also reports that took five, seven, and also eight months, from the previous report, to be released by the SG. However, they are the minority of the reports issued. Indeed, the vast majority of the reports were released three, four or six months after the previous report. In fact, more than half of all the SG reports on Timor-Leste were presented either three or six months after the previous report one. This indicates a clear consistency of the monitoring mechanisms and how close it was. Most importantly, this is a significant indication that the UN was monitoring Timorese conducts closely and constantly, which not only placed Timor-Leste under UN surveillance but its very actions under a periodic and constant international examination.

Fourth, the SG reports work also as an essential progress assessment mechanism. The SC, on its mandates, expressly requests these reports to be formulated by the SG, explicitly indicating both the timeframe in which the SG should deliver his report and the areas which the SC wants to have a progress assessment. Indeed, this request is pervasive through SC mandates regarding Timor-Leste as a way to perform a progress assessment of the Timorese conducts. Therefore, the SG reports play an essential role not only on placing Timor-Leste under surveillance and monitoring it, but also on evaluating how its conducts are being performed. In fact, this is a manner in which the SC scrutinizes whether the Timorese are conducting themselves accordingly to what was stipulated by the SC mandates regarding the several spheres observed by the reports. This is not something concealed or subliminal. Strikingly, several SG reports on Timor-Leste are literally named progress report. It is through this instrument that the UN sees whether Timor-Leste is behaving accordingly and also where corrections, regarding the Timorese conducts, may be needed.

Last, as obvious as it may sound, the SGRsSC are fundamental also due to their reporting character. There is no doubt that the UN has many other reporting mechanisms in order to inform the SC.[3] Nevertheless, the SGRSC is certainly a crucial one not only due to its regularity and broad area of scrutiny, but also because of the fact that it is delivered by a high-level office. This is important because, based on the progress assessment of what is working or not in the field, SG suggests corrections and adjustments to further UN actions on the ground are more likely to be accepted. Consequently, the SC regularly changes or creates new mandates based on recommendations formulated by the SG on his reports. Therefore, the SGRsSC did not merely report what was happening in Timor-Leste. Based on their progress assessment, they also proposed suggestions and modifications to the peace operation's mandate in the field. The SG, through his reports, made detailed recommendations regarding the future mandates ranging from activities to be performed to the size, structure and budget of the missions. In turn, the SC frequently not only acknowledged or welcomed the SG recommendations, but in fact incorporated them on the next mission mandate. As chapter 4 clearly evinced, in Timor-Leste this pattern was clear and present on SC mandates. In this way, not only the UN assessed the conducts of the Timorese state and its populations, but it was also able to make corrections where these behaviors were not conforming to what was expected. In other words, it is through this instrument that the UN, in light of progresses or regressions on the field, could actually modify its structuring and conducting toward Timor-Leste in order to seek to correct the conducts of the Timorese state and its population, so they could start conducting themselves normally.

At this point, it is clear that the SGRsSC are a pivotal piece of a larger process. These dynamics of rendering visible, individualizing, monitoring/

assessing, reporting, and correcting is clearly a disciplinary mechanism resembling those explored by Michel Foucault in his studies. While in Foucault's analysis the disciplinary mechanisms sought to discipline the deviant behaviors of the lepers, the poor, and the delinquent, in the international scenario it seeks to normalize the abnormal post-conflict states. It is in this context that the SGRsSC play an essential role; in regard to Timor-Leste, the SGRsSC is a fundamental instrument within the normalization process sought by the UN in the country. With it, Timor-Leste is placed within a network that might appear as merely technical, institutional or bureaucratic. However, these reports are far from being a part of a mere bureaucratic process; they position Timor-Leste inside a surveillance framework of a disciplinary process formed by several individual mechanisms—rendering visible, individualizing, monitoring/assessing, reporting, and correcting—that are interrelated and that collectively form a power framework that seeks to normalize the country. Indeed, in the case of Timor-Leste, the SGRSC was a refined instrument for rendering the Timorese reality visible and functioning as a steering and monitoring instrument of its normalization process, providing, therefore, updated and relevant information and recommendations so the SC could adjust the Timorese conduct whenever deemed necessary. Therefore, rather than a mere UN procedural process, the SGRSC is a crucial instrument of the normalizing state-building *dispositif* deployed by the UN which sought to shape, alter, and conduct Timorese behaviors so the country can be transformed into what is construed as a normal state within the international scenario.

Despite the fact that the SGRsSC play a central role in the normalization process sought by the UN, this process could not function properly without other complementing surveillance instruments. Apart from structuring and conducting the conducts of Timor-Leste as a state, and therefore ensuring that the country follows the proper and normal behavior of a country within the international system; in order to be more effective, the UN normalization process makes use of other instruments that follow the same rationale presented but work within the Timorese state. Although they are very much decentralized and quite often not related at all, it is important to notice that, combined, they are a part of an assemblage that places Timor-Leste into a framework of power that seeks to visualize, scrutinize, oversee, monitor, and correct several aspects of the country; seeking, in the end, both from within and from outside Timor-Leste, to normalize the country. Hence, it is important to shed some light on some of these instruments.

THE NATIONAL PRIORITIES PROGRAM

Another surveillance instrument worth mentioning is the National Priorities Program (NPP). This is, in fact, a Timorese mechanism within the Timorese state. NPP is an institutional mechanism that was created in order to face the challenges posed by the 2006 and 2008 crisis. Among other issues, the Timorese Government that took office in the beginning of August 2007 had to deal with several complex issues, such as: sixty-five IDP camps in Dili and the surrounding areas; nearly 400 former F-FDTL asking (sometimes violently) for their return to the military; the threat posed by Major Alfredo Reinaldo and his militia; martial arts gangs engaging in a series of violent acts; and a shrinking economy (Ministry of Finance, 2010: 11) to name just a few. Organized around a Secretariat and Working Groups (WG) focusing each on a determinate national priority, this was a mechanism designed essentially to construct the Timorese national priorities, through the prioritization of the Timorese challenges, and to plan, in an organized manner, the overcoming of these challenges. NPP was created, as a mechanism to enable the Timorese Government to primarily focus on these challenges and on the restoration of the public institutions (Ministry of Finance, 2010: 12). Therefore, this would be essentially a mechanism that would help the Timorese government to set the Timorese national priorities so the proper actions and focuses could be followed. Hence, it is fair to understand this mechanism as an instrument of national-priorities-building, where the Timorese national priorities are constructed. Indeed, for the UN, these national priorities were the pivotal instrument for the planning and implementation of the policies carried out by the Timorese government (Ministry of Finance, 2010: 12). Not surprisingly, the NPP would be, propagated by the UN, as a comprehensive planning and monitoring mechanism (UN, N/A-m). The Timorese National Priorities from 2008 to 2010 were: (1) for 2008—NP1: Public Safety and Security, NP2: Social Protection and Solidarity, NP3: Addressing the Needs of Youth, NP4: Employment and Income Generation, NP5: Improving Social Service Delivery, NP6: Clean and Effective Government; (2) for 2009—NP1: Food Security and Agriculture, NP2: Rural Development, NP3: Human Resources Development, NP4: Social Services and Social Protection, NP5: Public Safety and Security, NP6: Clean and Effective Government, NP7: Access to Justice; and (3) for 2010—NP1: Roads and Water (Infrastructure), NP2: Food Security (Focus on Productivity), NP3: Human Resources Development, NP4: Access to Justice, NP5: Social Services and Decentralized Services Delivery, NP6: Good Governance, NP7: Safety and Security (Ministry of Finance, 2010: 14).

Nevertheless, this is not the whole picture. NPP also functioned as an important entry point for international influence over the Timorese state and as an UN surveillance instrument in the sense that the UN sought to use it as a manner of shaping Timorese conducts not from outside the country but from within Timor-Leste. This can quite clearly be understood as an instrument for the UN not only influence the very process of setting the priorities, but also for monitoring the state actions in regard to the achievement of the priorities set. This was a direct consequence of the very structure of the mechanism. As mentioned, NPP was designed along two main elements: (1) a Secretariat, which was under the Ministry of Finance; and (2) the Working Groups (WGs), each one focusing on one national priority. The UN presence, and influence, is pervasive throughout the whole mechanism. Its influence was felt both in the Secretariat, whose main role is to coordinate, support with policy recommendations, and also monitor the overall process of building the Timorese national priorities, since it is a body assisted by the UN and other international actors; and in the Working Groups, which can be understood as a forum where different actors—such as ministries, secretaries of state, autonomous agencies, other branches of government, as well as development partners and international actors (not only the UN and its agencies/ programs, but also international financial institutions, and other states)— meet around a specific national priority. Due to the organization of the Working Groups, it was not uncommon for the UNMIT or a UN agency—like the WFP, UNICEF, or UNDP—to co-lead a Working Group.

The Secretariat is a body that, although led by the Ministry of Finance, is assisted by international experts from the World Bank and the UN and AusAID which has as its mains objective to make policy recommendations, focusing also on performance issues (Ministry of Finance, 2010: 13). It was the role of the Secretariat to provide assistance, regular monitoring and follow-ups to the Working Groups (UN, N/A-m). Meeting on a regular basis, each of these WGs is headed by a Timorese ministry, with the assistance of one or more than one international actor, which serves as lead assistants or co-leaders (Ministry of Finance, 2010: 13; UN, N/A-m). This is the case, for instance, of the UNMIT in the WG dealing with security (WG five in 2009) or the UNDP with the WG of the justice (WG seven in the same year) (UN, N/A-m). Consequently, each of the working groups identifies several objectives and targets that will be pursued in regard to each national priority and compile them into a matrix. Apart from this, the Secretariat also established a set of monitoring, tracking and evaluation systems in order to guide the WGs and to ensure that all WGs follow a common standard of operational performance (Ministry of Finance, 2010: 13). In this way, not only the work of each WG is under supervision and also monitored but also, and especially, the pursuit of the national priorities.[4]

The National Priorities Program might look like a mere institutional forum where a consensus-building is sought around what the Timorese national priorities should be and a bureaucratic mechanism where proper projects and actions in order to achieve each of them are thought. This might even be seen simply as a technical device built in order to harmonize and coordinate objectives, resources and actors toward the goals set in terms of national priorities, and an instrument to effectively analyze the proper progress of the projects and whether the goals set are being achieved or not. All of this is in fact true. In fact, this is a state management mechanism that might even be found in several states. Nevertheless, there is also another side to all this. There are at least two main points that should be also brought into light in regard to this mechanism, namely: (1) that this becomes a surveillance instrument through which Timorese state's actions turns out to be under a close international supervision; and (2) in line with other areas where the UN exercised its power, a deep amount of influence was exercised by international experts in a fundamental and structuring element of the process of building Timorese political policies.

In regard to the first point, the mechanism is recognized by the Timorese government, as an important tool to guide the government development efforts as well as to facilitate the engagement with international actors while strengthening their relationship (Ministry of Finance, 2010: 12). Therefore, this mechanism actually guides and directs the Timorese actions in terms of the projects elaborated and public policies formulated. However, the other side of this is that given the fact that this is a mechanism also constituted by major international actors—like the UN and its agencies, international financial institutions, and also national development agencies of other states like AusAID or USAID—a direct consequence of this constitution is that all the actions of the Timorese state immediately become under a close international watch. Rather than a mere bureaucratic mechanism, the National Priorities Program enables the international state-builders, those intervening in Timor-Leste, to have a great surveillance power over the Timorese state's actions, and therefore monitor and shape them accordingly. This is a mechanism that rather than a technical arrangement, it enables a close international scrutiny of the Timorese conducts.

Just as it will be further discussed in the next section, which deals with the United Nations Development Assistance Framework (UNDAF), this is done namely through the following elements: (1) the delineation of the goals and objectives, with their respective targets, to be achieved; (2) the clear temporization of each target, namely quarterly; and (3) the specification of where each actor involved is expected to act, in a clear delineation of responsibilities.[5] In addition to them, as it would be expectable, a whole set of tracking and evaluation systems were in place to ensure the proper progress of the activities. This is composed by "regular working group meetings/ monthly reports, analytical quarterly progress summaries, and a peer review every six months" (UN, N/A-m). Indeed, all these elements combined form a "robust monitoring framework" (UN, N/A-m). This robust monitoring framework not only servers the Timorese government to guide its own actions, but, obviously silently, also places its very actions under international scrutiny. It places Timor-Leste under a surveillance framework that makes visible what kind of policies the Timorese are pursuing and whether the Timorese are progressing accordingly or not; a framework that enables the shaping of the Timorese conducts so it can behave accordingly and in the end become a normal state within the international scenario.

In regard to the second point aforementioned—the influence exercised by international experts in a highly important and also structuring aspect of the Timorese political policy and policy-building—here again is perceived the normalizing power being exercised through the very role of the international experts through the already known power-denying notions like supporting, advising, capacity-building and so on. At this point, it is already well known that in post-conflict scenarios the international experts influence not only the implementation of national policies already designed by the national authorities, but also the very designing of these policies. In Timor-Leste, and also in other post-conflict countries, this went as far as these international experts actually being the authorities designing and implementing public policies. Observing the National Priorities Program it is visible that the influence of the international experts took a step further, by becoming institutionalized and highly influencing key processes of the Timorese political policy, such as, for instance, the process of thinking about what should be the national priorities, the process of setting these national priorities and also the process of pursuing the national priorities established.

Both points aforementioned place the international actors in a very privileged position within a fundamental state management mechanism that is hardly seen in an independent state. This, of course, does not mean that the international experts actually *decide* what will be the Timorese national priorities or the policies that it will be elaborated to accomplish the established targets. Nevertheless, they certainly seek to influence such decisions. Even further, the most important point here is to bring to light that the great amount of influence exercised by international state-builders—over the process of setting the Timorese national priorities and the achievement of them—is as deep as being even institutionalized in Timor-Leste. As already mentioned before, these priorities are references that guide the very public policies that will be designed in order to overcome the Timorese challenges. Consequently, through the influence over the process of setting these priorities and the priorities itself, the direct control and influence of the policies becomes less necessary (notwithstanding, this direct control does not disappear from the relationship between the Timorese and the internationals), since the influence was already exercised at the origin of the process; where it will structure these policies. Hence, what is seen with the NPP mechanism is the internationals exercising a high amount of power through the shaping and influencing, and perhaps most importantly the supervision, of key elements of the process of defining a pivotal element of a sovereign state—its own national priorities.

Attentively thinking about the National Priorities Program then, rather than a pure institutional bureaucracy that merely seeks to synchronize and bring together different objectives, projects and actors, the National Priorities Program, due to its own composition in regard to the presence of international actors and their relevance in the process, can also function as another surveillance instrument through which the Timorese state's actions becomes under a very close observation by international actors and under a great amount of influence by them. The framework and the *modus operandi* of the instrument in fact place all the actions of the Timorese government under a regular and periodic international scrutiny, placing a fundamental structure of Timor-Leste under an uninterrupted international examination and surveillance. Furthermore, observing this mechanism it is also observable that the Timorese actions are not only under a close scrutiny, but also its own process of deciding its own national priorities is under a severe amount of influence by international experts. Hence, this mechanism, more importantly, enables not only the conducting of the Timorese state by influencing the delineation of its own national priorities, but also the proper monitoring of the Timorese government actions in order to ensure that in the end, Timor, as a state, is more effectively normalized and therefore starts behaving accordingly in the international sphere.

THE UNITED NATIONS DEVELOPMENT ASSISTANCE FRAMEWORK

Another important surveillance instrument of the UN engagement with Timor-Leste is the United Nations Development Assistance Framework (UNDAF).[6] UNDAF is a UN document that is a key instrument for the UN action on the field, since it constitutes a framework where the actions of distinct actors on the field can become not only more operational but also more coherent. Nevertheless, rather than a mere technical UN instrument that seeks to harmonize different actors strategies/policies/activities and divergent objectives into a coherent platform, the UNDAF is pivotal for the normalizing state-building *dispositif* operating in Timor-Leste. The importance of this instrument is essentially threefold: (1) to group the several actors intervening in Timor-Leste together and to enable them to work as a one whole; (2) to work, from within Timor-Leste, as an important element in the disciplinary process that seeks to normalize the country; and (3) to attach the Timorese National Priorities to the Millennium Development Goals, in an effort of bringing Timor-Leste behavior closer to these standards.

In regard to the first importance of UNDAF aforementioned, this instrument seeks to be the framework that delineates the field where the development assistance carried out by the UN (and other international actors such as the international financial institutions and other states) will be performed. Therefore, all the actions and goals carried out by those several international actors on the field should, at least theoretically, align and converge according to this document. This enables the panoply of actors composed by UNMIT and the constellation of actors gravitating around it (each with its own set of disparate programs and objectives), to pursue coherence and coordination. It is the UNDAF that enables them to seek to work as a comprehensive and coherent whole.

Nevertheless, even if these actors and their actions lack coherence and coordination, the very existence of the instrument, and its high relevance in the intervention process in Timor-Leste, is important due to the reason that it enables the analyst to problematize this high variety of actors and disparate programs and objectives as a coherent whole. Most importantly, it clearly indicates that these diverse elements in fact form not only a coherent assemblage but an assemblage that seeks to function toward a common direction since it is there that are set the priorities to be followed and the overall objectives to be pursued. Therefore, this is an encompassing surveillance instrument that brings some sort of consistency and density to the whole normalization enterprise. This instrument facilitates the conduction of the conducts of Timor-Leste since it enables the actions and influences performed in the key pillar spheres of the country—the disciplinary, the political and economic, and the socio- and biopolitical ones—to be conducted toward a common end, obviously convenient to the internationals. Therefore, the UNDAF works by rendering operational, from within the country, the normalization process that Timor-Leste is subject to.

In order to better grasp the importance of UNDAF as a grouping mechanism, one should remember that there are nearly two dozen organizations—from the International Labor Organization (ILO), World Food Program (WFP), UNDP UNESCO, to UNICEF, the international (and regional) financial institutions, among others—gravitating around UNMIT that are part of the UN Country Team. Each one of them has several projects and programs, with innumerous objectives. Just to give a very brief idea of how encompassing it is, one might think, for instance, of: (1) numerous initiatives of the ILO in areas like the (1.1) employment promotion (ILO, N/A); and (1.3) labor market governance and working conditions; (2) the several activities performed by FAO in terms of a (2.1) national program of food security; (2.2) capacity building and technical assistance; and also (2.3) assistance in the increasing food production and enhancing sustainable food security (FAO, N/A; UN, N/A-i); (3) the fact that the ADB has more than thirty initiatives in areas ranging from microfinance (ADB, 2004), economic policies, and strategies for development planning (ADB, 2002) and infrastructure (ADB, 2005, 2007) to capacity-building in the areas macroeconomic policies (ADB, 2009), governance and public sector management (ADB, 2003), and ministries of infrastructure, planning and finance; (4) the activities performed by the WFP in areas such as (4.1) mother-and-child health and nutrition; (4.2) school feeding program; (4.3) food for work; and (4.4) capacity-building and technical assistance to ministries in order to enhance the food security and also food security monitoring systems (WFP, N/A); or (5) the wide scope of projects carried out by the UNDP touching areas as diverse as (5.1) democratic governance; (5.2) poverty reduction and achievement of the MDGs; (5.3) projects dealing with strengthening the national police capacity in Timor-Leste (UNDP, 2011c); and also (5.4) environment and sustainable development (UNDP, N/A-a, b, c, e); or even (6) the more than forty projects carried out by the World Bank touching on several aspects of the Timorese life as diverse as education (WB, 2006b, 2010); youth (WB, 2008); health (WB, 2007a); gas (WB, 2006a); petroleum (WB, 2007b); social protection (WB, 2011); and justice with its "Justice for the Poor" project (WB, N/A-b), to name just a few. These examples are by no means exhaustive. In fact, they are just a fraction of the whole picture. They merely give a small idea of the width of both the scope and the range of the normalizing assemblage operating in Timor-Leste.

In addition to the importance of the UNDAF as a grouping mechanism, it is also clear that the UNDAF works as a key instrument in the disciplinary process under which Timor-Leste is subject. This is the second reason why UNDAF in important to the UN engagement with Timor-Leste. Rather than a mere bureaucratic procedure seeking to harmonize the UN and other actors' actions and to optimize resources; the UNDAF also has other functions— such as individualizing, rendering visible, monitoring/assessing, reporting, and correcting—that are interrelated and that collectively form a power framework that seeks to conduct and normalize Timor-Leste. UNDAF's functions follow closely those of the SGRSC. However, whereas the SGRSC is an instrument that enables the normalization of Timor-Leste as a state and worked majorly from outside the country, the UNDAF is a pivotal instrument in the normalization process of Timorese spheres and worked within the country. It enables what could be seen as a huge and nebulous thing—a whole country with its several spheres—to become more tangible and, especially, more manageable and, consequently, its normalization more feasible.

The very first function of the UNDAF in the normalization process is, as the SGRSC, to individualize. Whereas the latter individualizes Timor-Leste as a post-conflict state, the former individualizes each sphere within this post-conflict state. Although the UN acts on several areas at once, through this document, each one of them is individualized and therefore can be focused individually. It is through this individualization process that what would at first be indistinct areas become distinct, and therefore enables the UN to act upon them. Furthermore, it is due to this process of individualizing the areas that these can be each one disaggregated into sub-elements and these, by their turn, into other sub-elements. This enables the Timorese reality to be rendered operational and therefore a vast sphere becomes workable and, most importantly, manageable. Secondly, as a consequence of the first function, the UNDAF functions also as a steering instrument. This brings the element of visibility to the normalization process in the sense that the Timorese reality in its diverse, but also distinct due to the individualization process, areas becomes visible for those who are intervening in Timor-Leste. It is through these functions that a field of visibility in regard to the Timorese reality is formed.

Consequently, the state-building *dispositif* can delineate the field where it will act and influence, and therefore seek to conduct the Timorese conducts. As a result, the intervening *dispositif* starts to be in the position to influence the fundamental spheres of a state—the disciplinary, political and economic governance, and the socio- and biopolitical spheres—giving a clearer picture of how wide and deep was the UN influence over Timorese spheres. In the UNDAF language used in the 2008 document (UNDP, 2008e: 5), this influence over those spheres was translated into the three major areas of intervention: (1) democratization and social cohesion, which includes also deepening state-building, and work on security and justice; (2) poverty reduction and sustainable livelihoods, focusing in particular vulnerable groups, including youth, women, IDPs and disaster-prone communities; and (3) basic social services, which includes education, health, nutrition, water and sanitation, and social welfare and social protection. Crosscutting these areas of intervention, subjects like gender, youth, human rights, prevention, and environment also have importance and would be fostered by the state-builders. These areas of intervention reflect, as it would be expected, a sort of continuation from the UNDAF document focusing on the period of 2003–2005 but with a different configuration. In this document (UNDP, 2002: 12–16) the areas of intervention were placed under the headings of: (1) Income Poverty and Hunger; (2) Education and Culture; (3) Health; (4) Gender; and (5) the Environment and Natural Resources. In the UNDAF document, the areas of intervention were disaggregated and became objectives. Each of these objectives, in turn, is composed by their own set of targets.[7] It is at this point that a field of visibility in regard to the Timorese reality becomes to be constructed. Moreover, this field of visibility is constantly fed by periodic documents, reports, surveys, publications, releases and so on, that by its turn, are supplied by periodic data collection instruments such as census, national statistics, governmental numbers, and so on.[8] All these elements not only provide a clearer picture, for those intervening, of the numerous spheres of Timor-Leste, but also frame what constitutes the Timorese reality in the eyes of those intervening. It is in this reality that international state-builders will intervene, making the areas that are not part of the UNDAF objectives simply invisible and, therefore, not part of the Timorese reality.

Not dissociated from the formation of the construction of a field of visibility through the delineation of the spheres of intervention (through the establishment of the aforementioned objectives), UNDAF has also a monitoring function. This function is what places Timor-Leste and the Timorese under a constant surveillance and a periodic examination. The UNDAF document enables a vast area of Timor-Leste and of the Timorese lives to become under a close international watch. One should also remember that what is under a very close scrutiny is whether the Timorese conducts, at the diverse areas aforementioned, are being shaped according to what was planned by the UN and its behaviors are being headed toward the documents' objectives. This is done essentially through five elements: (1) a very detailed delineation of the targets and objectives to be achieved; (2) the specification of the responsibilities and roles of each actor involved; (3) the exposition of the amount of resources that are allocated, by each intervening actor, to each intervened area's objective; (4) the signaling of the sources of verification of where the indicators of each objective must be reflected; this being a report, a document, the national statistics, or even a legislation when it is the case; and (5) the delineation of an evaluation calendar stipulating surveys, studies, and also reviews of the UNDAF itself in order to monitor the process. All these elements are compiled, as expected, along matrixes and tables throughout the document.[9] There, it was stipulated a whole set of surveys, studies, and reviews in order to assess and monitor the very UN surveillance instrument that UNDAF is so it can be changed and revised whenever necessary and, in turn, review and revise the very normalization process.

Separately, these tables and matrixes might perfectly pass as mere technical instruments that are pivotal for the management of any modern state. However, it should not pass unproblematically the fact that they are used by the UN in order to structure and influence Timorese conducts from within the country. Collectively, they form a pivotal instrument of the surveillance framework that was set up around Timor-Leste and the Timorese in order to shape several spheres of the country. Hence, they are far from mere technical instruments. Therefore, rather than mere a technical instrument, as Mitchell Dean (2010: 41) remembers, such instruments—like matrixes, tables, and so on—are what make it possible, on the one hand, to picture not only who and what will sought to have its conducts conducted, but also how different locales and agents are to be connected with one another, and the kind of objectives to be sought enabling the visualization of such diagram of power. In addition, on the other hand, rightly remembering Bruno Latour's phrase, Dean also sees that these instruments also enable one to "think with eyes and hands," bringing attention to the fact that seeing and acting are interconnected (Dean, 2010: 41). These matrixes, while enabling those intervening in Timor-Leste to think with eyes and hands, they, simultaneously, enable those intervening to visualize the Timorese reality, and also place the Timorese reality in their hands. In this way, Timor-Leste becomes not only manageable and conductible, but also the very process of conducting can be properly monitored.

Therefore, rather than a mere technical instrument, the UNDAF document gives a detailed image of the aims to be pursued in each intervening area; it indicates where each one involved in the intervention, either internationals or Timorese, should act, and also what must be done by each actor in each intervened area. It is through this clear picture that enables the proper monitoring of the Timorese conducts. One must also remember that an almost immediate consequence of this periodic scanning and monitoring that Timor-Leste, and the Timorese, are subject is a progress assessment. This evaluation assessment is what enables the UN to say that Timor-Leste is making the proper changes or not; whether Timor-Leste is properly conducted. This is what makes possible for the UN to follow the changes made in each of the intervened areas that compose the Timorese reality in the eyes of the UN. Indeed, this is what seeks to ensure that not only Timor-Leste will behave accordingly, but, specially, that, in the case of any misconduct in any specific area, it will be promptly pinpointed and properly corrected. It is the correction function that ensures that any misbehavior, when spotted, will be properly corrected so Timor-Leste, and the Timorese, can once more continue behaving accordingly. Indeed, this correction function is what completes the disciplinary process that fosters a normalization framework in Timor-Leste which the UNDAF is a key instrument.

Along with the two pillars presented previously underlying the importance of UNDAF as a pivotal instrument for the normalizing state-building *dispositif*, there is a third one: to append the Timorese National Priorities with the Millennium Development Goals (MDG),[10] in the effort to bring Timor-Leste, as a state, to behave more according to these standards. Hence, the UNDAF also plays an important role in the normalization of Timor-Leste, as a state, in the international scenario, but, once more, from within the country. The point here is not, obviously, to argue for or against the MDGs. This kind of discussion, in addition of being misplaced, certainly extrapolates the scope of this book. Nevertheless, one cannot avoid to understand the MDGs as elements of a state behavioral norm of the current international scenario, whether agreeing or not with them. Indeed, it is indisputable that the MDGs constitute a whole set of international standards that the UN fosters the states around the world to achieve. The UN seeks to provide a framework in which the states start behaving according to the established goals. These efforts, obviously, are denser and deeper in post-conflict states than in other states. In this case, the UN seeks to mold and shape the states' conducts in order to achieve those standards. In the end, the objective is that more states comply with those standards.

In the case of Timor-Leste, and other post-conflict states, the state-building *dispositif*, which has the UN as its core, emerges and seeks to normalize the country, including the areas of the MDGs. The UNDAF plays a key role in this. Apart from the elements already shown, the UNDAF is also important in the effort of seeking to make Timor-Leste, as a state, to behave according to the MDGs. This is done through the alignment of the Timorese national priorities for the country with the MDGs. In each of the major objectives of the UNDAF there is this grouping of the several objectives of the document and the national priorities seeking to make them head toward a common MDG. As a result, the Timorese state is expected to have a set of behaviors in these areas.[11]

Rather than a mere harmonization or synchronization of efforts and objectives, the UNDAF is an important element in connecting what is understood as a national priority with a set of international standards in order to make Timor-Leste, as a state, behave accordingly and become more of a normal state. It is true that the very core of the MDGs is to seek to improve and to enhance the population's lives. Nevertheless, one the other hand, it is also true that, precisely because of that, this process constitutes an exercise of a biopolitical power *par excellence*. Therefore, this does not weaken the instrument as an important surveillance instrument or the argument of the UN pursuit of the normalization of Timor-Leste. On the contrary, the pursuit of making Timor-Leste complying and behaving according to the MDGs, in fact, reinforces the argument of exposing the overall UN objective of seeking to make Timor-Leste behave as a normal state in the international scenario; of making it comply with these international standards.

Lastly, another element pervades the UNDAF document—the notion of good governance. The notion of good governance has mainly two functions: (1) through the noun governance, to structure the area where the intervention must occur; and (2) through the adjective good, to frame the kind of outcomes expected from the intervention performed. In the case of a normalization process, in which the UNDAF is a pivotal instrument, the interventions done in the key spheres of Timor-Leste are performed in light of, and underpinned by, the notion of good governance. It is true that the notion good governance does not appear literally in the current document in regard to Timor-Leste, as it was the case of the UNDAF document for the period of 2003–2005 where there is a specific section literally dealing with good governance and where one can clearly know the understanding of what it means for the UN (UNDP, 2002: 11–12). Nevertheless, closely observing the very areas of intervention delineated in the current document and the objectives pursued, it is clear that this notion underpins the intervention, even if not clearly explicitly.

In the UNDAF document for the period of 2003–2005, it is clear that, through the notion of good governance, not only the area of intervention was framed, but also the kind of intervention and the expected outcomes were delineated. Furthermore, one can also notice how this notion was expected to be fostered within the Timorese state. In this document one can read under the heading of "good governance" that, in the UN's understanding (UNDP, 2002: 11), the term, the western democratic tradition, brings the following set of characteristics: (1) political democracy; (2) decentralization; (3) transparency and free flow of information; (4) small government; (5) market liberalization; (6) elections; and (7) an impartial judicial system (UNDP, 2002: 11). This, as it was expectable, was designed to be fostered and encourage by the international experts. One could expect that this fostering of the good governance notion was something done in a concealed or secretly manner in the very exercise of advising, capacity-building and counseling. However, this is in fact clear in the very document when it states that fostering was to be done by the "international advisers whose primary function will be to transmit technical skills and know how, and to inculcate in their counterparts the values and attitudes normally associated with prevailing notions of 'good' governance" (UNDP, 2002: 11).

Observing the current UNDAF document for Timor-Leste, there is no reason to believe that this rationale changed. On the contrary, observing the very areas delineated for intervention and the objectives set to be achieved, one can clearly see the kind of economic and political reforms, and the focus on democratic principles, human rights and rule of law that characterize the notion of good governance (Wouters and Ryngaert, 2005: 69–77). Moreover, having also in mind that after the 2006 and 2008 crises the UN intervention became deeper and wider, one can only conclude that rather than a rupture between the two documents, one can in fact observe a clear continuity between them, indeed, a much denser continuity.

At this point is clear that the UNDAF document is a pivotal operative instrument in the normalization process carried out by the state-building *dispositif*. It is a refined instrument, working from within the post-conflict state, responsible for not only seeking to group the intervening assemblage—in regard to its actors, projects, and objectives—together, but also for placing the Timorese reality under a surveillance framework that seeks to make sure that fundamental spheres of Timor-Leste—the disciplinary, the political and economic, and the socio- and biopolitical ones—and its population, are actually behaving as it was designed and expected by the UN, and for signalizing when and in which areas the corrections are needed.

THE POLICE ARRANGEMENT AND
THE DISCIPLINING OF THE POLICE

Another field where the UN's exercise of its power and influence was deeply felt was at a key pillar of the disciplinary sphere of the Timorese state—the national police (PNTL). In the disciplinary sphere, the UN exercised its disciplining and normalization power namely in three dimensions: (1) the reform, restructuring and rebuilding of the police institutions and their functioning; (2) the normalization and disciplining of the very policemen/women; and (3) the manner and timing in which the Timorese police would conduct the police operations on its own country. Just as in other spheres, the UN intervention here also navigated between macro and micro aspects, going from the timing the Timorese would police their own country, and how their police institutions would look like and be internally organized, to shaping the conduct of the very individual policemen/women. All these elements were consolidated in an agreement between the UN and Timor-Leste that became known as the Police Arrangement (UN and DRTL, 2006). Rather than a mere technical agreement between two equal parts, this is a pivotal document that functions as a fundamental structuring instrument within the normalization process that Timor-Leste was subject to and the disciplining of the Timorese police. This was the document that framed and structured the UN actions within the field of the police. The aim was to produce a stable, predictable, disciplined police institution. Remarkably, in Timor-Leste, a sort of an apparent paradox is perceptible in this sphere—the formation of a disciplined discipline sphere. This means that the very disciplinary institutions of Timor-Leste were disciplined and built in a disciplinary manner. Hence, through rewards and punishments, not only their macro institutional configurations are shaped but even their micro detailed aspects are structured.[12] Therefore, the sphere which should be the definitive element of discipline in the country is in fact disciplined by internationals, being in fact a disciplinary institution that is under the constant gazing, shaping, structuring, and conducting of international actors.

In regard to the police institutions to be built, one must remember the fact that UNMIT was established as a reaction to the 2006 crisis. Hence, due to this environment, the institutions of the police received a considerable focus. This is perceptible, for instance, throughout the several mandates of the Security Council, either establishing or renewing the mission's mandate. In this area, the UN capacity-building efforts were not only aiming to completely (re)structure and (re)build the police institutions, but also to structure and build a certain kind of institutions. The institutions (re)built should follow a series of standards, which were pre-established by internationals, such as: (1) respect for national laws; (2) respect for international and national criminal justice norms and standards; (3) respect for democratic values and the values of the rule of law; (4) maintenance and promotion of respect for the rule of law, public safety, public order, security, and stability; (5) respect for human rights; (6) impartial, de-politicized, and non-partisan approach; (7) commanding of public respect and public confidence; and (8) rejection of all corrupt practices (UN and DRTL, 2006: 8–9). Once more, the point is not being either for or against these standards, but to shed light on the fact that a fundamental pillar of the disciplinary sphere of Timor-Leste would have its field of possible actions previously structured and comply with standards already structured by internationals.

The whole process of reform, restructuring, and rebuilding of the Timorese national police institutions focused on two dimensions—structural and procedural. Hence, the focus was not only on the formation of the institutions, but also on how they should work. Initially, UNMIT pursued a phase of a thorough assessment of several areas of the Timorese police such as the organizational, operational, administrative, managerial, logistical, budgetary, and financial; and the assessment of aspects like the internal accountability mechanisms, external oversight, support structures, human-resources management systems and procedures, internal discipline system, and its institutional arrangements for coordination with the defense sector (UN and DRTL, 2006: 9). After this initial assessment phase, which is, as already elucidated, an important phase of any disciplinary mechanism, the UN would pursue the actual rebuilding and restructuring of the institutions.

In the more macro and structural dimension, in the UN eyes the rebuilding should be aimed at: building a whole disciplinary system, capacity-building PNTL institutionally and in terms of how these institutions would operate, structuring their procedures, developing PNTL's administrative capacity, strengthening its administrative systems for budget, finance, and personnel (UN and DRTL, 2006: 9). The efforts were not only targeting the structural aspect of the police institution and the shaping of the internal manners of the Timorese national police; the UN also had in mind, characterizing a very disciplinary attitude and the disciplinary manner of the intervention, the detailed structuring of the very plan through which the rebuilding was pursued. The plan, in the eyes of the UN, should: (1) "contain a detailed statement of the aims and objectives to be achieved"; (2) "list specific actions to be taken for the purpose of achieving those aims and objectives"; (3) "clearly allocate responsibilities for the taking of those actions"; (4) "set out projected time-lines for the taking of those actions and the achievement of those aims and objectives"; (5) "elaborate benchmarks and performance targets to measure whether those aims and objectives have been met"; and (6) "set out the procedures and process by which the plan may be amended, if need be, and by whom" (UN and DRTL, 2006: 9–10). This provides a clear image of the vast and deep scope of the whole enterprise. In light of the crisis of 2006, the (re)building efforts in this area were thought to be drastic and profound. This document would later culminate and be supplemented by other capacity-building efforts and projects, with the assistance of UNMIT experts and UNDP consultants, throughout the UN intervention in this area with, for instance, the "Security Sector Review in Timor-Leste" (UNDP, 2008a), or, even, after the Timorese resumption of executive policing over its own country in March 2011 with, for instance, the UNDP "Project Strengthening the National Police Capacity in Timor-Leste" (2011c).

In parallel with all the capacity-building efforts of reform, restructuring, and rebuilding the institutions of the Timorese national police, another normalizing and disciplining practice was being performed—the training of policemen/women. This is the second dimension where the UN exercised its disciplining and normalization power over this fundamental part of the Timorese disciplinary sphere. Rather than a mere practice under the label of a practical or a technical assistance, the training of the policemen/women was another normalizing and disciplining mechanism portrayed as a capacity-building practice, just as the other several which Timor-Leste and the Timorese were subject to, presented with power-denying notions such as monitoring, counseling, supporting and so on. In regard to this practice, the normalizing and disciplining power was exercised through the power-denying program designed to issue a certification of the police officers. This was in essence a disciplinary and normalizing framework that through this certification program, the UN sought not only a different kind of police officers but, above all, a different kind of subject and subjectivity.

This "Registration and Certification Programme" was detailed in the Police Arrangement (UN and DRTL, 2006: annex). It was a program aiming at the training of the Timorese police officers. This might, at a first sight, look like an ordinary technical device deployed to train police officers, which in fact is something quite common in several states. Nevertheless, once more, this is far from being a mere technical device. Indeed, this mechanism places the Timorese police officers within a power framework which was already pre-established and previously structured by internationals in order to shape their behaviors so they behave and possess certain values that were also pre-determined by internationals. Therefore, rather than a mere training program, this in fact becomes a disciplining and normalizing mechanism directed to Timorese police officers which was composed by three parts: (1) identification and registration; (2) provisional certification; and (3) final certification.

The first part of this normalizing mechanism—the identification and registration—dealt essentially with the identification of the individuals who were serving the Timorese national police. These individuals should be properly identified and later registered by UNMIT as PNTL police officers (UN and DRTL, 2006: 14). This was an initial attempt, something that would be continued during the whole program, aimed at the construction of steering mechanisms and the creation of record-keeping instruments within the police. As already mentioned, a disciplinary mechanism can hardly function without the construction of such instruments. This first part was aiming essentially at the construction of instruments that would enable the UNMIT to know who these policemen/women were. Indeed, in the document it clearly states that the government should[13] give to the UNMIT all the documentation identifying those individuals serving the PNTL and all of its units (UN and DRTL, 2006: 17). This clearly characterizes not only the attempt of the UN to know who these individuals were, but also the very power hierarchy underpinning the process through the very words used in the document. This, as it will be later evinced, was not the only example.

After this first part of identification and registration, comes the second part of the provisional certification. Those who were properly registered were provisionally certified to be a PNTL police officer. However, this certification had to be proposed by the police commissioner (UN and DRTL, 2006: 14). Consequently, although the certification was issued by the Timorese government, the crucial element of this whole process is the police commissioner, who is the head of the whole police component of the UN on the field. As it will be seen soon, s/he is also responsible, or highly determinant, for key elements of the whole Timorese police chain, for instance the police operations, the promotion of the officers, and even the standards that the police officers must follow during the certification program and afterward. This provisional certification would be valid for six months with the possibility of renovation, upon agreement by the police commissioner, or successive periods of six months (UN and DRTL, 2006: 14). This certification renewal depended upon the successful completion of the training program.

Those provisionally certified would have a card certifying this, indicating when the provisional certification was granted and when the certification was renewed, if it ever was (UN and DRTL, 2006: 14). More than that, the Police Arrangement stated that the Timorese government had to require all those who were provisionally certified to provide UNMIT with information in regard to their "personal and professional conduct and activities, their financial dealings and their property holdings" (UN and DRTL, 2006: 17). Furthermore, in a very characterizing manner of a highly disproportionate power relation, the Police Arrangement clearly affirms that the Timorese government "shall, without delay, without restriction, qualification or exception and free of charge, make available to UNMIT such documentation, records or information within its possession or under its control" (UN and DRTL, 2006: 17). This information, apart from being a steering and record-keeping instrument, which also enabled the UN to place all of police officer's personal lives under a close surveillance and scrutiny, it would also underpin the police commissioner's decision "on the renewal of their provisional certification or the granting of final certification for service [of these police officers] with the PNTL" (UN and DRTL, 2006: 17). Hence this information would also be considered in the reward and punishing process of the disciplinary mechanism which is this certification program.

In fact, this provisional certification is what authorized the police officers to serve as police officers at the PNTL, which means that they could only be police officers after this screening, scrutinizing, and identification process. Nevertheless, although this is a key element of the normalization process, the most important part of this is that these police officers must be part of a training process. This is the part of the whole process that most directly sought to shape and conduct the conducts and behaviors of the policemen/ women seeking that they become not only normalized, but also had a different subjectivity. Indeed, all the policemen/women had to undergo the training process, which as designed, provided and carried out by UNMIT (UN and DRTL, 2006: 14).

In this training program, the performance of the police officers was individually assessed and evaluated, and the renewal of their certification depended upon the successful completion of these training activities. They would be evaluated in regard to aspects that an international actor, the police commissioner, would decide. The police commissioner was responsible for elaborating and disseminating detailed directives in regard to not only the training process but, specially, in regards to the performance standards that the police officers must comply (UN and DRTL, 2006: 15). The police officers would be evaluated not only in regard to operational aspects—such as their technical skills, professional conduct, or the performance of theirs tasks—but also in regard to deeper elements that characterize the pursue of certain kind of subjectivity, focusing on aspects like their: (1) demonstrated respect for human rights; (2) proven evidence of their gender sensitivity; and (3) recognized "adherence to standards of democratic policing and international and national criminal justice norms and standards" (UN and DRTL, 2006: 15). These were the parameters that would frame the whole training process and evaluation of the police officers. In addition to this frequent and individual evaluation, their evaluation would also be capilarized since the police officers would "be regularly evaluated by co-located United Nations police officers" (UN and DRTL, 2006: 15). This was by no means restricted to the police officers alone. In fact, the PNTL general commander was also subject to this kind of conducting since the police commissioner would assist his/her capacity-building "through constant mentoring, monitoring and supervision" (UN and DRTL, 2006: 15: 6).

Since the third, and final, part of the training process—the final certification—and the very promotion of the police officers depended on their complete compliance and fulfillment of these performance standards, the policemen/women ended up being put inside a power framework that through punishments (the nonrenovation of their certification and therefore prevent-

ing them from being police officers) and rewards (the renewal of their certification, their promotions inside the organization, and the possibility of obtaining a final certification) sought to shape and conduct their very behaviors.
Therefore, in addition to structure the institutions (and how they should
work) and to the fact that the entire institution was under the international
authority (the police commissioner) the instrument put the Timorese police
officers within an international disciplining framework that sought not only
to normalize them, but also to construct a specific kind of subjectivity on
them, a liberal one.

In addition to the two dimensions just exposed, one should not forget that
there was also a third dimension in which the exercise of the UN disciplining
and normalizing power in the sphere of the Timorese police was felt: the
manner and timing in which the Timorese police would conduct police operations in its own country. The manner in which the police officers would in
fact police their own country was a direct consequence of their normalization
pursued during their training program. Their policing would, undoubtedly, be
binding by the standards delineated by the UN police commissioner and that
was thought to be entrenched on them during the whole certification program. Otherwise, since their very possibility of continuing to be exercising
their police duties depended on following these standards, without their prov-
en adherence to, and in fact performance of, these standards they would not
be able to be police officers at all. This is certainly important since, as it was
evinced, these standards directed not only the very behaviors of the police-
men/women, but also the manner in which the Timorese would perform their
policing activities. Since, the police institution is a relevant institution within
any society—separating those who have a normal behavior from those who
have an abnormal and deviant one, and in the correction of these behaviors—
an important consequence of the disciplining and normalization of the Timorese national police attitude and behavior toward the very policing act is that
very understanding of what is perceived as a normal and deviant behavior
throughout the Timorese society and within the Timorese social body was
also, although indirectly, sought to be shaped and conducted. This is not a
small thing since those actions surpass, a lot, the power-denying shield of
technicality and expertise of policing, and affects the whole Timorese society. It is another effort, albeit indirectly but by no means less invasively, of
normalizing the Timorese society from within itself.

Finally, a second important aspect of this third dimension of the UN
normalizing and disciplining power directed at the sphere of the Timorese
police is the timing in which, and how, the Timorese would be allowed to
have the responsibility of the policing of their own country. This was clear in
the three-phased approach adopted: initial, consolidation, and full reconstitution phases. The initial phase was marked by the UN possessing full control
of, and the primary responsibility for, the whole policing activities through-

out Timor-Leste (UN and DRTL, 2006: 5). Although the operations would also be conducted by Timorese police officers that were certified, the main part of the job would be done by UN police officers. Furthermore, the police commissioner had overall command and control in regard to the whole chain of command of the police. He could appoint UN commanding officers who would have the command and control over the police operations within a determined district or unit (UN and DRTL, 2006: 6), and, as it was already evinced, the UN police commissioner would determinate the very rules and performance standards that the whole Timorese police should comply. In sum, this phase was characterized by the UN being the police *de facto* in Timor-Leste.

During the consolidation phase, the UN would begin to "progressively hand over (sic) responsibility for the conduct of police operations within Districts or by Units to the PNTL" (UN and DRTL, 2006: 6). This progressive hand-over would, once more, occur within a power framework where through punishments and rewards the fact of the Timorese becoming responsible for policing of their country was closely subject to alterations and corrections to the behavior of Timorese police institutions and Timorese police officers themselves. The hand-over of responsibility, which was still in regard to a district or unit and not for the overall policing operation, would occur once the UN police commissioner considered that the PNTL had achieved the standards and benchmarks previously established in regard to their behavior (UN and DRTL, 2006: 6). However, this hand-over was something very limited since the PTNL commanding officer of the district or unit that was subject to the hand-over would continue to be under the command and control of the UN police commissioner. Moreover, the UN police officers serving in a district or unit that was subject to the hand-over of responsibility would also continue under the exclusive command and control of the UN police commissioner (UN and DRTL, 2006: 6). Furthermore, even the Timorese police officer's conducts and behaviors of the Timorese police officers would continue to occur since the UN police officers would continue to serve alongside them and, most importantly, continue to advise and assist them in conducting police tasks (UN and DRTL, 2006: 6). In sum, the UN would remain continually correcting PNTL's behaviors.[14]

The third and final phase—full reconstitution—was characterized by the full hand-over of the responsibility for the conduct and the command and control of all police operations in Timor-Leste. Unsurprisingly, this would occur only when the UN police commissioner "certifie[d] that the PNTL [wa]s fully reconstituted and capable of conducting police functions throughout the territory of Timor-Leste in accordance with the benchmarks and performance targets set out" (UN and DRTL, 2006: 8). Indeed, a main part of this process is that "at least 80 percent of the officers in each district must be fully certified" (UN, N/A-c), and it was already evinced what were the standards they should follow.

Although the hand-over would be expected to occur in this phase, the UN disciplining and normalizing power would be far from terminating. Even after the hand-over, the UNMIT would continue to support the Timorese national police. Firstly, there would be no decrease in the number of UN police officers, and they would continue in the field in all districts (UN, N/A-c). Secondly, and most importantly, the UN would continue to daily advise and monitor the progress of PNTL officers (UN, N/A-c). As already predictable, this would place the Timorese police officers under a severe scrutiny and surveillance framework since, for the UN, this "[m]onitoring involves observing the response of the PNTL officers while they work. They will also keep records and evaluate the progress" (UN, N/A-c). Hence, the Timorese police officers, and the Timorese national police, as an institution, would remain under close international observation, even regaining the responsibility for policing their own country, which scrutinized how they would perform their policing, since the UN would continually and frequently asses the PNTL policing conduct and assure that the institution meet human rights standards (UN, N/A-c).

At this point it is clearly perceptible that the UN approach, often pursued through the power-denying notions like capacity-building, certification, training, assistance, and so on, to this pivotal element of the disciplinary sphere of Timor-Leste in fact placed the whole Timorese police, as an institution, and the very policemen/women inside this institution, within a three-layered disciplining and normalizing framework. This is also what brings a somewhat paradoxical situation of a disciplined discipline; a disciplined disciplinary institution. This is observable in not only the fact that the very process of reforming, restructuring and rebuilding the Timorese national police was fundamentally developed in a disciplinary manner but also in the fact that the Timorese police, that is supposed to be a crucial element of the application, and the maintenance, of the discipline in Timor-Leste, is essentially structured, shaped and conducted by international actors; international actors that during the whole process of its rebuilding, and even afterward, exert continued control, scrutiny, and supervision over the institution and the policemen/women.

Therefore, the three dimensions herein observed—the reform, restructuring, and rebuilding of the police institutions and its functioning; the normalization/disciplining of the very policemen/women; and the manner and timing in which the Timorese police would conduct the police operations in its own country—in fact, places the whole Timorese police institution and its officers within a framework that seeks to structure and to conduct their conducts. Indeed, rather than a mere bureaucratic mechanism of technical assistance, what is observable is a three-layered power framework that puts the Timorese police institution and the very policemen/women subject to a deep, and hierarchical, power relation that through their constant monitoring, supervision, correction, and continually making them to abide by internationally-built performance standards, pursues to discipline and to normalize them, and as a consequence the whole Timorese society.

THE MONTHLY GOVERNANCE REPORTS AND
THE LOCAL GOVERNANCE REPORTS

The Monthly Governance Reports and the Local Governance Reports[15] are two kinds of reports, issued by the Democratic Governance Support Unit of the UNMIT, that are directed precisely to seek to influence another fundamental sphere of Timor-Leste—the political and economic governance one. The reports seek to periodically shed light, in a very detailed manner, on several governance activities carried out at the state and the local levels, respectively. Rather than mere technical instrument used to merely describe and report what is being carried out on several fronts on the field, these reports are very capilarized monitoring instruments of the Timorese governance sphere. These are pivotal instruments through which the UNMIT places the whole Timorese political governance under a deep surveillance and scrutiny. Again, this is not something veiled or concealed. In fact, UNMIT openly states that it monitors very closely all the Timorese governmental activities (UN, N/A-l). Through the periodically (monthly) and detailed examination of several areas of the governance activities of Timor-Leste, in the end, these instruments in fact form a deep and encompassing surveillance framework frequently scanning, observing, and monitoring the Timorese actions within the governance sphere. Indeed, functioning as surveillance instruments *par excellence*, the whole Timorese governance sphere ends up being subjected to this international surveillance. This surveillance framework, especially in regard to the governance sphere, is pivotal for the normalization process that Timor-Leste is subject to.

It is not by coincidence that these reports are elaborated by the Democratic Governance Support Unit (DGSU) of UNMIT. This very fact is another evidence of the role played by these instruments in the normalization process in Timor-Leste; in the whole process of seeking to make Timor-Leste start abiding by international rules of governance and behaving as a democratic polity. The very subtitle, for instance, of the monthly governance reports—"The State of Democratic Governance in Timor-Leste"—is very indicative in this sense and leaves no room for doubt in regard to their role in the normalization process (see for instance UN, 2011a). These instruments, among others already explored, enable the UN to closely observe, in a very systematic and periodic manner, what is, and is not, being done in this field; it enables the UN to exam whether Timor-Leste is actually correcting its own conducts and behaving according to a normal state of the international system.

These monthly governance reports have under their scope a wide range of governance activities and focus on two different scales: (1) one at the level of the national government; and (2) the other at a more local government level. Whilst the monthly governance reports focus on the national state structures—such as the Office of the President, the National Parliament, the Council of Ministers, the Ministry of Finance, the National Police of Timor-Leste, and so on—the local governance report deals with the main activities of the district administration—such as its finance, activities, projects, and so on—of the several districts of Timor-Leste.[16] The level of scrutiny of the Timorese governance sphere, through the monitoring of these institutions, at both levels was profound. This occurs, as it is quite expectable in normalization processes, through a series of visualizing elements such as graphs and tables in order to clearly expose the government performance around several activities so they can be better monitored, and consequently corrected whenever needed. These documents are precisely a compilation of a series of these performance graphs and tables in regard to several governance issues.

At the level of the national government, the very first institution observed is the Office of the President of Timor-Leste. In regard to this institution, the performance graphs and tables of the Monthly Governance Reports focus on how many promulgations (decree laws, laws, presidential decrees and resolutions) were executed by the president each month; even the number of press releases made public by the President's Office, and their content, were under scrutiny. As it is expected, this quantitative scrutiny is accompanied by a more qualitative monitoring focusing also on what are the themes of the promulgations in a clear attention to the kind of promulgations done. Still, scrutinizing the President Office, the report also monitors the president's actions, the very action of being a president, through the monitoring of the diplomatic accreditations received by him/her and even his/her visits either overseas or to the Timorese districts.[17]

The same close monitoring framework was also in place in regard to the Timorese National parliament. The monitoring of the National Parliament is namely twofold: (1) through the monitoring of the parliament as a whole; and (2) through the monitoring of the political parties represented there, along with its very parliamentary members. In regard to the performance assessment of the parliament as a whole, on a more quantitative note, the performance graphs and tables focus, firstly, on the productivity of the parliament, focusing on the number of laws, resolutions and other legislative instruments approved in the parliament; and also the press releases made public. On a more qualitative note, this monitoring mechanism focuses on which subjects where approved. Furthermore, it is also focused on the plenary sessions of the parliament. Under scrutiny were the main issues that were on the agenda

and discussed, and the issues that were not on the agenda, along with the
ones that were raised in the plenary; even the parliamentary extraordinary
activities or announcements are under observation. Interestingly enough, the
report brings also a list of the pending issues to be approved by the parliament with their respective status, in a clear evidence that the UN is closely
tracking not only what was actually approved, but also what is pending to be
approved by the National Parliament.[18]

This mechanism is supplemented by a set of tables that expose the status
(published, being drafted, pending promulgation, and others) of all legal
acts—such as decree-laws, government decrees, government resolutions,
proposal of laws, national parliament resolutions, and presidential decrees—
since 2008. This, as already mentioned previously, not only forms the visibility of the whole legislative body, but also enables its close monitoring. The
bodies within the parliament are also subject to this surveillance framework.
This is the case of the specialized standing committees of the parliament,[19]
which are certainly not left out of this close scrutiny, in the sense that all the
main activities of each of the committees are also closely observed demon-
strating that the UN eyes closely monitors even what the parliament committees are discussing, approving and doing.

Still in regard to the surveillance of the Timorese parliament, another
aspect regularly monitored by the DGSU was the attendance of the members
of parliament to the plenary sessions. In fact, the UN went a step further and
literally compared the official and the actual attendance records. While the
official attendance records are the ones prepared by the secretariat of the
National Parliament, which are based on the signature of the congressmen/
women on the presence list of the National Parliament, the actual attendance
was a round-up average of attendance congressmen/women on the plenary
sessions elaborated by the Democratic Governance Support Unit of UNMIT,
which is based on actual counting of members of the parliament who were at
the beginning and at the end of the morning and afternoon plenary sessions.
This kind of monitoring is very much indicative of not only the hierarchical
manner in which the whole normalization process occurs, but also the very
degree of surveillance and scrutiny under which the Timorese state, and
population, are subject in their own country.[20]

The UN surveillance framework is pervasive throughout several Timorese institutions. This is clear, for instance, in regard to the surveillance of:
(1) the ministry of finance in terms of the state budget expenditure and
execution rate carried out; (2) the court of appeal through the monitoring of
the status of the penal and civil cases of the country; (3) the office of the
prosecutor-general in terms of the status of criminal cases; (4) the number of
cases and the very activities performed by the *Provedor* of Human Rights
and Justice, Inspector General, and Anti-Corruption Commission; among
many others. Even the legal acts approved by the Council of Ministers and

the issues analyzed during its meetings that took place during a certain month, along with the number of meetings of the National Priorities Working Groups and the matters discussed, are under UN close supervision.

The civil society was also not spared from this surveillance mechanism. In this regard, the report also paid a close attention to the range of activities, meetings, events, trainings, workshops, seminars, conferences and so on carried out at the Timor-Leste NGO Forum, which is a forum that seeks to congregate the NGOs, both national and international, working in Timor-Leste. In fact, they were not only under this surveillance mechanism, but also under the constant attempt, made by the international actors, of being conducted, in terms of being pushed, through funding, to carry out certain kind of projects that sometimes are not considered by the Timorese as their main concern. Unsurprisingly, this is not something specific to Timor-Leste. Just as in other post-conflict scenarios, this conduction is pursued, as it could be expected, through the disciplinary mechanism of funding, in the sense that certain kinds of projects find the necessary funding while others do not.

In regard to the local level, the local government reports, through its performance graphs and tables, scrutinizes several themes related to the governance aspects of each one of the Timorese districts. Therefore, enables the close monitoring of very crucial elements of the local governance, which also constitutes another element of the surveillance framework of the governance sphere of the country as a whole. The report monitors areas, among others, such as (1) the main activities (such as coordination and public meetings, events, ceremonies, among others) that were carried out at each district, focusing on their number and also the subjects dealt in these activities; (2) the very information flow of each district, monitoring not only the quantity of incoming/outgoing official documents in respect to each Timorese district, but also the very content of these documents, and therefore controlling the flow of information/instructions between the district and Dili, and among the districts themselves; (3) the finance of each district, monitoring both the amount of money received from each district and also from where that money comes; (4) the judicial activity in each district through the monitoring of the number and the status (new, solved, pending) of the civil and penal cases of the district courts; (5) the projects carried out in each district controlling both the number and the kind of projects, along with their status; (6) a crucial source of the development of any modern economy—electricity—through the monitoring of the electricity consumption, the current production and capacity to produce more of it by each Timorese district; (7) the compliance of the international standards fostered through the close attention to the number of the district civil servants officially trained and also to the subjects on which they are trained; (8) even the number of visits of senior state officials (the president, prime minister/vice prime minister, members of the parliament, minister/secretary of state, and others) to each district, and the reasons of the visit, were closely observed by the report.

Despite these several governance elements that are closely monitored by this surveillance instrument, the report is used also to monitor other elements of the districts apart from the governance sphere. This instrument enables, for instance, the UN also to better monitor and clearly picture its own presence in each district through the close observation of not only the number of UN staff in each district, but also which programs, projects, or activities are being carried out by UNMIT, and the constellation of UN actors that gravitate around it, in each Timorese district.

The civil society is also not out of this surveillance framework constructed by the UN. Through this surveillance instrument, the UN, for instance, monitors the information flow that passes through the community radios of each district. Apart from monitoring the number of hours that these radios broadcast, the UN also paid close attention to the radio programs broadcasted in each community radios. This enables the UN not only to know which radios broadcast, but also to observe which programs are being broadcasted through this channel, and perhaps most importantly, to observe whether its own programs were being broadcasted in each district. Another element that the UN also has under close observation is the NGOs' activities in each Timorese district. This surveillance instrument enabled the UN to see which NGO acts in which district and the very projects (advocacy, capacity-building, training, assistance, and so on), and sectors (education, health, justice, economy, and so on), that are being performed. Furthermore, as it would be expected, the biopolitical sphere of the population is also not left out of the surveillance framework. Through this instrument the UN also monitored several biopolitical processes such as: (1) the district education profile, (2) the district health care profile, or (3) the district demographic profile, through the monitorization of the population number, average growth rate, average household size, female and male population distribution, the average age at the first marriage, and the fertility rate, in each district.

All these examples leave little room for doubts in regard to the deep and encompassing surveillance framework that the Timorese governance sphere and also the Timorese people were subject to. This surveillance framework installed by the UN, through the use of several elements, which these monthly governance reports and the local governance reports are part, is a framework that seeks to closely monitor the Timorese conducts and actions. It is a framework that seeks to observe not only what kinds of activities and conducts the Timorese are performing, but especially whether the Timorese state, and population, are performing the activities and conducting themselves accordingly; whether these behaviors need to be fostered of corrected, and most importantly, whether Timor-Leste is closer to being, and behaving as, a normal state within the international scenario.

OTHER STEERING AND SCANNING INSTRUMENTS

In addition to all the instruments exposed and delineated so far, there are other instruments that have their structuring function somewhat diminished and are more characterized by their steering, scanning and monitoring functions. Although it is to some extent difficult to clearly dissociate these functions from one another, it is clear that there are some instruments in the normalizing state-building *dispositif* that have more the function of placing Timor-Leste into a permanent and constant framework of surveillance. This is certainly the case, for instance, of the index of laws of Timor-Leste (ILTL) (UN, 2012) and the Accountability Mechanism of Key Institutions (AMKI) (UN, 2011b). They both function as surveillance instruments; but whereas the former was directed to the Timorese laws, the latter was directed to its fundamental institutions.

The first instrument, the Index of Laws of Timor-Leste, is a document that was prepared by the UNMIT Democratic Governance Unit and the UNMIT Office of Legal Affairs. The intention was to consolidate in one document all the Timorese legislative instruments published in the Official Gazette of RDTL from May 20th 2002 to January 15th 2012. This index enables anyone to search through the Timorese laws by the general subject of legislation, by a more specialized subject, the reference of the law, by its title in Portuguese (along with its translation to English), and the date of publication (UN, 2011b). The second instrument, the Accountability Mechanism of Key Institutions, has more an examining function. This accountability mechanism is a document that focuses on several important Timorese institutions. The vast majority of them are within the Timorese state or state-related, such as the presidency, the national parliament, the central bank, the National Petroleum Authority, the National Electoral Commission, and others. The ones that are not part of the state are the Church, the NGO-forum, the chamber of commerce and the political parties. The document is intended to give a detailed account of the functioning, structures and explanation of the reason of each institution, with particular attention, to the state and state-related institutions. In this sense, this document focuses, independently of the kind of organization, on explaining and exposing the person at the head of the institution, the institution's role, its mission, the respective mandates and competencies, its organizational structure when it is the case, the legislative body that underpins that institution, its staffing profile, its institutional contacts and its respective budget (UN, 2011b).

There is no doubt that it can be very helpful, on the one hand, to consolidate the laws in one document, making it much easier to go through the Timorese legislative body and, on the other hand, to have a very clear picture of the functioning of the Timorese state and its respective institutions. In fact, both instruments could very much function as a powerful tool in the hands of active citizens that would like to demand services from the Timorese state, or even of some Timorese non-governmental organization that seeks to check the Timorese state power or to demand a certain kind of legislation in some determinate area. However, having these documents, in English, in a society where the vast majority does not have English as its primary, secondary, or even tertiary language is not of much help at all. Having these documents compiled in English is clearly not the best solution to foster accountability in a country where the vast majority of the people has a very limited command of the English language. Hence, the conclusion one can fairly reach is that the document was assembled by, and most importantly for, internationals.

In this way, on the one hand, the Index of Laws turns out to be another surveillance instrument, which facilitates a lot the monitoring, by the UN, of what is being legislated in each sphere. One should not distract from the fact that the consolidating of the Timorese legislative body—by subject, sub-subject, title, and its publication date—in one document is indeed a process of forming the very visibility of this sphere. It is the formation of this field of visibility of the Timorese legislative body that facilitates the process of enabling those intervening knowing, in a very fast and searchable manner, what kind of laws the Timorese state is passing in regard to each sphere. Hence, rather than a mere depoliticized bureaucratic document that seeks only to consolidate the laws in one place to better organize things, this index indeed places Timor-Leste under a regular surveillance due to the constant monitoring of its legislative production. Obliviously, the consequences of this, of course, are not limited solely to the legislative sphere. In fact, this has also consequences in the normalization process as a whole. A pivotal consequence of this monitoring of the legislative production of the Timorese state is that the monitoring of the whole normalization process that Timor-Leste is subject to becomes highly facilitated.

One the other hand, the Accountability Mechanism becomes a manner in which the internationals can keep scanning and mapping several Timorese institutions. Hence, in looking into all Timorese institutions, the Accountability Mechanism is more useful for those intervening in the country than to its population. Perhaps a clearer image of this mechanism is the image of an x-ray. Through the detailed delineation of each of these institutions, it is not only formed a field of visibility in regard to the Timorese state institutions, but, most importantly, this mechanism performs more of a scanning function. Through this scanning process, this mechanism would function as an instrument used to observe how these institutions are structured and assembled, whether there is some part missing, or whether there is something to be reformulated in terms of institutions in the normalizing process of the Timorese state institutions.

These instruments allow a kind of surveillance over Timor-Leste enables the visualization, by the UN, whether the changes envisaged (both within the

Timorese state and legislative body) were in fact performed. They enable the UN to observe whether the Timorese are actually changing its behavior (which could be exemplified in the kinds of laws passed and the functioning of state institutions). Therefore, it allows the UN to assess how Timorese normalizing process is progressing and see whether any correction in the process, or in the Timorese behavior, is needed.

CONCLUSION

This chapter explores a series of surveillance instruments that were deployed throughout Timor-Leste and which are essential operational instruments of the normalization *dispositif* deployed to the country. These are not central-ized and highly coordinated instruments; quite the contrary. However, they are instruments that although present in multiple and distinct sites, and not related to each other, they do form a coherent surveillance framework. Not-withstanding the fact that it is nearly impossible to delineate all steering, monitoring and structuring instruments that are actively operating throughout Timor-Leste, this chapter shed some light on the fundamental ones; namely the Secretary-General's Reports to the Security Council, the National Prior-ities Program, the United Nations Development Assistance Framework, the Police Arrangement and the Disciplining of the Police, the Monthly Govern-ance Reports and the Local Governance Reports, as well as the Index of Laws of Timor-Leste and the Accountability Mechanism of Key Institutions. Working both from within and from outside Timor-Leste, they are pivotal elements of the very functioning of the normalization state-building *dispositif* deployed to Timor-Leste. These are the instruments that enable not only the close monitoring and scrutiny of the conducts of the Timorese state, and its population, but especially the attempt of shaping them and, most importantly, their proper correction whenever necessary. The instruments herein explored, collectively, place Timor-Leste under a surveillance framework, which is what enables internationals to constantly and closely steer Timor-Leste, monitoring and scrutinizing fundamental spheres of the country, namely the disciplinary, political, and economic governance, and the socio- and biopolit-ical one. It is precisely due to the great amount of influence over these structural spheres that Timor-Leste was transformed into a governance state. The delineation of this process is the core of the next chapter.

NOTES

1. The last SGRSC released by the time of the writing of this chapter is dated from October 15th 2012. However, as long as the UN keeps a mission on the ground, the organization will continue releasing a SGRsSC.

2. By the time of the writing of this chapter, all Secretary-General's Reports to the Security Council dealing with Timor-Leste, including corrections and addenda, were: (S/1999/513; S/1999/595; S/1999/705; S/1999/803; S/1999/862; S/1999/1024; S/2000/53; S/2000/53/Add.1a; S/2000/53/Add.1b; S/2000/738; S/2001/42; S/2001/436; S/2001/719; S/2001/983; S/2001/983/Corr.1; S/2002/80; S/2002/432; S/2002/432/Add.1; S/2002/1223; S/2003/243; S/2003/449; S/2003/944; S/2004/117; S/2004/333; S/2004/669; S/2004/888; S/2005/99; S/2005/310; S/2005/533; S/2006/24; S/2006/251; S/2006/251/Corr.1; S/2006/580; S/2006/628; S/2007/50; S/2007/513; S/2008/26; S/2008/501; S/2009/72; S/2009/504; S/2010/85; S/2010/522; S/2011/32; S/2011/641; S/2012/43; S/2012/765).

3. For instance, the public briefings delivered at the SC meetings. Nevertheless, although this is one important reporting mechanism, since the situation in a given country is discussed and debated, these briefings are usually consolidated at the SGRsSC. However, they complement the picture of the observation of how monitored and supervised Timor-Leste was; the country was on the agenda of several SC meetings: (S/PV.3998; S/PV.4013; S/PV.4019; S/PV.4031; S/PV.4038; S/PV.4041; S/PV.4042; S/PV.4043a; S/PV.4043b; S/PV.4045; S/PV.4057; S/PV.4085; S/PV.4097; S/PV.4114; S/PV.4133; S/PV.4147; S/PV.4165; S/PV.4180; S/PV.4182; S/PV.4191; S/PV.4195; S/PV.4198; S/PV.4203; S/PV.4206; S/PV.4228; S/PV.4236; S/PV.4244; S/PV.4265a; S/PV.4265b; S/PV.4268; S/PV.4308; S/PV.4321a; S/PV.4321b; S/PV.4351a; S/PV.4351b; S/PV.4358; S/PV.4367; S/PV.4368; S/PV.4397; S/PV.4403a; S/PV.4403b; S/PV.4404; S/PV.4456; S/PV.4462a; S/PV.4462b; S/PV.4463; S/PV.4522a; S/PV.4522b; S/PV.4527); (S/PV.4534; S/PV.4537; S/PV.4540; S/PV.4542; S/PV.4598; S/PV.4646a; S/PV.4646b; S/PV.4715; S/PV.4735; S/PV.4744; S/PV.4755; S/PV.4758; S/PV.4843; S/PV.4913; S/PV.4963; S/PV.4965; S/PV.4968; S/PV.5024; S/PV.5074; S/PV.5076; S/PV.5079; S/PV.5132; S/PV.5171; S/PV.5179; S/PV.5180; S/PV.5251; S/PV.5351; S/PV.5432; S/PV.5436; S/PV.5445; S/PV.5457; S/PV.5469; S/PV.5512; S/PV.5514; S/PV.5516; S/PV.5628; S/PV.5634; S/PV.5682); (S/PV.5739; S/PV.5740; S/PV.5791; S/PV.5801; S/PV.5833; S/PV.5843; S/PV.5844; S/PV.5958; S/PV.5959; S/PV.6085; S/PV.6086; S/PV.6129) (S/PV.6205; S/PV.6275; S/PV.6276; S/PV.6278; S/PV.6332; S/PV.6405; S/PV.6485; S/PV.6487; S/PV.6664; S/PV.6714; S/PV.6720; S/PV.6721; S/PV.6858; S/PV.6859).

4. In order to have access to these matrixes for the years of 2009 and 2010, see for instance (Ministry of Finance, 2010: 25–46).

5. Once more, in order to have access to these matrixes for the years of 2009 and 2010, see for instance (Ministry of Finance, 2010: 25–46).

6. This section is based on the current United Nations Development Assistance Framework (UNDAF) for Timor-Leste (UNDP, 2008e) which covers the period of 2009–2013. Since the UNDAF is a standardized document, the rationale presented here is also valid for UNDAFs for previous periods, such as (UNDP, 2002).

7. For a further detailed observation of all 2009–2013–UNDAF objectives, see (UNDP, 2008e: Annex A).

8. For a clearer picture, see (UNDP, 2008e: annex B).

9. For more detailed and in depth information see (UNDP, 2008e: annexes A, B and C).

10. For more regarding the UN Millennium Development Goals see (UN, N/A-b).

11. This graphically illustrative in (UNDP, 2008e: 15).

12. For an analysis of such process in the case of Haiti, see (Zanotti, 2011: chapter 5).

13. The word used in the document is *shall*.

14. This correction of the Timorese policing behavior was a constant throughout the UN engagement with Timor-Leste.

15. Since the reports that deal with the same level of analysis, either national or local, are a standardized instrument with very few structural differences among them, this section will mention and problematize the report without specifying or referencing a month in particular, since the analysis developed is applicable for the whole instrument. These reports can be accessed at (UN, N/A-l).

16. The Timorese districts are: Aileu, Ainaro, Baucau, Bobonaro, Covalima, Dili, Ermera, Lautem, Liquica, Manatuto, Manufahi, Oecusse, and Viqueque.

17. For a graphic example of this, see (UN, 2010a: 2).

18. For a graphic example of this, see (UN, 2010a: 5).

19. The Specialized Standing Committees of the Timorese parliament are: Committee A—Constitutional Issues, Justice, Public Administration, Local Power and Government Legislation (12 members); Committee B—Foreign Affairs, Defence and National Security (10 members); Committee C—Economy, Finance and Anti-Corruption (12 members); Committee D—Agriculture, Fisheries, Forest, National Resources and Environment (10 members); Committee E—Poverty Elimination, Rural and Regional Development and Gender Equality (9 members); Committee F—Health, Education and Culture (8 members); Committee G—Infrastructures and Social Equipments (7 members); Committee H—Youth, Sports, Employment and Professional Training (5 members); Committee I—Internal Regulation, Ethics and Mandate of the Members of Parliament (5 members) (UN, 2011b: 14).

20. For a graphic example of this, see (UN, 2010a: 7).

Chapter Five

The Transformation of Timor-Leste into a Governance State

This chapter problematizes another fundamental dimension of the United Nations (UN) engagement with Timor-Leste—the transformation of Timor-Leste into a governance state. The chapter sheds light on the UN effort to exercise the technology of power of government by outlining the international will, led by the UN, to conduct Timor-Leste and Timorese. Hence, this chapter explores the attempts of conduction of the Timorese state's and population's conducts and on how it was rendered operational. This does mean that the UN *wants*, all the time, to conduct them and that this conduction is *detailed* and *consciously* planned. In fact, most of the time, when one talks to a UN official, one gets precisely the opposite narrative—they argue that what the organization seeks is that the Timorese state and population stand on their own feet. However, one should remember that this will to conduct is not visible in terms of an *obligation* to do something. On the contrary, government is a dispositional power. It is dispositional in the sense that a much subtler way to conduct is to dispose things and structures in a way that structure the field of possible actions of the other person or entity.

In Timor-Leste, this will to conduct is visible through the transformation of Timor-Leste into a governance state; through the international effort to influence, shape, and mold actions and process in pivotal dimensions of the state or population's lives. This certainly does not mean that the conduction pursued is always successful, in the sense that the UN is always successful in making the Timorese state or population behave accordingly. The main point here is to render visible the power structure that was set up by the normalizing state-building *dispositif* deployed to Timor-Leste which has as its purpose the effort of conducting the country. Obviously, this power structure is not rendered operational as such. On the contrary, it is structured through power-denying notions, through notions that precisely while exercising power deny its very exercise. In the case of Timor-Leste, this UN will to conduct becomes visible on several levels, such as: the structuring of the state deciding what institutions the Timorese would have; the formation of these institutions; or the structuring of the manner in which these institutions would function. These, by their turn, shape how the Timorese state will behave and function. This movement might be understood as a structuring of structures. Therefore, one can conduct a state not only by seeking to alter its behavior from outside, but also, from within, by structuring its own institutions and their respective *modus operandi*; especially when this is done with fundamental (structural) institutions, as it was done in Timor-Leste. This is certainly not the only dimension where this UN will to conduct can be felt. This will to conduct the Timorese is also visible on other dimensions such as the effort to influence the economic, social, security and political spheres; which, in essence, transforms Timor-Leste into a governance state. Certainly, this movement has a purpose. This attempt to conduct Timor-Leste and the pursuit to structure the field of its possible actions are an important part of the UN attempt to normalize the country. This will to normalize Timor-Leste seeks to turn Timor-Leste into a stable and predictable country; it seeks to make Timor-Leste start behaving more like a normal state within international relations.

In order to elucidate this process, this chapter clarifies the transformation of Timor-Leste into a governance state by exploring three fundamental moments of the UN engagement with the country. The chapter is structured in four sections. The first section delineates and further clarifies the notion of a governance state. Then, in the second section, the chapter explores the matter in which the UN shapes Timorese behavior, as voters, during the referendum process of 1999. The section delineates the UN attempt of constructing a liberal Timorese voter during UNAMET. The third section evinces UN's use of law-making as a dispositional instrument of structuring, and as a consequence conduct, present and future Timorese conducts. Therefore, it explores how the UN exercised its dispositional power by structuring pivotal structures of the Timorese reality. Finally, in its fourth section, the chapter sheds light on the international attempt, led by the UN, of influencing pivotal spheres of the Timorese state. Hence, the section evinces the international influence and supervision over crucial Timorese spheres such as: disciplinary; political and economic governance; and socio- and biopolitical.

TIMOR-LESTE AS A GOVERNANCE STATE

Observing the UN power exercised during its engagement with Timor-Leste, one might think that its power rested solely on its *de jure* sovereignty over

Timor-Leste. This understanding is quite reasonable. After all, according Jarat Chopra (2000) argues that the UN status in Timor-Leste, due to its executive, legislative and judiciary powers, was similar to a pre-constitutional monarch in a sovereign kingdom (Chopra, 2000: 29). This kind of power is visible in several occasions, for instance: (1) the fact that all executive, legislative and judicial powers were on the hands of one man—Sergio Vieira de Mello—who was the UN Transitional Administrator and understood his own role in Timor-Leste as a "benevolent despot" (Power, 2008: 302); (2) the centralization of decision-making within the UN, which not only failed on including the Timorese in processes, but also on making the UN accountable to them; (3) the UN obstruction of projects seeking to introduce local democracy where each sub-district would decide its own development priorities (Chopra, 2000: 29–33), which would certainly dilute the centralization of power; (4) the fact that the Timorese could only apply for the menial jobs (Chopra, 2000: 29–33); (5) the fact that the international staff working in the mission, in accordance with international conventions, had immunity from prosecution, while the Timorese were, obviously, subject to the laws and legally punished when an infraction was performed (Chopra, 2000: 29); (6) the UN exercising a sovereign role in agreements signed with international financial institutions, such as the World Bank (WB) (Chopra, 2000: 30); or even (7) the UN making itself the administrator of the "immovable or movable property, including monies, bank accounts, and other property of, or registered in the name of the Republic of Indonesia, or any of its subsidiary organs and agencies, which is in the territory of East Timor" on its very first legislative act (UNTAET/REG/1999/1). All these elements leads the analyst to conclude that the UN power was similar to a monarchical power in Timor-Leste (Chopra, 2000: 35) and that much of UN power rested, for instance, on its law-making monopoly.

Nevertheless, these indicators could lead the inattentive analyst to miss that much of the UN power rested and was exercised through a technology of power previously delineated—government. In regard to government, this is a more dispositional power in the sense that it is more concerned about "the disposition of things, that is to say, of employing tactics rather than laws, or, of as far as possible employing laws as tactics; arranging things so that this or that end may be achieved through a certain number of means" (Foucault, [1978] 2007: 137). Remembering Guillaume de La Perrière's definition of government, exposed by Foucault, government "is the right disposition of things, arranged so as to lead to a convenient end" (quoted by Foucault, [1978] 2007: 134). The convenient end, in the case of the UN in Timor-Leste, was certainly the construction of a liberal democratic state, which was underpinned by the attempt of implementing the liberal peace in Timor-Leste. This, as already discussed, is a kind of peace that is perceived as the very base of the stability of the international order (Richmond, 2011: 8). In the case of Timor-Leste, this has a close connection with the prevention of it becoming a failed state in the eyes of the international community. This process was pursued through the UN state-building process, which means the construction of stable, predictable, and disciplined institutions that in the end, hopefully, will shape a stable, predictable, disciplined, and, most importantly, normal state within the international scene.

In a more governmental exercise of power, the law-making is more a means to dispose and to shape a society aiming to achieve a determinate end, than a mere way of obtaining the population's compliance with the law. It is precisely in its dispositional character where rested the real power of the UN throughout its whole engagement with Timor-Leste. Fundamentally, the UN power is clearly visible in the transformation of Timor-Leste into a governance state. Mark Duffield (2007), using Graham Harrison's (2004) definition, says that a governance state "can briefly be described as a form of contingent sovereignty in which the international community exerts a good deal of control and oversight over the core economic, environmental and welfare functions of the state, that is, its core biopolitical functions" (2007: 82). This kind of relationship captures the fact that the core of Timor-Leste's functions as a state was, and continued to be, subject to a constant international influence and supervision. It is not an absurd to understand that these core state functions can be grouped around, interrelated and quite often overlapping, spheres such as: (1) disciplinary, which influences, shapes, and structures fields like policing, the military, law, and order; (2) political and economic governance, which is composed by the structures that carry out these processes, how they operate, and their very characteristics; and (3) socio- and biopolitical, which encompasses all the life-supporting processes of the population and its surrounding conditions. This certainly does not mean that these are clear-cut and hermetic spheres; one sphere definitely influences and is influenced by the other. In fact, some state functions can be fairly part of all of these spheres simultaneously. Hence, a governance state is a state where the disciplinary, political and economic governance, and the socio- and biopolitical spheres—the state's core—are highly influenced, structured, and shaped by internationals.

The transformation of Timor-Leste into a governance state happened along the whole UN engagement with the country and the dispositional character of the UN power, as it will be further evinced during this chapter, had different tones along its engagement with Timor-Leste. Initially, during UNAMET, it took it took the form of conducting the Timorese conduct in the sense of transforming the Timorese into a liberal voter. In essence, it took the form of teaching the Timorese of how to properly behave within an electoral environment. Then, during UNTAET, UN it was rendered operational through the structuring of Timorese structures. The importance of this structuring of structures is twofold. Firstly, this is important in order to match the

UN actions with the narratives and discourses, such as capacity building, frequently present along the UN engagement with Timor-Leste. This is what enables the UN to govern—to conduct conducts, to establish mechanisms and procedures that are destined to conduct Timor-Leste and the Timorese—*through* the very notion of capacity building. Is what enables the UN, unproblematically, to structure the possible field where, and how, the Timorese ownership or capacity might act and be exercised. One should remember that government neither necessarily collides with the governed perceived interests, nor presupposes that those who are governed are passive agents. One must bear in mind that government is not a repressive power. On the contrary, it is a power that fosters actions by those that are governed. In fact, to be most effective government *needs* active and free agents. There should be conducts to be conducted. Secondly, this structuring of structures performed by the UN power is what makes it possible, and enables, the UN to conduct the Timorese state and its population from more afar than, for instance, during the UNAMET period. In other words, with this structuring of structures of the first phase of the UN engagement, it was opened the possibility of not being imperative for the UN to directly and, most importantly manifestly, conduct the Timorese state. It made possible the conduction to be rendered operational much less noticeably.

This is fundamentally important after the Timorese legal/formal independence in 2002, since an open and visible conduct of Timor-Leste would look like a direct intervention in a sovereign state, and, most significantly, would also be contradictory and directly collide with the portrayal of UN previous actions of building the Timorese independence. Evidently, this does not mean that the UN exerted less power upon the Timorese after 2002, but that the tone in which it was exerted modified. It means that the conduct of Timor-Leste needed to become less manifest. Over the time, the conduct of Timor-Leste had to be exercised more *through* power-denying notions such as capacity-building, advising, counseling, training, consulting, monitoring, and mentoring in order to the shaping of Timorese conducts become less noticeable. This is an important feature of portraying the normalization process as a less invasive process, or even as a beneficial relationship in as much as these notions can easily be argued to be quite distinct from an indisputable and manifest control of the core disciplinary, economic, political, and biopolitical spheres of Timor-Leste. They can be easily portrayed as mere technical or bureaucratic assistance. Moreover, they allow a great amount of power, without a relevant local accountability, to be exercised unproblematically and enable a deep exercise of power to be performed without bearing much responsibility of its consequences. Precisely because of that, they are power-denying; they are power-denying exactly due to the fact that the great amount of power and influence is regularly exercised but clothed in a technical and bureaucratic character.

This kind of denial relationship and the governance state that Timor-Leste was transformed into are visible since the beginning of the UN engagement with the country. As already explored in chapter 4, one must remember that the since UNTAET, the UN peace operations not only already legislated over the country, but also, through the several Security Council (SC) mandates, was called, among other activities, to assist in the development of civil and social services; to ensure the coordination and delivery of humanitarian assistance, rehabilitation, and development assistance; to provide security and maintain law and order throughout the territory of Timor; to assist in the establishment of conditions for sustainable development; to establish an effective administration and to provide assistance to core administrative structures critical to the viability of the country; and to contribute to the maintenance of the external and internal security of Timor-Leste. Even with the beginning of UN's pull out of the country, this kind of relationship was thought to continue with UNOTIL and its advising, monitoring and supervision character. Moreover, it is true that this kind of relationship was undoubtedly accentuated in 2006 from the establishment of the UNMIT with its wide and deep mandate. However, the UN conduction of conducts felt by Timor-Leste and the country being characterized as a governance state is clear since the very beginning of the UN engagement with the country with UNAMET when the UN sought to shape a Timorese voter.

THE LIBERAL TIMORESE VOTER

The effort to conduct Timor-Leste and the Timorese is not something recent. In the case of the conduct of the Timorese, for instance, a fundamental effort began as early as the establishment of UNAMET. As already mentioned, UNAMET was responsible for organizing and monitoring the referendum in regard to the autonomy proposal advanced by Indonesia. Therefore, one of the very first things that the UN did was to teach the Timorese how to behave properly in an election environment. The whole set of practices expected to occur in a democratic election—such as campaigning, the interactions with the opposition, the formation of alliances, and the mobilization of supporters—needed to be taught and should occur within a framework pre-determined by the UN. Hence, the whole set of practices of the Timorese in the democratic environment that would begin was already defined by the UN through a pre-established framework. The UN, in this field, sought to transform the Timorese into liberal voters by conducting their behaviors; more precisely, by structuring the field of their possible behaviors, so they, in the end, would act appropriately in the UN's eyes.

This process was certainly not something hidden or veiled. On the contrary, the very name of the document that framed the behavior of the

Timorese during the popular consultation leaves little room for doubt: "Code of Conduct for Participants" (UN, 1999a). This document provided the code of conduct for the "participants" (how the Timorese are referred along the whole document) during the campaign period. The very Preamble of the code determines that the whole campaigning should be performed "strictly according to the Code of Conduct" (UN, 1999a: preamble). Therefore, the conducts of all "participants" "shall be bound" (UN, 1999a: preamble) by this Code of Conduct. From this, it should not be drawn the conclusion that the document induced the passivity of the Timorese. On the contrary, it encouraged their active participation in the election. The Code of Conduct sought to both positively and negatively structure their behaviors. The document sought not only to negatively limit the Timorese actions, in the sense of prohibiting them of having certain behaviors during the consultation process. The Code of Conduct also induced the Timorese to actively behave in a certain manner. Therefore, their behaviors were stimulated on a determined direction, in the sense that certain practices were fostered and encouraged rather than others (which were prohibited), seeking to shape their conducts toward a specific outcome, a specific kind of Timorese voter.

The effort to shape an active liberal voter is visible throughout the whole Code of Conduct. The document sought to structure several aspects, such as: freedom of speech and assembly; the language used during the campaign and the campaigning itself; the behaviors during the voting process; and the very acceptance of the results. At its very beginning, the document states that "[a]ll participants *shall actively* contribute to the creation of a climate of democratic tolerance" (UN, 1999a: paragraph 1; emphasis added). Moreover, the Timorese should behave accordingly by encouraging the democratic pluralism (UN, 1999a: paragraph 1). Other elements—such as freedom of assembly and of the press—were also included in the Code of Conduct that the Timorese should comply. The document went as far as noting to the Timorese that they should keep the secrecy of their vote but also "aid in maintaining the secrecy of the voting" (UN, 1999a: paragraph 16). Even the acceptance of the results was regulated when the document instead of asking the Timorese to accept the balloting results, it stated in advance that they should agree to accept the results of the consultation (UN, 1999a: paragraph 27).

As aforementioned, the document also identified the behaviors the Timorese should not have. The code sought to structure also the kind of language that the Timorese should use while campaigning, by stating that they "*shall at all times* avoid using language which is inflammatory, defamatory, or threatens or incites violence in any form" (UN, 1999a: paragraph 11; emphasis added). The Timorese were also requested to not be part and discourage (UN, 1999a: Paragraph 8) the prevention of people to attend, address, or form rallies, marches, or demonstrations; or even the destruction of posters and political material of adversaries. The document covered other aspects, like determining that "no participant shall" (UN, 1999a: paragraph 15): kill, torture, injure, intimidate, threaten, forcefully compel someone to take part on the campaign or to vote in any direction on the ballot, or offer monetary incentive for other voters. The document goes on also pointing that the Timorese "shall not" procure the support of officials to promote or interfere on any campaign (UN, 1999a: paragraph 19), and shall also cooperate with the voting officials in order to have a peaceful voting (UN, 1999a: paragraph 20).

Obviously, most of the elements delineated in the document—from freedom of speech and assembly to the prevention of the use of violence or the attempt to avoid corruption—are valid and should be carried out in a democratic election process. Nevertheless, it should not pass unproblematically through the eyes of an attentive analyst the kind of freedom one have when performing a sovereign act of choosing and selecting an outcome in an election within an environment that is very much beforehand pre-established by the internationals; an environment structurally built with no voice at all of the Timorese. Furthermore, this process evinces a very paradoxical, and frequent, feature of the UN engagement with Timor-Leste—the Timorese decision (or not) for its very legal independence, perhaps the most iconic example of the exercise of a sovereign act of a population, being performed within an environment that was a result of a decision-making process that clearly prevented the Timorese participation, while structuring their behaviors in their own country. In fact, this is a clear indication of how the conduct of Timor-Leste and of the Timorese was pursued through the very exercise of their freedom. This is visible precisely in the fact that the very exercise of their freedom to choose which way the country should go—either annexing to Indonesia or not—was performed in a field structured beforehand by the UN. Surely the Timorese could choose whichever path they preferred, but within the field of action previously structured by the internationals seeking to conduct the Timorese behavior, and also the behavior of the Timorese state.

THE STRUCTURING OF
TIMORESE STRUCTURES: LAWS AS TACTICS

The structuring, by the UN, of the field of action in which the behaviors of Timor-Leste and the Timorese could be performed certainly did stop after the referendum. In fact, it became much denser and deeper. After the referendum, during UNTAET, a huge amount of UN power rested on its ability to legislate. After all, the UN had the monopoly of the law-making in the country during this period. Nevertheless, the real power of the UN rested on the dispositional character in which the UN exercised this power. The dispositional power of the UN at that point took the form of structuring Timorese structures so they can shape the future behaviors of the Timorese state and the Timorese conducts toward a determinate end. With this process, the UN normalizing *dispositif* sought precisely to structure stable, predictable and disciplined Timorese institutions which, in turn, would structure a stable, predictable, disciplined and, most importantly, a normal Timor-Leste within the international scenario.

During the UNTAET period, as already mentioned, the UN exercised legislative power in Timor-Leste, along with administrations of justice and the executive power. This power was exercised through four UN legislative instruments: regulations, executive orders, directives, and notifications. Nevertheless, these four legislative instruments were used less as a means of obtaining the compliance of the law by the Timorese, than used in a dispositional and governmental manner. This UN dispositional power is clearly visible being exercised on different spheres, namely the ones which characterize a governance state (disciplinary, political and economic governance, and socio- and biopolitical). Furthermore, it was also exercised on distinct levels—macro and micro ones. Hence, the UN legislative instruments navigated, in distinct spheres, through a macro level of structuring state institutions and their functioning and also on a more capillary one exercised over very micro aspects of the Timorese state and people's lives. This means that they sought not only to structure the configuration of the future Timorese state, but also that the Timorese were placed on a UN power network that reached also micro aspects of their lives. Therefore, this is a power that was characterized by both its structuring and pervasive character.

This pervasiveness of UN power certainly makes one remember what Foucault exposed as the microphysics of power. To Roberto Machado (1979), Foucault understood the microphysics of power precisely as the fact that the power was exercised not only at the macro level and at the state mechanisms, but also at a micro level throughout the social body. In this way, the power was exercised not only above the people but also penetrated their very daily lives (Machado, 1979: xii). This is precisely what is observable while analyzing UNTAET legislative instruments—the UN power present not only above the Timorese, through the structuring of the state mechanisms but also reaching the molecular aspects of the Timorese lives. Taking each aspect targeted by the UN legislative instruments individually, one can grasp neither the depth nor the capillarity of the UN dispositional power in Timor-Leste. It is by taking a step back and seeking to understand them collectively that a clearer picture emerges. Therefore, rather than an exhaustive delineation of the areas where the UN legislated, the following examples give a clearer picture of the dispositional and structuring power exercised over Timor-Leste and its reach. Most importantly, it enables the visualization of the width of the normalizing *dispositif* deployed to Timor-

Leste and also the depth of the process of making Timor-Leste a governance state. Taking all the aspects legislated combined, it is clear that UN measures are not senseless disparate and distinct actions. Notwithstanding the fact that they are indeed very often disparate, distinct and not related at all, they do form a coherent whole that exercise a great amount of influence over fundamental spheres of Timor-Leste. In essence, collectively, they sought to structure the behavior of the future Timorese state and, in turn, of the Timorese. In the end, it is precisely through these apparently disparate legislative instruments that the UN sought to discipline Timor-Leste from within, by structuring its structures and forming the very behavior the Timorese state would have.

In regard to foundational elements of the future Timorese state, both on a macro structural level and on a micro capillary one, it is observable that the UN dispositional power reached several spheres. The construction of these elements is not something bad per se. However, this certainly constitutes a governmental power since those elements unquestionably shape and structure the future constitution and *modus operandi* of the Timorese state. Hence, the field of possible actions of the future Timorese state becomes structured *a priori*. The result is a future Timorese state that has its own functioning very much structured by elements that were created during a process that proceeded with marginal hearing of the Timorese population, a process in which the Timorese had little, if any, participation.

In regard to the political and economic governance sphere, on the one hand, on a macro level, the UN dispositional power is visible, for instance, in legislative instruments dealing with structuring issues, such as: the Code of Ethics which the judges and prosecutors should comply with[1]; the creation of a Central Fiscal Authority[2]; the creation of a Central Payments Office[3]; the determination of the currency of the United States of America, the US dollar, as the official currency of Timor-Leste and its bank notes and coins as the legal tender of the country[4]; and the creation of a border regime for Timor-Leste.[5] Furthermore, UNTAET also shaped pivotal elements in regard to the management of the future Timorese state by structuring: the taxation system[6]; the budget and financial management[7]; the bank licensing and supervision[8]; and the banking and payments authority.[9] The structuring of the very organic of these institutions and of the future Timorese state was certainly not bypassed either. The number of ministries, their *raison d'être* and responsibilities, their political management and the composing bodies of each ministry was also structured.[10] The UN went as far as regulating some operating rules of the Council of Ministers, such as how often they should meet (once a week), and the very working languages to be used (Portuguese and Tetum).[11] Strikingly, even though these were fundamental structures of the future Timorese state, once more, most of the Timorese had not say on the matter. On the other hand, the UN power was not confined to the macro aspects of the state mechanisms. Its power was also experienced on a more capillary level. This is visible, for instance, in legislative instruments dealing with micro aspects, such as, the establishment of a table in regard to the payment of taxes on the importation of products like soft drinks and other flavored waters, beers, wines, other alcoholic beverages, tobacco and tobacco products, perfumes, electronics, and others.[12] Moreover, it also stipulated fees regarding the landing and taking-off of aircrafts[13] and the use of Timo-rese ports.[14]

In regard to the biopolitical sphere, the UN dispositional power also navi-gated through both macro and micro levels. The legislative instruments de-ployed by the UN dealt with biopolitical processes of the Timorese popula-tion, such as, communication, movement, and labor. Regarding the commu-nication, the UN power reached, for instance, the radio and television broad-casting over Timorese territory.[15] In regard to the second, movement, the establishment of road traffic rules[16] is a clear aspect of it. The capillarity of UN power in such a matter went as far as, for instance, determining the side of the road that should be driven on, the speed limit, determining places where parking was prohibited (UNTAET/DIR/2001/7) and even determining the kind of traffic infringement notice for traffic offences.[17] Regarding the third process mentioned, labor, the dispositional power of the UN was felt, for instance, on the UN elaborating the very labor code of Timor-Leste.[18] In this matter, the capillarity of the UN power reached, for instance, how labor disputes should be settled,[19] how many hours should the Timorese work, their vacations and sick leaves, overtime compensations, the period of notice for terminating an employment contract, and the minimum elements that this contract should have,[20] to point out just a few examples. Still on the biopolit-ical sphere, the UN power also touched more molecular aspects of the Timo-rese daily life. There were legislative instruments dealing with the registra-tion of businesses[21] and charitable organizations,[22] the decriminalization of both defamation[23] and even adultery.[24] Moreover, the spheres the UN dealt with went as far as regulating matters like the fees regarding the use of water[25]; and the use of electricity and the price of the kilowatt-hour (kWh).[26] The capillarity of the UN power reached as far as, on the one hand, establish-ing the fees for the postal service, literally defining the prices for sending letters, postcards, and even for photocopying[27]; and, on the other hand, deter-mining the public holidays in Timor-Leste.[28] In addition of being clear exam-ples of the deep reach of the UN power, once more, even though these elements surrounded the very life-supporting processes of the Timorese, most of them did not have any participation on the decision-making process.

While, on the one hand, all these efforts, and certainly others not men-tioned, of shaping the Timorese state institutions sought to correct its deviant or abnormal behavior through their normalization mirroring what is under-stood as normal for its interventionist peers and seeking to construct a normal state on the international community's eyes; on the other hand, it was also important to deal with the deviant and abnormal behaviors within the Timorese social body, such as the criminals or the delinquents, in order to normalize them and the Timorese social body. Hence, the UN dispositional power was also felt in the disciplinary sphere. In regard to the disciplinary sphere, as expected, the UN dispositional power in this sphere also navigated through macro and micro levels.

On the one hand, on a macro level of the disciplinary sphere the UN dispositional power structured fundamental pillars of it, such as the police force,[29] the prison service,[30] and the justice system[31] dealing not only with their institutional framework but also with the manner in which they should operate. Regarding the first pillar, the police, the UN power went from structuring the very functioning of the police organization (establishing its general duties and competencies, hierarchy and chain of command),[32] to the establishment of the very criteria that should be followed to the appointment of the commissioner of the police, and the personal and professional requirements for someone to be appointed as commissioner[33] and as a cadet.[34] This pattern was also felt, for instance, in regard to the second pillar, the prison services, where the UN structured not only its duties and functioning, but also the very functions of the director and prison officers of the penal institutions.[35] Lastly, in regard to the last pillar mentioned, the power of the UN of structuring structures went as far as structuring a fundamental element of it—the criminal procedures applicable to Timor-Leste.[36] Still on the macro level, the development of a disciplinary sphere cannot exist without being accompanied by the construction of mechanisms which enable the Timorese state with instruments to properly see its own population and the deviant people amongst them. For this to happen, it is necessary to create record-keeping instruments. On the one hand, in order to see the deviant people, such as the criminals or the delinquents, it was stipulated that all penal institutions should keep records of all its inmates and the respective accusations and crimes[37]; on the other hand, to see all population, and render them visible, the Central Civil Registry was created[38] whose main objective was to maintain a register of the residents in Timor-Leste.

On the other hand, on a micro level of the disciplinary sphere, the UN legislative instruments dealt with capillary details of such sphere, but details that in the end constituted the very essence of this sphere. Such detailed structuring of several aspects was felt, for instance, on the criminal procedures established in Timor-Leste with the UN structuring elements such as trial proceedings, criminal jurisdiction and even procedure for *habeas corpus*.[39] In regard to the pillar of the police, the capillarity of the UN dispositional power went as far as stipulating, for instance, that while identifying, and recording, a suspect of a crime the police officers should also register the following information of the person: the name and address, nationality, prints (fingers, palm, toes, foot), photographs, and measurements (weight, height).[40] Still in the micro level of structuring structures of the disciplinary sphere, in regard to the pillar of the prison system, the UN power went as far as stipulating how the Timorese should handle and deal with its own inmates. It was stipulated, for example: the inmate's information that should be recorded (inmate's identity, fingerprints, body measurements, charges, day an hour of admission, and so on); whether force should be used or not in case of inmate's disobedience of orders; how the inmate's should be separated inside a prison institution (by gender, age, trial process, and so on); and that the prisoner shall be required to work. The UN detailed even the behaviors that would be interpreted as offences against discipline inside the prison institution, with their respective punishments (such as a warning or reprimand; a loss of privileges; performance of extra duties; confinement in the inmates sleeping quarters for a maximum of seven days; restitution; or confiscation of property associated with the offence).[41] Moreover, the UN power went as capillary as specifying the manner in which the recordkeeping of the punishments should be done, saying that in the case of a punishment, the manager of the prison "shall enter, in the Punishment Book, a statement of the nature of the offence, the date of the offence, the name of the offender and the punishment imposed and shall sign and date the entry" (UNTAET/REG/ 2001/23). This detailed structuring of micro, and fundamental, aspects of the disciplinary sphere was also felt on the pillar of the civil registry. The UN disciplinary power went as capillary as stipulating, for instance, even the kind of information about the Timorese that should be collected (such as: the family and given names; the gender; the date and place of birth; the residential address; a digital photograph of such person; the signature or thumb print of such person; and even the height and the color of the eyes of a person).[42]

There is no doubt that the examples aforementioned are not exhaustive regarding the governmental power exercised by the UN over Timor-Leste. There are several others in the same line. Nevertheless, they are certainly sufficient to characterize the kind of power exercised by the UN which used its legislative power in a dispositional manner. The pattern usually followed the action on two dimensions: a more macro institutional and a more micro and capillary one. Hence, in addition to the institutional structuring and the very functioning of the organizations created, the UN structuring power also sought to structure micro aspects of their functioning in detail. Despite the deep structuring being operated, the elements aforementioned appear as if they were mere technical aspects of the functioning of the structures. Nevertheless, it is precisely through these apparently technical aspects that the UN sought to structure the Timorese structures and shape the Timorese state and discipline it from within. Strikingly, even being a fundamental part of the formation of their state, most of the Timorese had no participation in the process.

On the contrary, both the Timorese population and the newly created institutions ended up being in a complex network of power which sought to shape their conducts. All these legislative instruments were used, as already said, in a dispositional and a governmental matter seeking to normalize the Timorese state and in turn its population, focusing more prominently, at this phase, on the state. Most importantly, this phase of structuring of structures sought also, as a consequence, to structure the future behaviors of the Timorese state. The expected end result of all these efforts was, as already said, the construction of stable, predictable and disciplined institutions that in the end, by extrapolation, would decisively shape a stable, predictable, disciplined—and most importantly—a normal state within the international scene. Nevertheless, needless to say, this kind and magnitude of normalization procedure, through a deep structuring of structures, in a legally independent Timor-Leste, in order to continue operating, would have to change its tone.

UNMIT AND ITS CONSTELLATION

The picture delineated so far not only exposes the pervasiveness and the microphysical characteristic of the UN dispositional power in Timor-Leste, but also its structuring character. Obviously, this kind of engagement neither ended after Timor-Leste achieved its legal independence nor the country ceased to be a governance state. Nevertheless, the tonality of the exercise of UN power and the manner in which Timor-Leste was handled as a governance state had to change. It means that the structuring of Timor-Leste and Timorese conducts had to become less noticeable and power-denying notions such as advising, capacitating, and counseling were essential, especially with the UN pulling out with UNOTIL. However, as already mentioned, after the 2006 crisis what was also at stake with this recurrence of violence was the issue of Timor-Leste being perceived as a failure. A perceived UN failure in Timor-Leste could jeopardize the UN's own reputation as an effective conflict-transformation actor. Therefore, the UN response was the deployment of a wider and deeper peace operation to Timor-Leste—UNMIT. This in fact constituted the reinforcement of the UN normalizing state-building *dispositif* and the strengthening of the character of Timor-Leste as a governance state. After all, as previously referred in chapter 4, UNMIT activities encompassed several areas, among others, such as: enhance democratic-governance culture; assistance regarding political and legal affairs; build capacity in regard to administration of justice; engagement in activities dealing with humanitarian affairs and HIV/AIDS; and mainstream children, youth, and gender issues through policies, programs, and activities throughout the country. Furthermore, the mission was tasked to cooperate and coordinate with UN agencies, funds and programs, along with the international financing institutions and donors to assist the Timorese government to design programs and strategies to reduce poverty and promote economic growth.

Therefore, Timor-Leste as a governance state was subject to a normalizing state-building *dispositif* that had UNMIT as its core but composed also by the constellation of actors—such as the UN agencies, funds and programs, and the international financing institutions—that gravitated around it. On can think, for instance, of organizations/programmes such as: the Food and Agricultural Organization (FAO), the International Labour Organization (ILO), the International Organization for Migration (IOM), the Office of the High Commissioner for Human Rights (OHCHR), the United Nations Capital Development Fund (UNCDF), the United Nations Development Programme (UNDP), the United Nations Education, Scientific and Cultural Organization (UNESCO), the United Nations Population Fund (UNFPA), the United Nations High Commissioner for Refugees (UNHCR), the United Nations Children's Fund (UNICEF), the United Nations Industrial Development Organization (UNIDO), the United Nations Development Fund for Women (UNIFEM), the United Nations Office for Project Services (UNOPS), the United Nations Volunteers (UNV), the World Food Programme (WFP), the World Health Organization (WHO), the Asian Development Bank (ADB), and the World Bank (WB).

In addition, one should not forget that each of them had several projects directed to a number of spheres of the lives of the Timorese population, seeking to influence, structure and oversee almost every core function—such as disciplinary, economic, political, and biopolitical processes—of the Timorese state. With this in mind, it is possible to have a clearer picture that Timor-Leste was placed under a vast and profound normalizing *dispositif* where its core processes as a state and its populations were under a constant and continued monitoring and supervision. The normalizing state-building *dispositif* operating in Timor-Leste is not something recent. As a matter of fact, many of these actors and their projects are in Timor-Leste for a long time. However, with the deployment of UNMIT, the normalizing *dispositif* became undoubtedly deeper, wider, and denser. In regard to the core of the normalizing *dispositif* operating in Timor-Leste, UNMIT was divided in several inter-related subjects such as—UN police, security, rule of law, democratic governance, and development—each of them with its sub-components and orientations. Nevertheless, the normalizing *dispositif* operating in Timor-Leste, as already mentioned, went further than the actions of the UNMIT. Observing the fields where these actors operate, it is clear that several areas of the Timorese lives and state were under continued scrutiny and international action. These areas are as disparate as, and its scope as wide as feeding, sheltering, government structures, economic policies, infrastructure, nutrition, labor, gender, or health. Hence, their actions encompass a comprehensive range of spheres, from development, passing through security and political and economic governance matters. These fields, along with those where UNMIT acts, can be fairly grouped around those spheres where a governance state is subject to a great amount of international surveillance and influence—the disciplinary, the political and economic governance, and the socio- and biopolitical ones. Indeed, closely observing this normalizing *dispositif*, it is patent that Timor-Leste's disciplinary, political and economic governance, and socio- and biopolitical spheres were under a frequent international gaze and influence in order to constantly seek to shape Timorese conducts on these fields so Timor-Leste starts to behave accordingly and in the end becomes normalized.

Although disparate, diverse, and not rarely conflicting, all these elements and actors combined form a coherent and comprehensive assemblage encompassing, and, most important, seeking to influence, shape, and oversee a wide range of Timorese's state and population conducts. In fact, this move toward understanding all these elements as a coherent and comprehensive assemblage is also present in the very effort that the UN itself pursues when it seeks a One UN approach. Furthermore, the fact that this normalizing *dispositif* places Timorese disciplinary, political and economic governance, and socio- and biopolitical spheres under scrutiny and constantly open for international influence is evident in the very areas that the United Nations Development Assistance Framework (UNDAF) focuses. This is a fundamental document of the UN engagement with Timor-Leste and a key component of the normalizing *dispositif* by having the function of holding all those elements and actors together and seeking to make them work as a whole. The areas focused by the document (UNDP, 2008e: 5), which frame and structure the actions of all actors inside the normalizing *dispositif*, are: (1) democratization and social cohesion, which includes also deepening state-building, and work on security and justice; (2) poverty reduction and sustainable livelihoods, focusing in particular vulnerable groups, including youth, women, internally displaced people (IDP) and disaster-prone communities; and (3) basic social services, which includes education, health, nutrition, water and sanitation, and social welfare and social protection.

In order to have a clearer picture of the width and depth of the normalizing state-building *dispositif* operating in Timor-Leste, it is necessary to further clarify its very structure. Hence, it is needed to outline the Timorese spheres that were under constant international supervision, influence, and conduction. It is necessary to shed some light in the wide scope of the innumerous projects developed in the key spheres of the Timorese state. This delineation of the spheres under international influence is, by no means, intended to be exhaustive. On the contrary, this delineation serves the purpose of merely giving a clearer idea of how Timor-Leste was in fact a governance state; a state where although it is legally sovereign, its sovereignty is contingent due to the fact that the internationals have a great amount of surveillance, influence, and power over several processes within pivotal spheres of the country.

The Disciplinary Sphere

The international influence over the disciplinary sphere of Timor-Leste was exercised essentially over the basic three pillars of such sphere: (1) the police, (2) the military, and (3) the rule of law. Within the disciplinary sphere of a state, the institution of the police is undisputable pivotal. The main objective of the field handled by the UN police, present throughout several Security Council resolutions dealing with UNMIT (S/RES/1704; S/RES/1745; S/RES/1802), was twofold. Firstly, developing capacity and capability of the national police (*Polícia Nacional de Timor-Leste*—PNTL), and the Ministry of Interior, which could be fairly labeled as capacity-building; and, secondly, restoring and maintaining the public security in the country. These objectives would culminate in a document that established the basis of the UNMIT assistance to Timor-Leste, in terms of the restoration and maintenance of public security in the country and of the assistance to the "reform, restructuring and rebuilding" of the national police, which became known as the Police Arrangement (UN and DRTL, 2006).

In order to perform such tasks, UNMIT field directed to deal with the pillar of the police was organized around several units: (1) the National Investigation Department, which was composed by the Criminal Investigation team; a Prosecutions Support Unit; a Vulnerable Person's Unit; an Evidence, Handling, and Forensics Unit; and a Criminal Records Management Unit; (2) the Operations Department, which was formed by a National Operations Center, a Community Policing and Humanitarian Unit; the coordination of the Formed Police Units; the National Traffic Coordination Office; the Close Security Protection Unit; the Special Operations Unit; the Border Patrol Coordination Office; and the Electoral Security and Planning Unit; (3) the Strategic Information Department, which comprised the Information Processing Unit and the Criminal Intelligence Unit; (4) the District United Nations Police, which was composed by thirteen UN Police District Headquarters responsible for a specific geographical area (District HQ); (5) the Reform, Restructuring and Rebuilding Coordination Unit, which was composed by the Vetting, Selection, Registration and Certification of National Police Unit, the Specialized Units of Advisers and Mentors, the Legislative Review and Advisory Unit, the Unit of Advisers and Mentors who worked at the headquarters of the PNTL, and the Training Unit; (6) the Strategic Planning Unit, which was composed by the Policy Development Unit, the Program Development and Project Coordination Unit, and the Operational Readiness Inspections, Evaluation and Assessment Unit; and (7) the Professional Standards and Discipline Unit, which was formed by the Conduct and Discipline

Unit, the Internal Investigation Unit, and the Audit and Evaluation Unit (UN, N/A-j).

Observing how the pillar of the police was organized, one can have a clearer idea of how wide was the collective directed to influence a key element of the disciplinary sphere of Timor-Leste through the capacity building of the Timorese police. This was sought, evidently, through power-denying notions such as training, capacity building, institutional development, and strengthening of the Timorese police, which, in fact, hide the deep power relations involved in such engagement. The purpose (the deep reorganization of the police institutions, and the normalization of the very policemen/women) and the means (through power-denying notions like training, support, mentoring, institutional development and strengthening, training) to achieve that purpose were certainly not veiled. Indeed, these were clearly expressed along the mandates. Moreover, observing, for instance, the "Arrangement" between the UN and Timor-Leste, the very name of the document calls for the "reform, restructuring and rebuilding" of the Timorese National Police and Ministry of Interior (UN and DRTL, 2006: 1). Regarding the manner in which the restructuring would be pursued, once more, the very names of some of the components of the UN Police on the field are instructive regarding power relations being rendered operational through power-denying notions. They were for instance: Specialized Units of Advisers and Mentors; Legislative Review and Advisory Unit; Unit of Advisers and Mentors; and Training Unit.

The activities under the sign of the capacity building of the Timorese police would aim to several aspects, going from "developing the operational capacity of the PNTL, including by rationalizing its organizational structure and operational practices," to "developing the PNTL's administrative capacity, including by building and strengthening its administrative systems for budget, finance, personnel, procurement, logistics and assets management" (UN and DRTL, 2006: 9). Just as in the capacity-building processes in other spheres, it aimed not only to the (re)formation of the institutions per se, but also at their very functioning, even if this bypassed Timorese laws and diminished the powers of Timorese officials. This was clear, for instance, regarding the Ministry of the Interior where its decrease of power was clear. The Police Arrangement clearly stated that the minister "shall not exercise any authority or powers that he or she may enjoy under or pursuant to the national laws of Timor-Leste to take decisions or to issue directives, standing orders, instructions or orders with respect to (…) the conduct of police operations; or (…) the maintenance and enforcement of good conduct, good order and discipline" (UN and DRTL, 2006: 4). In a clear hierarchy of powers, it was also very clear in the Police Arrangement that the minister "shall consult with the UNMIT Deputy SRSG for Security and the Rule of Law on any decision" regarding the policing or the maintenance and enforcement of the order in the country (UN and DRTL, 2006: 4–5).

In parallel with the capacity-building task, and until the PNTL was properly capacity-built, the UN police should also continue to assure the maintenance of public order in the country, which could include interim law enforcement and public security. For this task, the UN took what it called a phased approach going from the UN policing of the country to the final handout phase where the Timorese would once more be responsible for their own policing.[43] This meant that the Timorese would gradually, in consequence of substantial changes in institutions and the training of police officers in accordance to international established standards, regain the policing of its own country, which is a disciplinary framework *par excellence*. As for the UN police officers, although they were the police *de facto* of the country and were endowed with all police powers, the same vested by Timorese police officers. However, unsurprisingly, they were under the command and disciplinary authority of the UN Police Commissioner (UN and DRTL, 2006: 4). Furthermore, one should not forget that the UN was not only influencing and reconstructing the very core of the disciplinary sphere of Timor-Leste. Indeed, for a quite long period, this cluster was not merely *influencing* a key element of the disciplinary mechanism of Timor-Leste but it was in fact *being* the disciplinary mechanism of the country; which gives a clearer picture of the intensity of the character of Timor-Leste as a governance state.

Still in the disciplinary sphere, UNMIT exercised its influence and structuring power also on a second pillar—the military. Within this subject, the Security Council, through several resolutions (S/RES/1704; S/RES/1745; S/RES/1802; S/RES/1867; S/RES/1912; S/RES/1969), asked UNMIT to have a pivotal role in the security sector. The approach and the means to this task was the usual—a deep institutional reform and capacity-building efforts done through advisors and consultants. UNMIT was responsible to perform a wide assessment of the Timorese security sector and then reform it. Indeed, UNMIT, right on 2006, is asked to conduct "a comprehensive review of the future role and needs of the security sector, including the *Falintil-Forças Armadas de Defesa Timor-Leste*, the Ministry of Defence, the PNTL and the Ministry of Interior" (S/RES/1704), in order to support the government on this area. Hence, the assistance would need to go beyond the reform of the police to include other crucial elements of this sphere.

The means to achieve it was the usual—through advisors focusing on strengthening institutional capacity building (S/RES/1704). Hence, the pattern of UN power exercise certainly remained since deep structural reconstructions, influencing, structuring, and shaping a core sphere of a state—the disciplinary one—was to be operated through the power-denying and euphemistic notions of advising and capacity building. This kind of intervention was even further downplayed by the UN when it implies that this kind of activity is recurrently performed in states throughout the world (UN, N/A-g). Even if it is true, which is at least questionable, this in fact reinforces the denial and downplaying of the deep power relation present in the UN engagement with Timor-Leste. Indeed, this is even portrayed as a beneficial and even empowering relationship, since to the UN, this review and reform of the security sector is vital for Timor-Leste be prepared to deal with any future crisis without any external assistance (UN, N/A-g).

In addition, it is clear the presence of the UNDP in this sphere.[44] One might think, for instance, about the security sector assessment project initiated in June 2008 by the UNDP (2008a), in collaboration with UNMIT, that had essentially two pillars—"Security Sector Review in Timor-Leste" and a "Capacity Building Facility." The main objectives of each pillar were, respectively: (1) to support Timor-Leste in making its security sector reform, identifying the needs for any specific technical assistance and capacity development in this area (UNDP, N/A-f); and (2) to assist Timor-Leste in developing national capacity to manage the security sector through in four sectors—civilian oversight, operational management, financial accountability, and policy research capacity (UNDP, N/A-f). As expected, the project was envisioned to be implemented with a heavy assistance of UNDP experts and consultants. This project was pivotal to the capacity-building efforts of reform, restructuring, and rebuilding the key institutions of the disciplinary sphere dealing with policing and the military, in the sense that this was the element that would indicate the holes to be filled and what needed to be done in this area, therefore shaping and structuring the whole rebuilding process. Furthermore, there were other UNDP projects in this sphere. They dealt, for instance, with strengthening of civilian oversight and management capacity in the security sector (UNDP, 2011a) and strengthening the national police capacity (UNDP, 2011c). Whereas the former sought to enhance civilian oversight, management capacity, improve research and training capacity in the security sector, provide technical assistance for policy oversight, legal and institutional development, and also capacity building for the parliament, the Secretariats of State for Defense and Security, and the Office of the President (UNDP, 2011a: 1); the latter sought to develop management and administration capacity of the police, strengthen and enhance its training capacity and internal oversight mechanisms, and provide technical assistance to the Secretariat of State for Security (UNDP, 2011c: 1).

The third pillar, the rule of law, represented a clear international influence in another pivotal process of the disciplinary sphere of Timor-Leste, this time regarding the area of Justice. This pillar was essentially organized around the following areas: (1) laws and decrees; (2) human rights; (3) serious crimes investigation team; (4) transitional justice; (4) administration of justice support; (5) the justice system of Timor-Leste. Once more, the approach was directed to deep institutional reforms and the structuring and conducting power of the UN being operated through power-denying notions like capacity building, assisting or mentoring. An important element of this pillar is the Serious Crimes Investigation Team (SCIT) which was mandated with an investigative task. Its main function was to assist the Office of the Prosecutor-General of Timor-Leste investigating the cases of serious human rights violations committed in the country in 1999 (UN, N/A-h). Although the SCIT worked under the supervision of the Office of the Prosecutor-General, this was another clear case of a highly sensitive matter being highly influenced by internationals; hence in line with the governance state characterization of Timor-Leste.

Nevertheless, there were more pervasive processes in this same pillar. This was the case, for instance, of the Human Rights and Transitional Justice Section (HRTJS) of UNMIT. This unit was established to assist the strengthening of the Timorese capacity to monitor and promote human rights, justice, and reconciliation (UN, N/A-f). At a first sight, this might pass, to an inattentive observer, as one among many UN efforts to shape and conduct the Timorese conducts; as another key process of the Timorese state highly influenced by internationals. However, this unit has an important task inside the normalizing *dispositif* deployed to Timor-Leste. This unit was responsible for, on the one hand, providing capacity-building the Timorese in regard to human rights and, on the other hand, to ensure that Timor-Leste's laws, regulations and policies were in line with international human rights standards and benchmarks (UN, N/A-f). Furthermore, this unit was responsible for ensuring that the Timorese state institutions are in compliance with international standards on civil, political, economic, social, and cultural rights that it is had committed to abide (UN, N/A-f). In fact, this human rights unit observes the human right situation in Timor-Leste and disseminates it locally and internationally (UN, N/A-f). With this unit, rather than preaching human rights to Timor-Leste from outside, the UN was ensuring its structuring from within the country.

Here, again, the presence of the UNDP is substantial and its *modus operandi* the same—its power and influence is exercised through the power-denying notion of capacity building. The UNDP's (2009) project "Human Rights Capacity Building of the *Provedoria for Human Rights and Justice*" (PDHJ in Portuguese) seeks to capacity-build and to strengthen "the human rights capacity of the PDHJ to ensure its effectiveness in developing and implementing programmes in accordance with its mandate for human rights" (UNDP, 2009: 2). This would be done namely by enhancing the human rights knowledge of the PDHJ staff, and strengthening the PDHJ's capacity to educate in regard to human rights, and its ability to reach out to the Timorese and to build strategic networks with regional and international human rights actors (UNDP, 2009: 2). Hence, this project sought precisely to capacity-build the institutional actor, within the Timorese state, that would be not only one important transmission link of the international human rights standards within Timor-Leste but also a crucial actor responsible for ensuring that the Timorese institutions actually abide by these standards. At this point, it is already quite clear that this framework of ensuring compliance with standards, monitoring, reporting, and so on, is a patent normalizing framework as evinced in the chapter 2. Hence, this HRTJS unit was thought to play an important role in the normalization process conducting and influencing the Timorese state's conducts seeking to ensure that Timor-Leste complied with international standards regarding human rights—to make it a normal state in the international scenario concerning this matter. Furthermore, it also seeks to make sure that this kind of behavior is internalized within Timor-Leste, overseeing its incorporation in the very legislative corpus of the country. Through the power-denying notions of assistance and monitoring, UN-MIT sought not only to conduct the government of Timor-Leste through the conduct of its conducts but also the Timorese self-government. It sought to make Timor-Leste self-govern itself, to monitor and to conduct its own conducts, in the very light of these international standards advanced by UNMIT. For this end, there is nothing more effective than seeking that the Timorese themselves write these international standards on their own legislative body, which would clearly represent self-government effort *par excellence*.

Still within the pillar of the rule of law, another two areas that are indicative of the great influence exercised over this disciplinary sphere of Timor-Leste are the Administration of Justice Support Unit (AJSU) and the Justice System Needs Assessment Report. Both can be seen as a consequence of the UNMIT mandate, where supporting, strengthening and building the capacity of state institutions namely the justice system was seen as key. The former's objective was strengthening the Timorese state capacity in regard to the judicial area. This was sought through, on the one hand, the provision of advices regarding legal and technical issues and corrections regarding the judicial institutions and framework and also, on the other hand, through the very training and specialization of lawyers and judges (UN, N/A-d). Complementarily, the Justice System Needs Assessment (Rapoza et al., 2009) was basically a report which the objective was mainly to identify existing needs of the Timorese judicial system and to make recommendations for proper improvements. These two elements evince once more that a key component of the disciplinary sphere of Timor-Leste, its legislative sphere, was under the gaze and great influence of internationals, seeking to shape and structure its functioning. Again, the UN power was navigated between macro aspects—such as the (re)construction of institutions or the adoption of foreign legislative models not always consistent with the Timorese reality—and micro features of the legislative practice such as the very drafting of laws (Rapoza et al., 2009: 10–11).

These elements also had a close relationship with other UNDP projects. Since the UNDP has a considerable presence within the disciplinary sphere, the area of justice was also under its wide scope of action. At this area, it is worth mentioning, for instance, the UNDP project "Strengthening the Justice System in Timor-Leste" (UNDP, 2008b), which in essence was, just as the several others that Timor-Leste was subject to, a capacity-building effort. This project focused on the strengthening of institutional capacity of the justice system of Timor-Leste to enlarge the rule of law and improve access to justice of the Timorese (UNDP, 2008b: 16). Hence, the project pursued: (1) to enhance the skills of the actors within the justice sector; (2) the decentralization of the justice system and capacitating the district courts; (3) the strengthening of the prosecution service; (4) to strength the capacity of the correction services; and (5) improve the access to justice (UNDP, 2008b: 16–17).

The UNDP was certainly not the only international actor influencing and shaping the area of justice in Timor-Leste; there were also other UN agencies, international financial institutions, state development agencies, NGOs, and individual states. This was the case, for instance, of: (1) the UNFPA implementing a gender-based initiative in the realm of justice, or helping in drafting the law on domestic violence; (2) UNICEF's assistance on juvenile justice, children protection and the drafting of the Timorese juvenile justice legislation; (3) the World Bank's monitoring mechanism for institutional efficiency of the institutions related to the justice sector and its "justice for the poor" project; (4) the Agency for International Development of the Australian Government (AusAID) with its project "Justice Facility" focusing on enhancing the provision of equal access to justice, the institutional capacity building in the realm of the justice sector for state institutions and civil society organizations; (5) the Agency for International Development of the Government of the United States of America (USAID) assistance to the superior councils of the Judiciary and Prosecution by supporting the recruitment of international judges and prosecutor inspectors; (6) Portugal, through its Development Cooperation Agency (IPAD), assisting the Ministry of Justice not only on overall legal advice but also, among other things, on legislative drafting and the establishment of the undergraduate law faculty at the National University of Timor-Leste (*Universidade Nacional de Timor-Leste*; UNTL in Portuguese); (7) Brazil providing technical expertise through the participation of Brazilian judges, prosecutors, public defenders and administrative staff within the judiciary in Timor-Leste (UNDP, 2008b: 10–11); among many others.

This brief sampling of areas gives a clear idea of the amount of international influence the Timorese disciplinary sphere was subjected to. Nevertheless, this was not the only sphere where this happened. This amount of international influence and supervision was also present in the political and economic governance as well as in the socio- and biopolitical spheres.

The Political and Economic Governance Sphere

This sphere is composed by the structures and institutions that carry out the political and economic processes, along with their own functioning and characteristics. It is no secret that the UN has exercised a considerable amount of power and influence on this sphere since the very beginning of its engagement with Timor-Leste. In fact, for a long period of time the UN operated this sphere directly. After Timor-Leste's juridical independence this influence continued. Although the UNMIT, due to the 2006 and 2008 crises, placed a big emphasis on the disciplinary sphere, this political and economic governance sphere was by no means left out of its influence and will to conduct.[45] The UNMIT efforts on this sphere were concentrated on the subject of "democratic governance." This subject rested essentially on two pillars: (1) electoral assistance; and (2) the enhancement of the democratic culture in Timor-Leste. In fact, they were the very first UNMIT objectives delineated in the UN Security Council's (S/RES/1704) mandate that assembled the mission. This was thought to be accomplished through the exercise of a power and influence that were characteristic for its monitoring and oversight, and at the same time denying, tone. Rather than directly operating this sphere, the UN would, through supporting, advising, close monitoring and overseeing, make sure that Timor-Leste corrected its behavior and started to behave accordingly what is constructed as a normal behavior within international relations.

In regard to the first pillar, the electoral assistance, UNMIT was tasked by the SC, at a first moment, to support the country in the presidential and parliamentary 2007 elections[46] through technical support and electoral policy advice (S/RES/1704). Hence, during the 2007 elections the UNMIT strongly assisted the Timorese electoral institutions—the Technical Secretariat for Electoral Administration (*Secretariado Técnico de Administração Eleitoral*—STAE) and the National Commission for Elections (*Comissão Nacional de Eleições*—CNE)—both materially and in terms of advices (UN, N/A-e). The UNMIT continued its influence by institutional and personal capacity building not only at the STAE and CNE but also in the political parties (UN, N/A-e). Unsurprisingly, the capacity-building effort was pursued through advising and mentoring carried out by internationals within these institutions.

At this pillar, once more, the UNDP influence was felt. Through its project "Support to the Timorese Electoral Cycle" (UNDP, 2008d), UNDP partnered with UNMIT in capacity building the Timorese with, firstly, material assistance, and secondly focusing more on capacity-building both individuals and institutions (UNDP, 2008d: 2). The UNDP influence rested essentially in three elements (UNDP, 2008d: 5): (1) supporting electoral institutions, through the development of capacity and professionalism of the STAE and CNE at both national and sub-national levels; (2) supporting electoral processes, through legal reform, revision of the electoral procedures, and civic education in terms of the electoral institutions; and (3) supporting political parties, through the development of capacity of the parties in areas such as institutional organization, inter-election functions and civic education, and also through discussions and workshops. This is a project that was key to a crucial overall objective of the UN normalizing *dispositif* deployed to Timor-Leste—to bring democratic procedures to its political sphere. An overall objective of this project was to "help strengthen and widen the principles of democracy and good governance, enhance participation and thus contribute to political stabilization in Timor-Leste" (UNDP, 2008d: 5). In fact, this UNDP project was the pivotal element of the whole UN assistance in regard to electoral processes. Indeed, this project was understood as "the umbrella for all UN electoral assistance, whether it is being channeled through UNDP or provided through UNMIT's mandate" (UNDP, 2008d: 2).

These elements give a clear indication of how wide the scope of the UN intervention in this sphere was, and also, and perhaps most importantly, how pervasive the UN attempt to influence over this matter was. It is clear that through this approach, not only the institutions that should oversee the political development of the country, but also the very actors of the political field were under the influence and supervision of the UN. In this way, not only the political field where those actors would carry out its functions was being structured, but also the actors themselves, the political parties, were under the shaping and conducting power of the UN.

Regarding the second pillar of the UN intervention in this sphere, UNMIT was responsible, tasked by the Security Council, for "enhancing a culture of democratic governance" in Timor-Leste (S/RES/1704). This meant that the UNMIT also became responsible for a deeper and structural aspect of the Timorese political institutions—their culture. With this, more than the structuring of the Timorese state institutions, something that was heavily done in the past during UNTAET, the UN was targeting simultaneously also the very environment where these institutions act. This is not to argue that the institution-building in the sphere of governance had ceased, because it certainly continued, but to say that a lot of attention was placed also on the shaping and structuring—through the already well-known power-denying notions of capacity building, advising or mentoring—of their own *ethos*. Hence, it was not sufficient to target the structuring of institutions and its procedures, something that the UN already structured when it was the *de facto* and *de jure* power in the country; it was necessary to go beyond it. Indeed, enhancing a culture of democratic governance, for the UN, involved the capacity building of the Timorese in areas like: (1) the separation and independence of powers; (2) the exercise of power in accordance with the rule of law; (3) the respect for human rights; and (4) having a local and national civil service that is transparent and accountable (UN, N/A-k). Furthermore, the UN would call for an "integrated approach" so the Timorese state would welcome "a wide scope of political participation embracing a pluralistic system of political parties, a vibrant civil society and media (. . .) [and] promote and integrate women and minorities in all levels of the Government and society as a whole" (UN, N/A-k).

An important actor of these pillars was the Democratic Governance Support Unit (DGSU) of UNMIT. This unit was responsible for making sure that Timor-Leste would behave accordingly in terms of its political governance monitoring it and making proper corrections when necessary. This was a key unit responsible for having Timor-Leste and its political governance under scrutiny and international oversight. At this point, once more, this profound and deep power is not exercised in a concealed or hidden matter as it could be expected; after all, this can be understood as a great amount of control over a core process of a sovereign state that the UN seeks to promote as a success case. On the contrary, Timor-Leste was transformed in a governance state, and this is constantly portrayed as a beneficial relationship. Indeed, the amount of power exercised over Timor-Leste is as clear as the very goals of the unit. According to the UN, the DGSU would seek to enhance a culture of democratic governance by, on the one hand, monitoring the Timorese government in regard to its activities and, on the other hand, providing recommendations in regard to the democratic governance of the country (UN, N/A-l). Indeed, the DGSU had the function of overseeing the activities of the four Timorese constitutional organs: (1) the executive, (2) the government, (3) the parliament, and (4) the judiciary. It has the function of assessing how these institutions were functioning and, above all, ensure that they were behaving properly (UN, N/A-l).

This is another point where the presence and influence of the UNDP is felt. In fact, the UN agency has a whole segment of its activities directed, literally, to "Democratic Governance" projects (UNDP, N/A-b).[47] Apart from its initiatives in the realm of the electoral processes through the capacity building of key institutions and political parties, the UNDP was also an important actor in the very construction and shaping of the governance sphere of the Timorese national politics. This influence was felt not only in the judiciary sphere, as it was aforementioned, but also on the legislative sphere. One could mention, for instance, the UNDP project "Strengthening the Institutional Capacity of the Office of the President" (UNDP, 2007b), with the main objective of building the capacity of the Timorese President's Office in institutional and advisory terms. The project was responsible for (UNDP, 2007b: 3): (1) building an institutional and an organizational structure for the office; (2) designing the office's systems and processes; (3)

training the office's staff in order to improve the agenda management, coordination and communications of the office; and (4) enhancing the office's ability in the realm of policy analysis and advisory capacity in order to better support the Timorese president. At this point, again, despite the fact that the project would (re)construct the whole presidential office; once more, the means of the UN intervention was the power-denying notion of capacity building.

Another area where the presence of the UNDP was clear in this sphere was at the capacity-building efforts in regard to the Timorese parliament. At this point, there are two projects worth mentioning—the "Strengthening Parliamentary Democracy in Timor-Leste" (UNDP, 2006b) and the "Strengthening Institutional Capacity of the National Parliament in Timor-Leste" (UNDP, 2011b). The former was an extension of a UNDP project carried out since in 2003 (UNDP, 2003) which was also directed to the strengthening of the parliamentary democracy in Timor-Leste and, through the capacity building of the parliamentarians, focused on "building capacity among Deputies and Secretariat staff so that they may shape policies and laws that promote democratic governance" (UNDP, 2003: 2). The 2006 revised project (UNDP, 2006b: 2) would, through training, advising, and capacity building, focus on five areas: (1) building oversight capacity, through the consolidation of parliamentarian support systems and process that could provide the tools needed so the parliamentarians could not only control and monitor the government activities and expenditures, but also debate and analyze the national budget; (2) legislative support, through the provision of experts and legal advisors that would train the Timorese parliamentarians in law drafting, and also in scrutinizing, debating and amending the bills proposed by the government; (3) democratic representation, through the consolidation of systems within the parliament so the representatives could engage more with the population, and therefore incorporating more the popular demands; (4) gender mainstreaming, through the encouragement of making gender-related issues a transversal matter in the parliament, and also through helping women representatives in designing policies in regard of issues that concern Timorese women; and (5) developing capacity of the Secretariat, through its capacity building on administrative services to the parliament's members and organs, and on their ability to provide advisory services in several issues like economy, legal, political, and so on.

The second UNDP project—the Strengthening Institutional Capacity of the National Parliament in Timor-Leste—is also directed to the capacity building of the Timorese parliament. The project seeks, in essence, to "strengthen the democratic foundations" of the Timorese parliament through the enhancement of its oversight, accountability and transparency (UNDP, 2011b: 9). Just as in the disciplinary sphere, the intervention seeks to produce predicted, regular, and stable institutions so this can be extrapolate to Timor-

Leste as a country. In the case of the Timorese parliament, this would be done through: (1) institutional capacity-building; and (2) the enhancing of the knowledge of both the parliamentary members and the expertise of the parliament' staff (UNDP, 2011b: 9).

Hence, this capacity-building effort directed to the Timorese parliament would be focused on four areas (UNDP, 2011b: 10–11): (1) strengthening the expertise of the parliament's staff, aiming at enhancing the human resources capacity of the parliament; (2) improving the capacity of the parliamentarians to initiate and draft laws and also monitor and scrutinize the bills proposed by the government; (3) enhancing the parliament's oversight capacity through the improvement of its capacities to analyze, debate and approve the national budget, be an oversight of the government's actions and financial expenditures, as well as incorporating the inputs from civil society on the law-making process; and (4) improving the Timorese parliament's relations with other parliaments from Portuguese-speaking countries. This wide and deep project puts a crucial element of the Timorese state—its parliament—under a close and constant international scrutiny and influence. It shapes, and closely monitors, not only the parliament's institutional structures, but also, and most importantly, the very behavior of the institution. This constant and permanent scrutiny of the parliament is done through the monitoring and supervision of issues, among others, such as the number of the initiatives designed to oversee the government's actions, the quality of the parliamentary debates, and the number and quality of the laws proposed. Even how well the parliamentarians use their question hour in debates and whether they, and the parliament's staff, attend Portuguese language classes (and how well they perform in acquiring work competence in Portuguese) was monitored, and under the scrutiny of the UN (UNDP, 2011b: 9–10).

The influence of the UNDP was also felt on other areas of the governance sphere. The other two worth mentioning deals with the local governance and the civil service. The former was influenced and shaped by the UNDP project focused on supporting the local governance in Timor-Leste (UNDP, 2007a). This is a project that succeeded two other projects, the Local Development Programme and the Local Government Options Study, and focused on building a local government system in Timor-Leste. In order to achieve this, the project focused on (UNDP, 2007a: 7): (1) the development of a local government system through the development of several procedures and processes, and the continuity of fostering the local government assemblies in order to foster decentralization; (2) the provision of technical support to the government in order to improve its capacity on designing a comprehensive legal and regulatory framework on decentralization and local government; and (3) assisting the government on actually implementing the reforms toward a functioning local government system. This kind of actions advanced by the UN are a clear indication that its will to shape and influence the Timorese governance sphere is not limited to the central political structures like the government and the parliament, but it also sought to exercise its power on the level of the local government creating a wider power network.

Another crucial area of this sphere where the UNDP had its activities focused is the civil service. The Support to Civil Service Reform project (UNDP, 2008c) is a capacity-building effort in regard to public management. It sought to develop capacities "(at systemic, organizational and individual levels) necessary to the enhancement of professionalism and integrity in public service management" in Timor-Leste (UNDP, 2008c: 1). The Support to Civil Service Reform was underpinned by four pillars (UNDP, 2008c: 1): (1) a Management Information System that would enhance the ability for both operational matters like the personnel processing and more strategic ones like the strategic planning in regard of human resources of the civil service; (2) the enhancement of the strategic management of civil service, through the development of organizational plans, plans for capacity development, and action plans seeking also to improve the understanding of public sector management issues and roles; (3) the creation of a mechanism capable of providing, managing, and monitoring the technical assistance needed, and the mobilization of these technical assistance resources; and (4) efficiency and sustainability of the capacity-building efforts, through the targeted training and development of civil servants in order to increase the core capacities of the government.

The Support to Civil Service Reform is in fact a revision, and a consolidation, of three previous projects which ended in 2006: the Human Resource Management (HRM), the Institutional Capacity Development Support (ICDS), and the Development Advisory Services (DAS) (UNDP, 2008c: 2). Hence, this project marked a clear continuity of the UNDP influence and shaping power exercised, through the power-denying notion of capacity building, over the field of the Timorese public management and service. Indeed, during the ICDS,[48] which was another capacity-building effort aiming to shape three areas—skills and knowledge; systems and processes; and attitudes and behaviors—the UNDP filled 118 "critical" posts throughout several Timorese ministries with advisors in order to build and improve the Timorese governance capacity (UNDP, 2005).

The Socio- and Biopolitical Sphere

The socio- and biopolitical sphere was another core sphere of the Timorese state where a great amount of international influence and shaping was felt. This sphere is composed essentially by the life-supporting processes of the population and its surrounding conditions. In a few words, this is the sphere formed by the set of phenomena that bind the population together; of the processes related to the Timorese lives and by the environment that influence those processes. This is a sphere under a great international scrutiny and influence; a sphere under the oversight of several distinct actors such as UNDP, UNMIT, UNICEF, and so on, and where their actions seek to touch a very wide range of fields going from food and health to education and nutrition.

Two elements of UNMIT were directed to this sphere—the development and the humanitarian one. The first element was headed by the Socio-Economic Development Unit which was responsible for producing advice on poverty reduction and socio-economic policies and strategies. The second element was headed by the Humanitarian Coordination Unit which seeks to coordinate the work of several actors who are present on the humanitarian field. These elements act on a socio-biopolitical sphere *par excellence*. They are under constant supervision that seeks to influence and shape the Timorese policies and actions not only in the socio-economic sphere—such as infrastructure, poverty-reduction strategies, agriculture, and so on—as a whole but also specific biopolitical areas—like social services, food security, health, water and sanitation, sheltering, health, nutrition, or education, among others.

In regard to the development area, the international power was exercised, among other channels, through the influence over the Timorese policies which were grouped around a National Priorities Program (NPP). As already explored in chapter 4, NPP was clearly an institutional response that represented an effort to overcome the still present effects of the 2006 crisis, which ranged from IDPs, the militia, of Major Alfredo Reinaldo, the weak economy, among others. As previously mentioned, the very organization of NPP (organized around a Secretariat and Working Groups focusing each on a determinate national priority) institutionalized the international influence within the Timorese state. This influence was felt through policy recommendations, monitoring of the overall process of shaping the Timorese national priorities, and assistance. The international influence was felt even through the very leadership that, for instance, UNMIT or a UN agency—UNDP had on some Working Groups. Hence, it is not unreasonable to point to the fact that the UN influence in terms of its development area is entrenched not only at the endpoint of the chain through the implementation of projects in the field, but also, in the very beginning of the chain; seeking to influence the very process of building the goals—the Timorese national priorities—which will shape and structure all the rest of the chain. This, by its turn, inevitably leads the UN to influence which projects will be pursued and the manner in which the priorities set will be achieved.

At this point, on the one hand, it was clear that due to this influence certain areas received more attention than others. Here is very instructive, for instance, the focus received by the pillars of the disciplinary sphere, such as the rule of law or the police and the military (which were pivotal in the sense of making Timor-Leste a stable country in the international scenario) in comparison to sanitation or water (which still nowadays remain a fundamental challenge), for example. On the other hand, the NPP was also another instrument through which the UN could shape and structure the Timorese social and economic model from its very inception, from the very moment when the objectives are being designed.

In regard to the humanitarian branch of UNMIT, this was developed around what the UN calls a "cluster system" (UN, N/A-a). [49] This instrument consists in grouping together different actors—like UN agencies, NGOs, and other international institutions—around common areas within the humanitarian field. Each of these common areas constitute a cluster, and one of the main objectives of each of the clusters is to be a sort of forum and contact point for several actors, either part of the UN system or not, working around a certain field. This cluster system is a key example of the wide scope of the biopolitical power of several international actors, in particular the UN through UNMIT and its agencies, exercised over the life-supporting processes of the Timorese population. In Timor-Leste, this mechanism was put in place essentially as a response to the crisis of 2006 and to assist the Timorese on their recovery. The cluster system in Timor-Leste was composed by ten clusters. They were: (1) camp coordination and camp management and emergency shelter; (2) early recovery; (3) education; (4) emergency telecommunications; (5) food security; (6) health; (7) logistics; (8) nutrition; (9) protection; and (10) water, sanitation, and hygiene.

Notwithstanding the fact that this pillar was thought to cope with the 2006 tragedy, its influence kept being felt afterward. Its areas are a clear indication of the international influence over pivotal biopolitical processes of the Timorese population. It is clear their influence over multi-dimensional processes going from basic services to social dimensions. In all these clusters is perceptible the presence not only of the actions of UNMIT, but also the influence being exercised through projects, programs and action of other UN related organizations like, for instance, IOM, ILO, UNDP, UNHCR, UNICEF, WFP, WHO, FAO, among others. [50] Despite of the biopolitical tone that all aforementioned clusters have, in the sense that they in several manners touch and seek to influence processes that are important to the lives of the Timorese population, some other clusters that are in place in Timor-Leste are biopolitical *par excellence*, in the sense that they influence and shape processes that are the cornerstone of the Timorese lives. This is the case, for instance, of education, health, food, nutrition, water, sanitation, and even hygiene.

The cluster of education, for instance, sought to be a sort of a meeting forum for all the organizations working on the field of education in Timor-Leste. Among other things, this cluster sought to capacity-build and strengthen the education sector through the development of programs related to the education of the Timorese having due attention to priority cross-cutting issues such as diversity/inclusiveness, gender, HIV/AIDS and human rights (UN, 2009a). Another cluster rendered operational in Timor-Leste, the food security one, sought not only to prepare and coordinate food security programs and activities, but also to ensure adequate food security contingency and preparedness planning. Apart from dealing with issues regarding the Timorese population, the cluster also seeks to capacity-build the Timorese government to deal with the issue (UN, 2009c). In turn, the cluster that dealt with health had as its main objectives not only the coordination of actors within this sphere, but also the enhancement of the planning and the provision of health sector activities in Timor-Leste (UN, 2009b); while the nutrition cluster sought to intervene in order to ensure appropriate nutrition services for the Timorese population and also the technical quality of the programs in the area (UN, 2009d). Finally, the cluster dealing with water, sanitation, and hygiene focused on issues, for instance, such as: the water supply, excreta disposal, solid waste management, and hygiene promotion (UN, 2009e).

Each of the clusters of this cluster system functioned, as in several other spheres of the UN intervention, through the power-denying notion of capacity building. It functioned by identifying gaps in the Timorese policies that needed to be improved, and developing plans and programs to address such gaps and also to capacity-build Timor-Leste to have an appropriate preparedness and response to such challenges. However, what this approach masks is the pervasive power that was exercised over the biopolitical sphere of Timor-Leste and the kind of international influence and supervision that the Timorese are subject to. These clusters formed a sort of a biopolitical web that is a crystallization of a biopolitical power *par excellence* due to its constant international influence, shaping and supervision in regard to a wide number of life-supporting and life-related processes—like sanitation, health, education, food, water, and even hygiene, to name a few—of the Timorese population. This cluster system is a clear evidence of not only the width but also the scope of the exercise of the biopolitical power of the UN in Timor-Leste and the depth in which the country was transformed into a governance state.

CONCLUSION

This chapter outlines the transformation of Timor-Leste into a governance state and also the UN efforts to conduct the country. The chapter delineates the governmental power that the UN exercised over Timor-Leste, which was a kind of power that the UN directed to Timor-Leste and the Timorese since the very beginning of its engagement with the country. Its pervasiveness is perceived throughout several spheres and levels, such as structuring of the political field where the Timorese referendum would take place and the discipline of Timor-Leste as a state; the attempt of influencing biopolitical processes of the Timorese population; and a more capillary power sought to be exercised over very micro aspects of the Timorese state and people. Moreover, the chapter clearly illuminates the great amount of international influence in the very shaping and functioning of Timorese disciplinary, economic, and political and biopolitical spheres; putting them under a constant international supervision, influence, and conduct, which reinforces the characterization of Timor-Leste as a governance state. Hence, the chapter explores the UN effort to conduct Timor-Leste, aiming toward its normalization, being performed through the reform and (re)construction also of its pivotal spheres, namely through the (re)structuring of its institutions, the shaping of their ethos, and the influencing of pivotal life-supporting processes of the Timorese population. Moreover, the chapter evinces not only the panoply of actors of the normalizing *dispositif* which Timor-Leste is subject to, but also the wide scope and the high number of projects and programs that were deployed to these spheres. Through this delineation, it is possible to have a clearer idea of the width of the normalizing *dispositif* operating in Timor-Leste, which is rendered operational through power-denying notions such as capacity building, advising, and mentoring. This chapter also evinces the UN normalizing power which seeks to normalize the Timorese state through structuring its institutions into stable, predicting institutions, and most importantly, into institutions that behave accordingly international standards. Consequently, it is envisioned that, through the structuring of the disciplinary, governance and biopolitical spheres, Timor-Leste itself would become a stable and predicting country and, in turn, it would start to behave more like a normal state within the international relations. Finally, the transformation of Timor-Leste into a governance state evinces also a process of building peace that, in essence, is very hierarchical, top-down, and entrenched in a deep and highly unequal power relation. Therefore, the kind of peace built hardly becomes rooted in Timorese structures. As a result, this is a process that lays, contrary to what might be perceived at its surface, a foundation that can easily fall apart. This is particularly concerning because this process renders visible the very unstable base in which the future of Timor-Leste and the Timorese was built.

NOTES

1. See, for instance, (UNTAET/REG/1999/3).
2. See, for instance, (UNTAET/NOT/2000/2; UNTAET/NOT/2000/5; UNTAET/NOT/2001/19; UNTAET/REG/2000/1).
3. See, for instance, (UNTAET/NOT/2000/3; UNTAET/NOT/2000/6; UNTAET/NOT/2000/15; UNTAET/NOT/2001/24; UNTAET/REG/2000/6).
4. See, for instance, (UNTAET/REG/2000/7; UNTAET/REG/2001/14).
5. See, for instance, (UNTAET/REG/2000/9; UNTAET/REG/2001/17).

6. See, for instance, (UNTAET/DIR/2001/1; UNTAET/DIR/2001/2; UNTAET/REG/ 2000/18; UNTAET/REG/2000/32; UNTAET/REG/2000/35; UNTAET/REG/2001/16; UN-TAET/REG/2001/17; UNTAET/REG/2001/20).
7. See, for instance, (UNTAET/REG/2000/20; UNTAET/REG/2001/13).
8. See, for instance, (UNTAET/REG/2000/8).
9. See, for instance, (UNTAET/NOT/2002/14; UNTAET/ORD/2002/6; UNTAET/REG/ 2001/30).
10. See, for instance, (UNTAET/DIR/2002/08; UNTAET/REG/2002/07).
11. See, for instance, (UNTAET/REG/2002/07).
12. See, for instance, (UNTAET/REG/2000/12).
13. See, for instance, (UNTAET/NOT/2000/13).
14. See, for instance, (UNTAET/NOT/2000/11).
15. See, for instance, (UNTAET/ORD/2001/3; UNTAET/ORD/2001/5; UNTAET/ORD/ 2002/3; UNTAET/REG/2002/6).
16. See, for instance, (UNTAET/DIR/2001/7).
17. See, for instance, (UNTAET/NOT/2001/23).
18. See, for instance, (UNTAET/REG/2002/5).
19. See, for instance, (UNTAET/ORD/2001/1).
20. See, for instance, (UNTAET/REG/2002/5).
21. See, for instance, (UNTAET/REG/2000/4; UNTAET/REG/2002/4).
22. See, for instance, (UNTAET/DIR/2000/7).
23. See, for instance, (UNTAET/ORD/2000/2).
24. See, for instance, (UNTAET/ORD/2001/6).
25. See, for instance, (UNTAET/NOT/2000/9; UNTAET/NOT/2001/15).
26. See, for instance, (UNTAET/DIR/2001/10; UNTAET/DIR/2002/07; UNTAET/NOT/ 2000/12; UNTAET/NOT/2000/22).
27. See, for instance, (UNTAET/NOT/2000/10).
28. See, for instance, (UNTAET/NOT/2000/4; UNTAET/NOT/2002/12; UNTAET/ORD/ 2000/1).
29. See, for instance, (UNTAET/REG/2001/22).
30. See, for instance, (UNTAET/REG/2001/23; UNTAET/REG/2001/27).
31. See, for instance, (UNTAET/REG/2000/11).
32. See, for instance, (UNTAET/REG/2001/22).
33. See, for instance, (UNTAET/DIR/2001/12).
34. See, for instance, (UNTAET/REG/2001/22).
35. See, for instance (UNTAET/REG/2001/23).
36. See, for instance, (UNTAET/REG/2000/30).
37. See, for instance, (UNTAET/REG/2001/23).
38. See, for instance, (UNTAET/REG/2001/3).
39. See, for instance, (UNTAET/REG/2000/30).
40. See, for instance, (UNTAET/REG/2001/22).
41. See, for instance (UNTAET/REG/2001/23).
42. See, for instance, (UNTAET/REG/2001/3).
43. On March 27th 2011, the PNTL recovered the responsibility for the conduct, command and control of all police operations in Timor-Leste (SG, 2011b: paragraph 8). Nevertheless, the PNTL will continue under UN Police oversight and normalization process through capacity-building, training, skills enhancement, specific advisory functions, and operational support (SG, 2011a: paragraph 60).
44. The fact that the UNDP, a development UN agency, is part in the reform, restructuring and rebuilding of the disciplinary sphere might evoke a discussion about the security-development nexus. However, such discussion is off the limits of this book. For more about it see for instance (Duffield, 2010; Hettne, 2010; McCormack, 2011; Stern and Öjendal, 2010).
45. One should not forget the role of other actors on these conducting efforts in this sphere, and others like the biopolitical one, and their shaping during the whole UN engagement with Timor-Leste had the collaboration of several other actors. This is certainly the case, for instance, of the several structuring capacity-building projects carried out, in several areas, by the

World Bank, the International Monetary Fund, and the Asian Development Bank. Due to the scope of this book, this section will focus on the actions of the UN. For more on their actions and projects in Timor-Leste—which include actions on local governance, capacity-building efforts on political and financial structures and ministries, influence on the oil funds, among many others—see, for instance (ADB, N/A; IMF, N/A; WB, N/A-a).

46. This was in fact the fourth election carried out in Timor-Leste (the others were the referendum in 1999, the elections for the Constituent Assembly in 2001, and the presidential election of 2002) but the first one carried out in Timor-Leste as a legal independent country.

47. For more information regarding this segment of the UNDP activities, see (UNDP, N/A-b).

48. For more about the project, see for instance (UNDP, 2005, N/A-d).

49. For more regarding the UN cluster system, the clusters in Timor-Leste, and the cluster-specific documents and information, see (UN, N/A-a).

50. One can also see the presence of other kinds of organizations such as the ADB, IMF, the European Commission's European Community Humanitarian Office, AusAID, USAID, GIZ, Caritas, CARE, Red Cross, Oxfam, Save the Children, and others.

Conclusion

This book problematizes the construction of peace in the current international scenario, seeking essentially to unnaturalize what is quite often perceived as something natural, especially in contemporary efforts directed toward overcoming violent conflict throughout the globe. In order to advance its problematization, this book proposes a critical examination of the state-building process using theoretical and conceptual tools developed by the French philosopher Michel Foucault. Aiming at a distinct observation of the process, the book argues that the construction of peace in our current international scenario, the current reconstruction efforts in post-conflict settings, is an attempt, by those intervening, to normalize the post-conflict states and their populations. In order to render operational and clarify the argument, the book focuses on the UN intervention in Timor-Leste. In addition to delineating the structure and instruments through which the UN rendered operational its normalization effort directed to Timor-Leste, the book also clearly evinces that this normalization practice advanced by the UN in its state-building efforts, in fact, transforms the state into a governance state. Therefore, rather than enhancing and advancing the independency and autonomy in these states, which is the very surface of UN practices in post-conflict scenarios (especially in Timor-Leste), the post-conflict state in case turns out to have its sovereignty highly dependent on internationals since its fundamental spheres are under a constant international influence, scrutiny, and supervision. More concerning, the book sheds light on the fact that this kind of process, since it is highly hierarchical and top-down, constantly blocks local participation. Consequently, it cannot have deep roots in local structures. As a result, the outcomes achieved by the UN state-building efforts might have the propensity to be merely superficial and in need of a constant international monitoring. This was certainly the case of Timor-Leste.

The normalization process pursued by the UN, as explained throughout the book, is essentially the attempt made by those intervening to make the post-conflict state start behaving less as an abnormal state and more as a normal state within international relations. The normalization is a process in which those states perceived as abnormal are intervened and have their behaviors shaped in order to have their actions resemble more the ones of a normal state. Obviously, there are no ontological kinds of conditions that are naturally normal or abnormal. As could not be different, these abnormal and normal conditions in the international sphere are, just as within societies, constructed through narratives, practices, and, evidently, power relations. Within the international scene, as discussed, the perception of what a normal condition means is underpinned by a dual understanding. On the one hand, there is the assumption, even though not always verbalized, that the path which developed in Western Europe, in regard to the political entities becoming what is commonly understood as the modern state, is *the* correct and perhaps only path to be pursued in terms of both organizing a society politically and developing a political entity. It is due to this assumption that it is often pursued, in post-conflict reconstruction efforts, the implementation of what were the main outcomes of that path, namely: a centralized bureaucracy, which has the monopoly of the legitimate law making and use of violence; the rule of law; and a government that was accountable to its population. On the other hand, the second pillar that underpins the understanding of what a normal behavior means in the international sphere is the strong narrative, which is often veiled but certainly present, that naturally equates peace and prosperity with liberal values. Therefore, it is not by coincidence that what is perceived while analyzing the interventions in post-conflict states is exactly the attempt of shaping their behaviors in order to make these states, along with their populations, behave as liberal entities and subjects.

The other side of this same coin has to do with the construction of what an abnormal entity within the international relations means. This construction is rendered operational through the concept of "failed states." On the one hand, their abnormality is elaborated through analogies, quite often pathological, like "degenerative disease" or "serious mental or physical illness." Underpinning such analogies there is a subliminal and unspoken dichotomy which also defines what is understood as a successful and healthy state, which are the ones that have the elements that resulted from the state formation process that took place in Western Europe and have liberal values. On the other hand, the other pillar of the construction of the abnormality of these states is their constructed association with global insecurities and underdevelopment. Under this rationale, the picture portrayed is that the very existence of this kind of states, or the very threat of a state becoming one of them, poses not only a threat to the whole international system—due to the easiness in which the insecurities can move around the globe nowadays—but also retards the overall development of the global population.

Therefore, from this point of view, the normalization processes are perceived as an essential process for the proper regulation of the international system. This line of thinking is perhaps best exemplified in a presentation made by the a former British foreign secretary, Jack Straw, titled "Failed and Failing States," at the European Research Institute at the University of Birmingham. For him, "preventing states from failing and resuscitating those that fail is one of the strategic imperatives of our times" (Straw, 2002). In this rationale, different situations require different normalization processes. This picture is perhaps most iconic in a different part of the presentation when he says that in order to deal with this kind of states

> [w]e have a range of tools available. Some are developmental—the provision of direct aid, debt relief, institutional capacity building and security sector reform. Some are diplomatic—including the application of political pressure, international mediation and international agreements to remove contributing factors to conflicts such as conflict diamonds and small arms control. And some are more coercive, such as sanctions and direct military action. (Straw, 2002)

All of these tools aim at the modification of the failed state's behavior; some are portrayed as beneficial relationships whereas others are certainly more difficult to disguise because they are more directly and visually aggressive. Usually, different kinds of normalization tools, often coupled with different degrees of aggressiveness, are rendered operational by the construction of different kinds of abnormality and abnormal other. It is certainly not by coincidence that, in the case of peace, for instance, its operacionalization is performed through the notions of failed and failing states. This is a notion that immediately brings the idea, though unconsciously, of reconstructing, fixing even, something that is performing wrongly, and, simultaneously, the idea of how this reconstruction must be done due to its underpinning successful state framework. One cannot avoid from noticing, for instance, that more aggressive normalization processes, through more drastic measures such as direct military actions and invasions for example, are rendered operational through the notion of rogue state, bringing both the notion of an entity behaving in a very unacceptable way and that the correction of the behaviors of this entity must come through a severe punishment; quite often a violent one.

Moreover, this presentation of former foreign secretary Straw is also instructive in the sense of evincing the medical rationale that is pervasive when addressing these issues and the pathological analogies that underpin the problematization of failed states. In a different part of the presentation, for instance, former secretary Straw (2002) clearly argues that "[r]ather than waiting for states to fail, we should aim to avoid state failure wherever possible. Returning to my medical analogy, prevention is better than cure. It is easier, cheaper and less painful for all concerned." In this way, whereas the failed states are portrayed as pathologies of the international system, nothing more natural than portraying the intervention, even though pervasive with deep and entrenched asymmetric power relations, as therapeutic and as something beneficial for all parts involved. This is precisely the case of the construction of peace in post-conflict settings.

Hence, the construction of peace is just one among other tools used as a normalization process within international relations. This is a process especially directed toward post-conflict states. As regard to the construction of peace in the international scene, this normalization process is rendered operational by a state-building *dispositif*. As already discussed, a *dispositif*—an assemblage of actors, narratives, concepts, theories, institutions—emerges as a response to an *urgent need*. In the international scenario, this *urgent need* is precisely the perceived emergency in dealing with those states that are understood as being failed states and preventing those that are perceived as becoming "failed" from getting into this condition.

This was certainly the case of Timor-Leste. In this case, the country became an *urgent* international *need* after a long process that culminated with a massive UN intervention in the country. In combination with all the humanitarian concerns that were directed to Timor-Leste, which in several cases were indeed very genuine and true, there was a real fear of Timor-Leste becoming a failed state. This fear, under the orthodox rationale aforementioned, equated Timor-Leste with a potential threat and an obstacle to global development, even though not always openly verbalized. Therefore, a state-building *dispositif* was deployed to the country.

By pursuing a distinct understanding of the international reality and the practices performed there, which is the very aim of this book, one can have refined observation of the construction of peace in our time. This distinct understanding certainly enables the observation of the fact that the construction of peace is essentially a pursuit of making post-conflict states behaving less as abnormal states and more as normal states in the international scenario and complying with what is portrayed as international standards. Therefore, what an attentive observation of the reconstruction efforts performed in post-conflict countries brings, and certainly Timor-Leste is not an exception, is the understanding that the state-building *dispositif*, notwithstanding its rhetoric of building peace and preventing and transforming violent conflicts throughout the globe which are perceived in its very surface, is a pivotal element of the regulation of the international system.

The normalization process, as previously elucidated, works through the attempt of governing post-conflict states and their population's lives, which although constructed to be perceived as being merely a bureaucratic and technical endeavor of (re)building the post-conflict apparatuses is sought through the pursuit of disciplining these states and exercising a biopolitical power over their populations. Consequently, post-conflict states, and especially the case herein presented, turns out to be transformed into governance states. The book rendered visible such process by exploring in Timor-Leste namely five dimensions previously discussed—(1) visibility, by discussing how the UN actually renders Timor-Leste and its spheres visible so it can act upon them, such as using a set of reports, tables or matrixes; (2) *techne*, by evincing the instruments through which the UN rendered such process operational such as the SGRsSC, UNDAF, NPP, or the Police Arrangement; (3) *episteme*, by problematizing the notions and concepts that are fundamental to the functioning of the process, such as liberal peace, failed state, good governance, and capacity building; (4) identification, by delineating the kind of behaviors the UN attempted to shape and, most importantly, the kind of behaviors the UN have set to Timor-Leste through several objectives and standards that the country had to comply; and (5) the role of experts, by identifying several areas where the UN, through its several advisors, attempted to shape and conduct Timorese conducts.

Therefore, the book evinced that the UN normalization process directed toward post-conflict states is pursued through the setting up of a surveillance framework, which is formed by a variety of instruments that were discussed in previous chapters. In the case herein problematized, this surveillance framework enables the close monitoring of Timor-Leste's and Timorese conducts placing the state apparatus and the country's several spheres, along with its population, under a constant and frequent international scrutiny and observation. This close scrutiny, monitoring, and assessment is what enables the very exercise of the dispositional power of the internationals in general, and the UN in particular, allowing the arrangement of pivotal and structural elements of the country in order to achieve the right disposition of things, remembering La Perrière's definition of government exposed by Foucault. This framework is what allows the UN to pursue the conduct of Timor-Leste in the sense of seeking conduct and shape its conducts and behaviors toward a determinate end. This convenient end is what is understood as a "normal" behavior within international relations—state institutions and population pervasive with liberal *modus operandi* and values, even though shallowly.

As discussed previously, this surveillance framework is formed by instruments that worked both from outside and from within the Timorese state. This is certainly a natural consequence of the very functioning of the normalization process operating in Timor-Leste, which works essentially two-dimensionally—on an international and national levels. In both dimensions, Timor-Leste and the Timorese were put into a mechanism of rendering visible, individualizing, monitoring/assessing, reporting, and correcting their actions and behaviors, which is clearly a disciplinary mechanism; a mechanism that seeks to shape, alter, and conduct behaviors so Timor-Leste, and other post-conflict states, become a "normal" state within the international scenario.

This mechanism, directed not only toward the state per se but also toward several aspects of the Timorese "reality," operates through the interplay of several instruments delineated previously—such as the SGRsSC, the UN-DAF, the NPP, the Police Arrangement, or the Index of Laws—and is what underpins the attempt of normalizing Timor-Leste. This process, as explored throughout the book, is coupled with the attempt of a massive exercise of a biopolitical power, which is rendered operational through the transformation of Timor-Leste into a governance state, a state where its sovereignty is dependent due to the fact that its fundamental spheres—the disciplinary, political and economic governance, and the socio- and biopolitical ones—are under a great amount of international control and oversight (Duffield, 2007: 82). A pivotal characteristic of the normalization process that takes place in Timor-Leste is that all these practices, no matter how deep, operate through very power-denying, almost even benign, notions such as capacity building, good governance, mentoring, advising, empowerment, and so on.

Nevertheless, underneath this thin layer of technical and bureaucratic appearance, lays deep-rooted power, and hierarchical and patronizing relations. By exploring these relations, the book brings several kinds of uneven engagements and interactions that are entrenched in current state-building practices to the discussion. Therefore, this book brings to light not only some key flaws and major implementation's incongruities of the UN engagement with Timor-Leste, but, especially, some concealed processes and veiled power relations entrenched in this process. Most importantly, the book allows a profound reframing of how current state-building practices are understood. Rather than an effort of seeking to develop post-conflict states and enable their actions internationally, the book evinces that, on the contrary, the construction of peace can be instrumentalized as a fundamental device in the regulation of the current international relations.

As a consequence, the research herein presented enhances the discussion about the theme and also opens new research avenues to be further developed. Most importantly, this book enables the possibility of (re)conceptualizing and (re)problematizating some crucial concepts, notions, and processes of international relations, in general, and peace and conflict studies, in particular, such as failed states, good governance, capacity-building, state-building, peacebuilding, and, most importantly, peace. Drawing on the insights produced by this book, it becomes clearer that the real changes regarding the transformation of the conflicts and the construction of solid foundations for the emergency of a sustainable peace comes, necessarily, from a critical understanding and thought regarding the reflection about these processes. It comes, invariably, by the exhibition of the violence(s) of the orthodox truth surrounding current practices and by the deep rethinking of the very manner in which the transformation of violent conflicts is thought in the first place. It comes, therefore, by the search and observation of new facts, by the observation of the same fact but with different lenses, and by the construction and exposition of different truths.

Therefore, the research that follows could not be different from seeking a different kind of thinking when problematizing peace. Rather than simply seeking to correct and adjust current practices, the research that follows is firmly rooted in the understanding that the real changes in regard to current state-building practices must come necessarily from a profound reconstruction of how peace, and peacebuilding efforts, are thought. Most importantly, it follows the advice of the Portuguese sociologist Boaventura de Sousa Santos (2000), of not satisfying ourselves with merely thinking about alternatives; but, instead, by pursuing an "alternative thinking of alternatives" (Santos, 2000: 29). Since most of peacebuilding efforts are carried out in post-conflict states in the global south, and their character is highly entrenched in deep-power relations, the research that follows will walk through the path of seeking to problematize such practices departing from southern epistemologies[1] and decolonial reflections.[2]

This path clearly follows the understanding of the Slovenian philosopher Slavoj Žižek that there are times and situations, so grave, where the most *practical* thing to really *do* something is exactly to engage in a critical analysis of the surrounding reality (Žižek, 2009: 6). Bearing this in mind, it is quite hard not to agree with Foucault when he says that "the real political task in a society such as ours is to criticize the working of institutions which appear to be both neutral and independent" (Foucault apud Rabinow, 1984: 6). The point of engaging in such endeavor is precisely to "criticize them in such a manner that the political violence which has always exercised itself obscurely through them will be unmasked, so that one can fight them" (Foucault apud Rabinow, 1984: 6). Hence, the real task of someone concerned with the surrounding reality, especially academics, is to actively exercise criticism.

This was the point of this book and it is the core of the research that follows—to pursue a critical analysis of the construction of peace in our contemporary international relations. Nevertheless, one must thus have in mind what the exercise of *criticism* means. The exercise of *critique* is not merely "a matter of saying that things are not right as they are. It is a matter of pointing out on what kinds of assumptions, what kinds of familiar, unchallenged, unconsidered modes of thought the practices that we accept rest" (Foucault, 1988: 154). It is about stretching the field of *possible* questions, the extension of the very terms of the political debate (Rose, 1999: 277), broadening the spectrum of the visible. It is about enabling the thinking and acting otherwise regarding the practices and processes that are usually taken for granted and perceived as natural. Therefore, inverting Žižek's point, there

are times and situations where to *do something* is the least practical engagement one can have. Our current time is certainly one of those moments. We
live in a time where the utmost important engagement that one can have,
especially those in academia, in order to practically engage with our surrounding reality is precisely to *think*; most importantly, to think *critically*.

NOTES

1. For more, see for instance (Santos and Meneses, 2009).
2. For more in regard to these discussions, see for instance (Mignolo, 2000).

References

(A/47/277) "An Agenda for Peace—A/47/277—S/24111" 17th June 1992, (http://daccess-dds-ny.un.org/doc/UNDOC/GEN/N92/259/61/PDF/N9225961.pdf?OpenElement), [10th November 2008].

(A/50/60) "Supplement to an Agenda for Peace—A/50/60—S/1995/1" 3rd January 1995, (http://www.un.org/Docs/SG/agsupp.html), [15th November 2008].

(A/54/380) "Financing of the United Nations Mission in East Timor—A/54/380" 21st September 1999, (http://daccess-dds-ny.un.org/doc/UNDOC/GEN/N99/271/77/PDF/N9927177.pdf?OpenElement), [21st October 2011].

(A/55/305) "Report of the Panel on United Nations Peace Operations—A/55/305–S/2000/809" 21st August 2000, (http://secint24.un.org/documents/ga/docs/55/a55305.pdf), [13th December 2008].

(A/RES/1514) "Declaration on the Granting of Independence to Colonial Countries and Peoples—A/RES/1514" 12th December 1960, (http://daccess-dds-ny.un.org/doc/RESOLUTION/GEN/NR0/152/88/IMG/NR015288.pdf?OpenElement), [20th January 2010].

(A/RES/1542) "Transmission of Information under Article 73 of the Charter—A/RES/1542 (XV)" 15th December 1960, (http://www.un.org/ga/search/view_doc.asp?symbol=A/RES/1542(XV)&Lang=E&Area=RESOLUTION), [22nd February 2013].

(E/CN.4/S-4/CRP.1) "Report of the High Commissioner for Human Rights on the Human Rights Situation in East Timor—E/CN.4/S-4/CRP.1" 17th September 1999, (http://www.unhchr.ch/Huridocda/Huridoca.nsf/(Symbol)/E.CN.4.S-4.CRP.1.En?Opendocument), [21th June 2011].

(S/1999/513) "Question of East Timor—Report of the Secretary-General—S/1999/513" 5th May 1999, (http://daccess-dds-ny.un.org/doc/UNDOC/GEN/N99/126/29/IMG/N9912629.pdf?OpenElement), [23rd October 2011].

(S/1999/595) "Question of East Timor—Report of the Secretary-General—S/1999/595" 22nd May 1999, (http://daccess-dds-ny.un.org/doc/UNDOC/GEN/N99/151/14/PDF/N9915114.pdf?OpenElement), [5th January 2012].

(S/1999/705) "Question of East Timor—Report of the Secretary-General—S/1999/705" 22nd June 1999, (http://daccess-dds-ny.un.org/doc/UNDOC/GEN/N99/181/73/PDF/N9918173.pdf?OpenElement), [5th January 2012].

(S/1999/803) "Question of East Timor—Report of the Secretary-General—S/1999/803" 20th July 1999, (http://daccess-dds-ny.un.org/doc/UNDOC/GEN/N99/212/26/PDF/N9921226.pdf?OpenElement), [5th January 2012].

(S/1999/830) "Letter from the Secretary-General Addressed to the President of the Security Council—S/1999/830" 28th July 1999, (http://daccess-dds-ny.un.org/doc/UNDOC/GEN/N99/221/16/PDF/N9922116.pdf?OpenElement), [21st June 2011].

200   *References*

(S/1999/862) "Question of East Timor—Report of the Secretary-General—S/1999/862" 9th August 1999, (http://daccess-dds-ny.un.org/doc/UNDOC/GEN/N99/231/60/PDF/N9923160.pdf?OpenElement), [15th January 2012].

(S/1999/944) "Letter from the Secretary-General Addressed to the President of the Security Council—S/1999/944" 3rd September 1999, (http://www.undemocracy.com/S-1999-944.pdf), [21st June 2011].

(S/1999/976) "Report of the Security Council Mission to Jakarta and Dili, 8 to 12 September 1999—S/1999/976" 14th September 1999, (http://daccess-dds-ny.un.org/doc/UNDOC/GEN/N99/262/20/PDF/N9926220.pdf?OpenElement), [21st June 2011].

(S/1999/1024) "Report of the Secretary-General on the Situation in East Timor—S/1999/1024" 4th October 1999, (http://daccess-dds-ny.un.org/doc/UNDOC/GEN/N99/283/77/IMG/N9928377.pdf?OpenElement), [5th January 2012].

(S/1999/1025) "Letter from the Secretary-General Addressed to the President of the Security Council—S/1999/1025" 4th October 1999, (http://daccess-dds-ny.un.org/doc/UNDOC/GEN/N99/285/78/PDF/N9928578.pdf?OpenElement), [21st June 2011].

(S/2000/53) "Report of the Secretary-General on the United Nations on the Transitional Administration in East Timor—S/2000/53" 26th January 2000, (http://daccess-dds-ny.un.org/doc/UNDOC/GEN/N00/261/62/PDF/N0026162.pdf?OpenElement), [5th January 2012].

(S/2000/53/Add.1a) "Report of the Secretary-General on the United Nations on the Transitional Administration in East Timor—S/2000/53/Add.1 (1 of 2)" 8th February 2000, (http://daccess-dds-ny.un.org/doc/UNDOC/GEN/N00/286/18/IMG/N0028618.pdf?OpenElement), [5th January 2012].

(S/2000/53/Add.1b) "Report of the Secretary-General on the United Nations on the Transitional Administration in East Timor—S/2000/53/Add.1 (2 of 2)" 8th February 2000, (http://daccess-dds-ny.un.org/doc/UNDOC/GEN/N00/286/18/IMG/N0028618.pdf?OpenElement), [5th January 2012].

(S/2000/738) "Report of the Secretary-General on the United Nations Transitional Administration in East Timor—S/2000/738" 26th July 2000, (http://daccess-dds-ny.un.org/doc/UNDOC/GEN/N00/550/73/PDF/N0055073.pdf?OpenElement), [5th January 2012]

(S/2001/42) "Report of the Secretary-General on the United Nations Transitional Administration in East Timor—S/2001/42" 16th January 2001, (http://daccess-dds-ny.un.org/doc/UNDOC/GEN/N01/213/11/IMG/N0121311.pdf?OpenElement), [5th January 2012].

(S/2001/436) "Interim report of the Secretary-General on the United Nations Transitional Administration in East Timor—S/2001/436" 2nd May 2001, (http://daccess-dds-ny.un.org/doc/UNDOC/GEN/N01/357/82/PDF/N0135782.pdf?OpenElement), [5th January 2012].

(S/2001/719) "Progress Report of the Secretary-General on the United Nations Transitional Administration in East Timor—S/2001/719" 24th July 2001, (http://daccess-dds-ny.un.org/doc/UNDOC/GEN/N01/464/30/PDF/N0146430.pdf?OpenElement), [5th January 2012].

(S/2001/983) "Report of the Secretary-General on the United Nations Transitional Administration in East Timor—S/2001/983" 18th October 2001, (http://daccess-dds-ny.un.org/doc/UNDOC/GEN/N01/583/27/IMG/N0158327.pdf?OpenElement), [3rd August 2011].

(S/2001/983/Corr.1) "Report of the Secretary-General on the United Nations Transitional Administration in East Timor—S/2001/983/Corr.1" 22nd October 2001, (http://daccess-dds-ny.un.org/doc/UNDOC/GEN/N01/595/79/PDF/N0159579.pdf?OpenElement), [5th January 2012].

(S/2002/80) "Report of the Secretary-General on the United Nations Transitional Administration in East Timor—S/2002/80" 17th January 2002, (http://daccess-dds-ny.un.org/doc/UNDOC/GEN/N02/215/64/PDF/N0221564.pdf?OpenElement), [5th January 2012].

(S/2002/432) "Report of the Secretary-General on the United Nations Transitional Administration in East Timor—S/2002/432" 17th April 2002, (http://daccess-dds-ny.un.org/doc/UNDOC/GEN/N02/327/74/IMG/N0232774.pdf?OpenElement), [5th January 2012].

(S/2002/432/Add.1) "Report of the Secretary-General on the United Nations Transitional Administration in East Timor—S/2002/432/Add.1" 24th April 2002, (http://daccess-dds-ny.un.org/doc/UNDOC/GEN/N02/352/33/PDF/N0235233.pdf?OpenElement), [5th January 2012].

(S/2002/1223) "Report of the Secretary-General on the United Nations Transitional Administration in East Timor—S/2002/1223" 6th November 2002, (http://daccess-dds-ny.un.org/doc/UNDOC/GEN/N02/675/89/IMG/N0267589.pdf?OpenElement), [5th January 2012].

(S/2003/243) "Special Report of the Secretary-General on the United Nations Mission of Support in East Timor—S/2003/243" 3rd March 2003, (http://daccess-dds-ny.un.org/doc/UNDOC/GEN/N03/262/56/IMG/N0326256.pdf?OpenElement), [5th January 2012].

(S/2003/449) "Report of the Secretary-General on the United Nations Mission of Support in East Timor—S/2003/449" 21st April 2003, (http://daccess-dds-ny.un.org/doc/UNDOC/GEN/N03/328/84/IMG/N0332884.pdf?OpenElement), [5th January 2012].

(S/2003/944) "Report of the Secretary-General on the United Nations Mission of Support in East Timor—S/2003/944" 6th October 2003, (http://daccess-dds-ny.un.org/doc/UNDOC/GEN/N03/535/96/IMG/N0353596.pdf?OpenElement), [5th January 2012].

(S/2004/117) "Special Report of the Secretary-General on the United Nations Mission of Support in East Timor—S/2004/117" 13th February 2004, (http://daccess-dds-ny.un.org/doc/UNDOC/GEN/N04/233/19/IMG/N0423319.pdf?OpenElement), [5th January 2012].

(S/2004/333) "Report of the Secretary-General on the United Nations Mission of Support in East Timor—S/2004/333" 29th April 2004, (http://daccess-dds-ny.un.org/doc/UNDOC/GEN/N04/323/42/IMG/N0432342.pdf?OpenElement), [5th January 2012].

(S/2004/669) "Progress Report of the Secretary-General on the United Nations Mission of Support in East Timor—S/2004/669" 13th August 2004, (http://daccess-dds-ny.un.org/doc/UNDOC/GEN/N04/460/76/IMG/N0446076.pdf?OpenElement), [5th January 2012].

(S/2004/888) "Progress Report of the Secretary-General on the United Nations Mission of Support in East Timor—S/2004/888" 9th November 2004, (http://daccess-dds-ny.un.org/doc/UNDOC/GEN/N04/587/60/PDF/N0458760.pdf?OpenElement), [5th January 2012].

(S/2005/99) "Progress report of the Secretary-General on the United Nations Mission of Support in East Timor—S/2005/99" 18th February 2005, (http://daccess-dds-ny.un.org/doc/UNDOC/GEN/N05/238/59/PDF/N0523859.pdf?OpenElement), [5th January 2012].

(S/2005/310) "End of Mandate Report of the Secretary-General on the United Nations Mission of Support in East Timor—S/2005/310" 12th May 2005, (http://daccess-dds-ny.un.org/doc/UNDOC/GEN/N05/339/40/IMG/N0533940.pdf?OpenElement), [5th January 2012].

(S/2005/533) "Progress Report of the Secretary-General on the United Nations Office in Timor-Leste—S/2005/533" 18th August 2005, (http://daccess-dds-ny.un.org/doc/UNDOC/GEN/N05/463/09/PDF/N0546309.pdf?OpenElement), [5th January 2012].

(S/2006/24) "Progress Report of the Secretary-General on the United Nations Office in Timor-Leste—S/2006/24" 17th January 2006, (http://daccess-dds-ny.un.org/doc/UNDOC/GEN/N06/204/62/PDF/N0620462.pdf?OpenElement), [5th January 2012].

(S/2006/251) "End of Mandate Report of the Secretary-General on the United Nations Office in Timor-Leste—S/2006/251" 20th April 2006, (http://daccess-dds-ny.un.org/doc/UNDOC/GEN/N06/311/37/PDF/N0631137.pdf?OpenElement), [5th January 2012].

(S/2006/251/Corr.1) "End of Mandate Report of the Secretary-General on the United Nations Office in Timor-Leste—S/2006/251/Corr.1" 15th May 2006, (http://daccess-dds-ny.un.org/doc/UNDOC/GEN/N06/349/01/PDF/N0634901.pdf?OpenElement), [5th January 2012].

(S/2006/319) "Letter from the Secretary-General Addressed to the President of the Security Council—S/2006/319" 24th May 2006, (http://daccess-dds-ny.un.org/doc/UNDOC/GEN/N06/361/35/PDF/N0636135.pdf?OpenElement), [25th October 2011].

(S/2006/580) "Report of the Secretary-General on Justice and Reconciliation for Timor-Leste—S/2006/580" 26th July 2006, (http://daccess-dds-ny.un.org/doc/UNDOC/GEN/N06/446/74/PDF/N0644674.pdf?OpenElement), [5th January 2012].

(S/2006/628) "Report of the Secretary-General on Timor-Leste pursuant to Security Council Resolution 1690 (2006)—S/2006/628" 8th August 2006, (http://www.un.org/ga/search/view_doc.asp?symbol=S/2006/628), [3rd August 2011].

(S/2007/50) "Report of the Secretary-General on the United Nations Integrated Mission in Timor-Leste—S/2007/50" 1st February 2007, (http://daccess-dds-ny.un.org/doc/UNDOC/GEN/N07/223/04/PDF/N0722304.pdf?OpenElement), [5th January 2012].

(S/2007/513) "Report of the Secretary-General on the United Nations Integrated Mission in Timor-Leste—S/2007/513" 28th August 2007, (http://daccess-dds-ny.un.org/doc/UNDOC/GEN/N07/488/27/PDF/N0748827.pdf?OpenElement), [5th January 2012].

(S/2007/711) "Report of the Security Council mission to Timor-Leste, 24 to 30 November 2007—S/2007/711" 6th December 2007, (http://daccess-dds-ny.un.org/doc/UNDOC/GEN/N07/630/45/PDF/N0763045.pdf?OpenElement), [12th July 2011].

(S/2008/26) "Report of the Secretary-General on the United Nations Integrated Mission in Timor-Leste—S/2008/26" 17th January 2008, (http://daccess-dds-ny.un.org/doc/UNDOC/GEN/N08/208/18/PDF/N0820818.pdf?OpenElement), [5th January 2012].

(S/2008/501) "Report of the Secretary-General on the United Nations Integrated Mission in Timor-Leste—S/2008/501" 29th July 2008, (http://daccess-dds-ny.un.org/doc/UNDOC/GEN/N08/432/24/PDF/N0843224.pdf?OpenElement), [5th January 2012].

(S/2009/72) "Report of the Secretary-General on the United Nations Integrated Mission in Timor-Leste—S/2009/72" 4th February 2009, (http://daccess-dds-ny.un.org/doc/UNDOC/GEN/N09/222/46/PDF/N0922246.pdf?OpenElement), [5th January 2012].

(S/2009/504) "Report of the Secretary-General on the United Nations Integrated Mission in Timor-Leste—S/2009/504" 2nd October 2009, (http://daccess-dds-ny.un.org/doc/UNDOC/GEN/N09/525/36/PDF/N0952536.pdf?OpenElement), [5th January 2012].

(S/2010/85) "Report of the Secretary-General on the United Nations Integrated Mission in Timor-Leste—S/2010/85" 12th February 2010, (http://daccess-dds-ny.un.org/doc/UNDOC/GEN/N10/231/61/PDF/N1023161.pdf?OpenElement), [5th January 2012].

(S/2010/522) "Report of the Secretary-General on the United Nations Integrated Mission in Timor-Leste—S/2010/522" 13th October 2010, (http://daccess-dds-ny.un.org/doc/UNDOC/GEN/N10/569/52/PDF/N1056952.pdf?OpenElement), [5th January 2012].

(S/2011/32) "Report of the Secretary-General on the United Nations Integrated Mission in Timor-Leste—S/2011/32" 25th January 2011, (http://daccess-dds-ny.un.org/doc/UNDOC/GEN/N11/212/59/PDF/N1121259.pdf?OpenElement), [5th January 2012].

(S/2011/641) "Report of the Secretary-General on the United Nations Integrated Mission in Timor-Leste—S/2011/641" 14th October 2011, (http://daccess-dds-ny.un.org/doc/UNDOC/GEN/N11/536/23/PDF/N1153623.pdf?OpenElement), [5th January 2012].

(S/2012/43) "Report of the Secretary-General on the United Nations Integrated Mission in Timor-Leste—S/2012/43" 18th January 2012, (http://daccess-dds-ny.un.org/doc/UNDOC/GEN/N12/208/75/PDF/N1220875.pdf?OpenElement), [8th February 2012].

(S/2012/765) "Report of the Secretary-General on the United Nations Integrated Mission in Timor-Leste—S/2012/765" 15th October 2012, (http://unmit.unmissions.org/LinkClick.aspx?fileticket=67uhymFErqA%3d&tabid=12032&language=en-US), [8th November 2012].

(S/PV.3998) "UN Security Council 3998th Meeting—S/PV.3998" 7th May 1999, (http://daccess-dds-ny.un.org/doc/UNDOC/PRO/N99/853/42/PDF/N9985342.pdf?OpenElement), [5th January 2012].

(S/PV.4013) "UN Security Council 4013th Meeting—S/PV.4013" 11th June 1999, (http://daccess-dds-ny.un.org/doc/UNDOC/PRO/N99/854/62/PDF/N9985462.pdf?OpenElement), [5th January 2012].

(S/PV.4019) "UN Security Council 4019th Meeting—S/PV.4019" 29th June 1999, (http://daccess-dds-ny.un.org/doc/UNDOC/PRO/N99/855/10/PDF/N9985510.pdf?OpenElement), [5th January 2012].

(S/PV.4031) "UN Security Council 4031th Meeting—S/PV.4031" 3rd August 1999, (http://daccess-dds-ny.un.org/doc/UNDOC/PRO/N99/856/54/PDF/N9985654.pdf?OpenElement), [5th January 2012].

(S/PV.4038) "UN Security Council 4038th Meeting—S/PV.4038" 27th August 1999, (http://daccess-dds-ny.un.org/doc/UNDOC/PRO/N99/856/96/PDF/N9985696.pdf?OpenElement), [5th January 2012].

(S/PV.4041) "UN Security Council 4041th Meeting—S/PV.4041" 3rd September 1999, (http://daccess-dds-ny.un.org/doc/UNDOC/PRO/N99/857/38/PDF/N9985738.pdf?OpenElement), [5th January 2012].

(S/PV.4042) "UN Security Council 4042th Meeting—S/PV.4042" 3rd September 1999, (http://daccess-dds-ny.un.org/doc/UNDOC/PRO/N99/857/44/PDF/N9985744.pdf?OpenElement), [5th January 2012].

(S/PV.4043a) "UN Security Council 4043th Meeting—S/PV.4043" 11th September 1999, (http://daccess-dds-ny.un.org/doc/UNDOC/PRO/N99/857/50/PDF/N9985750.pdf?OpenElement), [5th January 2012].

(S/PV.4043b) "UN Security Council 4043th Meeting—S/PV.4043—(Resumption)" 11th September 1999, (http://daccess-dds-ny.un.org/doc/UNDOC/PRO/N99/857/56/PDF/N9985756.pdf?OpenElement), [5th January 2012].

(S/PV.4045) "UN Security Council 4045th Meeting—S/PV.4045" 15th September 1999, (http://daccess-dds-ny.un.org/doc/UNDOC/PRO/N99/857/92/PDF/N9985792.pdf?OpenElement), [5th January 2012].

(S/PV.4057) "UN Security Council 4057th Meeting—S/PV.4057" 25th October 1999, (http://daccess-dds-ny.un.org/doc/UNDOC/PRO/N99/862/27/PDF/N9986227.pdf?OpenElement), [5th January 2012].

(S/PV.4085) "UN Security Council 4085th Meeting—S/PV.4085" 22nd December 1999, (http://daccess-dds-ny.un.org/doc/UNDOC/PRO/N99/868/13/PDF/N9986813.pdf?OpenElement), [5th January 2012].

(S/PV.4097) "UN Security Council 4097th Meeting—S/PV.4097" 3rd February 2000, (http://daccess-dds-ny.un.org/doc/UNDOC/PRO/N00/277/36/PDF/N0027736.pdf?OpenElement), [5th January 2012].

(S/PV.4114) "UN Security Council 4114th Meeting—S/PV.4114" 21st March 2000, (http://daccess-dds-ny.un.org/doc/UNDOC/PRO/N00/352/50/PDF/N0035250.pdf?OpenElement), [5th January 2012].

(S/PV.4133) "UN Security Council 4133th Meeting—S/PV.4133" 27th April 2000, (http://daccess-dds-ny.un.org/doc/UNDOC/GEN/N00/406/57/PDF/N0040657.pdf?OpenElement), [5th January 2012].

(S/PV.4147) "UN Security Council 4147th Meeting—S/PV.4147" 25th May 2000, (http://daccess-dds-ny.un.org/doc/UNDOC/PRO/N00/449/96/PDF/N0044996.pdf?OpenElement), [5th January 2012].

(S/PV.4165) "UN Security Council 4165th Meeting—S/PV.4165" 27th June 2000, (http://daccess-dds-ny.un.org/doc/UNDOC/PRO/N00/503/15/PDF/N0050315.pdf?OpenElement), [5th January 2012].

(S/PV.4180) "UN Security Council 4180th Meeting—S/PV.4180" 28th July 2000, (http://daccess-dds-ny.un.org/doc/UNDOC/PRO/N00/558/65/PDF/N0055865.pdf?OpenElement), [5th January 2012].

(S/PV.4182) "UN Security Council 4182th Meeting—S/PV.4182" 3rd August 2000, (http://daccess-dds-ny.un.org/doc/UNDOC/PRO/N00/589/65/PDF/N0058965.pdf?OpenElement), [5th January 2012].

(S/PV.4191) "UN Security Council 4191th Meeting—S/PV.4191" 29th August 2000, (http://daccess-dds-ny.un.org/doc/UNDOC/PRO/N00/624/17/PDF/N0062417.pdf?OpenElement), [5th January 2012].

(S/PV.4195) "UN Security Council 4195th Meeting—S/PV.4195" 8th September 2000, (http://daccess-dds-ny.un.org/doc/UNDOC/PRO/N00/636/03/PDF/N0063603.pdf?OpenElement), [5th January 2012].

(S/PV.4198) "UN Security Council 4198th Meeting—S/PV.4198" 20th September 2000, (http://daccess-dds-ny.un.org/doc/UNDOC/GEN/N00/649/62/PDF/N0064962.pdf?OpenElement), [5th January 2012].

(S/PV.4203) "UN Security Council 4203th Meeting—S/PV.4203" 29th September 2000, (http://daccess-dds-ny.un.org/doc/UNDOC/PRO/N00/664/88/PDF/N0066488.pdf?OpenElement), [5th January 2012].

(S/PV.4206) "UN Security Council 4206th Meeting—S/PV.4206" 12th October 2000, (http://daccess-dds-ny.un.org/doc/UNDOC/GEN/N00/686/76/PDF/N0068676.pdf?OpenElement), [5th January 2012].

(S/PV.4228) "UN Security Council 4228th Meeting—S/PV.4228" 20th November 2000, (http://daccess-dds-ny.un.org/doc/UNDOC/GEN/N00/755/69/PDF/N0075569.pdf?OpenElement), [5th January 2012].

(S/PV.4236) "UN Security Council 4236th Meeting—S/PV.4236" 28th November 2000, (http://daccess-dds-ny.un.org/doc/UNDOC/PRO/N00/766/32/PDF/N0076632.pdf?OpenElement), [5th January 2012].

(S/PV.4244) "UN Security Council 4244th Meeting—S/PV.4244" 6th December 2000, (http://daccess-dds-ny.un.org/doc/UNDOC/PRO/N00/783/42/PDF/N0078342.pdf?OpenElement), [5th January 2012].

(S/PV.4265a) "UN Security Council 4265th Meeting—S/PV.4265" 26th January 2001, (http://daccess-dds-ny.un.org/doc/UNDOC/PRO/N01/228/44/PDF/N0122844.pdf?OpenElement), [5th January 2012].

(S/PV.4265b) "UN Security Council 4265th Meeting—S/PV.4265—Resumption 1" 26th January 2001, (http://daccess-dds-ny.un.org/doc/UNDOC/PRO/N01/228/77/PDF/N0122877.pdf?OpenElement), [5th January 2012].

(S/PV.4268) "UN Security Council 4268th Meeting—S/PV.4268" 31st January 2001, (http://daccess-dds-ny.un.org/doc/UNDOC/PRO/N01/233/84/PDF/N0123384.pdf?OpenElement), [5th January 2012].

(S/PV.4308) "UN Security Council 4308th Meeting—S/PV.4308" 5th April 2001, (http://daccess-dds-ny.un.org/doc/UNDOC/PRO/N01/320/66/PDF/N0132066.pdf?OpenElement), [5th January 2012].

(S/PV.4321a) "UN Security Council 4321th Meeting—S/PV.4321" 18th May 2001, (http://daccess-dds-ny.un.org/doc/UNDOC/PRO/N01/376/79/PDF/N0137679.pdf?OpenElement), [5th January 2012].

(S/PV.4321b) "UN Security Council 4321th Meeting—S/PV.4321—Resumption 1" 18th May 2001, (http://daccess-dds-ny.un.org/doc/UNDOC/PRO/N01/377/51/PDF/N0137751.pdf?OpenElement), [5th January 2012].

(S/PV.4351a) "UN Security Council 4351th Meeting—S/PV.4351" 30th July 2001, (http://daccess-dds-ny.un.org/doc/UNDOC/PRO/N01/472/63/PDF/N0147263.pdf?OpenElement), [5th January 2012].

(S/PV.4351b) "UN Security Council 4351th Meeting—S/PV.4351—Resumption 1" 30th July 2001, (http://daccess-dds-ny.un.org/doc/UNDOC/PRO/N01/473/74/PDF/N0147374.pdf?OpenElement), [5th January 2012].

(S/PV.4358) "UN Security Council 4358th Meeting—S/PV.4358" 23rd August 2001, (http://daccess-dds-ny.un.org/doc/UNDOC/GEN/N01/516/41/PDF/N0151641.pdf?OpenElement), [5th January 2012].

(S/PV.4367) "UN Security Council 4367th Meeting—S/PV.4367" 10th September 2001, (http://daccess-dds-ny.un.org/doc/UNDOC/PRO/N01/531/71/PDF/N0153171.pdf?OpenElement), [5th January 2012].

(S/PV.4368) "UN Security Council 4368th Meeting—S/PV.4368" 10th September 2001, (http://daccess-dds-ny.un.org/doc/UNDOC/PRO/N01/531/77/PDF/N0153177.pdf?OpenElement), [5th January 2012].

(S/PV.4397) "UN Security Council 4397th Meeting—S/PV.4397" 25th October 2001, (http://daccess-dds-ny.un.org/doc/UNDOC/GEN/N01/603/35/PDF/N0160335.pdf?OpenElement), [5th January 2012].

(S/PV.4403a) "UN Security Council 4403th Meeting—S/PV.4403" 31st October 2001, (http://daccess-dds-ny.un.org/doc/UNDOC/PRO/N01/611/42/PDF/N0161142.pdf?OpenElement), [5th January 2012].

(S/PV.4403b) "UN Security Council 4403th Meeting—S/PV.4403—Resumption 1" 31st October 2001, (http://daccess-dds-ny.un.org/doc/UNDOC/PRO/N01/612/68/PDF/N0161268.pdf?OpenElement), [5th January 2012].

(S/PV.4404) "UN Security Council 4404th Meeting—S/PV.4404" 31st October 2001, (http://daccess-dds-ny.un.org/doc/UNDOC/PRO/N01/613/64/PDF/N0161364.pdf?OpenElement), [5th January 2012].

(S/PV.4456) "UN Security Council 4456th Meeting—S/PV.4456" 23rd January 2002, (http://daccess-dds-ny.un.org/doc/UNDOC/GEN/N02/228/29/PDF/N0222829.pdf?OpenElement), [5th January 2012].

(S/PV.4462a) "UN Security Council 4462th Meeting—S/PV.4462" 30th January 2002, (http://daccess-dds-ny.un.org/doc/UNDOC/PRO/N02/235/33/PDF/N0223533.pdf?OpenElement), [5th January 2012].

(S/PV.4462b) "UN Security Council 4462th Meeting—S/PV.4462—Resumption 1" 30th January 2002, (http://daccess-dds-ny.un.org/doc/UNDOC/PRO/N02/236/49/PDF/N0223649.pdf?OpenElement), [5th January 2012].

(S/PV.4463) "UN Security Council 4463th Meeting—S/PV.4463" 31st January 2002, (http://daccess-dds-ny.un.org/doc/UNDOC/PRO/N02/238/09/PDF/N0223809.pdf?OpenElement), [5th January 2012].

(S/PV.4522a) "UN Security Council 4522th Meeting—S/PV.4522" 26th April 2002, (http://daccess-dds-ny.un.org/doc/UNDOC/PRO/N02/354/67/PDF/N0235467.pdf?OpenElement), [5th January 2012].

(S/PV.4522b) "UN Security Council 4522th Meeting—S/PV.4522—Resumption 1" 29th April 2002, (http://daccess-dds-ny.un.org/doc/UNDOC/PRO/N02/356/80/PDF/N0235680.pdf?OpenElement), [5th January 2012].

(S/PV.4527) "UN Security Council 4527th Meeting—S/PV.4527" 6th May 2002, (http://daccess-dds-ny.un.org/doc/UNDOC/GEN/N02/369/29/PDF/N0236929.pdf?OpenElement), [5th January 2012].

(S/PV.4534) "UN Security Council 4534th Meeting—S/PV.4534" 17th May 2002, (http://daccess-dds-ny.un.org/doc/UNDOC/PRO/N02/386/12/PDF/N0238612.pdf?OpenElement), [5th January 2012].

(S/PV.4537) "UN Security Council 4537th Meeting—S/PV.4537" 20th May 2002, (http://daccess-dds-ny.un.org/doc/UNDOC/PRO/N02/389/06/PDF/N0238906.pdf?OpenElement), [5th January 2012].

(S/PV.4540) "UN Security Council 4540th Meeting—S/PV.4540" 22th May 2002, (http://daccess-dds-ny.un.org/doc/UNDOC/PRO/N02/395/29/PDF/N0239529.pdf?OpenElement), [5th January 2012].

(S/PV.4542) "UN Security Council 4542th Meeting—S/PV.4542" 23rd May 2002, (http://daccess-dds-ny.un.org/doc/UNDOC/PRO/N02/395/61/PDF/N0239561.pdf?OpenElement), [5th January 2012].

(S/PV.4598) "UN Security Council 4598th Meeting—S/PV.4598" 13th August 2002, (http://daccess-dds-ny.un.org/doc/UNDOC/GEN/N02/521/40/PDF/N0252140.pdf?OpenElement), [5th January 2012].

(S/PV.4646a) "UN Security Council 4646th Meeting—S/PV.4646" 14th November 2002, (http://daccess-dds-ny.un.org/doc/UNDOC/PRO/N02/692/75/PDF/N0269275.pdf?OpenElement), [5th January 2012].

(S/PV.4646b) "UN Security Council 4646th Meeting—S/PV.4646—Resumption 1" 14th November 2002, (http://daccess-dds-ny.un.org/doc/UNDOC/PRO/N02/694/32/PDF/N0269432.pdf?OpenElement), [5th January 2012].

(S/PV.4715) "UN Security Council 4715th Meeting—S/PV.4715" 10th March 2003, (http://daccess-dds-ny.un.org/doc/UNDOC/PRO/N03/272/59/PDF/N0327259.pdf?OpenElement), [5th January 2012].

(S/PV.4735) "UN Security Council 4735th Meeting—S/PV.4735" 4th April 2003, (http://daccess-dds-ny.un.org/doc/UNDOC/PRO/N03/308/96/PDF/N0330896.pdf?OpenElement), [5th January 2012].

(S/PV.4744) "UN Security Council 4744th Meeting—S/PV.4744" 28th April 2003, (http://daccess-dds-ny.un.org/doc/UNDOC/PRO/N03/336/36/PDF/N0333636.pdf?OpenElement), [5th January 2012].

(S/PV.4755) "UN Security Council 4755th Meeting—S/PV.4755" 16th May 2003, (http://daccess-dds-ny.un.org/doc/UNDOC/GEN/N03/361/60/PDF/N0336160.pdf?OpenElement), [5th January 2012].

(S/PV.4758) "UN Security Council 4758th Meeting—S/PV.4758" 19th May 2003, (http://daccess-dds-ny.un.org/doc/UNDOC/PRO/N03/362/47/PDF/N0336247.pdf?OpenElement), [5th January 2012].
(S/PV.4843) "UN Security Council 4843th Meeting—S/PV.4843" 15th October 2003, (http://daccess-dds-ny.un.org/doc/UNDOC/PRO/N03/558/78/PDF/N0355878.pdf?OpenElement), [5th January 2012].
(S/PV.4913) "UN Security Council 4913th Meeting—S/PV.4913" 20th February 2004, (http://daccess-dds-ny.un.org/doc/UNDOC/PRO/N04/245/66/PDF/N0424566.pdf?OpenElement), [5th January 2012].
(S/PV.4963) "UN Security Council 4963th Meeting—S/PV.4963" 6th May 2004, (http://daccess-dds-ny.un.org/doc/UNDOC/GEN/N04/341/40/PDF/N0434140.pdf?OpenElement), [5th January 2012].
(S/PV.4965) "UN Security Council 4965th Meeting—S/PV.4965" 10th May 2004, (http://daccess-dds-ny.un.org/doc/UNDOC/PRO/N04/343/06/PDF/N0434306.pdf?OpenElement), [5th January 2012].
(S/PV.4968) "UN Security Council 4968th Meeting—S/PV.4968" 14th May 2004, (http://daccess-dds-ny.un.org/doc/UNDOC/PRO/N04/350/59/PDF/N0435059.pdf?OpenElement), [5th January 2012].
(S/PV.5024) "UN Security Council 5024th Meeting—S/PV.5024" 24th August 2004, (http://daccess-dds-ny.un.org/doc/UNDOC/GEN/N04/467/42/PDF/N0446742.pdf?OpenElement), [5th January 2012].
(S/PV.5074) "UN Security Council 5074th Meeting—S/PV.5074" 11th November 2004, (http://daccess-dds-ny.un.org/doc/UNDOC/GEN/N04/602/66/PDF/N0460266.pdf?OpenElement), [5th January 2012].
(S/PV.5076) "UN Security Council 5076th Meeting—S/PV.5076" 15th November 2004, (http://daccess-dds-ny.un.org/doc/UNDOC/PRO/N04/604/93/PDF/N0460493.pdf?OpenElement), [5th January 2012].
(S/PV.5079) "UN Security Council 5079th Meeting—S/PV.5079" 16th November 2004, (http://daccess-dds-ny.un.org/doc/UNDOC/PRO/N04/609/35/PDF/N0460935.pdf?OpenElement), [5th January 2012].
(S/PV.5132) "UN Security Council 5132th Meeting—S/PV.5132" 28th February 2005, (http://daccess-dds-ny.un.org/doc/UNDOC/PRO/N05/250/17/PDF/N0525017.pdf?OpenElement), [5th January 2012].
(S/PV.5171) "UN Security Council 5171th Meeting—S/PV.5171" 28th April 2005, (http://daccess-dds-ny.un.org/doc/UNDOC/PRO/N05/325/39/PDF/N0532539.pdf?OpenElement), [5th January 2012].
(S/PV.5179) "UN Security Council 5179th Meeting—S/PV.5179" 16th May 2005, (http://daccess-dds-ny.un.org/doc/UNDOC/PRO/N05/345/72/PDF/N0534572.pdf?OpenElement), [5th January 2012].
(S/PV.5180) "UN Security Council 5180th Meeting—S/PV.5180" 16th May 2005, (http://daccess-dds-ny.un.org/doc/UNDOC/PRO/N05/344/45/PDF/N0534445.pdf?OpenElement), [5th January 2012].
(S/PV.5251) "UN Security Council 5251th Meeting—S/PV.5251" 29th August 2005, (http://daccess-dds-ny.un.org/doc/UNDOC/PRO/N05/474/37/PDF/N0547437.pdf?OpenElement), [5th January 2012].
(S/PV.5351) "UN Security Council 5351th Meeting—S/PV.5351" 23rd January 2006, (http://daccess-dds-ny.un.org/doc/UNDOC/PRO/N06/217/38/PDF/N0621738.pdf?OpenElement), [5th January 2012].
(S/PV.5432) "UN Security Council 5432th Meeting—S/PV.5432" 5th May 2006, (http://daccess-dds-ny.un.org/doc/UNDOC/PRO/N06/339/83/PDF/N0633983.pdf?OpenElement), [5th January 2012].
(S/PV.5436) "UN Security Council 5436th Meeting—S/PV.5436" 12th May 2006, (http://daccess-dds-ny.un.org/doc/UNDOC/PRO/N06/346/39/PDF/N0634639.pdf?OpenElement), [5th January 2012].

(S/RES/1246) "UN Security Council Resolution 1246—S/RES/1246" 11th June 1999, (http://daccess-dds-ny.un.org/doc/UNDOC/GEN/N99/174/13/PDF/N9917413.pdf?OpenElement), [20th June 2011].
(S/RES/1257) "UN Security Council Resolution 1257—S/RES/1257" 3rd August 1999, (http://daccess-dds-ny.un.org/doc/UNDOC/GEN/N99/226/69/PDF/N9922669.pdf?OpenElement), [20th June 2011].
(S/RES/1262) "UN Security Council Resolution 1262—S/RES/1262" 27th August 1999, (http://daccess-dds-ny.un.org/doc/UNDOC/GEN/N99/247/47/PDF/N9924747.pdf?OpenElement), [20th June 2011].
(S/RES/1264) "UN Security Council Resolution 1264—S/RES/1264" 15th September 1999, (http://daccess-dds-ny.un.org/doc/UNDOC/GEN/N99/264/81/PDF/N9926481.pdf?OpenElement), [2nd August 2011].
(S/RES/1272) "UN Security Council Resolution 1272—S/RES/1272" 25th October 1999, (http://daccess-dds-ny.un.org/doc/UNDOC/GEN/N99/312/77/PDF/N9931277.pdf?OpenElement), [23rd April 2010].
(S/RES/1338) "UN Security Council Resolution 1338—S/RES/1338" 31st January 2001, (http://daccess-dds-ny.un.org/doc/UNDOC/GEN/N01/234/39/PDF/N0123439.pdf?OpenElement), [23rd April 2010].
(S/RES/1392) "UN Security Council Resolution 1392—S/RES/1392" 31st January 2002, (http://www.undemocracy.com/S-RES-1392(2002).pdf), [23rd April 2010].
(S/RES/1410) "UN Security Council Resolution 1410—S/RES/1410" 17th May 2002, (http://www.unhchr.ch/Huridocda/Huridoca.nsf/(Symbol)/S.RES.1410+(2002).En?Opendocument), [2nd August 2011].
(S/RES/1480) "UN Security Council Resolution 1480—S/RES/1480" 19th May 2003, (http://www.undemocracy.com/S-RES-1480(2003).pdf), [3rd August 2011].
(S/RES/1543) "UN Security Council Resolution 1543—S/RES/1543" 14th May 2004, (http://www.worldlii.org/int/other/UNSCRsn/2004/22.pdf), [3rd August 2011].
(S/RES/1573) "UN Security Council Resolution 1573—S/RES/1573" 16th November 2004, (http://www.undemocracy.com/S-RES-1573(2004).pdf), [3rd August 2011].
(S/RES/1599) "UN Security Council Resolution 1599—S/RES/1599" 28th April 2005, (http://www.undemocracy.com/S-RES-1599(2005).pdf), [3rd August 2011].
(S/RES/1677) "UN Security Council Resolution 1677—S/RES/1677" 12th May 2006, (http://www.undemocracy.com/S-RES-1677(2006).pdf), [3rd August 2011].
(S/RES/1690) "UN Security Council Resolution 1690—S/RES/1690" 20th June 2006, (http://www.securitycouncilreport.org/atf/cf/%7B65BFCF9B-6D27-4E9C-8CD3-CF6E4FF96FF9%7D/TL SRES 1690.pdf), [3rd August 2011].
(S/RES/1703) "UN Security Council Resolution 1703—S/RES/1703" 18th August 2006, (http://www.un.org/ga/search/view_doc.asp?symbol=S/RES/1703(2006)), [3rd August 2011].
(S/RES/1704) "UN Security Council Resolution 1704—S/RES/1704" 25th August 2006, (http://www.un.org/ga/search/view_doc.asp?symbol=S/RES/1704(2006)), [3rd August 2011].
(S/RES/1745) "UN Security Council Resolution 1745—S/RES/1745" 22nd February 2007, (http://www.un.org/ga/search/view_doc.asp?symbol=S/RES/1745(2007)), [3rd August 2011].
(S/RES/1802) "UN Security Council Resolution 1802—S/RES/1802" 25th February 2008, (http://daccess-dds-ny.un.org/doc/UNDOC/GEN/N08/251/41/PDF/N0825141.pdf?OpenElement), [20th March 2011].
(S/RES/1867) "UN Security Council Resolution 1867—S/RES/1867" 26th February 2009, (http://daccess-dds-ny.un.org/doc/UNDOC/GEN/N09/250/24/PDF/N0925024.pdf?OpenElement), [3rd August 2011].
(S/RES/1912) "UN Security Council Resolution 1912—S/RES/1912" 26th February 2010, (http://daccess-dds-ny.un.org/doc/UNDOC/GEN/N10/253/13/PDF/N1025313.pdf?OpenElement), [3rd August 2011].

(S/RES/1969) "UN Security Council Resolution 1969—S/RES/1969" 24th February 2011, (http://daccess-dds-ny.un.org/doc/UNDOC/GEN/N11/242/86/PDF/ N1124286.pdf?OpenElement), [3rd August 2011].

(S/RES/2037) "UN Security Council Resolution 2037—S/RES/2037" 23rd February 2012, (http://daccess-dds-ny.un.org/doc/UNDOC/GEN/N12/240/01/PDF/ N1224001.pdf?OpenElement), [28th February 2012].

(UNTAET/DIR/2000/7) "Directive no. 2000/7 on the Registration of Charitable Organizations—UNTAET/DIR/2000/7" 21st November 2000, (http://www.unmit.org/legal/UNTAET-Law/Directives English/Dir2000-07.pdf), [5th January 2012].

(UNTAET/DIR/2001/1) "Directive no. 2001/1 on Certain Income Taxation Provisions—UNTAET/DIR/2001/1" 23rd January 2001, (http://www.unmit.org/legal/UNTAET-Law/Directives English/Dir2001-01.pdf), [5th January 2012].

(UNTAET/DIR/2001/2) "Directive no. 2001/2 on the Calculation of Taxable Income of Taxpayers and Administrative Matters Relating to the Income Tax—UNTAET/DIR/2001/2" 31st March 2001, (http://www.unmit.org/legal/UNTAET-Law/Directives English/Dir2001-02.pdf), [5th January 2012].

(UNTAET/DIR/2001/7) "Directive no. 2001/7 on the Establishment of Road Traffic Rules in East Timor—UNTAET/DIR/2001/7" 26th June 2001, (http://www.unmit.org/legal/UNTAET-Law/Directives English/Dir2001-07.pdf), [5th January 2012].

(UNTAET/DIR/2001/10) "Directive on Fees and Charges for Electricity and Related Services—UNTAET/DIR/2001/10" 16th August 2001, (http://www.unmit.org/legal/UNTAET-Law/Directives English/Dir2001-10.pdf), [5th January 2012].

(UNTAET/DIR/2001/12) "Directive no. 2001/12 on the Criteria for Appointment of a Commissioner for the East Timor Police Service—UNTAET/DIR/2001/12" 15th October 2001, (http://www.unmit.org/legal/UNTAET-Law/Directives English/Dir2001-12.pdf), [5th January 2012].

(UNTAET/DIR/2002/07) "Directive no. 2002/07 Amendment on the Schedule of Fees and Charges for Electricity and Related Services—UNTAET/DIR/2002/07" 10th May 2002, (http://www.unmit.org/legal/UNTAET-Law/Directives English/Dir2002-07.pdf), [5th January 2012].

(UNTAET/DIR/2002/08) "Directive no. 2002/08 on the Organic Structure of the Ministries and Secretariats of State of the Second Transitional Government of East Timor—UNTAET/DIR/2002/08" 18th May 2002, (http://www.unmit.org/legal/UNTAET-Law/Directives English/Dir2002-08.pdf), [5th January 2012].

(UNTAET/NOT/2000/2) "Notification on the Appointment of the Acting Head and Acting Deputy Head of the Central Fiscal Authority of East Timor—UNTAET/NOT/2000/2" 26th July 2000, (http://www.unmit.org/legal/UNTAET-Law/Notifications English/Not2000-02.pdf), [5th January 2012].

(UNTAET/NOT/2000/3) "Notification on the Appointment of the Acting General Manager and Acting Deputy Acting Manager of the Central Payments office of East Timor—UNTAET/NOT/2000/3" (http://www.unmit.org/legal/UNTAET-Law/Notifications English/Not2000-03.pdf), [5th January 2012].

(UNTAET/NOT/2000/4) "Notification on the Designation of International Labour Day as a Public Holiday for East Timor on Monday, 1 May 2000—UNTAET/NOT/2000/4" 26th April 2000, (http://www.unmit.org/legal/UNTAET-Law/Notifications English/Not2000-04.pdf), [5th January 2012].

(UNTAET/NOT/2000/5) "Notification on the Appointment of the Head and Deputy Head of the Central Fiscal Authority of East Timor—UNTAET/NOT/2000/5" (http://www.unmit.org/legal/UNTAET-Law/Notifications English/Not2000-05.pdf), [5th January 2012].

(UNTAET/NOT/2000/6) "Notification on the Appointment of the General Manager and the Deputy General Manager for supervision of the Central Payments office of East Timor—UNTAET/NOT/2000/6" 30th November 2000, (http://www.unmit.org/legal/UNTAET-Law/Notifications English/Not2000-06.pdf), [5th January 2012].

(UNTAET/NOT/2000/9) "Notification on Fees in Relation to Water Services—UNTAET/NOT/2000/9" 26th July 2000, (http://www.unmit.org/legal/UNTAET-Law/Notifications English/Not2000-09.pdf), [5th January 2012].

(UNTAET/NOT/2000/10) "Notification on Fees in Relation to Postal Services—UNTAET/NOT/2000/10" 26th July 2000, (http://www.unmit.org/legal/UNTAET-Law/Notifications English/Not2000-10.pdf), [5th January 2012].

(UNTAET/NOT/2000/11) "Notification on Fees in Relation to Port Services—UNTAET/NOT/2000/11" 26th July 2000, (http://www.unmit.org/legal/UNTAET-Law/Notifications English/Not2000-11.pdf), [5th January 2012].

(UNTAET/NOT/2000/12) "Notification on Fees in Relation to Electricity Services—UNTAET/NOT/2000/12" 26th July 2000, (http://www.unmit.org/legal/UNTAET-Law/Notifications English/Not2000-12.pdf), [5th January 2012].

(UNTAET/NOT/2000/13) "Notification on Fees in Relation to Aviation Services—UNTAET/NOT/2000/13" 26th July 2000, (http://www.unmit.org/legal/UNTAET-Law/Notifications English/Not2000-13.pdf), [5th January 2012].

(UNTAET/NOT/2000/15) "Notification on the Appointment of the Deputy General Manager for payments of the Central Payments Office of East Timor—UNTAET/NOT/2000/15" 2nd August 2000, (http://www.unmit.org/legal/UNTAET-Law/Notifications English/Not2000-15.pdf), [5th January 2012].

(UNTAET/NOT/2000/22) "Notification on Fees in Relation to Electricity Services—UNTAET/NOT/2000/22" 30th November 2000, (http://www.unmit.org/legal/UNTAET-Law/Notifications English/Not2000-22.pdf), [5th January 2012].

(UNTAET/NOT/2001/15) "Notification on Fees in Relation to Water Supply Connection for the Bidau-Santa Ana Metiaut Zone—UNTAET/NOT/2001/15" 8th August 2001, (http://www.unmit.org/legal/UNTAET-Law/Notifications English/Not2001-15rev2.pdf), [5th January 2012].

(UNTAET/NOT/2001/19) "Notification on the Appointment of the Head and Deputy Head of the Central Fiscal Authority of East Timor—UNTAET/NOT/2001/19" (http://www.unmit.org/legal/UNTAET-Law/Notifications English/Not2001-19.pdf), [5th January 2012].

(UNTAET/NOT/2001/23) "Notification on the Traffic Infringement Notice for Traffic Offences in East Timor—UNTAET/NOT/2001/23" 31st October 2001, (http://www.unmit.org/legal/UNTAET-Law/Notifications English/Not2001-23.pdf), [5th January 2012].

(UNTAET/NOT/2001/24) "Notification on the Appointment of the Deputy General Manager for Payments of the Central Payments Office of East Timor—UNTAET/NOT/2001/24" (http://www.unmit.org/legal/UNTAET-Law/Notifications English/Not2001-24.pdf), [5th January 2012].

(UNTAET/NOT/2002/12) "Notification no. 2002/12 on the Declaration of an Official Holiday—UNTAET/NOT/2002/12" 26th March 2002, (http://www.unmit.org/legal/UNTAET-Law/Notifications English/Not2002-12.pdf), [5th January 2012].

(UNTAET/NOT/2002/14) "Notification no. 2002/14 on the Appointment of the General Manager of the Banking and Payments Authority of East Timor—UNTAET/NOT/2002/14" 1st April 2002, (http://www.unmit.org/legal/UNTAET-Law/Notifications English/Not2002-14.pdf), [5th January 2012].

(UNTAET/ORD/2000/1) "Executive Order no. 2000/1 on the Designation of Public Holidays in East Timor—UNTAET/ORD/2000/1" June 2000, (http://www.unmit.org/legal/UNTAET-Law/Executive Orders/Ord2000-01.pdf), [5th January 2012].

(UNTAET/ORD/2000/2) "Executive Order no. 2000/2 on the Decriminalization of Defamation—UNTAET/ORD/2000/2" 7th September 2000, (http://www.unmit.org/legal/UNTAET-Law/Executive Orders/Ord2000-02.pdf), [5th January 2012].

(UNTAET/ORD/2001/1) "Executive Order no. 2001/1 on an Interim Procedure to Settle Disputes Arising from the Termination of Labour Contracts—UNTAET/ORD/2001/1" 5th February 2001, (http://www.unmit.org/legal/UNTAET-Law/Executive Orders/Ord2001-01.pdf), [5th January 2012].

(UNTAET/ORD/2001/3) "Executive Order on the Prohibition of Unlicensed Radio and other Broadcast Transmissions Utilizing the Airwaves of East Timor—UNTAET/ORD/2001/3" 26th April 2001, (http://www.unmit.org/legal/UNTAET-Law/Executive Orders/Ord2001-03.pdf), [5th January 2012].

(UNTAET/ORD/2001/5) "Executive Order on the Prohibition of Unlicensed Radio and Other Broadcast Transmissions Utilizing the Airwaves of East Timor—UNTAET/ORD/2001/5" 8th August 2001, (http://www.unmit.org/legal/UNTAET-Law/Executive Orders/Ord2001-05.pdf), [5th January 2012].

(UNTAET/ORD/2001/6) "Executive Order no. 2001/6 on the Decriminalization of Adultery—UNTAET/ORD/2001/6" 23rd August 2001, (http://www.unmit.org/legal/UNTAET-Law/Executive Orders/Ord2001-06.pdf), [5th January 2012].

(UNTAET/ORD/2002/3) "Executive Order no. 2002/3 on the Prohibition of Unlicensed Radio and Other Broadcast Transmissions Utilizing the Airwaves of East Timor—UNTAET/ORD/2002/3" 19th February 2002, (http://www.unmit.org/legal/UNTAET-Law/Executive Orders/Ord2002-03.pdf), [5th January 2012].

(UNTAET/ORD/2002/6) "Executive Order no. 2002/6 on Provisional Governance Arrangements for the Banking and Payments Authority of East Timor—UNTAET/ORD/2002/6" 17th April 2002, (http://www.unmit.org/legal/UNTAET-Law/Executive Orders/Ord2002-06.pdf), [5th January 2012].

(UNTAET/REG/1999/1) "Regulation no. 1999/1 on the Authority of the Transitional Administration in East Timor—UNTAET/REG/1999/1" 27th November 1999, (http://www.un.org/en/peacekeeping/missions/past/etimor/untaetR/etreg1.htm), [22nd November 2011].

(UNTAET/REG/1999/2) "Regulation no. 1999/2 on the Establishment of a National Consultative Council—UNTAET/REG/1999/2" 2nd December 1999, (http://www.un.org/en/peacekeeping/missions/past/etimor/untaetR/etreg2.htm), [22nd November 2011].

(UNTAET/REG/1999/3) "Regulation no. 1999/3 on the Establishment of a Transitional Judicial Service Commission—UNTAET/REG/1999/3" 3rd December 1999, (http://www.un.org/en/peacekeeping/missions/past/etimor/untaetR/etreg3.htm), [21st November 2011].

(UNTAET/REG/2000/1) "Regulation no. 2000/1 on the Establishment of the Central Fiscal Authority of East Timor—UNTAET/REG/2000/1" 14th January 2000, (http://www.unmit.org/legal/UNTAET-Law/Regulations English/Reg2000-01.pdf), [5th January 2011].

(UNTAET/REG/2000/4) "Regulation no. 2000/4 on the Registration of Businesses—UNTAET/REG/2000/4" 20th January 2000, (http://www.un.org/en/peacekeeping/missions/past/etimor/untaetR/Reg004E.pdf), [5th January 2012].

(UNTAET/REG/2000/6) "Regulation no. 2000/6 on the Establishment of a Central Payments Office of East Timor—UNTAET/REG/2000/6" 22nd January 2000, (http://www.unmit.org/legal/UNTAET-Law/Regulations English/Reg2000-06.pdf), [5th January 2012].

(UNTAET/REG/2000/7) "Regulation no. 2000/7 on the Establishment of a Legal Tender for East Timor—UNTAET/REG/2000/7" 24th January 2000, (http://www.unmit.org/legal/UNTAET-Law/Regulations English/Reg2000-07.pdf), [5th January 2012].

(UNTAET/REG/2000/8) "Regulation no. 2000/8 on Bank Licensing and Supervision—UNTAET/REG/2000/8" 25th February 2000, (http://www.unmit.org/legal/UNTAET-Law/Regulations English/Reg2000-08.pdf), [5th January 2012].

(UNTAET/REG/2000/9) "Regulation no. 2000/9 on the Establishment of a Border Regime for East Timor—UNTAET/REG/2000/9" 25th February 2000, (http://www.unmit.org/legal/UNTAET-Law/Regulations English/Reg2000-09.pdf), [5th January 2011].

(UNTAET/REG/2000/11) "Regulation no. 2000/11 on the Organization of Courts in East Timor—UNTAET/REG/2000/11" 6th March 2000, (http://www.unmit.org/legal/UNTAET-Law/Regulations English/Reg2000-11.pdf), [5th January 2012].

(UNTAET/REG/2000/12) "Regulation no. 2000/12 on a Provisional Tax and Customs Regime for East Timor—UNTAET/REG/2000/12" 8th March 2000, (http://www.unmit.org/legal/UNTAET-Law/Regulations English/Reg2000-12.pdf), [5th January 2012].

(UNTAET/REG/2000/18) "Regulation no. 2000/18 on a Taxation System for East Timor—UNTAET/REG/2000/18" 30th June 2000, (http://www.unmit.org/legal/UNTAET-Law/Regulations English/Reg2000-18.pdf), [5th January 2012].

(UNTAET/REG/2000/20) "Regulation no. 2000/20 on Budget and Financial Management—UNTAET/REG/2000/20" 30th June 2000, (http://www.unmit.org/legal/UNTAET-Law/Regulations English/Reg2000-20.pdf), [5th January 2012].

(UNTAET/REG/2000/30) "Regulation no. 2000/30 on Transitional Rules of Criminal Procedure—UNTAET/REG/2000/30" 25th September 2000, (http://www.unmit.org/legal/UN-TAET-Law/Regulations English/Reg2000-30.pdf), [5th January 2012].

(UNTAET/REG/2000/32) "Regulation no. 2000/32 to Amend Regulation nos 2000/12 and 2000/18—UNTAET/REG/2000/32" 29th September 2000, (http://www.unmit.org/legal/UNTAET-Law/Regulations English/Reg2000-32.pdf), [5th January 2012].

(UNTAET/REG/2000/35) "Regulation no. 2000/35 to Amend Regulation no. 2000/18 on a Revenue System for East Timor (as amended by UNTAET Regulation 2000/32)—UN-TAET/REG/2000/35" 20th December 2000, (http://www.unmit.org/legal/UNTAET-Law/Regulations English/Reg2000-35.pdf), [5th January 2012].

(UNTAET/REG/2001/3) "Regulation no. 2001/3 on the Establishment of the Central Civil Registry for East Timor—UNTAET/REG/2001/3" 16th March 2001, (http://www.unmit.org/legal/UNTAET-Law/Regulations English/Reg2001-03.pdf), [5th January 2012].

(UNTAET/REG/2001/13) "Regulation no. 2001/13 on Budget and Financial Management—UNTAET/REG/2001/13" 20th July 2001, (http://www.unmit.org/legal/UNTAET-Law/Regulations English/Reg2001-13.pdf), [5th January 2012].

(UNTAET/REG/2001/14) "Regulation no. 2001/14 on the Official Currency and Legal Tender of East Timor—UNTAET/REG/2001/14" 20th July 2001, (http://www.unmit.org/legal/UN-TAET-Law/Regulations English/Reg2001-14.pdf), [5th January 2012].

(UNTAET/REG/2001/16) "Regulation no. 2001/16 to Amend Regulation no. 2000/18 on a Revenue System for East Timor—UNTAET/REG/2001/16" 21st July 2001, (http://www.unmit.org/legal/UNTAET-Law/Regulations English/Reg2001-16.pdf), [5th January 2012].

(UNTAET/REG/2001/17) "Regulation no. 2001/17 to Amend Regulation no. 2000/18 on a Revenue System for East Timor; and to Amend Regulation no. 2000/9 on the Establishment of a Border Regime for East Timor—UNTAET/REG/2001/17" 21st July 2001, (http://www.unmit.org/legal/UNTAET-Law/Regulations English/Reg2001-17.pdf), [5th January 2012].

(UNTAET/REG/2001/20) "Regulation no. 2001/20 to Amend Regulation no. 2000/18 on a Revenue System for East Timor—UNTAET/REG/2001/20" 21st July 2001, (http://www.unmit.org/legal/UNTAET-Law/Regulations English/Reg2001-20.pdf), [5th January 2012].

(UNTAET/REG/2001/22) "Regulation no. 2001/22 on the Establishment of the East Timor Police Service—UNTAET/REG/2001/22" 10th August 2001, (http://www.unmit.org/legal/UNTAET-Law/Regulations English/Reg2001-22.pdf), [5th January 2012].

(UNTAET/REG/2001/23) "Establishment of a Prison Service in East Timor—UNTAET/REG/2001/23" 28th August 2001, (http://www.unmit.org/legal/UNTAET-Law/Regulations English/Reg2001-23.pdf), [5th January 2012].

(UNTAET/REG/2001/27) "Regulation 2001/27 on the Amendment of UNTAET Regulation no.2001/23 on the Establishment of a Prison Service in East Timor—UNTAET/REG/2001/27" 19th September 2001, (http://www.unmit.org/legal/UNTAET-Law/Regulations English/Reg2001-27.pdf), [5th January 2012].

(UNTAET/REG/2001/30) "Regulation no. 2001/30 on the Banking and Payments Authority of East Timor—UNTAET/REG/2001/30" 30th November 2001, (http://www.unmit.org/legal/UNTAET-Law/Regulations English/Reg2001-30.pdf), [5th January 2012].

(UNTAET/REG/2002/4) "Regulation no 2002/4 on the Replacement of Regulation 2000/4 on Registration of Businesses—UNTAET/REG/2002/4" 23rd April 2002, (http://www.un.org/en/peacekeeping/missions/past/etimor/untaetR/2002_04.pdf), [5th January 2012].

(UNTAET/REG/2002/5) "Regulation no. 2002/5 on the Establishment of a Labour Code for East Timor—UNTAET/REG/2002/5" 1st May 2002, (http://www.unmit.org/legal/UN-TAET-Law/Regulations English/Reg2002-05.pdf), [5th January 2012].

(UNTAET/REG/2002/6) "Regulation no. 2002/6 on the Establishment of the Public Broadcasting Service of East Timor—UNTAET/REG/2002/6" 9th May 2002, (http://www.unmit.org/legal/UNTAET-Law/Regulations English/Reg2002-06.pdf), [5th January 2012].

(UNTAET/REG/2002/07) "Regulation no. 2002/07 on the Organic Structure of the Second Transitional Government of East Timor and to Amend UNTAET Regulation no. 2001/28—UNTAET/REG/2002/07" 18th May 2002, (http://www.unmit.org/legal/UNTAET-Law/Regulations English/Reg2002-07.pdf), [5th January 2012].

ADB, Asian Development Bank (2002) "TA-3803 TIM: Economic Policies and Strategies for Development Planning" March 2002, (http://www2.adb.org/Documents/TACRs/TIM/34400-TIM-TACR.pdf), [10th April 2012].

ADB, Asian Development Bank (2003) "TA:TIM 34020 Capacity Building to Strengthen Public Sector Management and Governance Skills" December 2003, (http://www2.adb.org/Documents/TARs/TIM/tar_tim_34020.pdf), [10th April 2012].

ADB, Asian Development Bank (2004) "TA-4509 TIM: Strengthening Microfinance Operations" December 2004, (http://www2.adb.org/Documents/TARs/TIM/tar-tim-38213.pdf), [10th April 2012].

ADB, Asian Development Bank (2005) "TA-4609 TIM: Infrastructure Sectors Capacity Development (previously Institutional Capacity Building for the Infrastructure Sectors)" July 2005, (http://www2.adb.org/Documents/TARs/TIM/tar-tim-38212.pdf), [10th April 2012].

ADB, Asian Development Bank (2007) "TA-4942 TIM: Infrastructure Project Management" May 2007, (http://www2.adb.org/Documents/TARs/TIM/39151-TIM-TAR.pdf), [10th April 2012].

ADB, Asian Development Bank (2009) "TA-7401 TIM: Statistical and Macroeconomic Capacity Building" December 2009, (http://www2.adb.org/documents/tars/tim/43142-tim-tar.pdf), [10th April 2012].

ADB, Asian Development Bank (N/A) "Timor-Leste—All Projects" N/A, (http://www2.adb.org/projects/summaries.asp?query=&browse=1&mode=1&ctry=TIM&year=ALL), [10th April 2012].

Agamben, Giorgio (1998) *Homo Sacer: Sovereign Power and Bare Life.* Stanford: Stanford University Press.

Agamben, Giorgio (2009) *What Is an Apparatus?—and Other Essays.* Stanford: Stanford University Press.

Alves, José Augusto Lindgren (2001) *Relações Internacionais e Temas Sociais: A Década das Conferências.* Brasília: IBRI.

Anderson, Benedict (1983) *Imagined Communities: Reflections on the Origin and Spread of Nationalism.* New York: Verso.

Aoi, Chiyuki; Coning, Cedric de; Thakur, Ramesh (Eds.) (2007) *Unintended Consequences of Peacekeeping Operations.* Tokyo, New York, Paris: United Nations University Press.

Ashworth, Lucian (2002) "Did the Realist-Idealist Great Debate Really Happen? A Revisionist History of International Relations" *International Relations.* 16 (1), 33–51.

Azar, Edward (1990) *The Management of Protracted Social Conflict: Theory and Cases.* Hampshire: Dartmouth Publishers.

Baranyi, Stephen (Ed.) (2008) *The Paradoxes of Peacebuilding Post-9/11.* Vancouver: University of British Columbia Press.

Barnett, Michael; Kim, Hunjoon; O'Donnell, Madalene; Sitea, Laura (2007) "Peacebuilding: What is in a Name?" *Global Governance.* 13 (1), 35–58.

Barnett, Michael; Zürcher, Christoph (2009) "The Peacebuilder's Contract: How External Statebuilding Reinforces Weak Statehood" in Paris, Roland; Sisk, Timothy (Eds.), *The Dilemmas of Statebuilding—Confronting the Contradictions of Postwar Peace Operations.* New York: Routledge, 23–52.

Beauvais, Joel C. (2001) "'Benevolent Despotism: A Critique of UN State-Building in East Timor" *New York University Journal of International Law and Politics.* 33 (4), 1101–11078.

Bellamy, Alex J.; William, Paul; Griffin, Stuart (2010) *Understanding Peacekeeping.* Cambridge: Polity Press.

Bellamy, Alex; Williams, Paul (2004a) "Conclusion: What Future for Peace Operations? Brahimi and Beyond" *International Peacekeeping.* 11 (1), 183–212.

Bellamy, Alex; Williams, Paul (2004b) "Introduction: Thinking Anew about Peace Operations" *International Peacekeeping.* 11 (1), 1–15.

Bendaña, Alejandro (2005) "From Peace-building to State-building: One Step Forward and Two Backwards" *Development.* 48 (3), 5–15.

Bercovitch, Jacob; Dean, Richard (2012) *Conflict Resolution in the Twenty-First Century: Principles, Methods, and Approaches.* Ann Arbor: The University of Michigan Press.

Berdal, Mats (2009) *Building Peace After War.* London: Routledge.

Bickerton, Christopher (2007) "State-Building: Exporting State-Failure" in Bickerton, Cunliffe & Gourevitch (Ed.) *Politics without Sovereignty: A Critique of Contemporary International Relations.* London: University College London Press, 93–111.

Blanco, Ramon (2013) "The Modern State in Western Europe: Three Narratives of Its Formation" *Revista Debates.* 7 (3), 169–184.

Blanco, Ramon (2014) "Del Mantenimiento de la Paz al Proceso de Formación del Estado: Un Esbozo de los Esfuerzos de la ONU para la Paz Internacional" *Foro Internacional.* 216 (2), 266–318.

Blanco, Ramon (2015) "The UN Peacebuilding Process: An Analysis of Its Shortcomings in Timor-Leste" *Revista Brasileira de Política Internacional.* 58 (1), 42–62.

Blanco, Ramon (2017) "Normalizando Anormais na Sociedade Internacional: Operações de Paz, Foucault e a Escola Inglesa" *Relações Internacionais.* 53 83–107.

Boege, Volker; Brown, M. Anne; Clements, Kevin P.; Nolan, Anna (2008) "States Emerging from Hybrid Political Orders—Pacific Experiences" *The Australian Centre for Peace and Conflict Studies—Occasional Papers Series.* 11 (September), i–41.

Boege, Volker; Brown, M. Anne; Clements, Kevin P.; Nolan, Anna (2009) "On Hybrid Political Orders and Emerging States: What Is Failing—States in the Global South or Research and Politics in the West?" *The Berghof Handbook Dialogue Series.* (8), 15–36.

Boege, Volker; Brown, M. Anne; Clements, Kevin P.; Nolan, Anna (2010) "Challenging State-building as Peacebuilding—Working with Hybrid Political Orders to Build Peace" in Richmond, Oliver (Ed.) *Palgrave Advances in Peacebuilding—Critical Developments and Approaches.* London and New York: Palgrave, 100-115.

Booth, Ken (1991) "Security and Emancipation" *Review of International Studies.* 17 (4), 313–326.

Brahimi, Lakhadar (2007) "State Building in Crisis and Post-Conflict Countries," Presented at *Global Forum on Reinventing Government, Building Trust in Government* Viena—Austria 26–29 June 2007 (http://unpan1.un.org/intradoc/groups/public/documents/UN/UN-PAN026305.pdf) [15th May 2008].

Brainard, Lael; Chollet, Derek; LaFleur, Vinca (2007) "The Tangled Web: The Poverty-Insecurity Nexus" in Brainard, Lael; Chollet, Derek (Eds.), *Too Poor for Peace?: Global Poverty, Conflict, and Security in the 21st Century.* Washington D.C.: Brookings Institution Press, 1–30.

Breen, Bob (2001) *Mission Accomplished, East Timor: The Australian Defence Force Participation in the International Forces East Timor (INTERFET).* Sydney: Allen & Unwin.

Bröckling, Ulrich; Krasmann, Susanne; Lemke, Thomas (2011) "From Foucault's Lectures at the Collège de France to Studies of Governmentality: An Introduction" in Bröckling, Ulrich; Krasmann, Susanne; Lemke, Thomas (Eds.), *Governmentality: Current Issues and Future Challenges.* 1–33.

Bull, Hedley (1977) *The Anarchical Society: A Study of Order in World Politics.* Basingstoke: Palgrave.

Bull, Hedley (1992) "Martin Wight and the Theory of International Relations" in Wight, Gabriele; Porter, Brian (Eds.), *International Theory: The Three Traditions.* New York: Holmes & Meier, xi–xxxiii.

Burchell, Graham; Gordon, Colin; Miller, Peter (Eds.) (1991) *The Foucault Effect: Studies in Governmentality.* Chicago: University of Chicago Press.

Burchill, Scott; Linklater, Andrew; Devetak, Richard; Donnelly, Jack; Paterson, Matthew; Reus-Smit, Christian; True, Jacqui (2005) *Theories of International Relations.* New York: Palgrave.

Bures, Oldrich (2007) "Wanted: A Mid-Range Theory of International Peacekeeping" *International Studies Review.* 9 407–436.

Burton, John (Ed.) (1990) *Conflict: Human Needs Theory.* New York: St Martin's Press.

Butler, Michael J. (2009) *International Conflict Management.* Abingdon: Routlege.

Buzan, Barry (2014) *An Introduction to the English School of International Relations: The Societal Approach.* Cambridge: Polity.

Buzan, Barry; Hansen, Lene (2009) *The Evolution of International Security Studies.* Cambridge: Cambridge University Press.

Call, Charles T. (2008) "Building States to Build Peace? A Critical Analysis" *Journal of Peacebuilding & Development.* 4 (2), 60–14.

Caplan, Richard (2005a) *Europe and the Recognition of New States in Yugoslavia.* Cambridge: Cambridge University Press.

Caplan, Richard (2005b) *International Governance of War-Torn Territories: Rule and Reconstruction.* Oxford: Oxford University Press.

Carey, Peter; Bentley, G. Carter (Eds.) (1995) *East Timor at the Crossroads: The Forging of a Nation.* Honolulu: University of Hawaii Press.

Carvalho, Maria José Albarran de (2001) "Panorama Linguístico de Timor. Identidade Regional, Nacional e Pessoal" *Camões—Revista de Letras e Culturas Lusófonas.* 14 (Julho-Setembro), 65–79.

Chandler, David (2005) "Introduction: Peace without Politics?" *International Peacekeeping.* 12 (3), 307–321.

Chandler, David (2006) *The Empire in Denial—The Politics of State-Building.* London: Pluto Press.

Chandler, David (2008) "Introduction" in Chandler, David (Ed.) *Statebuilding and Intervention: Policies, Practices and Paradigms.* London and New York: Routledge, 1–16.

Chandler, David (2010) *International Statebuilding—The Rise of Post-Liberal Governance.* Oxon: Routledge.

Chesterman, Simon (2004) *You, The People—The United Nations, Transitional Administration, and State-building.* Oxford: Oxford University Press.

Chesterman, Simon (2005) "From State Failure to State-Building: Problems and Prospects for a United Nations Peacebuilding Commission" *Journal of International Law and International Relations.* 2 (1), 155–175.

Chetail, Vincent (2009) "Post-Conflict Peacebuilding—Ambiguity and Identity" in Chetail, Vincent (Ed.) *Post-Conflict Peacebuilding: A Lexicon.* Oxford: Oxford University Press, 1–33.

Chopra, Jarat (2000) "The UN's Kingdom of East Timor" *Survival.* 42 (3), 27–39.

Chopra, Jarat (2002) "Building State Failure in East Timor" *Development and Change.* 33 (5), 979–1000.

Chopra, Tanja (2009) "When Peacebuilding Contradicts Statebuilding: Notes from the Arid Lands of Kenya" *International Peacekeeping.* 16 (4), 531–545.

CIGI, The Centre for International Governance Innovation (2009) "Security Sector Reform Monitor—Timor-Leste" *Security Sector Reform Monitor No 1,* December 2009, (http://fundasaunmahein.files.wordpress.com/2009/12/ssrm-east-timor-1.pdf), [August 01st 2012].

Collier, Paul (2009) *Wars, Guns and Votes: Democracy in Dangerous Places.* New York: Harper.

Collier, Paul; Hoeffler, Anke (2001) *Greed and Grievance in Civil War.* Washington, D.C: World Bank.

Collins, Cindy; Weiss, Thomas G. (1997) "An Overview and Assessment of 1989–1996 Peace Operations Publications" *Occasional Papers #28,* 1997, (http://watsoninstitute.org/pub/OP28.pdf), [May 16th 2012].

Couto, Mia (2002) *O Último Vôo do Flamingo.* Lisboa: Editorial Caminho.

Cox, Robert (1981) "Social Forces, States and World Orders: Beyond International Relations Theory" *Millennium—Journal of International Studies.* 10 (2), 126–155.

Cristalis, Irena (2009) *East Timor—A Nation's Bitter Dawn*. London and New York: Zed Books.

CTF, Commission of Truth and Friendship (CTF) Indonesia—Timor-Leste (2008) "Per Memoriam ad Spem—Final Report of the Commission of Truth and Friendship (CTF) Indonesia—Timor-Leste" 31st March 2008, (http://socrates.berkeley.edu/~warcrime/East_Timor_and_Indonesia/Reports/PER MEMORIAM AD SPEM Eng_ver.pdf), [21st June 2011].

Curtain, Richard (2006) "Crisis in Timor Leste: Looking Beyond the Surface Reality for Causes and Solutions" *State, Society and Governance in Melanesia Project*, 2006, (http://rspas.anu.edu.au/papers/melanesia/working_papers/06_01wp_Curtain.pdf), [August 3rd 2011].

David, Charles-Philippe (1999) "Does Peacebuilding Build Peace?: Liberal (Mis)steps in the Peace Process" *Security Dialogue*. 30 (1), 25–41.

Dean, Mitchell (2010) *Governmentality: Power and Rule in Modern Society*. London: SAGE Publications.

Deleuze, Gilles (2007) "What is a Dispositif" in Lapoujade, David (Ed.) *Two Regimes of Madness—Gilles Deleuze Texts and Interviews 1975–1995*. New York: Semiotext(e), 339–348.

Denis, Jett (1999) *Why Peacekeeping Fails*. New York: Palgrave.

DFID, Department for International Development (2009) "Building the State and Securing the Peace" *Emerging Policy Paper*, June 2009, (http://www.healthandfragilestates.org/index2.php?option=com_docman&task=doc_view&gid=60&Itemid=38), [20th October 2010].

DFID, Department for International Development (2010) "Building Peaceful States and Societies" *A DFID Practice Paper*, (http://www.gsdrc.org/docs/open/CON75.pdf), [28th December 2010].

Diamond, Larry; Linz, Juan J.; Lipset, Seymour Martin (Eds.) (1990) *Politics in Developing Countries: Comparing Experiences with Democracy*. Boulder: Lynne Rienner.

Diehl, Paul (1994) *International Peacekeeping*. Baltimore: Johns Hopkins University Press.

Diehl, Paul F. (1993) "Institutional Alternatives to Traditional U.N. Peacekeeping: An Assessment of Regional and Multinational Options" *Armed Forces & Society*. 19 (2), 209–230.

Diehl, Paul F. (2008) *Peace Operations*. Cambridge: Polity Press.

Diehl, Paul F.; Olsson, Louise; Rubinstein, Robert A.; Levine, Daniel H. (2010) "Peacekeeping" in Young, Nigel J. (Ed.) *The Oxford International Encyclopedia of Peace*. Oxford: Ofxord University Press, 386–406.

Dobbins, James (2003) "Nation-Building: the Inescapable Responsibility of the World's Only Superpower" *RAND Review*. 27 (2), 17–27.

Dobbins, James; Jones, Seth G.; Crane, Keith; Degrasse, Beth Cole (2007) *The Beginner's Guide to Nation-Building*. Santa Monica: RAND Corporation.

Dobbins, James; Jones, Seth G.; Crane, Keith; Rathmell, Andrew; Steele, Brett; Teltschik, Richard; Timilsina, Anga (2005) *The UN's Role in Nation-Building: From the Congo to Iraq*. Santa Monica: RAND Corporation.

Doornbos, Martin (2006) "Fragile States or Failing Models? Accounting for the Incidence of State Collapse" in Doornbos, Martin; Woodward, Susan; Roque, Silvia (Eds.), *Failing States or Failed States? The Role of Development Models: Collected Works*. Madrid: FRIDE Working Paper n° 19, 1–13.

Doyle, Michael (1983a) "Kant, Liberal Legacies, and Foreign Affairs, Part I" *Philosophy and Public Affairs*. 12 (3), 205–235.

Doyle, Michael (1983b) "Kant, Liberal Legacies, and Foreign Affairs, Part II" *Philosophy and Public Affairs*. 12 (4), 323–353.

Doyle, Michael (1986) "Liberalism and World Politics" *The American Political Science Review*. 80 (4), 1151–1169.

Doyle, Michael (2004) "Liberal Internationalism: Peace, War and Democracy." *Nobelprize.org*, 22nd June 2004, (http://nobelprize.org/nobel_prizes/peace/articles/doyle/), [20th December 2010].

Doyle, Michael; Recchia, Stefano (2011) "Liberalism in International Relations" in Badie, Bertrand; Berg-Schlosser, Dirk; Morlino, Leonardo (Eds.), *International Encyclopedia of Political Science*. Los Angeles: SAGE, 1434–1439.

Doyle, Michael W.; Sambanis, Nicholas (2006) *Making War and Building Peace: United Nations Peace Operations*. New Jersey: Princeton University Press.

Duffield, Mark (2001) *Global Governance and the New Wars*. London: Zed Books.

Duffield, Mark (2007) *Development, Security and Unending War—Governing the World of Peoples*. Cambridge: Polity Press.

Duffield, Mark (2010) "The Liberal Way of Development and the Development--Security Impasse: Exploring the Global Life-Chance Divide" *Security Dialogue*. 41 (1), 53–76.

Dunn, James (2003) *East Timor—A Rough Passage to Independence*. Double Bay: Longueville Books.

Dunne, Tim (1998) *Inventing International Society: A History of the English School*. Basingstoke: Macmillan.

Durch, William J. (Ed.) (1993) *The Evolution of UN Peacekeeping: Case Studies and Comparative Analysis*. New York: St. Martin's Press.

Durch, William J. (1996) *UN Peacekeeping, American Politics, and the Uncivil Wars of the 1990s*. New York: St. Martin's Press.

Durch, William J.; Berkman, Tobias C. (2006) "Restoring and Maintaining Peace: What We Know So Far" in Durch, William J. (Ed.) *Twenty-First-Century Peace Operations*. Washington: United States Institute of Peace and The Henry L. Stimson Center, 1–48.

Elman, Miriam Fendius (Ed.) (1997) *Paths to Peace: Is Democracy the Answer?* Cambridge: MIT Press.

Encarnación, Omar G. (2005) "The Follies of Democratic Imperialism" *World Policy Journal*. 22 (1), 47–60.

Englebert, Pierre; Tull, Denis M. (2008) "Postconflict Reconstruction in Africa: Flawed Ideas about Failed States" *International Security*. 32 (4), 106–139.

Ertman, Thomas (2005) "State Formation and State Building in Europe" in Janoski, Thomas; Alford, Robert R.; Hicks, Alexander M.; Schwarts, Mildred A. (Eds.), *The Handbook of Political Sociology—States, Civil Societies, and Globalization*. Cambridge: Cambridge University Press, 367–383.

FAO, Food and Agricultural Organization (N/A) "Timor-Leste" N/A, (http://www.fao.org/countries/55528/en/tls/), [March 06 2012].

Fearon, James; Laitin, David (2004) "Neotrusteeship and the Problem of Weak States" *International Security*. 28 (4), 5–43.

Fernandes, José Pedro Teixeira (2011) *Teorias das Relações Internacionais: Da Abordagem Clássica ao Debate Pós-Positivista*. Coimbra: Editora Almedina.

Fischer, Markus (2000) "Liberal Peace: Ethical, Historical, and Philosophical Aspects" *BCSIA Discussion Paper 2000–2007, Kennedy School of Government, Harvard University*, April 2000, (http://belfercenter.ksg.harvard.edu/files/fischer.pdf), [April 15th 2011].

Fortna, Vginia Page (2008) *Does Peacekeeping Work? Shaping Belligerents' Choices after Civil War*. New Jersey: Princeton University Press.

Fortna, Viginia Page (2004) "Interstate Peacekeeping: Causal Mechanisms and Empirical Effects" *World Politcs*. 56 (4), 481–519.

Foucault, Michel (1980) in Gordon, Colin (Ed.) *Power/Knowledge: Selected Interviews and Other Writings, 1972–1977*. New York: Pantheon Books,

Foucault, Michel (1988) "Practicing Criticism" in Kritzman, Lawrence D. (Ed.) *Michel Foucault—Politics, Philosophy, Culture: Interviews and Other Writings 1977–1984*. New York and London: Routledge, 152–158.

Foucault, Michel (1994) "The Ethics of the Self as a Practice of Freedom" in Bernauer, James; Rasmussen, David (Eds.), *The Final Foucault*. Cambridge: MIT Press, 1–20.

Foucault, Michel ([1974] 1994) "Prisons et asiles dans le mécanisme du pouvoir" *Dits et Ecrits, t. II*. Paris: Gallimard, 521–525.

Foucault, Michel ([1976] 1978) *The History of Sexuality—Volume I: An Introduction*. New York: Pantheon Books.

Foucault, Michel ([1976] 2003) *Society Must Be Defended*. New York: Picador.

Foucault, Michel ([1978] 2007) *Security, Territory, Population.* Basingstoke: Palgrave Macmillan.

Foucault, Michel ([1979] 2008) *The Birth of Biopolitics—Lectures at the Collège de France, 1978–1979.* Basingstoke: Palgrave Macmillan.

Foucault, Michel ([1980] 2009) *Do Governo dos Vivos—Curso no Collège de France, 1979–1980 (aulas de 09 e 30 de janeiro de 1980).* São Paulo: Centro de Cultura Social.

Foucault, Michel ([1982] 2000) "The Subject and Power" in Faubion, James D. (Ed.) *The Essential Works of Foucault 1954–1984. Volume 3: Power.* New York: New York Press, 326–348.

Fritz, Verena; Menocal, Alina Rocha (2007) "Understanding State-Building from a Political Economy Perspective—An Analytical and Conceptual Paper on Processes, Embedded Tensions and Lessons for International Engagement" *Report for DFID's Effective and Fragile States Teams* September 2007, (http://www.odi.org.uk/resources/download/1340.pdf), [27th December 2010].

Fukuyama, Francis (1989) "The End of History?" *National Interest.* 16 (Summer), 3–18.

Fukuyama, Francis (1992) *The End of History and the Last Man.* New York: Free Press.

Fukuyama, Francis (2004) *State-Building: Governance and World Order in the Twenty-first Century.* London: Profile Book.

Fukuyama, Francis (2011) *The Origins of Political Order—From Prehuman Times to the French Revolution.* New York: Farrar, Straus and Giroux.

Galtung, Johan (1969) "Violence, Peace, and Peach Research" *Journal of Peace Research.* 6 (3), 167–191.

Galtung, Johan (1976) "Three Approaches to Peace: Peacekeeping, Peacemaking and Peacebuilding" in Galtung, Johan (Ed.) *Peace, War and Defence—Essays in Peace Research Vol. 2.* Copenhagen: Christian Ejlers, 282–304.

Gama, Paulino (1995) "The War in the Hills, 1975–85: A Fretilin Commander Remembers" in Carey, Peter; Bentley, G. Carter (Eds.), *East Timor at the Crossroads: The Forging of a Nation.* Honolulu: University of Hawai'i Press, 97–105.

Gates, Scott; Knutsen, Torbjorn L.; Moses, Jonathon W. (1996) "Democracy and Peace: A More Skeptical View" *Journal of Peace Research.* 33 (1), 1–10.

Gellner, Ernest (1983) *Nations and Nationalism.* Ithaca: Cornell University Press.

Ghani, Ashraf; Lockhart, Clare (2008) *Fixing Failed States: A Framework for Rebuilding a Fractured World.* Oxford: Oxford University Press.

Ghani, Ashraf; Lockhart, Clare; Carnahan, Michael (2005) "Closing the Sovereignty Gap: an Approach to State-Building" *Overseas Development Institute Working Paper nº 253,* (http://www.odi.org.uk/resources/odi-publications/working-papers/253-sovereignty-gap-state-building.pdf), [15th December 2008].

Gilligan, Michael J.; Sergenti, Ernest J. (2008) "Do UN Interventions Cause Peace? Using Matching to Improve Causal Inference" *Quarterly Journal of Political Science.* 3 (2), 89–122.

Ginty, Roger Mac (2008) "Indigenous Peace-Making Versus the Liberal Peace" *Cooperation and Conflict.* 43 (2), 139–163.

Goetze, Catherine; Guzina, Dejan (2010) "Statebuilding and Nationbuilding" *International Studies Encyclopedia Online,* 2010, (http://www.isacompendium.com/subscriber/tocnode?id=g9781444336597_chunk_g978144433659718_ss1-12—Only for subscribers), [10th March 2010].

Goldstone, Anthony (2004) "UNTAET with Hindsight: The Peculiarities of Politics in an Incomplete State" *Global Governance.* 10, 83–98.

Gordon, Colin (1991) "Governmental Rationality: An Introduction" in Burchell, Graham; Gordon, Colin; Miller, Peter (Eds.), *The Foucault Effect: Studies in Governmentality.* Chicago: University of Chicago Press, 1–52.

Gourlay, Catriona (2009) *EU-UN Cooperation in Peacebuilding—Partners in Practice?* New York and Geneva: United Nations Publications.

Grindle, Merilee (2004) "Good Enough Governance: Poverty Reduction and Reform in Developing Countries" *Governance: An International Journal of Policy, Administration and Institutions.* 17 (4), 525–548.

Gros, Jean-Germain (1996) "Towards a Taxonomy of Failed States in the New World Order: Decaying Somalia, Liberia, Rwanda and Haiti" *Third World Quarterly.* 17 (3), 455–471.

Guerra, Lucas; Blanco, Ramon (2017) "A Minustah como uma Missão Civilizatória: Uma Análise Crítica da Política Internacional para a Estabilização do Haiti" *Revista de Estudos Internacionais (REI).* 8 (3), 259–275.

Guerra, Lucas; Blanco, Ramon (2018) "A Construção da Paz no Cenário Internacional: Do Peacekeeping Tradicional às Críticas ao Peacebuilding Liberal" *Revista Carta Internacional.* 13 (2), 5–30.

Gürkaynak, Esra Çuhadar; Dayton, Bruce; Paffenholz, Thania (2009) "Evaluation in Conflict Resolution and Peacebuilding" in Sandole, Dennis J. D.; Byrne, Sean; Sandole-Staroste, Ingrid; Senehi, Jessica (Eds.), *Handbook of Conflict Analysis and Resolution.* Oxon: Routledge, 286–299.

Harrison, Graham (2004) *The World Bank and Africa: The Construction of Governance States.* London and New York: Routledge.

Hay, Colin; Lister, Michael (2006) "Introduction: Theories of the State" in Hay, Colin; Lister, Michael; Marsh, David (Eds.), *The State—Theories and Issues.* London: Palgrave Macmillan, 1–20.

Hay, Colin; Lister, Michael; Marsh, David (Eds.) (2006) *The State—Theories and Issues.* London: Palgrave Macmillan.

Heathershaw, John (2008) "Unpacking the Liberal Peace: The Dividing and Merging of Peacebuilding Discourses" *Millennium—Journal of International Studies.* 36 (3), 597–621.

Heininger, Janet E. (1994) *Peacekeeping in Transition: The United Nations in Cambodia.* New York: Twentieth Century Fund Press.

Helman, Gerald B.; Rather, Steven R. (1992) "Saving Failed States" *Foreign Policy.* 89 (Winter), 3–20.

Herbst, Jeffrey (2003) "Let Them Fail: State Failure in Theory and Practice: Implications for Policy" in Rotberg, Robert (Ed.) *When States Fail: Causes and Consequences.* Princeton: Princeton University Press, 302–318.

Hettne, Björn (2010) "Development and Security: Origins and Future" *Security Dialogue.* 41 (1), 31–52.

Hill, Jonathan (2005) "Beyond the Other? A Postcolonial Critique of the Failed State Thesis" *African Identities.* 3 (2), 139–154.

Hobsbawm, Eric (1992) *Nations and Nationalism Since 1780: Programme, Myth, Reality.* Cambridge: Cambridge University Press.

Howard, Lise Morj'e (2008) *UN Peacekeeping in Civil Wars.* Cambridge: Cambridge University Press.

ICG, International Crisis Group (2006) "Resolving Timor-Leste's Crisis" *Asia Report No 120*, 10 October 2006, (http://www.crisisgroup.org/~/media/Files/asia/south-east-asia/timor-leste/120_resolving_timor_lestes_crisis.pdf), [September 20th 2010].

ICG, International Crisis Group (2008) "Timor-Leste: Security Sector Reform" *Asian Report No 143*, 17 January 2008, (http://www.crisisgroup.org/~/media/Files/asia/south-east-asia/timor-leste/143_timor_leste___security_sector_reform.pdf), [September 20th 2010].

IFP, Initiative for Peacebuilding (2009) "Security Sector Reform in Timor-Leste" June 2009, (http://www.initiativeforpeacebuilding.eu/pdf/Security_Sector_Reform_in_Timor_Leste.pdf), [October 20th 2011].

Ignatieff, Michael (2003) *Empire Lite: Nation Building in Bosnia, Kosovo, Afghanistan.* London: Vintage.

ILO, International Labor Organization (N/A) "Youth Employment Promotion Programme (Timor-Leste)" N/A, (http://www.ilo.org/jakarta/whatwedo/projects/WCMS_114992/lang--en/index.htm), [April 10th 2012].

IMF, International Monetary Fund (N/A) "All Reports—Timor-Leste" N/A, (http://www.imf.org/external/pubs/cat/shortres.aspx?TITLE=&auth_ed=&subject=timor&ser_note=All&datecrit=During&Lang_F=All&brtype=Date&YEAR=Year&submit=Search), [April 10th 2012].

Ingram, Sue (2010) *Key Concepts and Operational Implications in Two Fragile States: The Case of Sierra Leona and Liberia.* The World Bank—UNDP.

Jackson, Robert (1990) *Quasi-States: Sovereignty, International Relations, and the Third World.* Cambridge: Cambridge University Press.

Jackson, Robert (2000) *The Global Covenant: Human Conduct in a World of States.* Oxford: Oxford University Press.

Jahn, Beate (2007a) "The Tragedy of Liberal Diplomacy: Democratization, Intervention, State-building (Part I)" *Journal of Intervention and Statebuilding.* 1 (1), 87–106.

Jahn, Beate (2007b) "The Tragedy of Liberal Diplomacy: Democratization, Intervention, State-building (Part II)" *Journal of Intervention and Statebuilding.* 1 (2), 211–229.

Jakobsen, Peter Viggo (2002) "The Transformation of United Nations Peace Operations in the 1990s: Adding Globalization to the Conventional 'End of the Cold War Explanation'" *Cooperation and Conflict.* 37 (3), 267–282.

James, Alan (1995) "Peacekeeping in the Post-Cold War Era" *International Journal.* 50 (2), 241–265.

Jarstad, Anna K.; Sisk, Timothy D. (Eds.) (2008) *From War to Democracy: Dilemmas of Peacebuilding.* Cambridge: Cambridge University Press.

Jones, Bruce (2001) *"The Challenges of Strategic Coordination: Containing Opposition and Sustaining Implementation of Peace Agreements in Civil Wars."* *IPA Policy Paper Series on Peace Implementation.* New York: International Peace Academy.

Kant, Immanuel (1905 [1795]) *Perpetual Peace—A Philosophical Essay.* London: George Allen & Unwin Ltd.

Kelly, Mark G. E. (2009) *The Political Philosophy of Michel Foucault.* New York: Routledge.

Kemer, Thaíse; Pereira, Alexsandro Eugenio; Blanco, Ramon (2016) "A Construção da Paz em um Mundo em Transformação: O Debate e a Crítica sobre o Conceito de Peacebuilding" *Revista de Sociologia e Política.* 56 (2), 122–143.

Kenkel, Kai Michael (2013) "Five Generations of Peace Operations: From the "Thin Blue Line" to "Painting a Country Blue" *Revista Brasileira de Política Internacional.* 56 (2), 122–143.

Keohane, Robert O. (2003) "Political Authority After Intervention: Gradations in Sovereignty" in Holzgrefe, J. L.; Keohane, Robert O. (Eds.), *Humanitarian Intervention: Ethical, Legal and Political Dilemmas.* Cambridge: Cambridge University Press, 275–298.

Kingsbury, Damien (2009) *East Timor—The Price of Liberty.* New York: Palgrave Macmillan.

Knight, W. Andy (2007) "Democracy and Good Governance" in Daws, Sam; Weiss, Thomas G. (Eds.), *The Oxford Handbook on the United Nations.* Oxford: Oxford University Press, 620–633.

Krasner, Stephen (1999) *Sovereignty: Organized Hypocrisy.* Princeton: Princeton University Press.

Krasner, Stephen (2004) "Sharing Sovereignty: New Institutions for Collapsing and Failing States" *International Security.* 29 (2), 5–53.

Krasner, Stephen D.; Pascual, Carlos (2005) "Addressing State Failure" *Foreign Affairs.* 84 (4), 153–163

La'o Hamutuk (2009) "How Much Money Have International Donors Spent on and in Timor-Leste?" September 2009, (http://www.laohamutuk.org/reports/09bgnd/HowMuchAid-En.pdf), [August 13th 2012].

La'o Hamutuk (2012) "Timor-Leste Petroleum Fund" Last Update July 16th 2012, (http://www.laohamutuk.org/Oil/PetFund/05PFIndex.htm—sources), [August 13th 2012].

Larner, Wendy; Walters, William (Eds.) (2004) *Global Governmentality: Governing International Spaces.* London: Routledge.

League of Nations (1936) "Convention on Rights and Duties of States" *League of Nations Treaty Series.* Vol. 165 (n° 3802).

Lijn, Jaïr van der (2009) "If Only There Were a Blueprint! Factors for Success and Failure of UN Peace-Building Operations" *Journal of International Peacekeeping.* 13 (1–2), 45–71.

Linklater, Andrew (2005) "English School" in Burchill, Scott; Linklater, Andrew; Devetak, Richard; Donnelly, Jack; Paterson, Matthew; Reus-Smit, Christian; True, Jacqui (Eds.), *Theories of International Relations.* New York: Palgrave,

Linklater, Andrew; Suganami, Hidemi (2006) *The English School of International Relations: A Contemporary Reassessment.* Cambridge: Cambridge University Press.

Luttwak, Edward N. (1999) "Give War a Chance" *Foreign Affairs.* 78 (4), 36–44.

Machado, Roberto (1979) "Introdução—Por uma Genealogia do Poder" *Michel Foucault—A Microfísica do Poder.* Rio de Janeiro: Graal, vii–xxiii.

Magalhães, António Barbedo de (2007) *Timor-Leste—Interesses Internacionais e Actores Locais—3 Volumes.* Porto: Afrontamento.

Mallaby, Sebastian (2002) "The Reluctant Imperialist: Terrorism, Failed States, and the Case for American Empire" *Foreign Affairs.* 81 (2), 2–7.

Mansfield, Edward; Snyder, Jack (2005) *Electing to Fight: Why Emerging Democracies Go to War.* Cambridge: MIT Press.

Marker, Jamsheed (2003) *East Timor: A Memoir of the Negotiations for Independence.* Jefferson: McFarland.

Martin, Ian (2001) *Self-Determination in East Timor: The United Nations, the Ballot, and International Intervention.* Boulder: Lynner Rienner Publishers.

Martin, Ian; Mayer-Rieckh, Alexander (2005) "The United Nations and East Timor: From Self-Determination to State-Building" *International Peacekeeping.* 12 (1), 125–145.

Mayall, James (Ed.) (1996) *The New Interventionism, 1991–1994: United Nations Experience in Cambodia, Former Yugoslavia and Somalia.* Cambridge: Cambridge University Press.

McCormack, Tara (2011) "Human Security and the Separation of Security and Development" *Conflict, Security & Development.* 11 (2), 235–260.

Mendes, Nuno Canas (2005) *A Multidimensionalidade da Construção Identitária em Timor-Leste.* Lisbon: ISCSP.

Mendes, Nuno Canas; Saramago, André (2012) *Dimensions of State-Building: Timor-Leste in Focus.* Saarbrücken: Lambert Academic Publishing.

Mignolo, Walter D. (2000) *Local Histories/Global Designs—Coloniality, Subaltern Knownledges, and Border Thinking.* Princeton: Princeton University Press.

Miguel, Edward (2007) "Poverty and Violence: An Overview of Recent Research and Implications for Foreign Aid" in Brainard, Lael; Chollet, Derek (Eds.), *Too Poor for Peace?: Global Poverty, Conflict, and Security in the 21st Century.* Washington D.C.: Brookings Institution Press, 50–59.

Miller, Paul (2010) "Bush on Nation Building and Afghanistan" *Foreign Policy*, 17th November 2010, (http://shadow.foreignpolicy.com/posts/2010/11/17/bush_on_nation_building_and_afghanistan_0), [24th December 2010].

Ministry of Finance, Ministry of Finance of the Democratic Republic of Timor-Leste (2010) "Timor-Leste Development Partners Meeting—Background Paper" 7 April 2010, (http://www.mof.gov.tl/wp-content/uploads/2010/07/2010TLDPMBackgroundDocumentFINAL.pdf), [March 12th 2012].

Molnar, Andrea Katalin (2010) *Timor Leste—Politics, History and Culture.* New York: Routledge.

Montesquieu, Charles de Secondat, *baron de* (2002 [1748]) *The Spirit of the Laws.* Cambridge: Cambridge University Press.

Negri, Antonio; Hardt, Michael (2000) *Empire.* Cambridge: Harvard University Press.

Newman, Edward; Paris, Roland; Richmond, Oliver P. (2009) "Introduction" in Newman, Edward; Paris, Roland; Richmond, Oliver P. (Eds.), *New Perspectives on Liberal Peacebuilding.* Tokyo, New York, Paris: United Nations University Press, 3–25.

Niner, Sarah (Ed.) (2000) *To Resist Is to Win: The Autobiography of Xanana Gusmão.* Richmond (Aus): Aurora Books.

Nobel Foundation (1996) "The Nobel Peace Prize 1996" 1996, (http://www.nobelprize.org/nobel_prizes/peace/laureates/1996/), [21st February 2013].

NSS (2002) "The National Security Strategy of the United States of America" (http://www.whitehouse.gov/nsc/nss/2002/nss.pdf), [1st of November 2008].

OECD, Organization for Economic Cooperation and Development (2008) "State-building in Situations of Fragility—Initial Findings" August 2008, (http://www.oecd.org/dataoecd/62/9/41212290.pdf), [20th October 2010].

OECD, Organization for Economic Cooperation and Development (2010) "Do No Harm: International Support for Statebuilding" (http://browse.oecdbookshop.org/oecd/pdfs/browseit/4310041E.PDF), [28th December 2010].

Oliveira, Humberto de Luna de (2004) *Timor na História de Portugal—4 Volumes.* Lisboa: Fundação Oriente e Instituto do Oriente.

Olsson, Louise (2010) "Peacekeeping: Practices and Methods" in Young, Nigel J. (Ed.) *The Oxford International Encyclopedia of Peace.* Oxford: Ofxord University Press, 393–397.

Oneal, John R.; Russett, Bruce (1999) "The Kantian Peace: The Pacific Benefits of Democracy, Interdependence, and International Organizations, 1885–1992" *World Politics.* 52 (1), 1–37.

Ottaway, Marina (1999) "Nation-building and State Disintegration" in Mengisteab, Kidane; Daddieh, Cyril (Eds.), *State Building and Democratisation in Africa.* London: Praeger Publishers, 83–97.

Ottaway, Marina (2002) "Rebuilding State Institutions in Collapsed States" *Development and Change.* 33 (5), 1001–1023.

Owen, John (1994) "How Liberalism Produces Democratic Peace" *International Security.* 19 (2), 87–125.

Paris, Roland (1997) "Peacebuilding and the Limits of Liberal Internationalism" *International Security.* 22 (2), 54–89.

Paris, Roland (2000) "Broadening the Study of Peace Operations" *International Studies Review.* 2 (3), 27–44.

Paris, Roland (2002) "International Peacebuilding and the 'Mission Civilisatrice'" *Review of International Studies.* 28 (4), 637–656.

Paris, Roland (2004) *At War's End: Building Peace After Civil Conflict.* Cambridge: Cambridge University Press.

Paris, Roland (2009) "Understanding the "Coodination Problem" in Postwar Statebuilding" in Paris, Roland; Sisk, Timothy (Eds.), *The Dilemmas of Statebuilding: Confronting the Contradictions of Postwar Peace Operations.* New York: Routledge, 53–78.

Paris, Roland (2010) "Saving Liberal Peacebuilding" *Review of International Studies.* 36 (2), 337–365.

Paris, Roland; Sisk, Timothy (2007) "Managing Contradictions: the Inherant Dilemmas of Postwar Statebuilding" (http://www.ipacademy.org/asset/file/211/iparpps.pdf), [16th May 2008].

Paris, Roland; Sisk, Timothy (Eds.) (2009a) *The Dilemmas of Statebuilding: Confronting the Contradictions of Postwar Peace Operations.* New York: Routledge.

Paris, Roland; Sisk, Timothy (2009b) "Introduction: Understanding the Contradictions of Postwar Statebuilding" in Paris, Roland; Sisk, Timothy (Eds.), *The Dilemmas of Statebuilding: Confronting the Contradictions of Postwar Peace Operations.* New York: Routledge, 1–20.

Peoples, Columba; Vaughan-Williams, Nick (2010) *Critical Security Studies—An Introduction.* Oxon: Routledge.

Pinto, Maria do Céu (2007) *As Nações Unidas e a Manutenção da Paz e as Actividades de Peacekeeping doutras Organizações Internacionais.* Coimbra: Almedina.

Poggi, Gianfranco (2004) "Theories of State Formation" in Nash, Kate; Scott, Alan (Eds.), *The Blackwell Companion to Political Sociology.* Oxford: Blackwell Publishing, 95–106.

Portugal; Indonesia (1999a) "Agreement between the Republic of Indonesia and the Portuguese Republic on the Question of East Timor" May 5th 1999, (http://www.usip.org/files/file/resources/collections/peace_agreements/east_timor_05051999.pdf), [June 19th 2011].

Portugal; Indonesia (1999b) "Agreement Regarding the Modalities for the Popular Consultation of the East Timorese" May 5th 1999, (http://www.usip.org/files/file/resources/collections/peace_agreements/east_timor_05051999mod.pdf), [June 19th 2011].

Portugal; Indonesia (1999c) "East Timor Popular Consultation Agreement Regarding Security" May 5th 1999, (http://www.usip.org/files/file/resources/collections/peace_agreements/east_timor_05051999sec.pdf), [June 19th 2011].

Pouligny, Beatrice (2006) *Peace Operations Seen From Below—UN Missions and Local People.* C. Hurst & Co Publishers.

Power, Samantha (2008) *Chasing the Flame—Sergio Vieira de Mello and the Fight to Save the World.* New York: The Penguin Press.

PRTL, Permanent Representative of Timor-Leste (2004) "Letter dated 12 February 2004 from the Permanent Representative of Timor-Leste to the United Nations addressed to the Secretary-General—S/2004/114" 12 February 2004, (http://daccess-dds-ny.un.org/doc/UNDOC/GEN/N04/239/74/PDF/N0423974.pdf?OpenElement), [January 5th 2012].

Pugh, Michael (2005) "The Political Economy of Peacebuilding: A Critical Theory Perspective" *International Journal of Peace Studies.* 10 (2), 23–42.

Pureza, José Manuel (2001) "Quem Salvou Timor Leste? Novas Referências para o Internacionalismo Solidário" *Oficina do CES n° 164.* Outubro.

Pureza, José Manuel; Duffield, Mark; Mathews, Robert; Woodward, Susan; Sogge, David (2006) "Peacebuilding and Failed States: Some Theoretical Notes" *Oficina do CES n° 256.* Julho 1–36.

Pureza, José Manuel; Roque, Silvia; Rafael, Mónica; Cravo, Teresa (2007a) "Do States Fail or Are They Pushed? Lessons Learned from Three Fomer Portuguese Colonies" *Oficina do CES.* Abril (273), 1–24.

Pureza, José Manuel; Simões, Mónica Rafael; José, André Cristiano; Marcelino, Carla (2007b) "As Novas Operações de Paz das Nações Unidas. Os casos de Angola, Timor-Leste e Moçambique" *Oficina do CES n° 290.* Novembro 1–34.

Quinn, J. Michael; Mason, T. David; Gurses, Mehmet (2007) "Sustaining the Peace: Determinants of Civil War Recurrence" *International Interactions: Empirical and Theoretical Research in International Relations.* 33 (2), 167–193.

Rabinow, Paul (Ed.) (1984) *The Foucault Reader.* London: Penguim Books.

Rabinow, Paul; Rose, Nikolas (2003) "Introduction—Foucault Today" in Rabinow, Paul; Rose, Nikolas (Eds.), *The Essential Foucault: Selection from the Essential Works of Foucault, 1954-1984.* New York: New Press, vii–xxxv.

Rabinow, Paul; Rose, Nikolas (2006) "Biopower Today" *BioSocieties.* 1 (2), 195–217.

Ramos-Horta, José (1996) "Nobel Lecture" December 10, 1996, (http://www.nobelprize.org/nobel_prizes/peace/laureates/1996/ramos-horta-lecture.html—), [20th July 2011].

Ramsbotham, Oliver (2000) "Reflections on UN Post-Settlement Peacebuilding" *International Peacekeeping.* 7 (1), 169–189.

Ramsbotham, Oliver; Woodhouse, Tom (2000) "Introduction" *International Peacekeeping.* 7 (1), 1–7.

Ramsbotham, Oliver; Woodhouse, Tom; Miall, Hugh (2005) *Contemporary Conflict Resolution.* Cambridge: Polity Press.

Rapoza, Phillip; Bolieiro, Helena; Salibekova, Roza; Stompor, John (2009) "The Justice System of Timor-Leste—An Independent Comprehensive Needs Assessment" 13 October 2009, (http://unmit.unmissions.org/Portals/UNMIT/ICNA.pdf), [January 5th 2012].

Ratner, Steven R. (1995) *The New UN Peacekeeping: Building Peace in Lands of Conflict After the Cold War.* London: St. Martin's Press.

Rice, Susan E. (2003) "The New National Security Strategy: Focus on Failed States" *Brookings Policy Brief.* 116 (February), 1–8.

Rice, Susan E. (2007) "Poverty Breeds Insecurity" in Brainard, Lael; Chollet, Derek (Eds.), *Too Poor for Peace?: Global Poverty, Conflict, and Security in the 21st Century.* Washington D.C.: Brookings Institution Press, 31–49.

Richmond, Oliver (2004a) "The Globalization of Responses to Conflict and the Peacebuilding Consensus" *Cooperation and Conflict* 39 (2), 129–150.

Richmond, Oliver (2004b) "UN Peace Operations and the Dilemmas of the Peacebuilding Consensus" *International Peacekeeping.* 11 (1), 83–101.

Richmond, Oliver (2006) "The Problem of Peace: Understanding the 'Liberal Peace'" *Conflict, Security & Development.* 6 (3), 291-314.

Richmond, Oliver (2007a) "Critical Research Agendas for Peace: The Missing Link in the Study of International Relations" *Alternatives: Global, Local, Political.* 32 (2), 247–274.

Richmond, Oliver (2007b) *The Transformation of Peace.* New York: Palgrave Macmillan.

Richmond, Oliver (2008) *Peace in International Relations.* Abingdon: Routledge.

Richmond, Oliver (2009) "A Post-Liberal Peace: Eirenism and the Everyday" *Review of International Studies.* 35 (3), 557–580.

Richmond, Oliver (2011) *A Post-Liberal Peace.* Abingdon and New York: Routledge.

Richmond, Oliver; Franks, Jason (2007) "Liberal Hubris? Virtual Peace in Cambodia" *Security Dialogue.* 38 (1), 27–48.

Richmond, Oliver; Franks, Jason (2009) *Liberal Peace Transitions—Between Statebuilding and Peacebuilding*. Edinburgh: Edinburgh University Press.

Rocha Menocal, Alina (2009) "State-Building for Peace: A New Paradigm for International Engagement in Post-Conflict Fragile States?" *Workshop paper for the European Report on Development*, (http://www.odi.org.uk/resources/download/4553.pdf), [24th December 2010].

Rosato, Sebastian (2003) "The Flawed Logic of Democratic Peace Theory" *The American Political Science Review*. 97 (4), 585–602.

Rose, Nikolas (1999) *Powers of Freedom—Reframing Political Thought*. Cambridge: Cambridge University Press.

Rose, Nikolas; Miller, Peter (1992) "Political Power Beyond the State: Problematics of Government" *British Journal of Sociology*. 43 (2), 172–205.

Rotberg, Robert (2003) "Failed States, Collapsed States, Weak States: Causes and Indicators" in Rotberg, Robert (Ed.) *State Failure and State Weakness in a Time of Terror*. Washington D.C: Brookings Institution Press, 1–28.

Rotberg, Robert (2004) "The Failure and Collapse of Nation-States: Breakdown, Prevention and Repair" in Rotberg, Robert (Ed.) *When States Fail: Causes and Consequences*. Princeton: Princeton University Press, 1–50.

Rubin, Barnett R. (2006) "Peace Building and State-Building in Afghanistan: Constructing Sovereignty for Whose Security?" *Third World Quarterly*. 27 (1), 175–185.

Russett, Bruce (1993) *Grasping the Democratic Peace*. Princeton: Princeton University Press.

Samuels, Kirsti; Einsiedel, Sebastian von (2003) "The Future of UN State-Building: Strategic and Operational Challenges and the Legacy of Iraq" *International Peace Academy—Policy Report*, 14–16th November 2003, (http://www.ipinst.org/media/pdf/publications/future_of_un_state_building.pdf), [28th December 2010].

Santoro, Maurício; Blanco, Ramon (2012) "Segurança, Desenvolvimento e Democracia: Do Trilema da Guerra Fria à Simbiose Contemporânea" in Rosa, Renata; Avila, Carlos (Eds.), *América Latina no Labirinto Global: Economia, Política e Segurança—Volume 2*. Curitiba: Editora CRV, 241–256.

Santos, Antonio Marques dos (2002) "O Sistema Jurídico de Timor-Leste—Evolução e Perspectivas," Presented at *Deutsch-Lusitanische Juristenvereinigung e.V.* Erlangen November 22nd (http://www.fd.ul.pt/Portals/0/Docs/Institutos/ICJ/LusCommune/SantosAntonioMarques4.pdf) [29th September 2010].

Santos, Boaventura de Sousa (2000) *A Crítica da Razão Indolente: Contra o Desperdício da Experiência*. Porto: Edições Afrontamento.

Santos, Boaventura de Sousa; Meneses, Maria Paula (Eds.) (2009) *Epistemologias do Sul*. Coimbra: Almedina.

Scambary, James (2006) "A Survey of Gangs and Youth Groups in Dili, Timor-Leste" 15 September 2006, (http://www.etan.org/etanpdf/2006/Report_Youth_Gangs_in_Dili.pdf), [August 09th 2012].

Schumpeter, Joseph (1966 [1919]) "The Sociology of Imperialism" in Schumpeter, Joseph (Ed.) *Imperialism and Social Classes: Two essays by Joseph Schumpeter*. Cleaveland: Meridian Books, 2–98.

Scott, Zoe (2007) "Literature Review on State-Building" *International Development Department—Governance and Social Development Resource Centre Framework—University of Birmingham*, May 2007, (http://www.gsdrc.org/docs/open/HD528.pdf), [20th April 2009].

Sen, Amartya (2008) "Violence, Identity and Poverty" *Journal of Peace Research*. 45 (1), 5–15.

SG, Secretary-General (1999) "Report of the Secretary-General on the Situation in East Timor—S/1999/1024" 4th October 1999, (http://daccess-dds-ny.un.org/doc/UNDOC/GEN/N99/283/77/IMG/N9928377.pdf?OpenElement), [January 5th 2012].

SG, Secretary-General (2011a) "Report of the Secretary-General on the United Nations Integrated Mission in Timor-Leste—S/2011/32" 25 January 2011, (http://daccess-dds-ny.un.org/doc/UNDOC/GEN/N11/212/59/PDF/N1121259.pdf?OpenElement), [January 5th 2012].

SG, Secretary-General (2011b) "Report of the Secretary-General on the United Nations Integrated Mission in Timor-Leste—S/2011/641" 14 October 2011, (http://daccess-dds-ny.un.org/doc/UNDOC/GEN/N11/536/23/PDF/N1153623.pdf?OpenElement), [January 5th 2012].

Sisk, Timothy (2009) "Electoral Processes after Civil War" in Paris, Roland; Sisk, Timothy (Eds.), *The Dilemmas of Statebuilding: Confronting the Contradictions of Postwar Peace Operations.* New York: Routledge, 196–223.

Smart, Barry (2002) *Key Sociologists—Michel Foucault.* New York: Routledge.

Smith, Anthony D. (1998) *Nationalism and Modernism: A Critical Survey of Recent Theories of Nations and Nationalism.* London: Routledge.

Smith, Anthony D.; John, Hutchinson (Eds.) (1994) *Nationalism.* Oxford: Oxford University Press.

Smith, Michael G.; Dee, Moreen (2006) "East Timor" in Durch, William (Ed.) *Twenty-First-Century Peace Operations.* Washington, DC: United States Institute of Peace, 389–466.

Snyder, Jack (2000) *From Voting to Violence: Democratization and Nationalist Conflict.* New York: Norton.

STAE, Secretariado Técnico de Administração Eleitoral (2007a) "Eleições Parlamentares 2007—(Resultado)" NA, (http://www.stae.tl/elections/2007/parliament/results/), [August 09th 2012].

STAE, Secretariado Técnico de Administração Eleitoral (2007b) "Eleições Presidenciais 2007—(Resultado 2a volta)" NA, (http://www.stae.tl/elections/2007/president/results/second_round/), [August 09th 2012].

STAE, Secretariado Técnico de Administração Eleitoral (2012) "Rezultadu Provizorio Eleisaun Prezidensial 2012 Segundo Volta" NA, (http://www.stae.tl/elections/2012/rezultado/segunda/), [August 09th 2012].

Stern, Maria; Öjendal, Joakim (2010) "Mapping the Security-Development Nexus: Conflict, Complexity, Cacophony, Convergence?" *Security Dialogue.* 41 (1), 5–29.

Straw, Jack (2002) "Failed and Failing States," Presented at *European Research Institute, Birmingham September 6th* [July 10th 2011].

Suhrke, Astri (2001) "Peacekeepers as Nation-Builders: Dilemmas of the UN in East Timor" *International Peacekeeping.* 8 (4), 1–20.

Tanter, Richard (2008) "East Timor: The Crisis Behind the Coup" February 12th 2008, (http://www.isn.ethz.ch/isn/Current-Affairs/Security-Watch-Archive/Detail/?id=54125&lng=en), [August 3rd 2011].

Taylor, John G. (1999) *East Timor: The Price of Freedom.* London and New York: Zed Books.

Teles, Patrícia Galvão (1999a) "Autodeterminação em Timor Leste: dos acordos de Nova Iorque à consulta popular de 30 de Agosto de 1999" *Boletim Documentação e Direito Comparado.* 79-80 (Maio), 379–423.

Teles, Patrícia Galvão (1999b) "Autodeterminação em Timor Leste: dos acordos de Nova Iorque à consulta popular de 30 de Agosto de 1999" *Documentação e Direito Comparado.* 79-80 (Maio), 379–423.

Themnér, Lotta; Wallensteen, Peter (2011) "Armed Conflict, 1946–2010" *Journal of Peace Research.* 48 (4), 525–536.

Tilly, Charles (Ed.) (1975a) *The Formation of National States in Western Europe.* Princeton: Princeton University Press.

Tilly, Charles (1975b) "Reflections on the History of European State-Making" in Tilly, Charles (Ed.) *The Formation of National States in Western Europe.* Princeton: Princeton University Press, 3–83.

Traub, James (2000) "Inventing East Timor" *Foreign Affairs.* 79 (4), 74–89.

UN (2010a) "Monthly Governance Report—The State of Democratic Governance in Timor-Leste" 1st February 2011, (http://unmit.unmissions.org/Portals/UNMIT/DGSU/Monthly Governance Report_January 2010_English_21042011.pdf), [19th October 2011].

UN (2011a) "Monthly Governance Report—The State of Democratic Governance in Timor-Leste" 16th February 2011, (http://unmit.unmissions.org/Portals/UNMIT/DGSU/Monthly Governance Report_January 2011_English_18032011.pdf), [21st November 2011].

UN, United Nations (1945) "Charter of the United Nations" 24th October 1945, (http://www.un.org/en/documents/charter/index.shtml), [23rd December 2010].

UN, United Nations (1999a) "Code of Conduct for Participants" August 9th 1999, (http://www.un.org/peace/etimor99/code_frame.htm), [October 20th 2011].

UN, United Nations (1999b) "The United Nations and East Timor: A Chronology" 1999, (http://www.un.org/peace/etimor99/chrono/chrono_frame.html), [20th January 2011].

UN, United Nations (2001) "Final Election Results Announced Today in East Timor" 6th September 2001, (http://www.un.org/en/peacekeeping/missions/past/etimor/DB/db060901.htm), [15th November 2008].

UN, United Nations (2002a) "East Timor—UNTAET—Background" 2002, (http://www.un.org/en/peacekeeping/missions/past/etimor/UntaetB.htm), [August 2nd 2011].

UN, United Nations (2002b) "Gusmão Wins 82.7 percent of Vote in East Timor's UN-Run Election" 17th April 2002, (http://www.un.org/en/peacekeeping/missions/past/etimor/DB/db170402.htm), [15th November 2008].

UN, United Nations (2006) "East Timor—UNMISET—Background" 2006, (http://www.un.org/en/peacekeeping/missions/past/unmiset/background.html), [August 2nd 2011].

UN, United Nations (2009a) "Emergency Education Cluster—Terms of Reference" June 3rd 2009, (https://docs.google.com/viewer?a=v&pid=sites&srcid=ZGVmYXVsdGRvbWFpbnxjbHVzdGVyc3RpbW9ybGVzdGV8Z3g6MjUyYWY2YzhlZmQ2N2EzOQ), [April 9th 2012].

UN, United Nations (2009b) "Emergency Health Cluster/Coordination Group (EHCCG) in Timor-Leste—Terms of Reference" February 5th 2009, (https://docs.google.com/viewer?a=v&pid=sites&srcid=ZGVmYXVsdGRvbWFpbnxjbHVzdGVyc3RpbW9ybGVzdGV8Z3g6MTZjMTQwZDI4NDdiNTg4YQ), [April 9th 2012].

UN, United Nations (2009c) "Terms of Reference for Food Security Cluster" March 19th 2009, (https://docs.google.com/viewer?a=v&pid=sites&srcid=ZGVmYXVsdGRvbWFpbnxjbHVzdGVyc3RpbW9ybGVzdGV8Z3g6N2NkMjFjYjllYTkzM2M1Nw), [April 9th 2012].

UN, United Nations (2009d) "Terms of Reference for the Emergency Nutrition Cluster in Timor-Leste" March 20th 2009, (https://docs.google.com/viewer?a=v&pid=sites&srcid=ZGVmYXVsdGRvbWFpbnxjbHVzdGVyc3RpbW9ybGVzdGV8Z3g6MWE3MDY3Yjc0MTVkNmZkZg), [April 9th 2012].

UN, United Nations (2009e) "Water, Sanitation and Hygiene (WASH) Cluster in Timor-Leste—Terms of Reference" March 17th 2009, (https://docs.google.com/viewer?a=v&pid=sites&srcid=ZGVmYXVsdGRvbWFpbnxjbHVzdGVyc3RpbW9ybGVzdGV8Z3g6NWQ2YzNiNjQ2MzI2N2Y1MQ), [April 9th 2012].

UN, United Nations (2010b) "UN Peacebuilding: an Orientation" September 2010, (http://www.un.org/en/peacebuilding/pbso/pdf/peacebuilding_orientation.pdf), [May 16th 2012].

UN, United Nations (2011b) "Governance of the Democratic Republic of Timor-Leste—Accountability Mechanism of Key Institutions" December 2011, (http://unmit.unmissions.org/Portals/UNMIT/DGSU/Key Institutions Report_final_15 December_2011.pdf), [March 30th 2012].

UN, United Nations (2011c) "Timor-Leste: Recovery to Development—A Statistical Profile" May 2011, (http://unmit.unmissions.org/Portals/UNMIT/Socio Economic/Timor-Leste Statistical Profile_06052011.pdf), [February 28th 2012].

UN, United Nations (2012) "Index of Laws of Timor-Leste" 15 January 2012, (http://unmit.unmissions.org/Portals/UNMIT/Legal Affairs/Index of Laws T-L as of 15 Jan 2012.pdf), [March 30th 2012].

UN, United Nations (N/A-a) "The Cluster System in Timor-Leste" N/A, (http://sites.google.com/site/clusterstimorleste/Home), [April 5th 202].

UN, United Nations (N/A-b) "Millennium Development Goals" N/A, (http://www.un.org/millenniumgoals/index.shtml), [March 6th 2012].

UN, United Nations (N/A-c) "Police: Resumption of Responsibility" N/A, (http://unmit.unmissions.org/Portals/UNMIT/unpol/Brochure web PNTL.pdf), [March 23rd 2012].

UN, United Nations (N/A-d) "UNMIT—United Nations Integrated Mission in Timor-Leste—
Administration   of   Justice   Support"   N/A,   (http://unmit.unmissions.org/De-
fault.aspx?tabid=4966), [February 8th 2012].

UN, United Nations (N/A-e) "UNMIT—United Nations Integrated Mission in Timor-Leste—
Electoral" N/A, (http://unmit.unmissions.org/Default.aspx?tabid=190), [February 8th 2012].

UN, United Nations (N/A-f) "UNMIT—United Nations Integrated Mission in Timor-Leste—
Human Rights" N/A, (http://unmit.unmissions.org/Default.aspx?tabid=182), [February 8th
2012].

UN, United Nations (N/A-g) "UNMIT—United Nations Integrated Mission in Timor-Leste—
Security" N/A, (http://unmit.unmissions.org/Default.aspx?tabid=177), [February 8th 2012].

UN, United Nations (N/A-h) "UNMIT—United Nations Integrated Mission in Timor-Leste—
The Serious Crimes Investigation Team" N/A, (http://unmit.unmissions.org/De-
fault.aspx?tabid=4973), [February 8th 2012].

UN, United Nations (N/A-i) "UNMIT—United Nations Integrated Mission in Timor-Leste—
The United Nations Country Team in Timor-Leste" N/A, (http://unmit.unmissions.org/De-
fault.aspx?tabid=191), [February 8th 2012].

UN, United Nations (N/A-j) "UNMIT—United Nations Integrated Mission in Timor-Leste—
UN Police" N/A, (http://unmit.unmissions.org/Default.aspx?tabid=178), [February 8th
2012].

UN, United Nations (N/A-k) "UNMIT—United Nations Integrated Mission in Timor-Leste—
What   is   Democratic   Governance?"   N/A,   (http://unmit.unmissions.org/De-
fault.aspx?tabid=187), [February 8th 2012].

UN, United Nations (N/A-l) "UNMIT—United Nations Integrated Mission in Timor-Leste—
What is DGSU?" N/A, (http://unmit.unmissions.org/Default.aspx?tabid=188), [February 8th
2012].

UN, United Nations (N/A-m) "UNMIT—United Nations Integrated Mission in Timor-Leste—
International Compact" N/A, (http://unmit.unmissions.org/Default.aspx?tabid=436), [March
12th 2012].

UN, United Nations; DRTL, Democratic Republic of Timor-Leste (2006) "Arrangement on the
Restoration and Maintenance of Public Security in Timor Leste and on Assistance to the
Reform, Restructuring and Rebuilding of the Timorese National Police (PNTL) and the
Ministry of Interior—Supplemental to Agreement between the United Nations and the Dem-
ocratic Republic of Timor-Leste on the Status of the United Nations Integrated Mission in
Timor Leste (UNMIT)" December 1st 2006, (http://www.unmit.org/legal/Other-Docs/polic-
ing arrangement7.pdf), [January 5th 2012].

UN, United Nations Peacekeeping Department (2008) "United Nations Peacekeeping Operations   Principles   and   Guidelines"   (http://pbpu.unlb.org/PBPS/Library/Cap-
stone_Doctrine_ENG.pdf), [04th May 2009].

UNDP, United Nations Development Program (1990) *Human Development Report—Concept
and Measurement of Human Development.* New York and Oxford: Oxford University Press.

UNDP, United Nations Development Program (2002) "East Timor United Nations Development Assistance Framework (2003–2005)" 2002, (http://www.tl.undp.org/undp/TL-Coordi-
nation-Profile/UNDAF.pdf), [February 28th 2012].

UNDP, United Nations Development Program (2003) "Strengthening Parliamentary Democracy in Timor-Leste" June 2003, (http://www.undp.east-timor.org/documentsreports/Annex/
Annex14 Parliament.pdf), [April 10th 2012].

UNDP, United Nations Development Program (2005) "Institutional Capacity Development
Support Programme—Fact Sheet" February 2005, (http://www.undp.east-timor.org/ICDP/
documents/ICDS_FS.pdf), [April 10th 2012].

UNDP, United Nations Development Program (2006a) "Human Development Report 2006"
2006, (http://hdr.undp.org/en/media/HDR06-complete.pdf), [February 28th 2012].

UNDP, United Nations Development Program (2006b) "Strengthening Parliamentary Democracy in Timor-Leste" March 22nd 2006, (http://www.tl.undp.org/undp/what we do/Demo-
cratic Governance/Parliament/SignedProdocEn.pdf), [April 10th 2012].

UNDP, United Nations Development Program (2006c) "Timor-Leste Human Development Report 2006" 2006, (http://hdr.undp.org/en/reports/nationalreports/asiathepacific/timorleste/TIMOR_LESTE_2006_en.pdf), [February 28th 2012].

UNDP, United Nations Development Program (2007a) "Local Governance Support Programme Timor-Leste" January 2007, (http://www.tl.undp.org/undp/what we do/Democratic Governance/LGSP/LGSP Prodoc 2007_English.pdf), [April 10th 2012].

UNDP, United Nations Development Program (2007b) "Strengthening the Institutional Capacity of the Office of the President" December 2007, (http://www.tl.undp.org/undp/what we do/Democratic Governance/Office of the President/Prodoc OoP 08-10final Latest.pdf), [April 10th 2012].

UNDP, United Nations Development Program (2008a) "Project Document—Security Sector Review in Timor-Leste" June 2008, (http://www.tl.undp.org/undp/what we do/Crisis Prevention and Recovery/On going projects/SSR/SSR_ProDoc_ Signed.pdf), [January 5th 2012].

UNDP, United Nations Development Program (2008b) "Strengthening the Justice System in Timor-Leste" December 22nd 2008, (http://www.tl.undp.org/undp/what we do/Democratic Governance/Justice/Justice Project Doc.pdf), [April 10th 2012].

UNDP, United Nations Development Program (2008c) "Support to Civil Service Reform in Timor-Leste" (http://www.tl.undp.org/undp/what we do/Democratic Governance/Civil Services/Civil Services Prodoc.pdf), [January 2008].

UNDP, United Nations Development Program (2008d) "Support to the Timorese Electoral Cycle" February 2008, (http://www.tl.undp.org/undp/what we do/Democratic Governance/Election/Signed Prodoc Elections.pdf), [April 10th 2012].

UNDP, United Nations Development Program (2008e) "United Nations Development Assistance Framework UNDAF 2009–2013—Democratic Republic of Timor-Leste" 2008, (http://www.tl.undp.org/undp/UNDAF/00 Undaf December 181208.pdf), [February 28th 2012].

UNDP, United Nations Development Program (2009) "Human Rights Capacity Building of the Provedoria for Human Rights and Justice" July 2009, (http://www.tl.undp.org/undp/what we do/Democratic Governance/Provedor Project/Provedoria project doc (updated).pdf), [April 10th 2012].

UNDP, United Nations Development Program (2011a) "Strengthening Civilian Oversight and Management Capacity in the Security Sector" August 2011, (http://www.tl.undp.org/undp/what we do/Crisis Prevention and Recovery/On going projects/2011-Strengthening Civilian Oversight and Management Capacity in the Security Sector.pdf), [April 10th 2012].

UNDP, United Nations Development Program (2011b) "Strengthening institutional capacity of the National Parliament in Timor-Leste" July 21st 2011, (http://www.tl.undp.org/undp/what we do/Democratic Governance/Annex I—1st part.pdf and http://www.tl.undp.org/undp/what we do/Democratic Governance/Annex I—2nd part.pdf), [April 10th 2012].

UNDP, United Nations Development Program (2011c) "Strengthening the National Police Capacity in Timor-Leste" July 2011, (http://www.tl.undp.org/undp/what we do/Crisis Prevention and Recovery/On going projects/2011-Strengthening the National Police Capacity in Timor-Leste.pdf.pdf), [March 21st 2012].

UNDP, United Nations Development Program (2011d) "Timor-Leste—Human Development Report" 2011, (http://hdr.undp.org/en/reports/national/asiathepacific/timorleste/Timor-Leste_NHDR_2011_EN.pdf), [February 28th 2012].

UNDP, United Nations Development Program (N/A-a) "Crisis Prevention and Recovery's Ongoing Projects" N/A, (http://www.tl.undp.org/undp/recovery_ongoingproject.htm), [March 6th 2012].

UNDP, United Nations Development Program (N/A-b) "Democratic Governance's Ongoing Projects" N/A, (http://www.tl.undp.org/undp/democratic_ongoingproject.htm), [March 6th 2012].

UNDP, United Nations Development Program (N/A-c) "Environment and Sustainable Development's Ongoing Projects" N/A, (http://www.tl.undp.org/undp/environment_ongoingproject.htm), [March 6th 2012].

UNDP, United Nations Development Program (N/A-d) "Institutional Capacity Development Support Programme" N/A, (http://www.undp.east-timor.org/ICDP/ICDSP_home.html), [April 10th 2012].

UNDP, United Nations Development Program (N/A-e) "Poverty Reduction and Achievement of the MDGs' Ongoing Projects" N/A, (http://www.tl.undp.org/undp/poverty_ongoingproject.htm), [March 6th 2012].

UNDP, United Nations Development Program (N/A-f) "Programme Area Overview—Crisis Prevention & Recovery" N/A, (http://www.tl.undp.org/undp/what we do/Crisis Prevention and Recovery/On going projects/CPR Overview-new version-dec2010.pdf), [January 5th 2012].

Vincent, Andrew (1992) "Conceptions of the State" in Hawkesworth, Mary; Kogan, Maurice (Eds.), *Encyclopedia of Government and Politics—Volume I.* London: Routledge, 43-55.

Walker, R. B. J. (1993) *Inside/outside: International Relations as Political Theory.* Cambridge: Cambridge University Press.

Walton, C. Dale (2009) "The Case for Strategic Traditionalism: War, National Interest and Liberal Peacebuilding" *International Peacekeeping.* 16 (5), 717-734.

Watson, Adam (1990) "Systems of States" *Review of International Studies.* 16 (2), 99-109.

Watson, Adam (1992) "The Evolution of International Society: A Comparative Historical Analysis." London: Routledge,

WB, World Bank (1992) *Governance and Development.* Washington, D.C: World Bank.

WB, World Bank (2005) "International Development Association—Country Assistance Strategy for the Democratic Republic of Timor-Leste for the period FY06–FY08" 22th June 2005, (http://www-wds.worldbank.org/external/default/WDSContentServer/WDSP/IB/2005/06/27/000012009_20050627095435/Rendered/PDF/327000rev.pdf), [28th February 2012].

WB, World Bank (2006a) "Gas Seep Harvesting Project—P092055" September 26th 2006, (http://www-wds.worldbank.org/external/default/WDSContentServer/WDSP/IB/2006/07/13/000104615_20060713120929/Rendered/PDF/Project0Inform1nt010Appraisal0Stage.pdf), [April 10th 2012].

WB, World Bank (2006b) "TP-Education Sector Support—P095873" February 23rd 2006, (http://www-wds.worldbank.org/external/default/WDSContentServer/WDSP/IB/2006/03/12/000104615_20060313115524/Rendered/PDF/Project0Inform1ment010Concept0Stage.pdf), [April 10th 2012].

WB, World Bank (2007a) "Health Sector Strategic Plan Support Project—P104794" April 26th 2007, (http://www-wds.worldbank.org/external/default/WDSContentServer/WDSP/IB/2007/03/29/000104615_20070330110149/Rendered/PDF/Project0Inform10Stage010290March007.pdf), [April 10th 2012].

WB, World Bank (2007b) "Timor-Leste—First, Second Petroleum Technical Assistance Projects" June 24th 2007, (http://www-wds.worldbank.org/external/default/WDSContentServer/WDSP/IB/2007/08/17/000310607_20070817105006/Rendered/PDF/ICR0000453.pdf), [April 10th 2012].

WB, World Bank (2008) "Youth Development Project—P106220" May 5th 2008, (http://www-wds.worldbank.org/external/default/WDSContentServer/WDSP/IB/2008/05/05/000076092_20080506155224/Rendered/PDF/PID0Appraisal0Stage0AB3877.pdf), [April 10th 2012].

WB, World Bank (2010) "Timor-Leste—Second Chance Education Project—P120890" April 5th 2010, (http://www-wds.worldbank.org/external/default/WDSContentServer/WDSP/IB/2009/08/18/000104615_20090819100555/Rendered/PDF/Timor1Leste0Se1pt0Stage1Aug11812009.pdf), [April 10th 2012].

WB, World Bank (2011) "Timor-Leste Social Protection Administration Project—P125784" April 26th 2011, (http://www-wds.worldbank.org/external/default/WDSContentServer/WDSP/IB/2011/05/31/000001843_20110601142108/Rendered/PDF/P1257840PID00Appraisal0Stage0final.pdf), [April 10th 2012].

WB, World Bank (N/A-a) "All Projects—Timor-Leste" N/A, (http://www.worldbank.org/en/country/timor-leste/projects/all), [April 10th 2012].

WB, World Bank (N/A-b) "Justice for the Poor—Timor-Leste" N/A, (http://web.worldbank.org/WBSITE/EXTERNAL/TOPICS/EXTLAWJUSTICE/EXTJUSFOR-

POOR/0,,con-
tentMDK:22062225~menuPK:3282947~pagePK:148956~piPK:216618~theSitePK:328278
7,00.html), [April 10th 2012].

Weber, Max ([1922] 1978) in Roth, Guenther; Wittich, Claus (Eds.), *Economy and Society—An Outline of Interpretive Sociology*. Berkeley: University of California Press,

Weinstein, Jeremy M. (2005) "Autonomous Recovery and International Intervention in Comparative Perspective" *Working Paper Number 57—Center for Global Development*, April 2005, (http://stanford.edu/~jweinst/files/AutonomousRecovery_2005.pdf), [15th June 2010].

WFP, World Food Programme (N/A) "Timor-Leste—WFP Activities" N/A, (http://www.wfp.org/countries/timor-leste/operations), [March 6th 2012].

Whaites, Alan (2008) "States in Development: Understanding State-Building" *DFID Working Paper*, 2008, [27th December 2010].

White, Hugh (2008) "The Road to INTERFET: Reflections on Australian Strategic Decisions Concerning East Timor, December 1998–September 1999" *Security Challenges*. 4 (1), 69–87.

Wight, Gabriele; Porter, Brian (Eds.) (1992) *International Theory: The Three Traditions—Martin Wight*. New York: Holmes & Meier.

Wight, Martin (1977) *System of States*. Leicester: Leicester University Press.

Wight, Martin (1987) "An Anatomy of International Thought" *Review of International Studies*. 13 (3), 221–227.

Wilde, Ralp (2007) "Colonialism Redux? Territorial Administration by International Organizations, Colonial Echoes and the Legitimacy of the 'International'" in Hehir, Aidan; Robinson, Neil (Eds.), *State-building : theory and practice*. London and New York: Routledge, 29–49.

Wilson, Peter (1998) "The Myth of the "the First Great Debate"" *Review of International Studies*. 24 (5), 1–15.

Wouters, Jan; Ryngaert, Cedric (2005) "Good Governance: Lessons From International Organizations" in Curtin, Deirdre; Wessel, Ramses A. (Eds.), *Good Governance and the European Union—Reflections on Concepts, Institutions and Substance*. New York: Intersentia Publishers, 69–102.

Zanotti, Laura (2005) "Governmentalizing the Post-Cold War International Regime: The UN Debate on Democratization and Good Governance" *Alternatives: Global, Local, Political*. 30 (4), 461–487.

Zanotti, Laura (2011) *Governing Disorder—UN Peace Operations, International Security and Democratization in the Post-Cold War Era*. University Park: The Pennsylvania State University Press.

Zartman, William (1995) "Introduction: Posing the Problem of State Collapse" in Zartman, William (Ed.) *Collapsed States: The Disintegration and the Restoration of Legitimate Authority*. London and Boulder: Lynne Rienner, 1–11.

Žižek, Slavoj (2009) *Violence*. London: Profile Books.

Index

About the Author

Ramon Blanco is a professor at the Federal University of Latin-American Integration (UNILA-Brazil), where he coordinates the chair in Peace Studies.

www.ingramcontent.com/pod-product-compliance
Lightning Source LLC
Chambersburg PA
CBHW022308280326
41932CB00010B/1030